C. L. Elliott, Pinx[t] H. Wright Smith, Sc.

S. D. Bradford.

WORKS

OF

SAMUEL DEXTER BRADFORD, LL. D.

* * * "What is writ, is writ,—
Would it were worthier."
Childe Harold's Pilgrimage.

BOSTON:
PHILLIPS, SAMPSON & COMPANY,
13 WINTER STREET.
1858.

PRESS OF
S. Chism.—Franklin Printing House,
Corner of Franklin and Hawley Streets,
BOSTON.

DEDICATION.

To SAMUEL DEXTER BRADFORD, Junior, and JOHN HENRY BRADFORD:

MY DEAR SONS:

HAVING made a collection of some of my miscellaneous writings, I have concluded to inscribe them to you.

It was once the custom, on occasions of this kind, to make a selection of some distinguished name, to whom the author dedicated his work, and whose favor and protection he invoked in its behalf. When that distinguished philosopher, John Locke, Gent., had finished his great Essay concerning the Human Understanding, he dedicated it to the Right Honorable Thomas, Earl of Pembroke and Montgomery, with a list of other titles too long to enumerate, and he said, that, "as it had grown up under his Lordship's eye, he had a natural right to come to his Lordship for protection."

In the present case, I have no occasion to prefer a request of that nature to any one, as this collection has been made for circulation only amongst a few particular friends, so that it is not deemed necessary, (as is so often done,) to invoke even the tender mercies of critics or reviewers, should this work be ever so unfortunate, as to pass into their hands, and be considered worthy of their perusal.

The mode I have adopted of collecting my writings, and having them bound together in one volume, cannot fail to call your attention to them, and, if they do not interest you now, whilst you are so young, I cannot doubt they will do so presently, when you will naturally desire to know what your father's opinions were upon the various subjects discussed.

You will perceive the collection dates from the 19th October, 1813, more than forty-four years ago, at which time, you must remember, how inferior were the means of obtaining a good education, compared with those in use at present. Teachers, books, schools, colleges, were few and imperfect. I was almost twelve years old before I entered a school, or commenced the study of grammar. The appearance of things, around the mansion of my kind and most excellent father, in Roxbury, was very different then from that presented now. The house was almost surrounded by woods. Very little of the land was cleared or cultivated. Rabbits and wild squirrels were very abundant, not to mention other animals of a less pleasing description, which made sad havoc in the poultry yard. The woods were filled with wild pigeons, partridges, woodcocks, and quails, holding out such inducements for boys addicted to hunting, (as all such sports were then called,) as cannot be readily conceived of at the present time, when the forests are gone, the ground shot over by so many people, and almost without game of any kind. Like other boys of my age, I passed most of my time in the woods, with my dog and my gun. The beautiful white rabbits, which abounded in those days, had greater attractions for me than books of any kind.

On the seventh of September, 1807, I was persuaded, by the kindest and most affectionate of mothers, to enter the family of the Rev. Joshua Bates, of Dedham, who prepared me for college, and I was admitted a member of the Freshman Class at Cambridge, on the first of September, 1810, and graduated nearly three months before I was nineteen years of age. I mention this to account, in part, for the imperfection of my college exercises, a few of which are contained in this volume.

Of the kindness and attention I received from my preceptor, Dr. Bates, afterwards President of Middlebury College, I cannot speak in terms of too exalted praise. He was a scholar, and—what is more important—a wise and good man. He graduated at Cambridge in 1800, having obtained the first honor in a class, which contained Joseph Stevens Buckminster and Chief Justice Shaw amongst the graduates of that year.

I studied very hard at Cambridge; observed all the college rules and regulations; was never fined during the four years I remained there; was always commended by my teachers, and rewarded upon every suitable occasion. There were many in my class who were devoted to their studies; and some who have greatly distinguished themselves since. One of the number, William H. Prescott, the historian, has nearly as many titles to his name in the college catalogue as a Spanish grandee; and I will add that nearly every one, who has sustained a high reputation since, was a good scholar at Cambridge, thus confirming the observations of the great Lord Chancellor Eldon, who, as late as 1836, wrote the following most excellent advice to a grandson about to be entered at Oxford:

"It will depend much upon yourself what degree of benefit you may reap there. Of the young, it has been said, 'Gaudent, equis, canibusque, et aprici gramine campi,' or something to that effect. Of extravagant gratification of that passion in young men, I well remember the pains which were taken in Oxford to restrain it. What are precisely the rules of the university, in this respect, now, I cannot say; but so much I can say, that, after long and great experience, I never knew a young man who had indulged too much in those amusements at Oxford, to the neglect of very diligent, if not severe duty, who ever afterwards in life graced his friends, family or country, as I hope and pray you may hereafter grace them; and I never knew one who signally devoted his time at Oxford to study, who did not, in after life, become a blessing and ornament to his family and country.

"Be very select in the company you keep at Oxford, and never forget, what so many forget, that the university is not a place for amusement, but of constant study, to be interrupted only by necessary attention to health."

These are the words of Lord Eldon, but they are as wise as those of Solomon, and ought to be placarded in letters of gold upon tablets of silver within the walls of every college in the country. Let them sink deep into your hearts, and be impressed upon your memory, and time will prove how true and wise they are.

When I graduated, in August, 1814, the country was engaged in a disastrous war with Great Britain. Commerce was paralyzed. Our ships were perishing with the dry-rot at our wharves, or upon our rivers, where they had been towed to save them from seizure by the enemy. Our merchants were in despair.

Having a salutary dread of idleness, although inclined to become a merchant, I immediately entered the office of my uncle, the late Judge Ward of Boston, and commenced the study of the law, which, however, I abandoned at once, on the news of peace, in February, 1815, when I entered the counting-room of an importing house in Broad Street; was soon after admitted a partner; and embarked for England to conduct the business of the house there. I have visited that country many times since, and have resided there altogether about seventeen years, having been engaged in a large and laborious business, which occupied all my time and thoughts, left me no leisure to review the books I had studied at Cambridge, and often deprived me of the time required for recreation and health.

Knowing how busy I was for so many years, taking care of the affairs not only of my own house, but of another very extensive one, located in New York, Messrs. Peter Remsen & Co., you will not be surprised at any errors you may find in the volume inscribed to you; nor can you expect those graces of style and composition, which are found in the works of professed scholars, but are not expected in those of the active and busy merchant. I have endeavored, however, always to express myself with perspicuity, which always pleases the reader, as he is able so easily and readily to comprehend the author he is perusing.

You may not have decided yet to what you will turn your attention, after you have obtained your education ; but I trust that a perusal of the lives of great and good men, will stimulate in you a desire to excel ; that you will take a lofty model for your guide, and that you may fully appreciate the value and indispensable necessity of religion, industry, perseverance, and self-denial. Remember that, with these qualities, there is scarcely any eminence which may not be obtained ; and that without these no satisfactory progress can be made.

Remember the proverbs of Solomon : "My son, forget not my law, but let thy heart keep my commandments. For length of days, long life and peace shall they add to thee. Keep thy heart with all diligence, for out of it are the issues of life."

I will conclude with an Eastern apothegm, which I have always admired, not only for the beauty of the language, but also for the excellent moral it contains.

On parents' knees a naked, new-born child,
Weeping thou sat'st, whilst all around thee smiled ;
So live, that, sinking in thy last, long sleep,
Calm, thou may'st smile, whilst all around thee weep.

I remain your ever affectionate Father,

SAMUEL DEXTER BRADFORD.

West Roxbury, January 1st, 1858.

CONTENTS.

WORKS

OF

SAMUEL DEXTER BRADFORD, LL. D.

A LATIN ORATION.

NATIONIBUS GLORIAM LITTERÆ AFFERUNT.

INTER causas multas, quæ aliis temporibus addiderunt dignitatem honoremque nationibus, doctrina et eruditio conspicuum illustremque locum tenent.

Etsi Mars imperatorum votis respondeat, tamen est Minerva sola, "quæ dictis mœrentia pectora mulcet, animi motus sedat, et homines esse sapientes docet."

"Qui bene placarit Palladi, doctus erit."

Ille, qui hostes externos vicerit, urbes, quas subegit, e manibus suis eripi haud raro videt, et suas possessiones ferro invadi ab hostibus, quos ante contemserit; sed vetustas, quæ omnia alia consumit, artium scientiæque monumenta non delere potest, sed laude postera crescunt. Imperium Romanum jam pridem non levi ruina disjectum, at Virgilius, Horatius, Livius, Tacitusque omnis ævi oblectamenta-admiratioque manent, et manebunt. Doctrinam et eru, ditionem animos mollire, irasque temperare, barbararum et rudium gentium conditio maxime probat. "Pleni omnes sunt libri, plenæ sapientium voces, plena exemplorum vetustas, quæ jacerent in tenebris omnia, nisi lumen literarum accederet." "Antequam lux scientiæ in animos indoctorum et rudium hominum penetret, tempus per otium transigunt, nudi atque intecti, sicuti peregrinantes vivunt." Cum vero doctrinæ amore semel ardent, fortuna simul cum moribus immutatur. "Quæ homines arant, navigant, ædificant; virtuti omnia parent."

Hactenus nationum rudium conditionem contemplavimus, antequam artes utiles colentur; sed cum scientiæ fundamentum posuerint, ædificium artes ingenuæ elegantesque cito extruunt.

"Didicisse fideliter artes, emollit mores, nec sinit esse feros."

Cato ille censor fertur invidiam subiisse, quod artium Græcarum admissionem in Italiam impedire obniteretur. Tamen constat, eum a sententia sua non solum discessisse, sed senem Græcas literas didicisse. Etsi concedatur, rerum abundantiam opesque, cupiditates inanes nonnunquam gignere, et luxuriam doctrinæ et eruditionis comitem, tamen servitutem, paupertatem, miseriamque ignorantiæ comites, nemo negare potest.

Quod malum gravius hominis animum invadere possit, quam superstitio, quæ ex ignorantia procreatur, et timore alitur? Cum illa oculis nubem objicit, quid caliginem dispellere potest, nisi philosophia atque eruditio? Ut oriens sol rorem matutinum dispergit, sic lux scientiæ, cum animum ignorantia ac superstitione oppressum intraverit, tenebras mentis discutit, liberatque omni inani timore.

Alexander magnus, (ut Cicero ait) multos scriptores secum habuisse dicitur; atque is, cum in Sigeo ad Achillis tumulum adstitisset, "O fortunate," inquit, "adolescens, qui tuæ virtutis Homerum præconem inveneris." "Et jure optimo; nam nisi Ilias illa exstitisset, idem tumulus, qui ejus corpus contexerat, nomen etiam obruisset." Ii, qui inomni ævo damno aut pœna doctos afficere aggressi, aut tyranni, aut homines indocti rudesque fuerunt. Etsi tamen Caligula crudelis Virgilii Homerique libros perdere conatus est, tamen, cum ingenii egregia facinora, sicuti anima ipsa, immortalia sint, manent, manebunt in animis hominum in sæcula sæculorum.

"Trahimur omnes laudis studio, et optimus quisque maxime gloria ducitur."

Is itaque, qui viros laudem mereri spe famæ gloriæque incitet, magna æstimatione semper habendus est. Talis poeta et historiæ scriptor est, ad quos pertinet, magnorum, illustrium, et sapientium virorum res gestas posteris tradere. Hoc modo, nomen civis illustris, ac insignis imperatoris, non cum corpore peribit, sed postera laude crescet. Nisi Tyrtæus cecinisset, Lacedæmonii non vicissent. Igitur cum imperator prudentia atque virtute patriæ hostes fuderit, et sapiens civis improborum hominum clandestina consilia invenerit, poetæ et historiæ scriptori laudis aliquam partem tribuamus.

Sed ut hæc non falsa videantur, ad Græciam Romamque spectemus. In Græcia, tam inclyta non solum propter eruditionem artesque, sed etiam res prosperas in bello, militum duces oratores fuerunt, omnesque regebat eloquentia. Tanta Græcorum doctrina, et scientia, ut Græcia non terræ nomen, sed eruditionis et eloquentiæ habebatur.

Imperatores Græci, cum hostes externos vicerint, laurea atque omnium laude donati in urbem rediere. Post non multos dies, libris poetæ in cœlum tolluntur. Hac spe elati, Themistocles, Alcibiades, Pericles, atque Miltiades, ense in bello, consiliis sub placida pace, patriam defenderunt. Si ad Romam contra spectemus, omnem illustrem civem literis initiatum invenimus, et oratorem "qui (ut ait Pindarus) non pluvias aquas colligit, sed vivo gurgite exundat," quique dictis Romanorum animos tam diu regebat, doctrina atque optimarum artium studiis eruditissimum. Nam etsi Cicero se populi Romani saluti devovit, tamen libri, quos, posteritatem ut delectarent reliquit, ad ejus laudem plus contulerunt, quam labores, quos consul aut senator sustinuit. Historiam Romanam legentes, ducem illustrem magnanimumque admiratione, sed Ciceronem quadam pietate contemplamur.

Si dubitetur numspes laudis famæque sæpe homines alliciat de patria sua bene mereri, respondeo, omnium illustrium et insignium virorum vitas hanc sententiam confirmare. "Dum gloria est consentiens laus bonorum, et incorrupta vox bene judicantium de excellente virtute, hanc laudem mereri omnes decet." "Nullam enim virtus aliam mercedem laborum periculorumque desiderat, præter laudem ac gloriam."

Sed quid enumerem artium multitudinem, sine quibus vita omnino nulla esse possit? "Quis enim ægris subveniret, quæ esset oblectatio valentium, qui victus, aut cultus, nisi tam multæ nobis artes ministrarent, quibus rebus exculta hominum vita tantum distat a victu et cultu bestiarum?" Sed ut verbo uno dicam, quo plures sapientes viros ulla terra contineat, hoc felicior ac doctior erit. Talis gentis gloria, ut sol nulla nube obscuratus, summo splendore enitescit: atque cum in tali terra literæ auctoritate publica sustentantur, duplici laude florent.

Quamquam in nostra patria nunc rauco strepunt cornua cantu, atque pax, felicitas, honorque ab oculis eripiuntur, tamen diu expectatum diem venturum speramus, quando docti eruditique ab omnibus in maxima æstimatione habeantur, quando America in artibus et omni virtute Europam æmuletur; et omnes, qui in Senatus consiliis versantur, ut Hamilton, omni virtute præditi; et imperatores nostri, ut Washington, omni laude digni sint; Washington, quem omnes boni venerantur, amantque,

"Nil oriturum alias, nil ortum tale fatentes."

A DISSERTATION

ON THE RIGHT AND DUTY OF FREE INQUIRY IN MATTERS OF RELIGION.

1st of Corinthians, x. 15.—" I speak as to wise men, judge ye what I say."

It has ever been the lot of some opinions, as of some men, to have their claims acknowledged, because no one has had the confidence to dispute them, and to escape the censure of the public, because they were supported by rank and elevated station, or because they favored the indulgence of some favorite inclination. Perhaps, however, none has had more advocates, or been maintained with greater zeal, than the unreasonable maxim, that, as religion is a system, which we can but imperfectly comprehend, it should never be examined; that the Bible is a book, which demands implicit obedience and belief, though infinitely above our comprehension; and that, since it contains a variety of sacred doctrines, which it surpasses the strength of the human understanding to comprehend, we should resolve to live in ignorance of the reasons of its commands, and, at the same time, yield an unlimited obedience to its dictates. By some, the world is represented as lost in tenfold ignorance and error; the understanding as obscured by the degeneracy of our first parents; and the whole human race as incapable of every meritorious and virtuous action.

It has always been the practice of the artful and designing, when the absurdity of their opinions was about to be exposed by the light of reason, to declaim upon the fallibility of man, and the imperfections of the human mind. By these means, the grossest absurdities have been often imposed upon the credulity of the inexperienced and unlearned, by assuring them that the opinions they were solicited to embrace were mysteries and truths too abstruse for a vulgar understanding, but which, at the same time, demanded their confidence and belief. Doctrines, wholly contradictory to common sense, have been palmed upon mankind, under the veil of mystery, or the ignorant have confided in them, because an apparent sanctity had been thrown over them by time, or they have gained admittance by receiving the support of the great and powerful. Would to Heaven I could add that this mis taken zeal, that this artful policy, which has served so long to support the tottering throne of popery, had been confined to the Church of Rome; that it had prevailed in those countries alone, where the clergy were too profligate, and the impositions of hierarchy too daring and oppressive, to endure the clear and convincing light of reason, and impartial examination. But a portion of the same spirit has descended to later times, and prevailed in countries where the Bible is not taken from the possession of the people by the daring and unhallowed hand of public authority; where the clergy are highly distinguished for the purity of their lives, and the simplicity of their manners, no less than for eminent learning and zeal in their profession; and where civil government imposes no restraints upon the consciences of its subjects, but grants them religious liberty in its fullest extent.

Since, however, there is no unjust or impolitic measure, which has not some advocates, who pretend to assign the reasons of their support; and since it is a question of no small importance, whether the Christian should not be permitted and exhorted to exercise all his reasoning powers upon the subjects of religion; I propose, in the following observations, to consider the right and duty of private judgment, and free inquiry in the concerns of religion, and some of the objections, which have been made to the use of reason, in examining the truths of Christianity. I shall commence my observations with acknowledging it as an indisputable principle, that the understanding is naturally right, and capable of distinguishing truth from error, and right from wrong; because, to deny this maxim is to subvert the whole structure of society.

Like an ancient philosopher, we shall prove the fallacy of our reasoning, by saying that everything is doubtful, and, at the same time, making pretensions to the discovery, that it is certain, that everything is uncertain.

The right of examining the truths of religion is one of the most important and valuable we possess, and, as it constitutes one of those inalienable privileges, which belong to us in every situation in life, so it should never be resigned, while we make any pretensions to the name of reasonable beings, or to the inestimable right of religious liberty.

There are many other privileges, which are possessed in a state of nature, which require that a portion of them should be surrendered to civil authority for the public good. But, with respect to this, the case is far otherwise, and it can never be restrained or limited by civil government, without a surrender of an invaluable privilege and security. As the right of self-preservation can never be resigned, without exposing our temporal interest to a variety of dangers, so that of free inquiry into the concerns of religion can never be renounced, without hazarding our eternal welfare, and subjecting ourselves to be deceived by the wildest absurdities. As a right to the salubrious air is necessary to the health and vigor of the body, so this is no less requisite to the preservation of the same qualities in the human mind. The ambitious ruler may persuade a deluded people, to make a surrender of their natural liberty, and a spiritual despot may assume the privileges of infallibility, deceive with making claims to divine authority, or terrify by the thunders of the church; but all such pretensions are vain; and the arts of ambitious men, by which they hope to rise to eminence on the ruins of truth and reason, should therefore be rejected with that calm but firm and spirited opposition, which they so justly deserve.

Having said thus much upon the right of free inquiry, I proceed to inquire what is implied in an impartial examination of religion. When a number of persons are selected to decide upon the claims of two contending parties, it is always considered as a necessary qualification, that their judgment should be unbiassed, and open to conviction. He, likewise, who examines the doctrines of religion, and the opinions of the different sects into which the Christian world has been divided, should come to the inquiry with a mind free from prejudice, and ready to be convinced by sufficient evidence. He who desires to know the whole truth, will never suffer himself to be influenced by old prejudices and prepossessions, but will endeavor to preserve that state of equilibrium, which is so necessary in the examination of religious subjects. The person who wishes to discover the truth of a particular doctrine which suffers the indulgence of some favorite but criminal pursuit, will hardly listen to objections. The syren voice of pleasure will sound too sweetly in his ears to leave room for the harsh, yet certain voice of reason. The man who wishes an opinion to be true is half convinced of its truth already, will turn a deaf ear to all objections, and live as if there were none. But, if it requires fairness to collect the evidence of different religious tenets, it is likewise necessary that no less time than attention should be employed to estimate that evidence, and to give to each portion its proper degree of influence. Here the aid of reason, and the rules of fair criticism, are most required, and he who rejects their assistance, because they are sometimes perverted, and lead to dangerous consequences, acts a part no less absurd than he who, because his eyesight is sometimes injured by excess of light or other causes, resolves to extinguish his eyes at once, and grope in darkness. Here the scholar may display the depth of the metaphysician, the acuteness of the logician, and the candor of an honest man. Without these precautions, error will assume the specious garb of truth, delusions resemble the sound deductions of reason, and the dogmas of enthusiasm, the sacred appearance of inspiration. In the last place, judging with impartiality implies that, in assenting to a proposition, our belief be proportionate to its evidence. All truths are not equally obvious and incontestable. Many lie far beyond our sight; some just dawn upon the view; others appear in a clear and convincing light, while others glare upon us with all the force of demonstration. Without a just proportion of our assent, we shall hardly arrive at just conclusions; and if the intermediate degrees of evidence be omitted, the moralist, like the mathematician, who has lost some intermediate step in the demonstration, when about to infer the conclusion from the premises, will soon discover that the chain is imperfect, and that a new link must be supplied before he can arrive at certainty and satisfaction in the process.

The duty and the obligation which we are under of examining the doctrines and commands of Scripture, which I proposed secondly to consider, is no less obvious than the right. It is proved by the danger of submitting to the decisions of men fallible in their judgment, and often prejudiced in their determinations; by the circumstance of our being endowed with reason; but, above all, by the example and command of our blessed Savior. The motives which lead to erroneous sentiments in religion are extremely numerous. The spirit of party, the love of novelty, and an evil desire of reputation, all these are so many allurements which serve to draw mankind from the path of truth and reason.

The authority of men is one of the most fruitful sources of prejudice and error. Religious sentiments are sometimes firmly believed because they were professed by our parents, instructors, or friends; and antiquity seems often to cast a mist over the minds of men, which it seems impossible to dissipate. To place, however, implicit confidence in the opinions of our ancestors, because they were peculiar to them, and not because they are founded in truth, is to assign to ourselves but an inferior rank in the creation, to deny the gradual progress of the understanding in the pursuit of truth, and to suppose our ancestors the standard of all that is sublime and perfect in religion, or elegant and learned in literature. But had our ancestors no imperfections? Is the candle of the Lord, which has so long enlightened the human race, almost consumed, and will it consequently be soon extinguished? Or does it rather consist of more durable materials, and may we not expect that it will burn forever?

Indeed, to believe all that our predecessors have asserted, is to keep the mind in everlasting infancy, and to check every noble and exalted effort. Had such been the method pursued in former times, what would the world exhibit but a scene of error and superstition? In vain should we look for the sound and convincing reasoning of a Socrates, or the sublime and pathetic sentiments of a Cicero.

But had those who have preceded us, no heresies in religion, or absurdities in philosophy? The answer is obvious, and had succeeding generations been content with the discoveries and principles of their progenitors, the vast and comprehensive mind of Locke would have explored the regions of thought in vain, and the maxims of Aristotle been still the standard of perfection. The investigations of this wonderful man would have been considered as the productions of a lively imagination, instead of the sound deductions of reason. The everlasting law of gravitation, which holds the planets in their orbits, and subjects them to a regular revolution, would have still existed, but the concentric spheres of the ancients would have retained the confidence and belief of men. The earth would have continued to turn upon its axis, but it would still have been heresy to maintain and publish an opinion so contradictory to reason, and dangerous in its consequences. The opinions of our parents, and of the wise and virtuous, should be always treated with becoming deference, and, though we should embrace them as grounded in truth, before age and information have qualified us for an impartial examination, still there is a point beyond which belief is idle veneration, and submission slavery. Our Maker has given no human being a sovereignty over the faith of others, and he who assumes it usurps the empire of reason.

But, admitting that we ought to be determined in the articles of our faith by the authority of men, instead of drinking the draughts of knowledge and divine instruction from the pure and unruffled fountain of heavenly wisdom; to what sect or denomination of Christians shall we apply for information? There have been nearly as many sects as disputed opinions in the world, and there are but few truths which have not been questioned by different men. Thus, on whatever side we view the practice of adopting the opinions of others without examination, the experiment seems big with danger.

Our obligation to embrace no doctrines which have

been professed by others without sufficient evidence, is, in the next place, apparent from our being endowed with reason. No anatomist, when dissecting the human body, and explaining the several offices which belong to the different parts, could ever say, with truth, that a single portion of this complicated whole was useless. There may be a few small fibres, or other minute divisions of the human frame, the use of which he might not be able exactly to define; but no one, who possesses skill in his profession, or a just sense of the imperfections of human knowledge, would ever affirm that a single fibre was, in reality, without its legitimate and determined function.

Now if we apply the same mode of reasoning to the faculties of the mind, we may easily prove, that each has its appropriate sphere of action, from the single circumstance of its being implanted in our nature. As our eyes were formed for seeing, and our feet for walking, so was the faculty of reason implanted, to enable us to improve in moral and religious truth, to detect the errors of sophistry, and to arrive at just conclusions in all the employments and concerns of life. And what sublimer subjects can engage our attention, than those of religion? What concerns exercise our reason, or occupy our thoughts, upon which more depends, both in the present and a future world? The inventions of the arts and sciences, and all those things which administer to the comfort and ease of life, may employ our intellectual faculties, but these are but earthly cares. The pleasures of this life are like the bright days of winter, of flattering aspect, but of short duration, while the joys of heaven flow from a fountain which is inexhaustible in its nature, and never ruffled by commotion. Virtue alone can procure that independence, which is the end of human wishes.

Perhaps, however, the duty of exercising reason in the concerns of religion, receives the highest confirmation from the example of our blessed Savior. We can nowhere find, in the volume of inspiration, a single precept to be influenced in our faith by the authority of men, rather than by the conviction of our own minds. Our Lord and Master was always ready to submit his credentials to the examination of all. He always appealed to the judgment of his hearers, and, instead of demanding a blind obedience to the precepts he delivered, proved to them the authority of his mission by the miracles he performed. Do the multitude doubt his power over the confines of the grave, immediately he utters the solemn and memorable words, "Lazarus, come forth," and the grave gives up its dead. Do they distrust his power to heal the infirmities of the sick, or to restore the power of walking to the lame? No sooner does he utter the command, "Take up thy bed and walk," than the lame man rises, and returns to his own house. Before his awful summons, the demons are deprived of all their influence; at his command, the withered hand is restored to vigor, and the blind receive their sight. In short, the whole Bible seems clearly to testify, that our Savior required the exercise of reason in its fullest extent. He reproves the unbelieving Jews for the confidence they reposed in the Scribes and Pharisees, who were their spiritual guides, and exhorts them to examine for themselves. "But I," says Christ, "have greater witness than that of John; for the works that the Father hath given me to finish, the same works that I do bear witness of me, that the Father hath sent me." Such, too, I might easily show, was the method of instruction used by the apostles. They claimed not to be received without sufficient evidence of their authority; and it is the advice of St. Paul, "Prove all things; hold fast that which is good."

It appears, then, that all who discourage freedom of inquiry encroach upon the natural rights of mankind, and oppose their own authority to that of Christ and his apostles. I might easily mention many practices in the Christian church which have evidently this tendency. But, as they are well known to my learned and highly respected audience, it is unnecessary to mention them, and sufficient to notice some of their dangerous consequences. And it is obvious to remark, that they tend to check all religious knowledge and improvement, to confine the mind in useless chains and fetters, and to entail ignorance and superstition upon posterity. These, and many other inconveniences, are hardly to be balanced by the advantages which these practices seem to afford. It is asserted, however, that all these endeavors to restrain free inquiry, have been made with the purest intentions, and most disinterested motives; that, by these means, the church has been preserved from heretics, and those who are unsound in faith; those, in other words, who have never been accustomed to measure their piety by the number of speculative principles to which they could subscribe their names; or those who have not imbibed their sentiments from the confessions of men, but from the oracles of GOD.

The spirit of free inquiry, like most other blessings, has been sometimes carried to excess, and it is a melancholy truth, that so powerful are the allurements of novelty and singularity, and so overbearing the love of reputation for uncommon learning, that men are sometimes found weak enough to imagine that they can never think with sufficient freedom and independence, till they have rejected all that has been believed by their predecessors; men who support their pride and evil inclination, by endeavoring to undermine the sacred fabric of religion, instead of adding new pillars to support its weight. But these instances are not extremely frequent, and men are more prone to embrace the opinions of a court or majority, and blindly to follow their spiritual guides, than to expose themselves to the danger of losing the road to preferment and favor, while searching after the path that leads to truth.

There is a necessity of encouraging, rather than of depressing, a spirit of free and impartial inquiry; and I hold it as a maxim no less applicable to religion than politics, that few persons, who have once tasted the honey of favor, will readily consent to return to hunger and philosophy.

I shall now attempt briefly to answer some of the objections, which have been made against the principle I support. It has sometimes been asserted, that a free examination has a dangerous tendency to disturb the peace of the church with erroneous opinions and heresies, and that it exposes religion to the attacks of rash and unprincipled infidels. This objection seems grounded upon the supposition, that our religion is of such a nature, that it will not bear the test of examination, and that he, who investigates its principles, will necessarily be led to dangerous conclusions; and that his reason, instead of enlightening the path which leads to truth, will conduct to error. But is it the province of reason to mislead? Does history justify the conclusion? Is it not rather her province, to enlighten the ways of science, to "illumine what is dark," and to detect what is erroneous? If our religion be founded in truth, it has nothing to fear from impartial examination. Like a rock in the midst of the ocean, the waves of infidelity, and the violence of passion, may dash against its sides, but it will remain unmoved. The clouds of scepticism may hover round its surface, but it will still remain amidst all the gloom with which it is surrounded. It may be concealed for a season by the fog of error or superstition, but the full sunshine of reason will at last dissipate the darkness.

To magnify the dangers of free inquiry, is tacitly to confess that we doubt the truth of the system we support. Opinions founded in reason and revelation, have nothing to fear from the minutest investigation. The better they are understood, the more shall we discover of their intrinsic excellence; the better they are known, the greater will be our approbation. It is the nature of falsehood alone to shun the light of day, to involve itself in mystery, and to demand belief without examination. But truth solicits an investigation, and, being founded in the constitution of things, must ever remain the same while nature herself endures.

The doctrines of religion may sometimes be attacked by violent and ignorant opponents; but this is an evil, the remedy of which would be worse than the disease. Religious freedom is an inestimable blessing, but, like other privileges, is attended with some inconveniences. Our most exquisite joys, when they surpass a certain limit, are followed by the most painful consequences; and our most valuable mental endowments may subserve the cause of error and deception.

Another objection is drawn from the unsettled state of mind, which is supposed to attend a free inquiry in the concerns of religion. This, however, should always be expected, since our faculties are limited, and there are many questions, which are indeterminate in their nature. But the same difficulties are common to all the sciences, and we have nothing to apprehend from this source; since questions of this nature are generally such as are purely speculative, and possess but little influence on practice.

By accustoming ourselves to habits of close examination, we may possibly lessen the number of our tenets, but I doubt whether our piety will be diminished. We may lose some portion of our respect for men, but our reverence of God may be increased. A corrupt government may attempt to destroy the liberty of the press, because it serves to expose the baseness of their conduct, or to enlighten the public mind. A corrupt and prejudiced ecclesiastic may likewise conceal his ambition under the veil of piety, or rise to eminence, because the people are too ignorant to detect the imposition, or too enslaved to resist his measures. Yet the freedom of the press must always be regarded as the palladium of our civil liberties, and free inquiry as the only security from fraud and delusion.

But, though I think there is but little weight in all the objections, which have or can be made against freedom of inquiry, still I am of opinion that it should be conducted with prudence and moderation. There have been too many contentions for victory instead of truth, too many attempts to support a party instead of religion; and too much zeal, uninfluenced and undirected by charity. Those, who have engaged in controversies, have often displayed more of temper than argument, and a zeal "which was not according to knowledge." Instead of "speaking the truth in love," they have uttered their sentiments in the tone of anger and resentment. In short, polemic skill must always be regarded as a dangerous qualification, and, if not governed by charity, wisdom, and integrity, may betray the possessor into intemperate zeal, or absolute indifference for truth. Every object assumes an importance, in our estimation, in proportion to the labor and attention we bestow. But the real value of any doctrine can be determined only by its influence on the conduct of man with respect to himself, his fellow creatures, and his God. And it has been well observed, by an author, that "some kinds of error are so intimately connected with truth and virtue, as to render the separation of them impracticable without doing violence to both." It is better, therefore, according to our Savior's advice, to permit a few tares to grow up with the wheat, than to endanger the destruction of the wheat by rooting up the tares.

It now remains to make some application of the sentiments above advanced to our own condition.

If any class of persons are under an obligation to examine with care and attention the truths of our holy religion, it is certainly the duty of those who are favored with the means of intellectual and moral improvement. "To whom much is given, of him shall much be required," is a sacred declaration, but no less sacred than reasonable and important. If it be ever necessary, that we should entertain correct views of the doctrines and precepts of religion, the time has certainly arrived, when we should commence the duty to be performed.

There is a becoming respect, with which we should treat the opinions of our parents or early instructors, and those from whom we imbibed our first sentiments. This is but a just tribute to parental affection, and superior information and experience. But there is a season when we should examine for ourselves, and inquire into the foundation of the sentiments which we have embraced. We need never blush to maintain opinions, which differ from those of our parents and connections, if they have been adopted upon sufficient evidence.

To promote and encourage this impartial inquiry, is one of the objects of this society; and as our future conduct must, in no small degree, depend upon the sentiments we here embrace, it can surely be esteemed a duty of no minor consideration, that we endeavor, by reason and application, and, above all, by the kind assistance of our Maker, to discover those principles, which will guide us safely in our future career, and cultivate that spirit of piety, the exercise of which constitutes no inconsiderable portion of the Christian's happiness. It is vain and dangerous to suppose, that we can live in safety without any religious sentiments. The human mind resembles a piece of ground, which will, by no means, be wholly barren, but will either bring forth the noxious weeds of vice, or the wholesome fruits of righteousness, according as it is neglected or cultivated with care. The short period we here devote to the services and the duties we owe our God, cannot but be attended with improvement.

The prayer, in which we here engage, has a greater tendency, than more public forms of devotion, to revive, and fasten upon our minds, the general principles of religion. We are here permitted to particularize our necessities and wants in a greater degree than is practicable in the house of public worship; and it should always be remembered, that all forms of public adoration are less interesting than services of the kind in which we engage; and that the ardor of devotion is better supported, and the sympathy more easily propagated, through a small assembly connected by ties of familiarity than in the presence of a mixed congregation.

As the dangers to which youth is exposed seem to arise rather from thoughtlessness and levity than from any prejudice against religion, if we habituate ourselves to abstract our thoughts from the external objects which surround us, and with the intellectual eye to examine our own minds, we shall not only correct this dangerous habit, and fix our wavering thoughts and resolutions, but accomplish another important end of the society to which we belong. Religion is a subject upon which our present and future happiness depends; and, as it is often the topic of conversation and controversy, to have a comprehensive view of its evidences, and to be able to assign the reasons of our belief, should be the desire of all.

Having once obtained this object, we shall feel an assurance in our faith, which all the arts of infidelity will be unable to destroy. For unbelievers can only go round and round the same topics in an eternal circle, without advancing a single step. It produces no new forces; it only brings those again into the field, which have been already baffled and subdued. Let us not be prevented from the performance of our religious duties by the common complaint, that we have not time for the services of religion. The cares and avocations of this life are often urged as an excuse for our neglects, but they will have but little weight with him who reflects that we are placed in this world only to prepare for another, and that the troubles and solicitude of our earthly career are so many trials of our patience and fortitude. But we seem ever ready to forget that an unruffled flow of pleasures is not to be expected, and that there is no pursuit so important and interesting as to afford a continual subject of meditation, and to employ all the powers and faculties of our nature, except eternity. But, if we consider this world as only a passage to a more perfect state, and as a removal from a scene of confusion and discord to one of everlasting peace and happiness,

"To die is landing on some silent shore,
Where billows never beat, nor tempests roar,
Ere well we feel the friendly stroke, 't is o'er."

He who, with such prospects before him, can complain of heaven, and repine at death, acts a part no less absurd than he who, proposing to himself a delightful tour into an unknown country, should lament that he cannot take up his residence, and remain forever at the first noisy and inconvenient inn he meets with on the road.

From the above observations, we may likewise perceive the importance of acquiring all that knowledge and information, which may lead us to entertain just views of the important subjects of religion, and enable us to expose the "traditions of men." Ignorance is the road which is generally travelled by the idle, and we should always preserve a caution that we never mistake a lazy and blind devotion for an enlightened, generous, and industrious piety. But let us think no knowledge so important as that which pertains to religion. The glory which letters bestow is, no doubt, greatly desirable; yet it is difficult to acquire. It is much easier to live a life of virtue than a life of fame. We pardon a man though he be undignified in his manners and address, and unacquainted with all the elegances of polite literature, but we never forgive him, if he be deficient in goodness and honesty of character. On this subject, we perfectly accord with Themistocles, who observed, "that he loved the man without letters much better than letters without the man." If we owe much to the fathers of our bodies, how much more are we indebted to those who have formed our minds? For the knowledge of letters has a favorable tendency to produce within us just sentiments, elegant manners, and, what is far more important, to enable us to defend our religion.

That the world contains no substantial happiness, that, without the expectation of another, the soul has nothing upon which it may repose itself, is a common observation; but, though it be confirmed by a variety of examples, it seems to have but little influence upon our lives. The more we know of the world, its phantoms and enchantments, the more do we feel the want of some grand idea to elevate the soul above the discouragements which continually occur. When we engage in the pursuits of honor, fame, and gratitude, we find everywhere illusions and mistakes. If we make no uncommon exertion, and leave our vessel in the harbor, the success of others dazzles and disturbs us; if we spread our sails, we are the plaything of the winds. Activity, inactivity, ardor, indifference, all have their cares and difficulties. No person is sheltered from the caprices of fortune. Her wheel is forever in motion. We tremble on its summit, in the middle we are suspended, and, at the bottom, we are trampled under foot. When we have reached the summit of our wishes, sadness and languor are preparing to frustrate our hopes, and dissipate the enchantment. If such then be the instability of the world, and the uncertainty of all earthly possessions, to whom shall we go but unto God? And how shall we obtain his mercy but through the merits of his Son? It is virtue alone which can render us superior to fortune, and, if we quit her standard, the combat is no longer ours. Let not then the important work of salvation be longer neglected.

But the prayer of too many is, "Lord, make me virtuous and continent, but not too soon." "Wait, I beseech thee, till the season of pleasure be passed, and the ardor of passion subsided." "The time will come when I shall have little inclination for vice, and when satiety and disgust will prevent all danger of a relapse." To ask in such a manner, is, indeed, to ask in vain. If we would find our God, we must seek him early. How often have we witnessed the danger of postponing the duties of religion! With how many lessons for youth has experience furnished us! Let, then, our solicitude be in some proportion to our danger. Let us make it the important business of our lives to fix the purest and most sacred principles in our hearts, and lay the foundation of that solid peace through life, which, once lost, is never perfectly recovered; not even under the direction of the brightest understanding, and most fervent piety. If such be our conduct, we shall have but little reason to find fault with the difficulties of this life. Those who utter the loudest complaints have generally wasted or misimproved their time. "If the tumult of your souls," says St. Austin, "would subside, you would not be moved by outward noises. When the mind is calm, the confusion of outward objects is disregarded. In this happy state of the soul, neither the clouds which fly around us, or even the thunder which rolls over our heads, is able to disturb her serenity. Safe in the port, she beholds, but feels not, the tumult." "Behold, now is the accepted time; behold, now is the day of salvation.

DISSERTATION

ON THE IMPORTANCE OF THE DOCTRINE OF A FUTURE STATE.

One of the Subjects of the Bowdoin Prize Dissertations for 1814.

"He that cometh to God, must believe that he is; and that He is a rewarder of them that diligently seek Him."—HEBREWS x. 6.

IN religion, as in the arts and sciences, there are a few important principles, which serve as the support and foundation of all the rest. The great object, therefore, of the inquirer after truth should be, to ascertain, in every science, which is the subject of his examination, what are its fundamental truths. Having satisfied himself in this important inquiry, he has laid a solid basis, and will be able, without much difficulty, to raise the superstructure.

As religion is a concern not confined to any particular class of people, but universal in its obligations, and ever salutary in its effects, it is a circumstance which deserves our warmest gratitude to the Parent of the universe, that its two essential constituents are so clearly manifested to mankind, that they are discoverable by the light of reason. The existence of one God, and a future state of rewards and punishments, form the grand basis of this interesting and important science. He who would destroy or weaken the evidence of either of these doctrines, aims a deadly blow at the peace and happiness of mankind. To exemplify and display the influence of the persuasion of a future state of recompenses upon the order and well-being of society, is the design of the following dissertation.

To the Christian, who reflects how numerous have been the endeavors of unbelievers, in every age, to overturn this important doctrine, and to prove it to be the vain imagination of the enthusiast, and how ingenious have been the attempts of the profligate and wicked, to demonstrate the fallacy of an opinion, which they tremble to believe as true, it can afford no small degree of satisfaction, that the basis of the Christian's hopes is no less supported by reason than revelation, and that the infidel must destroy the dictates of reason, as well as the authority of revealed religion, before he can demolish or undermine the firm fabric of his faith. Those, who have wished to prove that the present life is the whole duration of our existence, and thus to destroy the validity of revelation, have argued, that the ancients had no expectation of a future state of recompenses, by comparing their different opinions with one another, and showing the diversity of sentiment, which prevailed amongst them. Should, however, the endeavors of this class of sceptics be crowned with complete success, and should it be demonstrated, that Aristotle, Plato and Cicero, had all different ideas, and confused notions of a future world; still, this mode of arguing can have no influence upon this interesting inquiry. A sufficient answer to all such unbelievers, is, that, prior to philosophy, or the existence of the school-men, there was everywhere a common consent on the subject of a future state; and should philosophy claim the honor of having discovered this important doctrine, its claims should be rejected, and we shall probably be indebted to tradition for this interesting truth. Now that such was the common persuasion of mankind, prior to revelation, is clearly proved from the appeal which is made by every writer on the subject, to the common consent of men, which is always used as one of their chief arguments. This almost universal agreement is the voice and law of nature, because that of which are all persuaded, must have had a common origin, and must, therefore, have proceeded, in the first instance, from the Parent of mankind. The fictions of the poets, and subtleties of the philosophers of antiquity upon this subject, are well known; but, however the notion may have been confused by them, the common consent of the universe, and the evidence of nature, are the same, and, though entangled by perplexities, can never be extinguished. The rational proofs of a future state can never be lost upon the sincere and pious Christian; and, since such is the preëminence of reason, that no opinion is to be credited when contrary to its dictates, the man of virtue and religion will feel no small gratification, when he discovers, that every part of revelation is grounded upon truth and reason. As it is the beauty of the laws by which a sovereign governs the people of a country, that they be established upon the immutable nature and constitution of man, so, likewise, it is the excellency of the Christian dispensation, that all the doctrines it contains, are not only reasonable, but so admirable in their nature, as no reason could discover.

Among the doctrines of revelation, that of a future state of rewards and punishments is one; and when the Christian finds that reason conspires with revealed religion, requires the same important duties, and enforces them by the same motives, with the additional advantage on the side of revelation, that it teaches us our whole duty; the Christian, I say, when he calls to mind all these circumstances, must feel a complacency and delight, which are wholly unknown to one who has never observed this perfect harmony and order.

Having premised the above observations upon the universality of the belief of a future state, I proceed to consider what is the immediate object of the dissertation, viz., its influence upon the order and well-being of society;

and, in prosecuting my design, I know of no more effectual method of showing its vast importance, to the peace and happiness of mankind, than by proving the insufficiency of all other motives to piety and virtue. Such is the frame of our nature, and so violent are the passions of mankind, that he, who should destroy the belief of the doctrine of a future life of recompenses, would abolish almost every motive to decency and order, and fill the world with every species of vice and immorality. He who attempts to overturn the religious sentiments of any class of believers, must always presume, that those, whose opinions he has controverted, will ask of him some new principles, which they may substitute, in the place of those which he has rejected with so much confidence. Accordingly, we find, that this method has been pursued in the controversy between the advocates of the truth of revelation, and those who have rejected the divine authority of Jesus Christ, and the latter, with much ingenuity and skill, have substituted every motive, which their imaginations could suggest. Since, however, in the commencement of their arguments, they had rejected the only powerful consideration to piety and religion, their endeavors have been unsuccessful, and no principle has been discovered, or alleged, which, like a state of future recompenses, operates at all times, and upon all descriptions of persons.

It has not unfrequently been asserted that, though there were no belief of a future state impressed upon the minds of men, yet that, since God is a being of infinite wisdom and unbounded goodness, mankind ought, and naturally would, adore and worship him, for these and other inestimable perfections. It is the argument of some, that, from the impulse of nature, we respect and esteem the wise and virtuous of the earth, and that, from the same principle, we should be led to worship and to reverence the Maker and Preserver of the universe without the intervention of a revelation.

That mankind owe unbounded gratitude, love and adoration, to him, who formed and upholds the world, will not be denied; but that the perfections of his character alone are sufficient to ensure the performance of these and other duties, is contradicted, both by the testimony of experience, and the consideration that the great mass of the people are not influenced by the contemplations and speculations of philosophers, but by the passions which reign within their own breasts. Every argument drawn from the perfections of the Deity, and the propriety of worshipping him on their account, is of no great weight when opposed to the passions and inclinations of mankind. Self-love is the great handle by which religion takes hold of the fears and affections of mankind. The same person who, under the persuasion that death was the extinction of his being, would defile himself with every species of vice, when assured of the certainty of a future state of recompenses, would sacrifice his disorderly passions to his duty, and lead a rational and virtuous life. Should it be said, that virtue and piety, to be acceptable to God, must proceed from purer motives than a servile fear of punishments, I answer, I am of the same opinion. But may not this fear in early life, sow the seeds of future piety and devotion? May not the man, who once acted chiefly from an apprehension of punishment, after a contemplation of the goodness of God and the duties which he owes to so benevolent a Father, be actuated by nobler motives? He, on the other hand, who has grown to manhood, under the impression that he shall never be required to answer for his conduct, will, at that period of his life, when reason is able to discover his obligations to his Maker, be destitute of those restraints upon his passions and inclinations, which are experienced by him, who has been educated under the opposite impression. While the latter comes to examine the truths of religion, uninfluenced by importunate inclinations; the former coming to the examination under the influence of prejudices, which he is unwilling to resign, and under the government of desires and feelings, which it is irksome to sacrifice to reason and propriety, will readily seek for objections to those doctrines, which he wishes to be false, slight all objections to the opposite opinions, and probably end the examination with a full conviction of the fallacy and unimportance of religion.

The insufficiency of every motive, except that of a future state, to lead men to the worship and reverence of God, and to a conduct conformable to his will, is most clearly proved by the concurrent testimony of history. To form hypotheses, when we possess the richest stores of information, derived from a knowledge of antiquity, is useless and absurd. In confirmation of the preceding observations, we find, that, in Greece and Rome, there were some philosophers, who believed in the immortality of the soul, and hence inferred the probability of future recompenses; but we likewise discover, that the lower classes of the community seldom perplexed themselves with the speculations of philosophers, and were almost wholly regardless of the consequences to be deduced from the nature of the soul; and we have the authority of Cicero for saying, that the thoughts of Socrates, himself, upon the immortality of the soul, were both fluctuating and undetermined. The generality of the people felt no interest in the subtleties of philosophy, and would certainly be at no trouble to discover the truth of a doctrine, which must either produce a change of conduct, or fill them with fears and apprehensions for their future welfare. The worship of one God is established in almost all parts of the habitable globe, because almost all are possessed of a belief in a future state of rewards and punishments, and he who should destroy this belief, would probably abolish every form of worship. Though it be true, that it is the will of God that we should adore and reverence his name, yet the greater part of mankind are too gross in their ideas of things, and too much enchained by the allurements of the world, to be influenced by this consideration alone; and whoever expects universal obedience from any arguments wholly addressed to the understanding of the human race, must be grossly ignorant of human nature.

I come now to consider another motive to piety and virtue, and which has been exalted to an high elevation in the writings of those, who have denied a future state, viz., a sense of honor and decorum. Though, in the estimation of different persons, this term seems to have a variety of senses, I know of none better, than that of a celebrated writer, who defines the laws of honor, to be "a system of rules constructed by people of fashion, to facilitate their intercourse with one another." Whatever candid person reflects, for a moment, how few are influenced by the laws of honor, and how many shelter themselves under those of the land, which, like Solon's, may possibly detect some daring offenders, but, like cobwebs, permit the greater number to escape with impunity, will hardly be so unfair, as to compare honor, as a principle of virtue, with a future state of recompenses. He, who has offered every argument in favor of its claims, must confess, that the sphere of its influence is extremely limited, and that, though this principle might have some influence upon men of rank and elevated station, still that the greater part of mankind are left wholly without the circle of its operation.

But, after all that can be said in favor of reputation, or the laws of etiquette, how are those rules of conduct worthy of much consideration, which have no other standard than custom, or the fashion of the day? If our conduct is to be directed by rules of this kind, those actions, which, in one age or period, are esteemed innocent, or even praise-worthy, may possibly, in the next, or at another period, be considered as highly criminal. Indeed, without some other standard, by which to judge of the propriety of our conduct, we may fall into the grossest absurdities, and the most dangerous practices. The state may be deprived of its most eminent warriors and statesmen, by the destructive habit of duelling, and he who meets disappointments or vexations in life, may, without the infringement of any law, terminate his existence by suicide.

The punishments of civil government, will, equally with the common opinion of the community, to which any person belongs, be too weak to ensure safety and peace either to the individual or magistrate. The rod, which is in the hand of the civil governor, and the sword which is wielded by public opinion, will be hardly sufficient to check the inroads of vice, or ensure the performance of moral duties. It is obvious to remark, that the influence of laws is confined within a narrow circle, and that a person may escape their animadversion, and, at the same time, be stained with some of the foulest actions.

The deficiency of laws seems to arise chiefly from two causes. First, that many actions are wholly without the sphere of their operation, because they possess no discriminate character, by which they may be defined. Secondly, because they are in their nature such as may easily be evaded. He who, with respect to the laws of the civil magistrate, is blameless, may still be destitute of humanity and benevolence, may plunge his afflicted country into unnecessary wars, in order to render his services desirable, may be treacherous in his friendships, and indeed destitute of every active virtue. The important duties of charity and humility may have never influenced one action of him, who in the eye of the law is wholly free from guilt.

The excellent doctrines of our holy religion, on the other hand, while they ensure the perfect security and encouragement of the sovereign, teach those humbler, but not less important duties, which constitute the glory and happiness, both of the individual, and the community. In case, however, these obligations should be disregarded, it does not appeal to the imperfect authority of a human sovereign, but to the tribunal of an almighty Judge. The sentence of the former may be influenced by a variety of motives, which may effect our deliverance, though not restore our innocence, but in the latter case we stand before a Judge of infinite wisdom, and unbounded goodness, but of perfect justice.

As, in all these instances, the penalties of human laws may be evaded, and the guilty escape with impunity; so there are many actions, concerning which we can only be interrogated at the tribunal of our own consciences. And yet conscience itself is a mere name, a mere bugbear, independent of the notion of a future retribution. Let us be cautious, then, how we weaken the authority of a Judge so faithful, energetic, and enlightened. Let us reflect, that, when we have overturned his powerful empire, we have opened the flood-gates of licentiousness and vice; that the cement is loosened, the cohesion broken, and that the torrent of immorality and wickedness must rise superior to every barrier.

Indeed, the supposition that public opinion can ever subdue the power of inclination, or restrain, within due bounds, the violence of passion, seems wholly unsupported by fact. Such an hypothesis is contradicted by the very nature of man, who, in order to persevere in the paths of rectitude, must be influenced by some adequate motive. Besides, those who are chiefly the objects of public attention, are not the low and impotent, but those who have attracted the admiration, or drawn upon themselves the detestation of the public, by eminent services, or notorious frauds. The opinion of the world exercises its authority over those, whose rank or employment throws some splendor upon their earthly career; while the conduct of the private individual is less within the circle of its influence. Those, therefore, whose time is devoted to dissipation, and whose behavior has no connexion with the grand interests of the community, are, in some measure, independent of the opinion of the world. Their actions are confined to too humble a condition to excite public admiration, or to draw forth much censure and rebuke. Thus a large portion of every community who are distinguished by no ornaments of riches or privilege of title, are uninfluenced by this love of reputation, or desire of fame, which has been ranked as so important a principle by many writers. "Every thing valuable seems therefore to depend upon religion. It surrounds the whole compass of morality, resembling that universal and mysterious force of physical nature which retains the planets in their orbits, and subjects them to a regular revolution, and which, amidst the general order it maintains, escapes the observation of many, and appears to their feeble sight unconscious of its own work."

Much has been written upon the loveliness of virtue, and the intrinsic excellency of certain actions, and the deformity of vice, and yet the observation and experience of mankind unite to prove that, however the world may admire, or be enamored of virtue, she is seldom chosen. Though I could never discover any internal goodness or immorality in actions, independent of the motives with which they were performed, yet it is not denied that some are found to lead to happiness, while others tend to make us miserable. Those of the former class may therefore be figuratively denominated virtuous, and those of the latter immoral, and destructive of happiness. Now it seems somewhat absurd, if not impious, to extol the beauty and excellency of virtue, and yet to suppose that, with all her claims to notice and consideration, a Being who delights in goodness has been regardless of her claims, and made no difference between herself and her irreconcilable enemies, vice and immorality. He, who believes in the goodness of God, must be mad to suppose that he can view vice and virtue with the same feelings. Yet upon the supposition that this life is the whole duration of our existence, we are compelled to admit the conclusion that virtue loses her reward, and that vice is completely successful. It is the test of a true patriot, when private advantage is opposed to public good, to sacrifice his own convenience to that of society. So likewise we may denominate him virtuous, who, when duty and inclination are at variance, sacrifices his propensity to the dictates of reason. If, however, mankind are actuated by no apprehensions of future consequences, it is no hard matter to predict which of these two principles of action will prevail. If virtue, without the authority she acquires from the consideration of a future life, be opposed to vice, with all the passions on her side, it would be absurd to suppose that she could possibly succeed against such powerful enemies, united by a common interest. Overpowered by superior force, she must soon be vanquished, and leave the field in the possession of her lawless and barbarous invaders. Many writers who have endeavored to prove that the consideration of a future state of recompenses is unnecessary to the support of piety and virtue, seem to have had very indeterminate notions of these important qualities in the Christian character. They do not consist of show or ostentation, or in performing a few hasty and benevolent actions, while under the influence of some violent emotion. Virtue, or an upright conduct towards our fellow-beings, and temperance as it respects ourselves, depends upon religion as its chief support; and he, who destroys the confidence of another in a future state, has taken from him the vital principle of his virtue. Those who maintain the opposite opinion seem never to have considered that piety is an internal principle of the heart, and that those who are flattered for their benevolence or liberality are often destitute of all true virtue.

There are but few who are so hardened as to commit such crimes as both reason and the laws condemn in the full sunshine of day; because, though possibly they might escape the cognizance of law, yet the natural sense of right and wrong found amongst all classes would condemn such actions, and the perpetrators be thus exposed to disgrace and ignominy. But since it is not always day, and since there is the greatest necessity for some internal principle which is obligatory at all times, and upon all descriptions of persons, but little reflection must be sufficient to convince us that all others are insufficient, and that a future state of recompenses alone is able to effect this important end. It is this alone which can restrain the dangerous machinations of him who would subvert the laws of his country. It is this alone which can defeat the wicked designs of the robber, murderer, or thief, and, without this belief to influence the actions of mankind, every species of vice and immorality must prevail. Without this fear, the unprincipled ruler may destroy the best interests of his country with impunity, and the ambitious general has nothing to prevent his rendering himself absolute as soon as he can obtain the consent of that army upon which he depends for his support. In short, were this principle banished from the world, all confidence and security in our fellow beings would be lost in the general confusion which must ensue.

Should it be said that the natural consequences of vice in this world are themselves sufficient to ensure the victory to sobriety over immorality and licentiousness, and that such are the salutary effects of virtue, that, to be admired, she needs but to be known, I answer that these natural consequences may, with justice, be alleged as proof of the manner in which God considers the virtuous and the vicious; but are certainly insufficient of themselves to maintain the supremacy of piety and virtue. How numerous are the instances of persons ruined in their fortunes, and depressed by sickness, on account of the irregularities of their past lives, and yet, how many do we find rushing inconsiderately into the same excesses, through looseness of principle, or the violence of passion! In other words, how many do we find "who need the smart of pain, to make them prudent"! Whatever may have been the losses or sufferings of others, in the same career, many will be always found who, having never made the experiment, will be led to believe that they shall be more successful.

Indeed, without the assurance or presumption of a future state, indulgence in sensual gratifications would hardly deserve the name of criminal; since the Governor of the universe, upon that supposition, makes no distinction between the virtuous and the vicious; and I see no sufficient reason why, upon that supposition, we should not adopt the language of the sensualist, "Let us eat and drink, for to-morrow we die." To-morrow we cease to exist, like the beasts which perish; and, whatever may have been our conduct in this world, our condition after death will be the same; since death is an eternal sleep.

Upon the hypothesis that the present life is the whole of our existence, the wicked are completely successful, while those of the opposite character must be exposed to ridicule and disgrace as solitary beings, who are continually perplexing themselves with possibilities, and passing their lives in a manner both disagreeable and absurd. Besides, it should never be forgotten that there are many actions highly criminal in their nature, which raise the perpetrators of them to places of honor and distinction, instead of bringing upon them the punishment they so justly deserve. The unprincipled usurper, for instance, is found to make his way to empire by the most barbarous and disgraceful actions, and afterwards to enjoy those privileges which, in justice, belong only to the lawful heir. The opulent and powerful baron has been often known to oppress his numerous dependents, and yet to escape the penalty of law, through the affluence of riches, or magnitude of authority. While mankind have the fear of a state of future recompenses to influence their conduct, the unfortunate and impotent have some protection and security against the wiles of the crafty and oppressive; but, without this restraint, they must be exposed to every species of injury and insult.

It here seems worthy of observation, that those writers, who, denying a future state of recompenses, have affirmed that a belief in it is unnecessary to the support of morality, have an advantage over those, who maintain the opposite opinion, which is hardly discerned at first, and which often passes wholly unnoticed. For those several motives, which they have substituted in the place of rewards and punishments, would be of but little, if any weight, when deprived of the support, which they derive from the same doctrine which they have attempted to prove fallacious. Our opponents, therefore, to reason with justice and candor, ought not to allege these motives as they now exist in the minds of those who enjoy the light of revelation, but should look for them, as they exist in that portion of the world which has never been visited by the genial influence of religion, and to those dark regions which have never been illuminated by the glorious light of revelation. They will find, upon inquiry, that, before the world had been favored by the Christian dispensation, amongst the most polished nations of antiquity, their sense of decency and decorum was not so delicate, but it would admit of the grossest obscenities, and actions too offensive to be named; that their sense of virtue was not so strong and determinate, but it would admit of the exposure of helpless infants and aged parents, whenever the infirmities of their nature, or the lapse of years, had rendered the latter unfit for the common business and duties of active life; that their conceptions of the gods were not so accurate and just, but they would allow them to suppose, that they felt no interest and concern in the affairs of mortals; in short, that their sense of honor was not so enlightened, but it would lead one of their most polished scholars and philosophers to remark, that "suicide was the noblest privilege which the gods had conferred on man." When, therefore, our opponents assert that the opinions and principles, which men must naturally imbibe from their intercourse with each other, would afford a sufficient encouragement to good morals and religion, they forget that all these principles are derived immediately from the doctrines of religion, and that connexion which subsists between the creature and Creator; and that, when you have destroyed religion, you have dried up the fountain from which these opinions are derived.

The instances we sometimes discover of sceptics who maintain good moral characters, has been likewise urged to prove the belief of a future state unnecessary to the support of virtue. Other reasons, however, than the internal loveliness of virtue, may easily be assigned to account for this phenomenon. Religion suffers nothing from the discovery. In the first place, those unbelievers who answer to this description, have been generally persons who had acquired habits of reflection and study, and contracted a love of scientific distinction, and had few temptations to resist, and few unlawful desires which they wished to gratify. As they were removed from the bustle of the world, and separated from those who might endanger their virtue, so they have been seldom found to fall into gross irregularities. Where this has not been the case, their conduct has been as wicked and profligate as their speculations have been absurd and impious. Bolingbroke may serve as a remarkable example, and striking illustration of the truth of this remark. Persons of the above description have often avoided the extremes of profanity, drunkenness, or debauchery; but they have likewise been destitute of those excellent feelings of the mind, and those nicer emotions of the heart, which distinguish and exalt the most humble Christian.

In the second place, it is worthy of remark, that unbelievers of the class now under consideration have been generally speculative men, and members of some sect, whose opinions they were bound to defend; and, as it has been their wish to increase their number, they have preserved that course of conduct, which has the greatest tendency to secure this end. Few of them have ever been in places of high responsibility and trust, subject to be seduced from the path of rectitude by flattery and intrigue, or exposed to the temptations of interest, or the dangers of pride and vanity. They were content with their humble condition, and have seldom risen to the honors of the world, which are justly termed the precipices of virtue. I know of no greater incitement to diligence and circumspection than that impulse of the soul, which always actuates him who meets opposition to prove the soundness of his principles by the propriety and virtue of his conduct.

Vice and immorality are not the only evils which arise from the disbelief of a future state of recompenses; but mankind would be extremely miserable, were not this doctrine founded in truth. The virtuous, but unfortunate person, when afflicted by the rod of the tyrant, or the injustice of the powerful, consoles himself with the reflection that this world is not his eternal home, or lasting residence; but, though a state of trial, that the time will come when the whole human race shall be rewarded according to their works, by a Judge of impartial justice and infinite knowledge. Upon the supposition that there is no state of future recompenses, reason, far from being a blessing or privilege to our species, must be considered as a quality of the mind, which serves no other purpose, but to disappoint and render us unhappy. It would serve as a lamp to light us to our solitary dungeon at our death, there to be deprived of existence, and never to rise again. The assurance of non-existence after death might liberate the wicked from those gloomy apprehensions and fears which disturb the guilty mind; yet the better part of the community must be deprived of their best hopes, which illuminate the dark and dreary path of life, and refresh the weary traveller at every stage of his long and tiresome pilgrimage. Every advantage arising from this unreasonable supposition, belongs to the profligate and wicked; that class of persons, in every community, which nothing but the apprehension of extreme punishment in a future world, can induce to sacrifice a single gratification to the peace and happiness of society. Persons of all descriptions would be extremely unhappy, though the wise and virtuous would lose more of their enjoyments than the hardened and abandoned sinner. Those who had devoted themselves to the pleasures and vanities of life would, at the approach of death, be very reluctant to leave a world of enjoyment for a dark and gloomy grave; which must forever terminate their existence. The virtuous, who had long endured all the sufferings of an earthly residence, and had been comforted, in every adversity, with the hopes of a happier existence beyond the tomb, when told that, after death, they were to rise no more, would be struck with astonishment and dismay; and their reason would exalt them above the brutes only to increase the sum of human misery. By a kind disposition of Providence, the brute creation are unable to foresee the approach of death, and are therefore deprived of no portion of present happiness by gloomy apprehension. But death, which, to the Christian, is often a place of refuge from the trials and persecutions of the world, to him who disbelieves the immortality of the soul, can afford but a gloomy prospect. Whatever may be said of the wisdom of the heathens, before the glorious light of revelation had burst upon the world, it cannot be denied, that, with no other guide but reason, we may fall into dangerous errors on the subject of religion. Revelation has displayed, with all the brightness and splendor of noonday, those truths, which were but imperfectly viewed through the dim twilight of reason. Reason, when applied to religion, is the sun in an eclipse; but revelation is the sun shining with his meridian splendor. Amongst heathen moralists, there prevailed great diversity of opinion on man's identity, and so discordant were their sentiments upon this and many other questions with respect to the body after death, that many were induced to reject the doctrine of the immortality of the soul, as the dogma of some philosopher. Their ideas upon the nature and duration of a future state were confused and indeterminate, while the

Christian can contemplate, with confidence and assurance, the existence and enjoyments of a future world.

He, who imagines himself the child of blind and undiscerning chance, has formed too grovelling an idea of his own nature, to permit him to aspire to virtue and distinction. He possesses a temporary faculty, which is denominated reason, but it is only to light him to the grave, and there to vanish for eternity. He has a soul capable of great improvement, and vast expansion, but it is only to continue during its infancy, and perishes before it can produce those salutary fruits, which fill the mind with insatiable delight.

Though man is the most excellent part of this lower creation, and though his intellectual faculties give him, in this world, a vast superiority over the rest of the beings of the earth, yet he is, on some accounts, the least provided for, if there be no future state. For what encouragement would there be, to sacrifice private interest to public good, or to deny present appetites and passions? What inducement to practise self-denial, and to seek the happiness of particular persons, if there be no future state of recompenses? What profit would be derived from the cultivation of our minds, and advancement in knowledge, if the progress of it is to end at death, and can last no longer? To be assured that our souls are immortal, revives the drooping spirits, and fills the mind with unspeakable delight. How pleasing is the thought, that we are to live beyond the grave, and that our condition, in that state of existence, will depend upon our conduct in the present; that there is no respect of persons, and that, in that scene, the weary traveller finds a heavenly home! Having burst asunder the chains which confine the soul, and divested ourselves of the external garment, how pleasing, how consoling, is the thought that we shall be clothed with an immortal robe! The greatest anxiety, the severest pains, which can surround a death-bed, are the fears of future punishments; but, if the soul can cast itself upon God, and place an entire confidence in the Rock of Ages, death is then no more than a sigh, or a short passage, from a world of trouble and perplexity, to a world of immortality and endless felicity.

Thus have I completed what I designed to say, upon the important and interesting subject of a future state. That the above observations are very obvious and common, and that the whole composition has probably many faults and imperfections, the writer has little doubt. That the subject, too, is but in part unfolded, and that many important observations, which arise from it have been omitted, is likewise probable. It is hoped, however, that its complicated nature, and its various connections and dependencies, will serve, in some measure, to extenuate those imperfections. Let it be remembered, that such is the nature of the subject, and so various its relations, that a full investigation could hardly be expected from one, whose attention has never been expressly and particularly devoted to the numerous and interesting subjects and speculations, which belong to religion, but distracted with a variety of studies and pursuits. It is now submitted, such as it is, to the candid examination of those, whose age and learning have supplied them with more enlarged views, but who are not unmindful of the difficulties which must attend the pursuits of those, who are just entering within the mazes of science, which must necessarily produce some uncertainty and confusion of thought. "Whatever may be the reception or fate of this performance," to use the words of another, "the writer flatters himself with the reflection, that it has not been wholly without advantage to himself, and that, in every stage of its progress, he has found in it, that alone, which can alleviate our pains, or give a zest to our enjoyments, occupation, and engagement."

A DELIBERATIVE DISCUSSION,

ON THE EXPEDIENCY OF ENCOURAGING MANUFACTURING ESTABLISHMENTS IN THE UNITED STATES.

It has generally been thought that our country is not yet ready to engage in manufactures with success. This opinion, which was expressed by some of our ablest writers, when our present government was formed, has lost but little of its truth, by change of circumstances. So long as the strength of a nation consists in the wealth, numbers, and character of its people, and manufactures are found to be incompatible with these objects of national grandeur and prosperity, so long it is no less the duty than the policy of our citizens, to discourage them. A successful prosecution of domestic manufactures can be the offspring only of an overflowing population, and ample capitals, but it is impracticable for the United States, containing extensive tracts of territory, which require but the hand of industry to produce the most abundant fruits. American manufactures will never increase our wealth, while our population is yet small, and the price of labor extremely high. Our citizens will never consent to sacrifice all the elegant and beautiful productions of European ingenuity, to humor the caprice, or to flatter the vanity, of any class of politicians, who, like the enlightened philosophers of China, imagine their own country to be a sort of paradise, amidst a degenerate and impoverished world; the seat of all that is elegant in literature, profound in science, or grand in nature. Whatever may be said of that noble independence which our country would enjoy, if it had no intercourse with foreign nations, the prudent politician will ever remember the useful maxim, "that national honor should never be viewed as distinct from national interest." The pursuit of independence, undirected by prudence, is a blind and romantic passion; and some reasons may be alleged to show that it is even desirable that our country should, in a degree, depend upon other nations. A situation of this nature restrains the violence of passion, and curbs that arrogance and national pride which are generated by prosperity, and not unfrequently induce the corrupt and unjust ruler to invade the unoffending provinces of neighboring empires. Commerce, which must always be regarded as the most fruitful source of national wealth, should never be impeded by the encouragement of domestic manufactures. But all the advantages to be derived from foreign intercourse may be lost, if, through a blind attachment to the productions of our own country, we neglect to form commercial relations with the nations of Europe in this infancy of our republic. When they have once discovered that our commerce is not necessary, either to their subsistence or prosperity, it may be too late to obtain the advantages of their trade. The dews of the morning will have passed, and we shall vainly attempt to pursue the chase by the meridian splendor. I am not anxious to accelerate the approach of that period, when our citizens, instead of enjoying in security the beauties of nature, shall be enveloped in the smoke of factories, or be dizzied with the hammering of presses, the clatter of engines, and the whirling of wheels; when, instead of gambolling and sporting in the rich ocean of commerce, they shall be compelled forever to behold the expert and active seaman transformed to the teamster; and the rapid and majestic motion of the merchant vessel exchanged for the slow, dull creaking of the wagon. If, therefore, our agriculture and commerce should be lost in an experiment to try how well our country would succeed without them, there is reason to apprehend that our situation would be indeed deplorable, and that we should become a nation of ferocious and stupid, and, at the same time, poor and sordid barbarians, without enjoyment and without hope. Private interest will ensure the wealth and prosperity of a country with much greater certainty than the refinements of state. The mistaken politician may imagine that he has augmented the happiness of his people by the support he affords to one species of labor, while he discourages another; or that the desire of gain will be more ardent when cherished by the favor of public authority; but in reality he has only attempted to increase what is already sufficiently vehement; "he has dashed with his oar to hasten the cataract, and waved with his fan to give speed to the winds."

It is the very nature of manufactures to afford but a precarious subsistence. A foreign war, or a change of fashion, (which, of all things, is most changeable,) are often sufficient to throw thousands out of employment, and to reduce them to the extreme of poverty. A person, while toiling in a factory, is exercising no faculties of his mind or body, which can ensure happiness or prosperity in declining years; when the decrepitude of age has succeeded to the strength of manhood, and the enfeebled limbs refuse to fulfil their respective offices. In short, the ignorant and impotent manufacturer has been justly denominated one of that class of persons whom we cannot prove to be a human being by any rational characteristic, but must admit to be so by a sort of *reductio ad absurdum*, because he cannot possibly be anything else; and I think it must be allowed by all, that the eighteen persons who, in an European factory, are engaged in manufacturing a single pin, fulfil an office which requires no very great exercise of the faculties of the mind. These and other circumstances, which might be mentioned, cannot be favorable to the increase of population, because, whatever impoverishes the parent, incapacitates him, in the same degree, for the maintenance and education of his children. In confirmation of this remark, it is computed that, in every manufacturing town in Europe, not one-third of the offspring of the poor arrive at maturity; and that, in England, whose extension of commerce and refinement in the arts during the last century, are unparalleled in the history of nations, the number of paupers in the same period has increased in a fourfold proportion, and is now rated at one-tenth of her whole population. The increase of our population by the emigration of foreigners has likewise been alleged as a reason why we should engage in the support of manufactures. That our numbers would be increased by the accession of foreigners, who might transplant themselves to America to engage in the pursuit of gain, will not be denied; but, before I can assent to the expediency of such a measure, I must be convinced that our republican institutions are sufficiently firm and durable to bear the ungoverned violence and daring innovations of so heterogeneous a mass of citizens. Patriotism, to become a powerful principle, must be impressed upon the mind by association and habit; or else it is the watchword of party, or a factitious spirit, which leads to disorder. But how, I would ask, can the bosoms of those glow with an enlightened love of country, who visit the United States only to increase their fortunes; who learn only from the speeches of our presidents, or from our public prints, that they are our countrymen; and who refuse to contribute to the support of government, while they possess a full share, though but little skill, in making our rulers? As well might we expect political virtue and an enlightened mind from the wandering Arab, or Indian hunter, as from the foreign artisan, whose only knowledge is that of his profession, whose only pursuit is gain. Those kinds of manufactures which are conducted in the household by persons under the inspection of guardians and friends, are probably highly beneficial to our country, because, while they increase its wealth, they do not pollute the morals, nor destroy the health. But those kinds which can be rendered profitable only by a minute division of labor, and by the employment of women and children separated from the care of connections, I cannot but condemn. I can discern in them no spirit favorable to our republican institutions; no circumstances, which are not hazardous to the morals, the patriotism, the happiness, and the lives of our countrymen. It is the glory and peculiar blessing of our country that its inhabitants are not, like some of the European nations, grouped in large collective bodies; and that the air which they breathe is uncontaminated with the destroying pestilence which pervades those manufacturing towns and cities which overflow with numbers. Places of this description are the seats of all that is hostile to civil liberty, to morality, and religion. An infuriated populace assumes the sovereign command, and the virtuous are compelled to enlist under their banners, because they are unable to resist their fury.

In seasons of public disorder, the advice of such as possess wisdom and integrity will be disregarded. The censure of the majority will be dreaded, and their favor sought. For the punishments inflicted by an enraged multitude are just causes of terror; and there are but few who can contemplate, with philosophical composure,

> "That baleful star, whose horrid hair
> Shakes forth the plagues of down and tar."

If, therefore, good morals are essential to the preservation of our republican institutions, and manufactures have a tendency to corrupt them, let us cordially unite in the wish, which was long since uttered by the third President of the United States, who, while contemplating, with the eye of unprejudiced reason, the circumstances of our country, expressed his desire, that, "while we have land to labor, our workshops might remain in Europe." Let us encourage no species of labor which is incompatible with the security and happiness of our country. And, may the tree of liberty, which was reared and nurtured by the care of our pious ancestors, be ever guarded by the vigilance, defended by the energy, and protected by the patriotism, of their descendants!

THESES RHETORICÆ.

RHETORICE ORNATE LOQUI, ET REBUS VERBA APTARE, DOCET.

Ut naturæ jura prius extiterunt, quam homines societate conjuncti, aut mores legibus formati sint, sic oratores fuerunt, antequam rhetores dicendi præcepta tradiderunt.

Loquendi consilia sunt quatuor; intellectui lucem afferre, imaginationem delectare; animi affectiones excitare; et voluntatem movere.

Evolvendi penitus auctores, qui de pietate, fortitudine, temperantia, et philosophia pæcipiunt; et rerum plurimarum scientia comprehendenda, sine qua orator frustra eloquens sit. "Nam eloquentia nihil aliud est, quam copiose loquens sapientia."

Omnis orationis vis et facultas in quatuor partes distributa est; invenire quid dicetur; inventa disponere; deinde ornare verbis; vel inventa eloqui; tum ad extremum agere ac pronuntiare cum dignitate ac venustate.

Apud antiquos genera tria orationis fuerunt: demonstrativum, deliberativum, et judiciale.

His aliud genus concionale nunc adjectum, quod in Dei templis exercetur.

Genus demonstrativum laudando et vituperando utitur. In genere deliberativo quæritur, quid utile, et in judiciali, quid justum sit.

Homines docere et emendare, atque eos a "peccatorum

via convertere," oratoris Christiani officium præcipuum est. Itaque incumbat, primum ut ii, qui audiant, cognoscant, quid elegendum et quid vitandum sit; et tum ad extremum virtutis amore arderent.

Tres sunt facti generales status; conjecturæ, finitionis, et qualitatis; aut tria sunt, quæ in omni disputatione quæruntur; An sit, quid sit, quale sit.

Partes orationis sunt exordium, propositio, probatio, ac peroratio.

Rhetores jubent exordire ita, ut eos, qui audiant, benevolos, et attentos, et dociles reddemus.

Deinde rem ita proponere, ut verisimilis, ut aperta, ut brevis narratio sit; ut auditores, facile cognoscant, quid confirmandum, aut refutandum sit.

Omnis probatio constat argumentis, quæ ex loco, tempore, et fine ducantur.

Peroratio sequitur, quæ rerum repetitione et congregatione constat. Hic si usquam, totos eloquentiæ aperire fontes, et hic auditorum animos possidere, totaque pandere possumus vela.

Pronuntiatio duas partes continet, vocem et motum; et affectus omnes languescant certum est, nisi orator voce, vultu, totius prope habitu corporis inardescat.

Omnis oratio causæ, auditoribus, personæ ac tempori accommodanda est.

In stylo necesse est, primum ut purus; deinde ornatus figurarum varietate, et ad rerum dignitatem accommodatus; sed ante omnia dilucidus; nam orationis virtus præcipua est perspicuitas.

SAMUEL D. BRADFORD.

CHARACTER OF BENJAMIN BILLINGS.

DIED, in Roxbury, on Thursday, August 20th, 1829, Mr. Benjamin Billings, aged sixty-four years. The decease of this excellent man will be a subject of deep regret to a large circle of relatives and friends, and to all, who had the privilege of his acquaintance. It appears to us, that, when the great and the good are taken away, whose lives have been distinguished by uncommon acts of virtue and kindness, they should not be permitted to be silently numbered with the dead, without that tribute of respect to their memory, which is the just reward of excellence.

The subject of this notice was a person of extraordinary worth; and we have never been called to mourn the death of any one, whose life was passed in the performance of more virtuous and disinterested actions.

His youth was marked by respect for his superiors in age and experience; by uncommon industry; and moral rectitude; and he formed, early in life, habits of close attention to business, which continued, without relaxation, in after years, and contributed so largely to his success. He was the friend of religion, and of good order in society; and was always ready to contribute liberally in aid of measures, which should benefit the interest of the town in which he resided. When any work of utility was to be accomplished, his name was among the very first, upon the list of contributors; although his acts of public munificence were few, compared with those of a private nature, which he was in the habit of constantly performing. His mode of life was quiet and unobtrusive. He avoided display and ostentation, and sought no other reward than that which he found in the approbation of his own conscience.

Of his domestic qualities, his affectionate devotion to his family and friends, (scenes which least attract public attention and notoriety,) we cannot speak in terms of too exalted praise. As a husband, he was attentive and affectionate; as a father, indulgent and kind; and, as a master, humane and merciful. He seemed particularly formed for domestic enjoyments; and it was in the circle of his family and friends that his character appeared to the greatest advantage. Indeed, by those, who were intimately acquainted with Mr. Billings, scarcely any degree of commendation would be deemed exaggeration.

We might dwell much longer upon the qualities of his heart, and speak of his perfect integrity, his love of truth, his hospitality, and the uncommon candor of his disposition. We might attempt to explain that power and influence about his manners and address, by which he was enabled to acquire so many friends, who survive deeply to lament his loss, and to whom his memory will be forever dear.

There are many, who feel that his death has dissolved some of the strongest ties, which human nature can know; but we forbear. The heart is now cold, which once glowed with friendship and philanthropy; and the ear, which was always open to the tale of distress, hears not our tribute of applause; but it is not possible that the impression, which his exemplary life and character have left upon our memories, can be easily or suddenly effaced.

No man, whom we have ever known, had more sincere and devoted friends; and, should we admit that he had any enemies, it would only prove that there are some hearts, which no degree of kindness can soften.

He displayed throughout his protracted sickness the most unbounded patience and fortitude, and in the last melancholy scene, the resignation which he discovered, evinced the efficacy of those religious principles, by which he had always been governed.

It may be deemed superfluous, to add, that, by the death of such a man, his afflicted family, his relatives and friends, the town in which he resided, and the religious society to which he belonged, have sustained an irreparable loss. But the event was ordered by better wisdom than ours, and Christianity would teach us rather to be grateful that his valuable and useful life was spared so long, than to complain that it was not continued longer.

"Thy fate, then, shall we ever mourn,
Placed, as thou art, in happier realms above?
No! — We scarce wish thee to return;
Sainted and blest, if virtue Heaven approve."

CHARACTER OF PETER REMSEN.

DIED, on Friday, August 26th, 1836, at his country seat at Newtown, Long Island, in the sixty-sixth year of his age, Peter Remsen, Esq., late principal of the house of Peter Remsen & Co., of New York.

The decease of such an eminent merchant, and excellent man, as was the subject of this notice, cannot fail to be a source of deep regret to a large circle of friends in this city and its vicinity. It will remind some, of numerous favors received; others, of the ties of a long cherished friendship, which are now forever broken; and all, who enjoyed his acquaintance, of the loss of an individual, who was highly valued, and who possessed a character of very uncommon excellence and worth.

The situation, which he filled so long, as the head of a commercial house, so extensively known and so highly esteemed, both at home and abroad, and the close connexion he sustained, for so many years, with all the most important interests of the city of New York, cannot fail to impart an interest to the announcement of his death, which will be deeply felt on both sides of the Atlantic.

He came to New York so early in life, and while that city was almost in a state of infancy, as respects its commercial relations, continued there so long, and for so many years filled so prominent a station, that the history of his commencement, his growth, and his prosperity, seems almost identified with that of the city itself. And it may well be so; for he held, for many years, the very first rank as the head of an establishment, second to none, at the time, in the union; and his industry, integrity, and unwavering regard to the interests of his correspondents, were followed by the usual reward of a rich harvest of wealth, honor, and esteem. He took a deep interest in the rising greatness of that city, to which he contributed by all the means in his power. By the establishment of a commercial house conducted on principles like his own, he offered powerful inducements to the merchants of other countries, to give the market of New York a preference over all others; and no plan could possibly have been adopted, more effectual to make the city of his adoption, what it has now become, the greatest commercial emporium upon the American continent.

No situation, however elevated, could make him forget the claims of those, who had done him a kindness, especially when he was commencing life with but slender means; and he used, in later years, to dwell with much pleasure, on the early confidence which was reposed in him by some friends at Boston, and especially by the late Francis C. Lowell, whose sagacious mind made an early discovery of Mr. Remsen's worth and fidelity. It may be truly said, that this kindness extended even to the descendants of these early patrons. This aid, thus promptly applied, no doubt quickened his advancement; but, at the same time, it is believed that he possessed such untiring industry, unwavering integrity, and close attention to the interests of his correspondents, as could not have failed, in time, to bring him into the foremost rank, even under circumstances less auspicious. His death will be especially regretted by many of thc young and middle-aged, who are now filling respectable and responsible stations in life, and who feel how great a debt of gratitude they owe to his memory; not only for the benefit of his valued counsel and advice, but also for his active exertion and substantial favors in their behalf; and probably the city of New York has never been called to mourn the loss of an individual, to whom so many of the junior members of society are indebted; for he had a most rational view of the worth of money, and considered it as valuable only in proportion as it confers happiness on the possessor, and those within his sphere of action.

He possessed, too, a mind of great discrimination, and a judgment which seldom erred in its decisions; and he could remain cool and under the influence of his reason, while all around him were under excitement, and the influence of temporary feeling; and this, no doubt, was one of the principal causes of his great success. His prudence and wisdom, in this respect, may be well recommended to persons of every age; and especially at the present crisis of affairs in our country. He was very kind and charitable to the poor, and, if his name was sometimes found wanting upon the numerous lists, which are so constantly presented to us at the present time, it was because his better judgment told him that some are of a nature, and for a purpose, from which the virtue is greater to withold, than to afford our aid and support. The example of such a man should not be slightly passed over, or soon forgotten. The lesson it teaches of the value of industry, integrity, and a faithful discharge of the duties of life, may be perused with benefit by all.

Mr. Remsen was never married, but those who knew him most intimately, felt assured that, had he taken upon himself the relations incident to that connexion, they would have been sustained with the same fidelity and steadiness, with which he fulfilled the other duties of life. He has left but few near relatives, but they knew how to appreciate his numerous virtues, and possessed his entire love, confidence and esteem; and, although the declining state of his health, for several years past, had forbidden the hope of his long continuance, his death will have inflicted a wound upon their hearts, which time only can cicatrize and heal.

LETTER FROM CARLSBAD.

[We hope that the length of the following letter will not deter any of our readers from its perusal, for it will be found to be of a very interesting character. The description of the venerable Coke, (to whom, we believe, the writer carried letters, from the President,) the warm friend of America, who made the motion, in the House of Commons, that "the thirteen American Colonies should be free," and carried up the Address to the Throne, for which he was never forgiven, will be read with great pleasure. The writer is a Boston merchant, of high standing and intelligence, and every way worthy of the liberal courtesy extended to him. We hope his tour may prove as beneficial to his health as it must gratifying to his feelings, and, in a short time, find him safely restored to the bosom of his very numerous friends here, who are awaiting his return with impatient anxiety.
Boston Post.]

KINGDOM OF BOHEMIA, BATHS OF CARLSBAD,
July 30, 1835.

MY DEAR SIR: — Soon after the date of my last letter, I proceeded, by invitation, to Holkham, in Norfolk, the residence of the celebrated agriculturalist, Mr. Coke, where I was detained, by his kindness and attention, nearly a week; was conducted, by him, over the greater part of his estate, consisting of 40,000 acres, and made acquainted with his numerous and valuable improvements in the art of agriculture. He also introduced me to several of his tenants, of which, he has a great number, and some of whom rent parcels of his land, amounting from 1500 to 2000 acres, paying for the same, £1800 to £2500 sterling, per annum. He gives no leases for less than twenty years, and some of his tenants are nearly as old as himself, possessing properties from £30,000 to £50,000 sterling, keeping a great number of horses, cows, and large flocks of sheep; and, in some instances, fine hunting horses, and packs of hounds. Mr. Coke retains about 1700 acres of his land, for his own use and cultivation; has 400 head of cattle, nearly all of the North Devon breed; 4000 sheep; a vast many swine, of the Neapolitan breed, and a great number of horses, for pleasure, and, also, for the use of the farm. His park is seven miles in circumference; and about 40,000 head of game are killed upon his whole estate, per annum. These consist of pheasants, partridges, woodcocks, snipes, hares, and rabbits. Mr. Coke, himself, is a great sportsman; and, although now eighty-two years old, seldom allows a fine day to pass, during the sporting season, without improving it. He went out every fine day, during my visit, and never missed a shot. His chaplain, Mr. Collier, records, in a book, the game which is killed, every day, by Mr. Coke himself, and his guests, describing the number of each sort.

Mr. Coke has been twice married. He had three daughters by his first wife — Lady Andover, Lady Anson, and Mrs. Spencer Stanhope, who are all living; and the two last named were making their annual visit, at Holkham, while I was there. I have never seen two ladies, who appeared to possess more excellent qualities, and shall ever feel indebted for the kindness and hospitality with which they treated me. Mr. Coke's present wife was Lady Ann Keppel, daughter of the Earl of Albemarle; and they were married on the 22d February, 1822. She was then nineteen years old, and he was sixty-nine years. By her, he has had five sons, and one daughter, all now living, and a more beautiful or promising family of children, I am quite sure, cannot be found in England. The eldest son, Thomas, goes to Eaton next year; and, when he is of age, will, no doubt, be Earl of Leicester. Mr. Coke, himself, has received the offer of a title seven times; but, having incurred the displeasure of George III., on account of his active measures, in concert with the late Mr. Fox, in favor of American Independence, he would never accept, afterwards, of any honor, which the court would confer. Indeed, he had risen, already, so high, that no title, even that of king, could make him greater.

I regretted, very much, being deprived of the society of Lady Anne Coke, during my visit; but she was confined to her room, having given birth to her fifth son, about ten days previous to my arrival. Before my departure, however, she requested Mr. Coke to have me conducted to her apartment; and, there, I found her reclining on a sofa. She gave me a most kind and hearty welcome to Holkham; regretted her indisposition had prevented her receiving me sooner, after my arrival; expressed a hope I should renew my visit, at a future time, and, on taking leave, presented me with engravings of the portraits of herself, and her four eldest boys. I had heard of her great personal attractions before, but they much exceeded my anticipations, and her whole countenance was marked by an expression of benevolence and kindness, which I have seldom, if ever, seen equalled. Indeed, I was ready to believe that she was, what Mr. Coke had previously assured me she was, "a perfect model of a wife and mother." She mingles very little with the gay world; and nearly all her time is devoted to the care of her family, and the wants of her numerous tenants.

Mr. Coke has an income of £70,000, sterling, per annum, and this immense wealth, possessed by two persons, of such unbounded benevolence and generosity, enables them to do a vast deal of good. Indeed, their tenants almost idolize them. I very much regret that our country, in general, is not sufficiently aware of what she owes to Mr. Coke. He has been the oldest, and firmest, and most active friend America ever had, in England. He was the bosom friend of Mr. Fox, and concerted, with him, most of the measures, in the British Parliament, which paved the way to the acknowledgment of the American Independence. In short, he made the motion, in the House of Commons, that "the thirteen American Colonies should be free," and carried up the Address to the Throne; and, for doing which, the king never forgave him. He was in thirteen consecutive parliaments, occupying a space of more than fifty years; and concluded his parliamentary life, by the passage of the Reform Bill, which passed through the House of Commons, just fifty years from the day on which Mr. Coke made his famous motion in Parliament in favor of reform. Mr. Coke pointed out to me, in his library, an engraving of the Declaration of Independence, which, he remarked, "had been sent to him by order of the American Congress, and which," he said, he "considered the greatest honor ever conferred upon him." I wish, however, that Congress would take some measures which should cause his services to be more known, and more justly appreciated by the whole American nation; for Mr. Coke, like Fox or Jefferson, has ever been the steady and consistent friend of civil and religious freedom throughout the world. Allow me, my dear sir, to invite your attention to this subject, and something valuable, I think, may be accomplished. Mr. Coke takes a lively interest in all the concerns of America; is a great admirer of General Jackson, and thinks him the best President we have had since the time of Washington. He told me that Earl Gray remarked to him, "that the late Ministry in England, having read many of the violent newspaper attacks on General Jackson, copied into the London papers, had anticipated difficulties in the negotiation with America, during the Presidentship of the General; but that, instead of anything unpleasant, "he had never conducted a correspondence, with any country, so agreeably, as with America, during the administration of

President Jackson." Mr. Coke says, there is no man living he so much wishes to see; and he has sent him, by me, an invitation, to visit Holkham, and insists upon it, that the general shall visit England, after his present term of office expires. "Tell him," says he, "it will do him much good, and that he is not too old, being quite a boy, compared to me." For myself, I can truly say, nothing could give me more pleasure; and I would readily consent to cross the Atlantic, the eleventh time, to accompany so illustrious a character. Indeed, I find the character of the President justly appreciated, and held in the most exalted estimation, in every part of Europe, which I have visited. No man, since Washington, has been so generally known, or so much admired. The fact is, that the people of Europe, with a sight undimmed by that film of prejudice, which the violence of party zeal has drawn over the eyes of the enemies of the administration in America, are doing, now, that justice to the great merits and services of General Jackson, which, a part of his ungrateful country-men, and which posterity, without any exception, are sure to render, after a time.

I left London for Paris, on the 10th of February, and, after remaining there three weeks, crossed the Alps, over Mount Cenis, on the 4th of March, and next day arrived at Turin. Fron Turin, I went to Genoa, Leghorn, Pisa, Florence, Rome, Naples, Bologna, Venice, and Milan, remaining in each principal city about three weeks; and, on the 4th of July, I left the Lakes of Maggiore and Como, intending to pass over the Rhætian Alps, through the Tyrol to Innsruch, Vienna, Prague, Dresden, Leipsic, and Berlin, to Lubec, on the Baltic sea, and there to take the steamboat for St. Petersburg. The distance is about 1200 miles, and I have already accomplished about 750 miles of it, having arrived here a few days ago from Prague, to see the most celebrated baths in Europe, and to drink the waters for a fortnight, for the further improvement of my health. I find travelling in Germany very agreeable. The posting is excellent; my carriage is light; I have fresh horses every nine miles, and accomplish about nine posts, or seventy-five miles a day. I travel, attended only by my servant, and have done so ever since I left Paris in February. It is sometimes rather solitary, and a little expensive; but I have a perfect command over my time and movements, and not having to consult with any travelling companion, there is no danger of any collision or quarrel, as to whether our hermitage shall be red or white. I hope to reach St. Petersburg by the 6th of September, and London by the 15th of October; and where, among my letters, I hope to find one from you. I wish you would arrange your affairs, so as to visit England, and travel with me in that country. It would do your health much good, and your acquaintance with the French language would make you feel quite at home in nearly every part of Europe. I think, too, it would cause you to estimate our excellent and free institutions, even more highly than you do at present. I wish that some of those persons in America, who complain "of the arbitrary measures" of the American government, would cross the Atlantic, and take a survey of some of the governments of Europe; that, for instance, of the king of Sardinia, Carlo Alberto, who is probably the most perfect model of a tyrant, which Europe contains. He maintains an immense army, at a great expense, not to guard his kingdom against foreign invaders, but to protect his own person against the indignation of his own subjects. In Genoa, only, he has 14,000 soldiers, and eight citadels with their guns all pointed towards the city. No soldier dares speak to a citizen, as they might contrive a plot together; and every person is watched, and even in his own house. This government fears and hates foreigners of every kind;

but especially those who are the subjects of free states. It was, perhaps, on this account I was imprisoned at Alexandria, (a very strongly fortified town,) on my way from Turin to Genoa. I had been in the town only four hours, and had left my hotel only twenty minutes before, when standing for a moment in the public highway, looking towards the citadel, I was suddenly arrested, (as also my servant,) by two soldiers belonging to the fortress, and taken before the governor of the citadel, on a false charge of having taken a drawing of the citadel—was reprimanded, and then handed over by him to the governor of the town, who refused to hear any explanation—addressed us in the most offensive language, and then committed us to another guard of soldiers, directing them to imprison us closely in one of the barriers of the town, and to wait for his further orders. This was soon done, and we were lodged in a place nine feet long, by eight broad, having on the floor a bed of oak, with a pillow of the same, and without any covering at that cold season of the year. Our persons were also searched, and everything in our pockets taken away, and conveyed to the governor. We could do nothing. Our passports were set at nought, as affording us no protection. After our liberation, (which was done also in a very offensive manner, and without any apology or excuse,) I learned that a respectable citizen of Leghorn, had a year ago been imprisoned eleven months, and supplied only with bread and water by this same governor, for having taken two letters of a stranger as he was leaving Marseilles in the steamboat for Genoa, and which, unknown to the passenger, happened to be addressed to some persons at Genoa, who were concerned in what is called "the rebellion of 1821." This man was wholly innocent, and never interfered with politics, and was liberated after a confinement of eleven months, only by the interference of the Grand

Duke of Tuscany, to whom Leghorn is subject. The treatment I received was shameful—I was perfectly innocent—had no materials about me for taking a drawing, and had never thought of attempting one. I have had the deposition of my servant taken before the American Consul at Rome, stating the facts of the case—I will have the case laid before the American Government for the vindication of my rights, and the protection of other Americans who may chance to travel through the dominions of that despicable tyrant, Carlo Alberto, king of Sardinia. Such is the nature of all governments which have no constitution, charter, or fixed laws. The person or property of no man is safe for a moment. There is no trial by jury in any of these arbitrary governments. The military are the judges, and accusation is generally equivalent to conviction and death; or, what is far worse, imprisonment in one of their charnel-houses. During my stay at Naples, the squadron arrived there from Gibraltar. This was a pleasing occurrence, and I had many very agreeable interviews with the officers; particularly with Captain Nicholson of the Delaware.

I cannot, of course, attempt to give you any account of the countries or things, which I have seen during my tour. The weather has been uniformly fine, and I can accomplish much in the long summer days. I wonder people will visit Italy, or any other country, in the winter. One should see Italy, at any rate, in the spring or summer. The most beautiful spot I have seen, was the Lake of Como, near Milan; and if heaven be a place, I cannot help thinking it is certainly something like the banks of this lake. But all such places must be seen in warm weather, and in summer. I am pleased with Carlsbad also. It is a pleasant place; and about 4,000 persons have already arrived here this year, to take the waters. They have produced some cures, which were almost miraculous.

The water of one of the springs is hot enough to make tea. The people place earthen ware in the water to have it baked hard. The Grand Duke, Michael, of Russia, is here, and many Russians, Poles, Germans and French. I have now almost travelled beyond the range of the English, and there are only two or three families here. It is a general remark, that the English are omnipresent; but I have never found them agreeable people on the continent. In their own country, they are hospitable, and have much to say; but, on the continent, they are silent when they meet you; or, if they speak, it is with the manner of a bad boy, whom his parents have just flogged, and who gives an answer, sullenly, to some question asked him.

I see that the English papers say that you are going on swimmingly in America. I also see that the United States Bank, just as its charter is expiring, has increased its loans to sixty millions. Beware. We may have "another crisis;" and, if we should, I predict it will be more severe, and ruin more people, than the last. There is no remark older, or more false, than, "that mankind grow wiser or more cautious by experience;" and I affirm, and will affirm, that a man who has once committed a rash or foolish deed, and suffered for it, is more likely to commit the same again, than another person, who has never done the foolish act, or acquired this "experience," as it is called. But I must conclude. My medical attendant, who has the care of my eyes, has just called, and, seeing my long letter, has blamed me for writing it.

To Hon. David Henshaw, Boston.

LETTER FROM MANCHESTER.

MANCHESTER, Dec. 24th, 1836.

DEAR SIR,—When we last met, you were pleased to express a desire that I should address you, occasionally, from this side of the water. A wish, on my part, to prove that I duly appreciate your politeness, and not the most distant hope that I can communicate any thing either new or interesting, impels me to comply with your request. At a time like the present, when Banks and Banking are almost the only topics of conversation, I might, perhaps, be thought inexcusable should I touch upon any subject but "the currency," which occupies, it would appear, the minds and thoughts of all on both sides of the Atlantic.

You will all have heard of the rise in the value of money here to 5 1-2 per cent; the curtailment of credit, and the dulness of trade. There have also been one or two stoppages of what are called "the Joint Stock Banks," and, in one instance, one of these institutions, viz., the Northern and Central Bank of England, (the head of which is located here,) has been obliged to ask aid of the Bank of England. This has been an occasion of regret to the friends of joint stock companies, but of great triumph to the bank itself. This institution, viz., the Northern and Central, has been doing an immense business, and had forty branches and agencies. They also issued bank notes payable on demand, and, in this way, offended the Bank of England, which, in March last, offered almost any accommodation, provided the Northern and Central would withdraw its own notes, and circulate those of the Bank of England. This offer was declined, and, in July last, a committee was raised by Parliament, "to inquire into the state of the joint stock banks, with leave to send for witnesses and papers."

This led to an exposition of the affairs of the Northern and Central Bank, by which it was discovered that, although its paid up capital was only £712,000, it had, in circulation of notes, £340,000; owed £379,000 to its depositors, and had allowed those with whom it had done business to overdraw their accounts to the extent of over a million of pounds! To meet these liabilities, all its ready money means amounted to only £87,000; and, in case of any panic, it depended solely upon re-discounting in London the notes receivable, which it had received of its customers; and it had formed the erroneous opinion that its security was so good there never could come a time when, with its securities, it could not re-discount in London its notes or bills receivable to any, the most unlimited extent. In this, the bank was deceived, and the examination of its chief manager, Mr. Cassels, having been published among the parliamentary papers, the public, seeing its condition, began to doubt its credit; the moneyed interest of London would not discount its bills, because the Bank of England would not take those bills again of the bill-brokers and bankers; and, in this emergency, the Northern and Central Bank was compelled to apply to the Bank of England, which, with true consistency, said to the directors,—"We know well enough that you are good, and safe, and solvent, and, although we would not take your bills when offered by the bill-brokers, still we will take them of you direct to the extent of £500,000 or more, if you request, on the condition that you will close and wind up your branches, all or nearly all, issue no more notes of yours, but circulate ours."

Humiliating as was the proposal, the Northern and Central could do no better, and accepted it, and the triumph of the National Bank was complete! So much for becoming extended, and doing too much business! Few persons appear to have any doubt, that the raising of the whole committee itself was a plan concerted on the part of the bank and a few of its friends, to put down the Northern and Central Bank, and similar institutions; and this opinion will be strengthened in the mind of any man, who will read the whole examination of witnesses, filling two hundred and fifty folio pages in the Parliamentary Reports. You will perceive, by the London papers, that, although the Bank of England has only about four millions of bullion in lieu of eight, which is the lowest sum it ever ought to have, when its liabilities are thirty-two millions of pounds, yet it continues to increase its securities or discounts, and appears to have very little regard to the foreign exchanges, which can be made favorable only by a curtailment of its discounts. The only way to account for this, is the opinion that, in case money affairs become worse, and the bank continues to lose its bullion, it intends to apply at once to the government to have the restriction repealed, by which it is compelled now to redeem its notes by its gold, in the same manner in which it was done in the time of Mr. Pitt. What a scene in England, and indeed everywhere else, would be produced by such a measure as this, I cannot attempt to describe. So much for raising up a mammoth institution, like the Bank of England, in copartnership with the government!

There can be no doubt, that joint stock banks, since their commencement in 1827, have been multiplied far beyond the wants of the country; have been, in some instances, very imprudently conducted, and have caused much over-trading; but these things are the natural effects of the want of proper bounds and restrictions in their charters, and an attempt will probably be made by Parliament, when it meets, to correct the errors which former legislators have committed.

These banks must, however, be all eventually safe; for every person who holds a single share of their stock, is liable to make good all their engagements to the last pound of property he possesses. The Northern and Central Bank, before mentioned, has 1264 shareholders. The influence of these banks will continue to increase, probably, and they are likely to do away, in a great measure, with private bankers, and eventually, perhaps, with the bank of England itself; for that institution has always failed to exercise that boasted salutary influence over "the currency," to which it has always laid claim. England, like the United States, appears destined to continue subject to alarming panics and violent revulsions; and, while they continue, we hear much of the cruelty of banks and bankers; "of their shameful disregard of contracts entered into before;" and their refusal to aid those of their friends who are "hard-pressed," and find it difficult or impossible to meet their engagements; whereas, there is reason to suspect, often, that the banks and bankers themselves, at such times, stand quite in as much need of aid, if not more in need, than their customers; and every panic which occurs should teach every man that banks and bankers are seldom ready to accommodate their friends at those times when their aid is most required, and is asked by those who need it most. It would appear that banks and bankers have a sort of prescriptive right to do what would be deemed highly improper in others, and generally they do it with impunity, because their victims are almost always indebted to them, and, on this account, dare not resist oppression.

The banks in America, resemble, in this respect, what are called spiel-huyses, in Amsterdam, which are crowded with females of easy virtue, for the accommodation of the public. The proprietors of these establishments entice their victims into their dens of misery and vice by furnishing them, in the first place, with fine clothes on their admission, by which means they become indebted to their keepers, and, after this is accomplished, they find no difficulty in practising upon them every kind of imposition, cruelty, and unfair usage. On this account, the moneyed institutions of the United States should be subjected to the severest discipline on the part of the Legislature; but here, again, the same difficulty occurs; and, from the lenient manner in which they are dealt with, when brought before their judges, there is great reason to fear many of the legislators themselves have long since put on the livery of the spiel-huys, and dare not do their duty like freemen, and independent members of the Legislature. In this way, many of the banks in the United States have become nuisances, which ought to be abated, and would not be tolerated in any other portion of the globe; and this proves that a country may have free and liberal institutions, and make their own laws, and yet, for want of the requisite virtue, and moral courage, which should always guide the counsels of such a free country, may be subject to a great many abuses of power, and subjected to numerous inconveniences, almost as great as those which exist under a despotic government. But we all admit these evils, but who shall point out the remedy? Alas! that question it is difficult to answer, for mankind do not grow wise by experience.

I wish it were in my power to report a more favorable state of things in England; but the improvement in the moneyed affairs of the country, which seemed near at hand a few days since, has not been realized, and most persons look forward to the future with considerable apprehension. The prices of manufactured goods, however, do not fall, and holders here, like the same class in America, appear resolved to make any sacrifice rather than to submit to a reduction in price.

It was supposed the shipments to the United States would almost cease, in a time like the present, especially as this is declared to be the only way in which trade can be brought back to its usual channels; the interest of money reduced, and business be conducted once more with any kind of satisfaction. Instead of this, however, the vessels now sailing for America, have full freights, and nearly as many manufactures as last year, but I should fear that, while this continues, the embarrassments at present existing in America, will not be removed. A rise in the necessaries of life has taken place here, very similar to what has occurred in the United States. Wheat has advanced from thirty-six shillings a quarter, (the price in July, 1835,) to sixty shillings. Potatoes, which usually bring six shillings and sixpence a load, are now twelve shillings and sixpence. Straw has advanced from three and two pence to seven shillings a stone, of fourteen pounds; and the price of hay has doubled. The poor, of course, feel this advance sensibly, but thus far, fortunately, the winter has been very mild, and much like the weather which is usual in the spring; although at sea there have been violent gales, and many vessels wrecked. The last three packets have made their passages from New York, each in seventeen days.

Believe me to remain, dear sir, very respectfully,

Your friend and obedient servant.

To C. G. GREENE, Esq.

Editor of the Boston Morning Post.

THE BOSTON BANKS.

THE subject of currency and banking, which has so much engaged the public attention of late, has, unluckily for the cause of truth, been so mingled with the party politics of the day as to induce many to suppose that there is some natural connexion between them. No two subjects, however, are more distinct in themselves, and all must regret the unfortunate coincidence, by which a connexion has appeared to subsist between them. It is no easy thing to establish the principles of a sound and safe currency for a great commercial country like our own, even when the mind comes to the inquiry unfettered by prejudice or passion. It is a topic on which the wise and good of both parties may agree to differ; but, when we look at the manner in which our banks in Boston, or (to speak with greater caution) some of our banks in Boston, have been conducted of late years, especially when one calls to mind the facts which have been disclosed during the past twelve months, all, it is believed, will admit that the time has arrived when the shareholders in those institutions should call the managers of them to a strict and "searching" examination.

Some years since, it was the boast of our city that a bank failure had never occurred in it, and that, during the commercial panics, in which the banks of other portions of our country, (including even New York and Philadelphia,) violating every principle of their charters, as well as every obligation of honor and honesty, had suspended specie payments, the banks of Boston had never swerved from the path of duty. Many of our merchants must remember when, some twenty or thirty years since, it was announced, in State street, that a deficiency had been found in the accounts of one of our bank officers. The news of a general war in Europe would scarcely produce such surprise and consternation at the present time. But what a sad reverse have we witnessed of late! Within the past twelve months, several banks in our city, and its immediate vicinity, have actually failed. In one or more instances, the managers, after purloining a part of the capital of the institution, absconded; and, in other instances, the shareholders have been obliged to dismiss certain leading officers for gross dereliction of duty. In most cases, where the probe has been made to enter, it has been found to pierce only rottenness and decay; and quite sufficient has come to light to excite our fears and alarms that, should the examination be persisted in, a further amount of decay and rottenness would be disclosed.

Much has been said and written upon what is called "the sub-treasury system of Mr. Van Buren," and upon the great risk of loss the public would incur, by entrusting large sums of the revenue to individuals called sub-treasury agents, instead of depositing the public money in our banks, governed and guarded, as they are, by twelve or more directors to each institution; and looking at what has occurred in Boston, as well as in many other places, one might dwell upon the fallacy of such an argument, were this the place for such a discussion. Enough, however, has come to light to convince any prudent and thinking man that the stocks of our banking companies can no longer be considered as furnishing safe investments for money, conducted as many of them have been of late years; and that a thorough reform has become a matter of absolute necessity. And when I consider that the banking capital of this city is over twenty millions of dollars, and that the funds of every class of our citizens, as also of our savings banks, and many other corporations, are invested in them; not to mention the property of the widows and orphans, whose all, in many instances, depends upon the upright management of those institutions; I am utterly astonished at the apathy with which this subject has been viewed, and at the surprising supineness with which the stockholders stand still, and see their property mismanaged, wasted, or purloined.

That these institutions ought, long since, to have been subjected to the most severe legislative enactments, and the infraction of them summarily punished, no person of just views can doubt; but experience forbids the expectation that any thing is to be hoped for in that quarter; and, therefore, the shareholders should take the business into their own hands, and that without a moment's delay. Let the proprietors of each and every bank appoint two or more persons amongst themselves, whose duty it shall be to visit, twice or more times a year, the several banks; to call for officers, clerks and papers, and to examine every evidence of property the banks have. Let them look sharply to the accounts of the presidents, cashiers, and directors themselves; see that no private ledger or portfolio is kept; that no due-bills on demand are set down as cash actually in possession; that no heavy loans are made to favored individuals, or to persons who have become so needy as to compel them to pay a usurious rate of interest for the accommodation. Let them inquire whether the bank which they are visiting, when the last dividend was declared, had actually the earnings on hand, or made it out of profits to be realized at a future day; or, (what is alleged to have been sometimes done,) borrowed the money at twelve per cent. per annum, to make a dividend to the stockholders at the rate of six per cent. Let them ascertain how many New York, and Philadelphia, and Baltimore notes the bank holds, which have been discounted at an usurious rate of interest for the accommodation of traders and speculators in those cities, and to enable them to take away the little foreign commerce which remains to our city, while the paper of our merchants and of our own young men, who have grown up amongst us, settled amongst us, and who have to pay our taxes, is thrown out, because a just regard to their rights or their credit would not allow them to pay over six per cent. for money. Let them further inquire whether the capital of the bank has been lent to its depositors and responsible customers, and in due proportion to each, and at the rate of interest established by the law of the State; or whether it has been disposed of to brokers, or needy applicants, or overgrown corporations in large sums on pledges, and at an illegal rate of interest. Let all these points be ascertained, and, if such practices have or do prevail, let the unjust stewards who are guilty of them be dismissed. Let each bank be directed by its stockholders to publish a quarterly account of its situation, that all the stockholders may have access to it, and judge for themselves. Let these measures be adopted, and we shall have no more bank failures, and no more derelictions of duty among the officers of the banks. The stocks of these institutions will no longer be selling at a discount of ten to twenty per cent.; the property of our widows and orphans will become safe again in their former depositories, and the banks of Boston will once more deserve and acquire the high character which they once maintained. CATO.

LETTER ON CURRENCY.

MANCHESTER, NOV. 30, 1839.

MY DEAR SIR: — I had last this pleasure, by the steamer, since which, nothing of much importance has occurred on this side the Atlantic. The pressure upon the money market is as great as ever; and the circulation is said to be as low as in 1822. In the issues of the Bank of England alone, there is a reduction of three millions sterling, and the deposits were never so small. These circumstances, occurring at the same time, have almost entirely removed all apprehension of a suspension of specie payments on the part of the bank, or of the issue of one pound notes. Commerce, in the mean time, is greatly depressed; people in trade find it very difficult to meet their engagements, and there is a general complaint of "bad times." Of the various causes which have produced this state of things, the heavy import of corn, the reckless and profligate course pursued by the Bank of Pennsylvania, and the disasters occasioned by it in America, the destruction of so much British property in China, in the shape of opium, and the necessary doubt how the trade with that empire is to be conducted in future, are the principal; and it is difficult, at this moment, to predict what the result may be. Our dates, from New York, are to the 8th of November, and are looked upon as more favorable — while the conduct of the New York and Boston Banks, in maintaining their integrity, is the theme of universal encomium. At the same time, Mr. Biddle, and his bank, are only mentioned in terms of execration, and will not soon be forgotten. We shall, very soon, expect to hear of a resumption, by the solvent banks of Philadelphia, Baltimore, and Virginia; for, with the exchange on London and Paris, at three and four per cent. below par, so that a remittance of gold or silver would produce a considerable loss, we cannot understand how solvent institutions can remain much longer in their present degraded condition. The question for every one, now, to ask himself, is, "How are we to avoid, in future, a recurrence of the events of the past three years, and save ourselves from becoming a nation of bankrupts?" for, if there be one plan more sure and efficacious than another, for converting the most moral and virtuous people upon earth into a nation of bankrupts, swindlers, and rogues, it may be found in just such a system of banking, and paper money as exists in the United States of America, at the present time. Among the various remedies recommended, that alone, which can be proposed to our State Legislatures, with any prospect of receiving their sanction, is the prohibition of bank notes under the denomination of twenty dollars; and the adoption of such a rule would give us a sound and healthy circulation. If you agree with me in this opinion, as I hope you do, permit me to implore you to use all the weight of your influence to produce this desirable reform, so essential to the best interests of our country. America, without the adoption of this plan, can never retain among her population such an amount of gold and silver as is absolutely essential to the stability of her moneyed institutions, or to the solvency and honorable standing of her merchants. Gold and silver will not long remain in a country having a paper circulation like that of our own. But let us appeal to facts.

In Great Britain, prior to 1822, and while the Bank of England remained, like the banks of Philadelphia now, in a state of suspense, and refused to redeem her paper, the circulation amounted to £64,000,000, and was made up thus:—

Bank of England Notes,	£30,000,000
Country Bank Notes,	23,000,000
Gold,	4,000,000
Silver,	7,000,000
Making in all	£64,000,000

In 1822, the bank was *compelled* by Parliament, amidst the predictions of universal ruin on the part of the Directors and the Tories, to return once more to specie payments, and to issue no notes under £5, and now let us see how the circulation was made up ten years after, in 1832, as given in Parliament by the Duke of Wellington. It was made up thus:—

Bank of England Notes,	£19,900,000
Country Bank Notes,	9,200,000
Gold,	28,000,000
Silver,	8,000,000
	£65,100,000

Need I add another line to establish the position assumed?

A question of this important kind, which concerns the honor of our country both at home and abroad, should never be mixed up with party considerations. Our future character as a nation, our rank as a great commercial people, the duty we owe ourselves, and the good example we should leave our children, demand an immediate, a radical, and a thorough reform in the circulation of the United States.

In my last, I had the pleasure of mentioning a very pleasant visit I had received from Mr. and Mrs. Van Buren who passed three days with myself and family on their way from the Duke of Cleaveland's to Bristol, to embark, and now I have the great satisfaction of recording a most agreeable visit just concluded, from our justly valued, and very talented minister, Mr. Stevenson, and his very amiable and accomplished lady.

You are aware how many difficult questions Mr. Stevenson has had to discuss with the British Cabinet, and how ably and triumphantly he has advocated the rights of his country. It always gratifies me to hear the way in which the English speak of him. He possesses great natural eloquence, improved by frequent practice and is a most beautiful and animated speaker. It is said his speeches at Glasgow, and before the British Institution at Birmingham, have seldom, if ever, been surpassed. I was pleased to hear that he had obtained of England the indemnity of £30,000 for the slaves which were unjustifiably set at liberty from a ship, which was wrecked at or near Nassau. If America has been fortunate in one thing more than in another from the peace of 1783, it has been in the character of the distinguished persons whom we have sent abroad to represent us in Europe; and what can be more important than to employ the most able men, since foreigners judge us so much by our ministers?

S. D. B.

To the Editor of the Boston Post.

CAPTURES IN THE AFRICAN SEAS.

[*From the Manchester Guardian, January* 15, 1842.]

UNITED STATES.—THE RIGHT OF SEARCH.

THE packet-ship *New York*, which arrived at Liverpool on Wednesday, has brought American papers to the 22d ult., but they do not contain any news of importance. The American editors, having pretty nearly disposed of M'LEOD, and the burning of the *Caroline*, are now busily engaged in discussing the merits of the correspondence between the English government and Mr. STEVENSON, the late American envoy, on the subject of certain alleged outrages upon American vessels by British cruisers on the coast of Africa. The tone of these discussions is, in general, abundantly angry and pugnacious; and we find, that parties connected with the United States, are not free from apprehensions of a war arising out of the misunderstanding which exists on this subject. To us, however, this apprehension seems a little chimerical; for the claims set up by the American envoy, and supported in the American papers, are so utterly unreasonable—we might, indeed, say absurd and preposterous—that any government which should resort to a war for the purpose of enforcing them would expose itself, not merely to the grave censures, but almost to the ridicule, of the civilized world. Put into plain English, and divested of extraneous topics, with which it is invested in the course of the discussion, the American claim amounts to this—that no vessel carrying the American flag shall be visited by a British cruiser, even for the purpose of ascertaining whether she is, or is not, entitled to carry that flag. It is true, that the Americans do not put their claim in this form, which would be too absurd for any diplomatist to venture upon;

but it is the real essence of what Mr. STEVENSON says upon the subject; and when that is pointed out by Lord PALMERSTON and Lord ABERDEEN, instead of showing that those noble lords have misunderstood his allegations, and that he really means something else, the American envoy shelters himself under vague generalities, which may mean any thing or nothing at all.

One fallacy under which Mr. STEVENSON seeks to cloak his meaning, or his want of meaning, is an allegation, which he repeats many times, and in support of which he quotes various authorities on international law,—to the effect that the right of search is a belligerent right; and that, as Great Britain is not at war, she has no right to ascertain the nationality of vessels bearing the American flag on the African coast. Mr. STEVENSON had no need to quote VATTEL, or Lord STOWELL, to prove his allegation; the right of search is belligerent; but then, what is a belligerent right? Why, in this case, nothing more than the right of one vessel to make war upon, and to capture other vessels. A national ship, of a country at war, that meets with an enemy's vessel,—any ship that meets with a pirate, the common enemy of all mankind,—any revenue cruiser that finds a smuggler,—and also any English, French, Spanish, or Portuguese ship of war, that meets with a slaver of any one of those nations,—has the undoubted right to attack it with fire and sword, to capture, and, if resisted to a sufficient extent, to destroy it, with its crew. These are all and equally belligerent rights; and they all and equally give the right of visitation of vessels under circumstances which induce a fair suspicion that they come within the category of enemies. The Americans, however, set up a claim to have all American vessels exempted from visitation by the cruisers engaged in putting down the slave trade; and they require that the simple display of an American ensign shall be taken as proof of national character. In other words, they require that all British, French, Spanish, or Portuguese slavers shall be enabled to shelter themselves, and carry on their horrid trade with impunity, by the very cheap expedient of carrying a piece of bunting, with certain stripes and stars upon it. But upon what definite grounds do they rest this extraordinary claim? We have searched in vain in Mr. Stevenson's notes, and in the leading articles of American newspapers, for any intelligible statement on this point. If the claim should be conceded by the English government (of which, by the way, there is very little danger,) we presume the next demand would be, that any suspicious-looking, lugger-rigged vessel that might be found lurking about the English or Irish coast, should be exempted, not merely from capture, but from visit and examination, by hoisting an American flag. The one demand is just as reasonable, just as consistent with common sense and international law, as the other, and just as likely to be conceded by the English government.

We confess that we have no fear of war on any such grounds. American envoys (especially when desirous of giving trouble to the government that has recalled them) may write waspish and unreasonable notes, and American editors may indite blustering articles, on such subjects; but the American government is not so destitute of common understanding, as to plunge their country into a war on any such ridiculous grounds.

[*From the Manchester Guardian, January* 22, 1842.]

ENGLAND AND THE UNITED STATES — THE RIGHT OF SEARCH.

We have received, from a highly respectable American gentleman resident in this town, the following letter in reference to an article on this subject, which recently appeared in the Guardian, with a request that we will give it insertion. To this request, we most readily accede; and, though the great length of the letter makes such a course somewhat inconvenient, we place it in the most prominent situation we can command for it; at the same time requesting that those of our readers who feel an interest in questions of international law will read it, not only with care and attention, but with that feeling of indulgence which ought always to be extended to a gentleman who comes forward in a foreign land to maintain his views of the interests and the honor of his country. In the present state of the relations between England and the United States, it is important that Englishmen should make themselves acquainted, not only with the real merits of the great questions that divide the two countries, but also with the interests and even the prejudices which prevent others from taking a just and dispassionate view of them. Inveterate prejudices are best worn away, as hard substances are polished, by rubbing them together; and we can conceive no practice more likely to abate certain unfriendly feelings prevailing on both sides of the Atlantic, than the practice of Englishmen in America, and Americans in England, stepping forward, as our correspondent has done, and fairly and fully advocating the opinions generally entertained by their fellow-countrymen.

With this preface, we give the letter above referred to, hoping that our readers will not be deterred by its length from giving it a perusal; and we subjoin some observations to which we beg also to direct their attention.

To the Editor of the Manchester Guardian:

Sir,—I have read with attention some editorial remarks contained in your paper of the 15th instant, under the head of "The Right of Search," relating to the recent correspondence between the American ambassador in London, and her majesty's late and present secretaries of state. The conclusions at which you appear to have arrived, seem to me so unsupported by the terms of that correspondence that I find it difficult to believe that you can have read it with your usual attention and care. The charge against Mr. Stevenson, the late American ambassador, that "he has sheltered himself under vague generalities," and that it would appear, by the tenor of his letters,—"that the Americans require that all British, French, Spanish and Portuguese slaves, shall be enabled to shelter themselves and carry on their horrid trade with impunity, by the cheap expedient of carrying a piece of bunting with certain stripes and stars upon it," has no foundation, so far as I can find, in the letters of the above-named individual. On the contrary, the subjects in dispute between the two countries appear to me to have been treated, on the part of Mr. Stevenson, with courtesy, dignity, and consummate ability; nor have I been able to find, in the replies of the British secretaries, any satisfactory answer to the powerful arguments advanced. On reference to the correspondence, I find no less than three letters from Lord Palmerston, in which he expressly disclaims all right, on the part of Great Britain, "to search and detain vessels, which are the property of citizens of the United States, when navigating the high seas." In his letter, dated 5th August, 1841, to Mr. Stevenson, who had called upon her majesty's government for reparation for losses sustained by a recent detention, by one of her majesty's cruisers, of an American vessel called the Douglas, his lordship does not undertake to justify the same by reason of any right of search, or detention, possessed by Great Britain, but assigns, as a reason and excuse for the proceeding, an agreement alleged to have been entered into by the American commander, Paine, of the American navy, with the commander of her majesty's cruisers in the African seas, according to each other, for a season, a mutual right of search; and his reply to Mr. Stevenson is in the following words: "Although it was indisputable that British cruisers have no right as such to search and detain vessels which are the property of citizens of the United States, even though such vessels may be engaged in the slave trade, yet, in these cases, these vessels acted in pursuance of a special engagement with a naval officer of the United States." Again, on the 27th August, Lord Palmerston informs Mr. Stevenson, "that the government had written to the commissioners of the British court, at Sierra Leone, that British ships of war were not authorized to visit and search American vessels on the high seas." And, in another letter of his lordship's, of the same date, he declares: "Such things, however, will not happen again, because orders have been given, which will prevent their recurrence;" and he adds, "her majesty's government do not pretend that her majesty's naval officers have any right to search American merchantmen, met with, in time of peace, at sea." Can any language be more decisive or unequivocal than this? But what will your intelligent readers say, when informed that, before concluding this same letter, after making, with more flippancy than good taste, some very indiscreet and uncourteous remarks upon the American flag, his lordship proceeds to cancel every thing which he had written before, and puts in the claim of Great Britain to the odious right of search, in a form never before avowed, and to an extent never before asserted? In this communication, with a sophistry which, in the history of special pleading, was never surpassed; and with a chicanery almost without parallel in the records of diplomacy, he undertakes to vindicate the claim of Great Britain, by attempting to prove a difference between the right of search and the act of arresting, visiting, and detaining a vessel upon the high seas, examining her papers, and ascertaining (to use the words of the secretary) "that she is a vessel of the United States, and navigated according to law." It is true, as remarked by Mr. Stevenson, that his lordship has omitted to mention by what law he required these American vessels to be navigated. To this communication, the American ambassador replies, under date of the tenth September, and most triumphantly refutes the sophistical reasoning of the British secretary. He proves, beyond all doubt, that the claim asserted by Great Britain is, undisguisedly, the same right of search, and the same attempt to exercise a jurisdiction upon the high seas, against which America has always contended; and to which she will never submit under any circumstances whatever. This is the letter in which Mr. Stevenson, with so much force, calls the attention of Lord Palmerston to a decision of the late Sir William Scott, in 1817, relating to a French slaver, which had been captured by an English cruiser, and condemned, as Sir William contended, against the law of nations. The words of that eminent and learned man are so remarkable, and apply with so much force to the dispute existing at present between England and America, I cannot forbear their quotation, "that no authority could be found, which gave any right of visitation or interruption over the vessels or navigation of other states on the high seas, except that which the right of war gives to belligerents against neutrals; and that Great Britain had no right to force her way to the liberation of Africa, by trampling upon the rights or independence of other nations, for any good, however eminent."

From the above premises, and the admissions and declarations of Lord Palmerston himself, the following conclusion is unavoidable, namely, that whereas, in his earlier communications, Lord Palmerston unequivocally disclaimed "a right to search American vessels on the high seas in time of peace," some circumstance must have occurred between the fifth and twenty-seventh of August, of no ordinary importance, to have induced the British cabinet to assume this new and unexpected position, and to assert the above-named odious claim in the manner already described. In seeking for the cause of this sudden change, the mind is carried at once to the treaty recently proclaimed as having been made by Great Britain with the other four great powers of Europe, and which Lord Palmerston, with so much complacency, has named "The Christian League." It is true that the treaty was openly proclaimed and published only a few weeks since; and all must remember with what a flourish of trumpets it was ushered in on the part of the British press, on account of the astounding effect it would have upon the United States; (no doubt in enabling Great Britain, after a trial of more than half a century, to establish the right of search;) but no one has informed us at what precise time its principal articles were agreed upon. Lord Palmerston, under date of 27th August, informs Mr. Stevenson, that "the treaty will be a dead letter," unless America will become a party to it, which proves his anxiety upon the subject; nor is it any violent presumption, that Great Britain, to carry her point, may have engaged with France, for instance, to require of the United States to accede to the terms of the treaty; and, in case of refusal, to force a compliance by a violation of her rights upon the highway of nations. Agreements of this character, in the form of what are called secret articles, are events of no uncommon occurrence between the crowned heads of Europe. France is understood to have been the power which hesitated the longest; and, looking at the character of that proud monarchy, and the well-known hatred and jealousy entertained by the people of that country towards Great Britain, it is no improbable supposition that the motive for her present compliance with the earnest solicitations of Great Britain may have been the hope of producing a war between her ancient rival and the United States. It would not be the first time that a British Secretary of State has been made the dupe of the crafty diplomacy of France; nor could the government of France have taken a safer position; for, if Great Britain shall determine to exercise the right asserted, war is inevitable.

And now, sir, since you have been pleased to pronounce the claims of America so "unreasonable," "absurd," and "preposterous," permit me to ask a few plain and simple questions. If the United States had placed themselves in a false position, or asserted unjust or unreasonable claims, why did Lord Palmerston, when called upon by the American government for reparation for losses sustained by the detention of certain American vessels upon the African seas, justify the same by reason of the agreement between the English and American naval commanders already mentioned? Why did he not say at once, "We had a right to arrest and detain these vessels, and shall do so again under similar circumstances?" What emergency has arisen to authorize Great Britain to interpolate the law of nations, or to render the surveillance of British cruisers necessary or just over the shipping of the United States? Twenty-six years have elapsed since the peace and treaty of Ghent were concluded, during which time the slave-trade has been carried on, as Mr. Buxton and others assure us, to the greatest extent upon the African and other seas; and yet, Great Britain has never ventured, until now, to assert the right of violating the American flag. Is America, with a population of seventeen millions, and a fleet treble in power to that she possessed in 1812, less able now to execute her laws for the suppression of the slave-trade than she has been? Is there a single inhabitant of Great Britain mad enough to suppose, that America will permit any nation upon the earth to dictate to her what she ought to do? Have not only the laws of nations, but of England too, as expounded by Sir William Scott, become changed, because what are called the five great powers of Europe (three of which can scarcely be called commercial nations) have ordered to be put the signatures of their respective ambassadors to a piece of parchment, called, by Lord Palmerston, "The Christian League?" And last, but not least, if Great Britain or her allies have a right to exercise the power claimed over American vessels, why has Great Britain, as stated by Lord Aberdeen in his letter of the 13th October last, deemed it necessary to request the permission of America, or, in other words, to solicit her to become a party to the treaty which should contain that permission?

The truth is, the position now maintained by America is not "any extraordinary claim," as has been asserted, but is as old as the American government. Its infringement by Great Britain was one of the principal causes of the war of 1812. As long ago as 1812, Mr. Madison, in his message to the American Congress, informs them, "that the British cruisers have been in the continued practice of violating the American flag on the great highway of nations, and of seizing and carrying off persons sailing under it, not in the exercise of a belligerent right, founded on the law of nations, against an enemy, but of a municipal prerogative over British subjects."—"British jurisdiction," says he, "is thus extended to neutral vessels in a situation where no laws can operate but the law of nations, and the laws of the country to which the vessels belong; and the practice is so far from affecting British subjects alone, that, under the pretext of searching for these, thousands of American citizens, under the safeguard of national law, and of their national flag, have been torn from their country and everything dear to them, have been dragged on board of ships of war of a foreign nation, and exposed under the severities of their discipline, to be exiled to the most distant and deadly climes, to risk their lives in the battle of their oppressors, and to be the melancholy instruments of taking away those of their own brethren."

Thus wrote President Madison, in his address to the American Congress, in June, 1812; and who, after its perusal, can feel any surprise that America should look with suspicion, in 1842, upon propositions touching this same right of search, and coming from the same British government, whose unjust and violent proceedings are detailed above in the year 1812? In the editorial remarks contained in the *Guardian* of the 5th instant, you impute the feeling of disaffection between England

and America to the contiguity of the possessions of the two countries, and to the large military force on foot in Canada; and you speak of "the remarkable patience" of the Americans, under what you appear to consider such a heavy grievance. I am quite at a loss, however, to understand what proof you have that America has ever considered the standing army in Canada as a grievance, or a subject of which she had any right to complain. I am not aware that any feeling of that character has ever manifested itself on the part of the American government or people; nor have they ever ventured to interfere as to the manner in which Great Britain should govern her foreign possessions in North America, or any other part of the globe. On the contrary, most well-informed Americans, I believe, have, for a long time, looked upon the Canadas as rather an expense and source of weakness to Great Britain than an advantage; and have commiserated her being obliged to retain her dominion over the Canadians by a standing army of 16,000 men, in a time of profound peace. They have seemed to me to entertain the opinion expressed by Lord Ashburton some time since in the House of Lords, in the debate upon the affairs of Canada, "that it may be well doubted if there be a power in Europe, possessing a foreign colony, which would not be advantaged by the loss of it."

Three questions now divide England and America: the boundary; the right of search or visitation of American vessels in the African seas; and the attack upon the Caroline. Respecting the first, you long since had the independence and candor to insert in the *Guardian*, a communication received from the United States, which you pronounced at the time quite satisfactory, as establishing the justice of the American claim. There are, however, as I conceive, intrinsic difficulties appertaining to that question which can never be surmounted, except by a reference of the whole dispute to the arbitration of some friendly power. As regards the second,—the right of search,—I have endeavored, in my previous remarks, to justify the conduct of the American government, as respects the demand of Great Britain, and I hope with impartiality. In the case of the Caroline, it is well known, that a company of her majesty's soldiers, under the command of a British officer, invaded the American territory, seized and burnt an American vessel, murdering one or more persons on board; that this act was contrary to the express orders of Sir Francis Head; that, notwithstanding, it has been since approved by Great Britain, and the commanding officer rewarded. America has demanded reparation; but it has not been given. Should she continue to press the demand, it may be, that Lord Aberdeen may persevere in denying her redress, and remind her present ambassador, as he did Mr. Stevenson, "that it is for the American government to determine what may be due to a just regard for the national dignity and national interests." His lordship may rest assured, that America will not be found wanting in the maintenance of either; and that, upon this occasion as upon others, she will strictly adhere to the rule laid down by that distinguished citizen and patriot, Andrew Jackson, "to ask nothing that is not clearly right, but to submit to nothing which is wrong."

The above language of Lord Aberdeen may well be denominated "pugnacious." It is that of pride and hauteur. It is the same which Great Britain has too often used to nations less powerful than herself. It will not be heeded in America, but will be answered only by resistance. War may be the result; but the United States, animated by the justice of their cause, will not wait to count the cost, when the question of national honor is concerned. Great Britain would not, it is believed, have ventured, under similar circumstances, to have used the same language to France. The navy of the latter is too powerful; the blood of Frenchmen is too warm; the British isles are too near to Cherbourg and Toulon. It is only the other day, in a war which Great Britain is waging for trade, and for the right of poisoning the Chinese, by introducing among them, against the edicts of the emperor, a deadly drug, upon which, we are informed, the profits have amounted to four millions sterling a year, that we have heard of an attack upon a fortified city called Amoy, when a mandarin came out to meet the attacking fleet with a flag of truce, inquiring "why so many ships had come there to trade at one time, and what commodities they required." What is still more remarkable, the despatch of the commanding officer, detailing the destruction of the citadel and capture of the town, presented the anomaly of having no list of persons killed, and there were only nine wounded. But let not Great Britain flatter herself that it will always be practicable to gain her victories upon such easy terms. One can easily call to mind engagements by land and upon the sea, where the result has been very different from the above. Finally, it is understood to be agreeable to the self-complacency of Englishmen, in reference to the extensive foreign possessions of Great Britain, to be called "the modern Romans." Let them, then, learn a lesson from the history of Rome, that a lawless ambition for conquest, and injustice towards the governments and people of other countries, are sure, sooner or later, to be followed by the decline and fall of the nation which avails itself of such unwarrantable means of aggrandizement.

AN AMERICAN.

January 20th, 1842.

In replying to this letter, we may as well observe, at the outset, that, for the present, at any rate, we shall abstain from any particular reference to a considerable number of subjects to which the writer has adverted. Not that we have the slightest disinclination to discuss, with our correspondent, his particular views of the burning of the Caroline, the situation of Canada, the war with China, or any other of the topics—somewhat extraneous to the question of the right of search—which he has introduced into his letter ; but because we hold that that question is of itself of sufficient magnitude and importance to require the undivided attention of both writer and reader ; and that the mixing up with it of other matters, though it may tend to mystify the subject, and to conceal unsound reasoning, can never aid in the elucidation of truth. We shall, therefore, in this article, confine ourselves strictly to the question—or rather the questions, for there are two—arising out of the recent correspondence between the American envoy and the British government, in reference to what is commonly, but rather inaccurately, termed " the right of search."

In commencing this task, we feel a difficulty, arising out of a fact which, we dare say, will have become apparent, from the perusal of the letter of An American to some of our readers who have paid attention to the subject; namely, that it scarcely presents a single definite or tangible proposition with which we contend. Though professedly written in reply to our article of Saturday last, it does not even attempt to answer one of our arguments against the claim which Mr. Stevenson sets up. Our correspondent denies our charge, that Mr. Stevenson has sheltered himself under generalities, instead of replying closely to the arguments of the British ministers. If we were not afraid of leading the minds of our readers from the main point at issue, we could easily prove our allegation by extracts from the correspondence; and An American must excuse us if we say that he has treated our article very much in the same way in which Mr. Stevenson treated Lord Palmerston's letters. After we had done our best to strip the real question at issue of all the unimportant considerations with which it had been loaded, our correspondent has been very successful in smothering it with extraneous topics, until its real shape is effectually concealed. Can any man, who reads the letter of An

American, deduce from it the actual points of difference between the English and American governments? We defy him to do so. When professing to describe the English claim, the writer huddles it up under the vague term "right of search," with an allegation, most inaccurate and unfounded, that it is the same claim which was advanced in and prior to 1812, and which gave rise to the war with America! As no discussion can proceed satisfactorily, until its basis is ascertained and defined, we shall proceed to state at once what are the two distinct questions arising out of the recent correspondence, and then show in what manner our correspondent has been misled, by mixing these two questions together.

The questions are these:

1st Have British ships a right to capture or detain American vessels known or suspected to be engaged in the slave trade?

2d. Has a British naval commander a right to visit a vessel displaying an American flag, but reasonably suspected to be, in fact, a British, French, Spanish, or Portuguese slaver; for the purpose of ascertaining, from her papers, whether she is an American or not?

These are questions so thoroughly separate and distinct, that any writer who mixes them together must either be mistaken himself, or endeavoring to mislead his readers. Yet, throughout the whole correspondence of Mr. Stevenson, there is an obvious disinclination to keep them separate; and he repeatedly answers the arguments of Lord Palmerston on one question, by allegations which really apply only to the other. Of course, it is not our business to impute motives to Mr. Stevenson; and all that we shall say about the course he has taken on this point is, that it has evidently misled our correspondent, who, through the whole of his letter, never once seems to suspect that two different questions had been under discussion; and hence he has fallen into some very extraordinary mistakes, and has charged Lord Palmerston with inconsistencies which have no existence, except in his own imagination.

For instance, complaints were made by Mr. Stevenson, to the effect that English vessels had captured vessels known to be American, which were found or alleged to be engaged in the slave trade; and these complaints gave rise to the first question above enumerated. Upon that question, and in answer to Mr. Stevenson's complaints, Lord Palmerston most distinctly stated, that Great Britain claimed no right, under the law of nations, or under any general treaty, to capture or detain any American vessel, or even to visit any vessel known to be American; and to this disclaimer he adhered throughout the whole of his correspondence. Subsequently, however, in answer to other complaints, not of capture, but of visitation and inspection of papers, which gave rise to the second of the two questions above stated, his lordship contended that the mere hoisting of an American flag could not be taken as proof of the nationality of a vessel; because that flag can be just as easily hoisted by an English, French, Brazilian or Spanish slaver, as by an American; and he claimed for British cruisers the right of visiting and examining any vessel which they had reason to suspect to be one of those which they were empowered to capture, and of ascertaining her real character from her papers. Of course, if she was found to be American, even if filled with slaves, all right of interference with her ceased at once; and she must be permitted to proceed on her voyage.

Now, in all this, we can see neither sophistry, nor special pleading, nor chicanery, nor inconsistency. It seems to us that the ground taken by Lord Palmerston, in reference to the two distinct questions brought under his notice, is perfectly clear, candid, straightforward, and consistent. That our correspondent (no doubt misled by Mr. Stevenson's letters,) has not understood the real points in dispute, is manifest from a question which he asks, as if he thought it conclusive of the whole matter. He says—

> "And now, sir, since you have been pleased to pronounce the claims of America so 'unreasonable,' 'absurd,' and 'preposterous,' permit me to ask a few plain, simple questions. If the United States had placed themselves in a false position, or asserted unjust or unreasonable claims, why did Lord Palmerston, when called upon by the American government for reparation for losses sustained by the detention of certain American vessels upon the African seas, justify the same by reason of the agreement between the English and American naval commanders already mentioned? Why did he not say at once, 'We had a right to arrest and detain these vessels, and shall do so again under similar circumstances'?"

We should have thought that even the slightest attention to the correspondence would have guarded our correspondent from the error into which he has here fallen, by following the example of Mr. Stevenson, and applying to one question the facts and the reasons which belong only to the other. Lord Palmerston could not, under a claim of right to visit vessels for the purpose of ascertaining their national character, justify the capture of a vessel ascertained to be an American ; and he, therefore, showed that where such capture had taken place, they had been made under a special convention concluded between the British and American naval commanders on the African coast. With respect to that convention, and to the captures made under it, all we shall say is, that the American government must settle with its own officer any complaints arising out of them ; and we have mentioned it now only for the purpose of showing the error into which our correspondent has fallen, respecting the real nature of the claim set up by the English government. A mistake of a similar character has given rise to another question of the same kind. Our correspondent asks,—

> "And last, but not least, if Great Britain or her allies have a right to exercise the power claimed over American vessels, why has Great Britain, as stated by Lord Aberdeen in his letter of the 13th October last, deemed it necessary to request the permission of America, or, in other words, to solicit her to become a party to the treaty which should contain that permission?"

To this question we again reply, that nobody claims a right to exercise any power over American vessels known to be such ; but, if America would become a party to the treaty of which our correspondent speaks so sneeringly, but the real nature of which he apparently does not understand, all the contracting parties would have a right to capture a slaver, even though known to be an American ; and the exercise of this right would do much to put down the slave-trade, for which the American flag is now almost the sole refuge,—which will sufficiently account for the anxiety of Lord Palmerston, that America should become a party to the treaty. That treaty, by the way, gives no new power to England, but merely puts the stipulations hitherto contained in separate treaties with different foreign powers, into one general convention executed jointly by all.

But, to return to the claim, advanced by England, of a right of visitation of vessels suspected to be engaged in the slave trade, and liable to capture by British vessels: we shall be glad if our correspondent, from whom we hope to hear again, will state his views as to the law of nations upon this, the only point at present really in dispute in connection with the subject of search. As he has asked some questions which did not bear upon the point, we will take the liberty of asking him one or two which, in our opinion, do bear upon it, and to which we shall be exceedingly glad to have his answers. He is, no doubt, well aware of the fact, pointedly alluded to in the message of President Tyler, and perfectly notorious to the world, that, in carrying on the slave-trade at the present time, "the American flag is greatly abused by the abandoned and profligate of other nations;" that, in fact, the Spanish slavers from Cuba almost invariably sail under it, and seek to protect themselves by assuming an American character. Now we beg that he, keeping this fact in mind, will reply to the following queries,—which, in our judgment, go to the root of the matter in dispute:

1. When a captain of an English cruiser, acting under a treaty with Spain for suppressing the slave-trade, sees a vessel which he has reason to believe to be a Spanish slaver, but which hoists an American flag, does our correspondent maintain that the English officer has no right to visit such vessel, and examine its papers?

2. Suppose the officer, though acting in good faith, should be mistaken, and that the vessel should prove to be an American, would such visit and inspection involve a breach of international law?

3. If so, upon what opinions, decisions, or analogies, does our correspondent rest his opinion?

We think that, if our correspondent will answer these questions candidly, sincerely, and dispassionately, he may do much good in the way of removing prejudice and misconception from the minds of others; and perhaps, in the course of the investigation which the framing of his answers will require, he may possibly discover that he has himself been a little mistaken; in which case we feel confident, that we only do him justice in believing that he will not shrink from avowing his change of opinion. At all events, it is exceedingly desirable that the merits of the question should be fully understood; and if the Americans will, as our correspondent intimates, go to war, provided the British claim of visitation be persisted in, we hope that they will, at any rate, take care to inform themselves as to what that claim really is, and not commence hostilities under an impression that it is the same claim of searching for and impressing seamen in American vessels, which gave rise to the last war between the two countries.

We purposely abstain from noticing some little topics of irritation, which we think would be much better omitted in discussions of international questions; but there is one point mentioned by our correspondent, on which we cannot help saying a few words. Our correspondent charges Lord Palmerston with flippant, indiscreet, and uncourteous remarks upon the American flag; but we think that a very little consideration will convince him that his charge has no good foundation. Of the real and genuine American flag, the emblem of the power and independence of the United States, neither Lord Palmerston nor any other sensible man would speak otherwise than with respect. But when a flag is forged and counterfeited,—when, instead of truly representing the national character of the vessel that bears it, it is made the cover of deceit and falsehood,—whether it may resemble the "star-spangled banner," or the union jack, it is nothing better than a fraudulent rag, and deserves no respect from anybody. Now, it was of this counterfeit and fraudulent flag that Lord Palmerston spoke in his letter; and we cannot but think, that the sensitiveness which our correspondent displays on the subject is very much misplaced.

[*From the Manchester Guardian, January* 29, 1842.]

THE RIGHT OF SEARCH.

We have received the following further communication from the writer of the letter which appeared in the *Guardian* of Saturday last:

To the Editor of the Manchester Guardian:

Sir,—In sending you a communication under date the 20th instant, nothing could be more distant from my thoughts than entering upon a newspaper controversy; nor is it my intention to continue a discussion which, I fear, must have already wearied the patience of your readers. It appeared to me, on the perusal of your editorial remarks of the fifteenth of January, upon the correspondence between Lords Palmerston and Aberdeen, and the American ambassador, that you had mis-stated, not to say perverted, unintentionally or otherwise, the true meaning of, at any rate, one of the writers; and, being a personal friend of Mr. Stevenson, and always desirous of defending the character of my country when unfairly attacked, my wish was solely to call the attention of your readers to the correspondence itself, hoping they might find in it a refutation of your statements, and a confirmation of my own. The prominent place assigned by you with so much courtesy to that communication, together with your remarks, leads me to believe that my object will have been attained; and, therefore, our correspondence must end with the present letter.

You commence your remarks by saying, that my communication, " though professedly written in reply to your article of Saturday, the fifteenth of January, does not even attempt to answer one of your arguments against the claim which Mr. Stevenson has set up." In answer to this, permit me to observe, that Mr. Stevenson " has set up no claim whatever." On the contrary, it is Great Britain, or rather her government, which " has set up a claim," as I trust I have proved in my first letter; and, if my communication of the twentieth instant was no reply to your article of the fifteenth instant, as asserted by you, I may truly aver that I have only followed the example which I had before me in your editorial remarks of the above-named date, upon the correspondence itself. After repeated reference to those remarks, I have been utterly unable to discover any thing which has even the semblance of "an argument." I was, therefore, compelled to have recourse to the correspondence itself; and, in commencing my observations, I spoke accordingly, not of your "arguments," but of "your remarks," "the conclusions at which you had arrived," and of "the charge against Mr. Stevenson." The greater part of the article is taken up in an attempt to define the word "belligerent right," in which I must think that you have succeeded wonderfully in introducing confusion into what was before quite plain and evident. After having called the claim alleged by you to have been set up by Mr. Stevenson "unreasonable," "absurd," and "preposterous," it was incumbent upon you to prove it so. Instead of this, after having, as it appears to me, mis-stated his argument, and charging him with claiming what he never did claim, you undertake to give your readers a list of what you assert may be called "belligerent rights."

You never attempt to prove the difference, (which however, you assert exists,) between a right to search for British seamen on board of American vessels, (which I have declared was one of the principal causes of the war of 1812,) and a search for slaves, which is the claim now set up by her majesty's government. But every one must perceive it can make no difference to America what may be the object of the search, provided a foreign nation shall have assumed it against her permission, and in violation of that freedom of the seas which is guarantied to her by the law of nations. If Great Britain, in consequence of having made a treaty with the four other great powers of Europe, can assume with impunity the right of establishing what a London journal has rightly denominated "a police," upon the high seas, and in the exercise of the same, can subject American vessels to search and detention, in pursuit of slaves, what can prevent her assumption of the same power for any other object she may desire to accomplish? We all know what these great powers have done upon the continent in the form of what are called passports, which subject every foreigner to expensive and vexatious detentions and annoyances from every petty custom-house subaltern met with on the road. We also know that British travellers have been the loudest and most violent in their condemnation and execration of this system, which they have denounced as the meanest and most degrading species of espionage, tyranny, and oppression. Indeed, many of them have openly resisted it. What, then, must be our surprise, when we now witness the attempt of the government of Great Britain to establish the same kind of offensive police upon the seas? Who would ever have expected to have found its establishment and exercise defended in the far-famed *Quarterly Review* upon the very same grounds? As if there was any analogy between the sea — the highway of nations — and the territory of a continental king, emperor, or petty prince, who possesses indisputably the right of establishing what regulations he pleases, upon his own territory, and over his own subjects, but whose power stops there. It only proves that the *Quarterly Review*, as also Lord Palmerston, Lord Aberdeen, and the editor of the *Guardian*, are ready to avail themselves of every species of aid, to acquire the jurisdiction, so long desired, over the freedom of the seas, and the ships of the commercial rival of Great Britain.

You have evaded an answer to my question, why Lord Palmerston, when called upon by Mr. Stevenson for reparation of losses sustained by the detention of certain vessels sailing under the American flag, availed himself of the alleged agreement between the English and American commanders, by attempting to prove that Mr. Stevenson's complaint respected "the capture" of a vessel sailing under the American flag, and not its search or detention. On reference to the correspondence, I do not find the word "capture," or any other word having its meaning, in one of the earlier letters of Mr. Stevenson, or of Lord Palmerston. In his lordship's note to Mr. Stevenson, dated the 17th August, 1841, he informs him, "that he sends him a copy of the agreements entered into between the English and American commanders, on the subject of the detention of the vessels, the Douglas, the Iago, and the Hero, by her majesty's cruisers." The first time we meet with the word "capture" is in Lord Palmerston's note of the 27th August, relating to the brig called the Mary. In this, his lordship, after having stated the circumstances under which that vessel was seized, remarks: "Under these circumstances, the undersigned is of opinion that the commander of her majesty's ship Forrester was fully justified in considering the Mary to be a Spanish vessel, and, consequently, in taking her before the British and Spanish court; and, accordingly, when the British commissioners reported to her majesty's government, that the judges had refused to allow the Mary to be libelled in that court, under the impression that the mere fact of her having the American flag hoisted should have protected her from visitation and search by a British cruiser, the British commissioners were told that there was, in the opinion of her majesty's government, reason to suppose that the Mary was a Spanish, and not an American, vessel; and that the judges ought, therefore, to have allowed her to be libelled in the British and Spanish court." You state, that I have confounded two things essentially different, and that "two distinct questions" were brought by Mr. Stevenson under the notice of Lord Palmerston. I have searched in vain to find "these two distinct questions" in the letters of Mr. Stevenson; nor does Lord Palmerston anywhere speak of them when called upon for reparation. The complaint of the first is always of the "detention" or "search" of certain vessels sailing under the American flag; and the reply of the latter is always the same, viz.,—"that it was done in consequence of the agreement" before mentioned. Again, Lord Palmerston, in his letter dated the 27th August, informs Mr. Stevenson, "that if, in some few cases, such merchant-men have been searched, when suspected of having been engaged in the slave trade, this has been done solely because the British officer who made the search imagined that he was acting in conformity with the wishes of the United States government." I would here call your attention to the reason assigned by the British commissioners for having refused to libel the Mary, viz.,—that, in their opinion, "the fact of her having the American flag hoisted should have protected her from visitation and search by a British cruiser." Permit me to inquire, why these commissioners came to this conclusion in the case of the Mary, unless they had always acted upon this principle in former cases of detention or seizure, which may have been brought under their notice; and, if so, does it not prove conclusively, that the British government, in giving them new instructions, are attempting to set up a new claim, as was asserted in my last communication; or, rather, that it has revived its claim "to the odious right of search in a form never before avowed, and to an extent never before asserted?"

You will please also, to observe, that Lord Palmerston explicitly disclaims all right to search American vessels, even "when suspected of having been engaged in the slave-trade," and apologizes for what had occurred in the same manner as before. Not a word is said about capturing prior to his letter of the 27th August. And now, will the editor of the *Guardian* inform his readers, in what possible way Great Britain can execute the treaty she has signed, without frequently violating the American flag in the manner already described, and which Lord Palmerston admits she has no right to do? And who, that reflects for a moment upon the incessant and interminable complaints and reclamations which the exercise of such a claim must inevitably produce between "two such energetic people," would desire to see it attempted?

Nor is your reply more successful to another question of mine; viz., Why, if Great Britain had a right to exercise the power claimed over American vessels, has she requested "permission" of America to do so, or, in other words, solicited her to become a party to a treaty which should contain that power? Here you assert that "I have fallen into another error," of "a similar character" to the first; and in consequence, so far as I can understand your meaning, of not comprehending the stipulations of the treaty concluded by the "Christian League." You claim to have a superior knowledge of the treaty; and, if so, why have you not stated what its terms are, to which Great Britain has solicited America to accede? If the principal article in it be not "the permission" to board, visit, or search vessels sailing under the American flag, in the African seas, what is it? Have you omitted to furnish the information required, because, as very conveniently alleged by you in reference to another declaration of mine, "you were afraid of leading the minds of your readers from the main point at issue?" You assert "that the treaty gives no new power to England;" but the *London Morning Post*, of the 21st December, declares, "that it gives extended powers to the right of search, in order to give the fuller effect to the provisions of the treaty." Which statement are we to believe? You intimate that the principal article respects "the right to capture a slaver, even though known to be an American;" in other words, to permit English cruisers to execute the laws which the United States have passed so many years since, for the suppression of the slave trade. But you have not informed your readers how an American or other vessel could be ascertained to be a slaver without first boarding, detaining, or searching her; and, therefore, that permission must also have been asked; for surely you would not have a vessel captured upon the African seas, when met with by one of her majesty's cruisers, without first ascertaining that she was a slaver. But if you have omitted to inform your readers what the treaty does contain, Lord Aberdeen has supplied that omission; for, in his letter of the 13th October, he declares "his proposal" to have been, not—what you have intimated—"the right to capture American vessels," but a right to search them. "A mutual right of search," says his lordship, "regulated in such a manner as to prevent the occurrence of any irritating circumstances, has always appeared to the undersigned as the most reasonable, the most simple, and most effectual method of attaining the great object which both governments have in view." Let your impartial readers compare this open declaration of Lord Aberdeen with the various passages contained in your article of the 22d instant, in which, unable to answer satisfactorily the questions proposed, you have charged me with having "misunderstood the real points in dispute," of "having fallen into an error," of "unsound reasoning," of "being a little mistaken," and of "smothering the real question with extraneous topics." May I not be permitted to repeat, what I stated in my first communication, that "I find it difficult to believe that you can have read the correspondence with your usual attention and care?" In my last communication, I stated that "the right of search," now claimed by Great Britain, is the same which was advanced in and prior to 1812, and which gave rise to the war with America. This assertion you have ridiculed as "most inaccurate and unfounded." What, then, will be the astonishment of your readers to be informed, that, if they will only refer to your editorial remarks contained in the *Guardian* of the 5th January, they will there find the same assertion made by yourself? In detailing the various causes of disaffection between England and America, you express yourself in the following words:—"Thus the old boundary question, which, as a matter of popular excitement, had slumbered from 1783 to 1836, has become exceedingly prominent on account of the supposed weakness of England, arising from the disaffection of the Canadian people; and the old and much-vexed question of the right of search has received new importance from the affair of the Caroline, and the recent captures or detentions of vessels, alleged to be American, on the coast of Africa"!

As respects the charge of my having spoken "sneeringly" of the treaty entered into by the "Christian League," it is too early to have heard what reception the news of its signature may have met with in the United States; but if its reception there be the same which it has encountered here, and from a journal too which may almost be denominated an Englishman's testament, the *London Times*, it is to be feared the self-complacency of Lord Palmerston will not be much gratified. In reference to that treaty, in the *London Times* of the twenty-second of December last, will be found the following remarks, which I recommend to the particular attention of the editor of the *Guardian*, and of his readers: "The French slave-trade, though nominally suppressed in 1819, has never ceased to be carried on systematically, and with vigor. Nor is very much gained, by the concession, on the part of Austria, Prussia, and Russia, that the same measure may be dealt to their subjects. It is not from these states, confined, as their power and influence is, to the eastern hemisphere, or even within narrower bounds, nor even from France, despoiled of her colonies, that we can look for any really effectual coöperation in putting an end to this standing iniquity. Prussia and Austria may well afford, (honest people !) to sit at home, and denounce and renounce all slave dealers, with their aiders and abettors, as if the colliers of Staffordshire and manufacturers of Derbyshire were to sign a round robin against smuggling of French brandy. Such documents cost little, and do little; but try Dorsetshire and the Isle of Wight.

"It is not your inland powers, with half-a-dozen seaports, and no trade beyond the Mediterranean or Baltic, however great their European credit, whose influence will be here effectual. Spain, Portugal, the Brazils, and America,—these are the criminals, and these only are the powers, from whose assistance, voluntary or otherwise, any true amelioration must result. And while, in spite of the meagre concessions which we have extorted from Spain by 'legitimate influence,' or bought from her by our gold, her Cuba merchants can show fortunes made in their infamous traffic, and complacently boast that, if but one out of three ventures escape the British cruisers, it well answers their purpose; while parliamentary evidence tells us that, before the court of Havana, established for the express purpose of condemning slavers, no seizure of a slave vessel has ever taken place but at the interference and denunciation of the British commissioners; and that, even then, such seizure has only been made to be followed by perfect acquittal in the Spanish tribunals; as long as this goes on on the spot, it is a mere farce to congratulate ourselves on the protest, noble protest it may be, of distant powers scarcely interested in the question, or able to exercise an influence upon it, as if we had gained any real and substantial victory. If we can believe Mr. M'Culloch, that, between the years 1680 and 1700, no less than three hundred thousand slaves were imported into the West Indies, and that, in the succeeding eighty-six years, six hundred and ten thousand were imported into Jamaica only, we cannot but feel thankful that these times of guilt seem, at any rate, gone for ever."

From the above statement of the number of slaves imported into Jamaica, the conclusion would seem to follow that, if importations of slaves have been made into the other colonies of her majesty upon a similar scale, they must be well stocked; and a person disposed to be uncharitable in his judgment of the motives of Great Britain, might attribute her extraordinary zeal to prevent the further extension of the slave-trade to the desire to increase the value of what persons in trade denominate "stock on hand;" for, although an Act of Parliament has emancipated the slaves in the British colonies, every one knows, that the value of a West India estate depends upon the price of sugar and coffee; and the readers of the *Guardian*, at any rate, cannot be ignorant, that the principal competitor, with which the British West India Proprietors have to contend, is the Brazils, into which slaves continue to be imported, as is affirmed, at the rate of fifty thousand a year.

And now, as respects the questions contained in your article of the twenty-second instant, were I disposed, I might deny the courtesy of your proposing questions to be answered by me, until you had first replied to those which I had previously put to you; and I trust I have proved, that to neither of my interrogatories can any answer be found in your article of the twenty-second instant. But I would not avail myself of any want of inclination or of ability on your part; and therefore, in reply to your first question, viz.,—"When a captain of an English cruiser, acting under a treaty with Spain, for suppressing the slave-trade, sees a vessel, which he has reason to believe to be a Spanish slaver, but which hoists an American flag, does our correspondent maintain that the English officer has no right to visit such vessel, and examine its papers?"—my answer is, that America seeks no jurisdiction over, nor does she protect the ships, be they slavers, suspected slavers, or what they may, of any foreign nation sailing under any flag they may choose to hoist; but does, and always will deny the right to stop, examine, detain, or interfere, in any way whatever, with American ships sailing under her own flag, in time of peace, upon the high seas; and that, if the right now claimed by Great Britain, in order to execute the terms of her treaty with the other great powers of Europe, cannot be exercised without "that visitation" or "interruption" over her vessels and navigation, described by Sir William Scott, and which he declares to be contrary to the law of nations, America will never submit to the exercise of that right, contrary to her consent, either on the part of Great Britain, or of any other nation upon the face of the globe.

From this it follows, in answer to your second question,—viz., "Suppose the officer, though acting in good faith, should be mistaken, and that the vessel should prove to be an American, would such visit and search involve a breach of international law?"—that such conduct would "involve a breach of international law." And, finally, to your third and last question—viz., "If so, upon what opinions, decisions, or analogies, does our correspondent rest his opinion?"—my answer is, that, in spite of your very friendly suggestion as respects "the investigation which the framing of my answers will require," after the decision so emphatically pronounced by Sir William Scott and resting upon a well-known law of nations, I would not be guilty of the presumption of adding another word upon a point which has been settled by such high authority, and which no one, to my knowledge, has ever ventured to call in question. I do not forget the courteous and feeling manner in which you solicited "the indulgence" of your readers for my last communication; but I must think that a newspaper discussion, upon a point so well established, would be deemed a work of supererogation, not only on the part of the humble individual who now addresses you, but even on that of the editor of the *Manchester Guardian.*

AN AMERICAN.

January 27th, 1842.

Of the preceding very long letter, the two last paragraphs, containing together about fifty lines, are to the purpose, because they relate to the only point now at issue between the British and American governments. As to the rest of the letter, with all due respect for our correspondent, we feel bound to say, that it has apparently been written for the purpose of keeping that point as much as possible out of sight, and diverting the attention of the reader to topics which are either wholly immaterial, or of comparatively small consequence. Perhaps we should have best consulted the taste and convenience of our readers, by confining our remarks entirely to the two paragraphs above specified; but we must crave their indulgence for a brief allusion to one or two points in the previous portion of the letter, which seems in some degree necessary for the purpose of clearing the way to the real question at issue.

It will be seen, that a large portion of the letter is devoted to a very elaborate attempt to prove, that the right of visitation, for the purpose of ascertaining national character, now claimed by Great Britain, is precisely the same right of search which was formerly resisted by the Americans, and which gave rise to the last war between the two countries. Our correspondent says, that we "never attempt to prove the difference between a right to search for British seamen on board of American vessels, and a search for slaves, which is the claim now set up by her majesty's government." If this statement was correct,—if the English government did set up any claim to search American vessels for slaves, there would be, at all events, some analogy between the two questions, and it might have been incumbent upon us to show the difference between them. But how stands the fact? Does Great Britain set up any claim of right to search American vessels for slaves? Nothing of the sort: any such right is distinctly and emphatically disclaimed by Lord Palmerston; and therefore there is not the slightest resemblance between the right of visitation now claimed (the exercise of which, in time of war, was never objected to by anybody,) and the power of examining and impressing the crews of American vessels, which the government of that country most strenuously, and, we think, with good reason, disputed and resisted.

This fact disposes at once of the greater part of our correspondent's remarks, and furnishes the ground of an answer to the two long paragraphs which our correspondent has devoted to a defence of the two questions contained in his former letter. He now intimates, that we were incorrect in saying, that Mr. Stevenson complained of the capture of certain American vessels, and says, that he can find no use of the word "capture," or any analogous word, in Mr. Stevenson's letters. Very likely not; but he will find a statement of facts, which amount to something very like capture. At all events, after the visitation for the purpose of ascertaining national character, vessels alleged to be, and appearing from their papers to be, American, were detained for several days. Yet our correspondent asked, Why did not Lord Palmerston seek to justify this protracted detention of a vessel known to be American, under the alleged right of visitation, for the purpose of ascertaining national character? He might just as well have asked, why his lordship did not set up that right of visitation as a justification of the burning of the Caroline. But such are the absurdities into which very acute men are perpetually driven when seeking to prop up a bad cause.

As to the allegation, that we have asserted the identity of the old question of the right of search with that which has recently sprung up, our correspondent must have been disposed to be facetious when he penned that part of his letter. The quotation from the *Guardian* bears no such meaning as that which he ascribes to it.

Enough, however, on these preliminary points. Our correspondent has, at last — and evidently with much reluctance, at which we do not wonder — come fairly up to the real point in dispute; and to that we shall address the few additional remarks which we have to make. It will be seen, that our correspondent, in replying to our questions (in one of which, by the way, he has, we hope, unintentionally made an important alteration, by substituting the word "search" for "inspection,") says, as we expected he would say, that a visitation of an American vessel, for the mere purpose of ascertaining her national character, though made under reasonable grounds of suspicion that she was Spanish, would involve a breach of international law; and he says, this is a well-established point, and has been settled by a decision of Sir William Scott, which is referred to by Mr. Stevenson, in his correspondence with Lord Aberdeen. From the way in which our correspondent speaks of this decision, those of our readers who have not paid much attention to the subject may probably suppose that it was made upon some case involving the point now in dispute; that Sir William Scott had actually pronounced a judgment upon the question of visitation, for the purpose of ascertaining national character. They will be somewhat surprised to learn, that no such point was involved in the case; which was one of actual capture and confiscation. A French vessel, engaged in the slave-trade, was taken by an English cruiser, at a time when there was no treaty between the two countries authorizing the capture. Sir William Scott, of course, pronounced the capture illegal; and the only wonder is, that any body should ever have held a contrary opinion. But this decision has no more bearing upon the right of visitation, than the judgment which displayed the wisdom of Solomon.

We should not, however, be acting candidly by our readers, if we did not state that, in giving his judgment as to the illegality of the capture, Sir William Scott made use of some expressions which, at first sight, seem to countenance the opinion advanced by our correspondent. Sir William said:

"I can find no authority that gives the right of interruption to the navigation of states upon the high seas, except that which the right of war gives to belligerents against neutrals. No nation can exercise a right of visitation and search upon the common and unappropriated parts of the ocean, except upon the belligerent claim."

Now this observation, inasmuch as it did not apply directly to the case before the court, was what lawyers call an *obiter dictum*, which is never considered as having the authority of a decision, nor indeed any authority at all in governing subsequent decisions. At the time when it was uttered, the question of the right of visitation, as now claimed by the English government, had never, so far as we know, been called in question, and had certainly not been argued before the court. Even supposing, therefore, that Sir William Scott had directly, and in express terms, intimated an opinion adverse to the right of visitation, that opinion would amount to little or nothing. But has he expressed any such opinion? He says that, except in particular cases, no nation can exercise a right of visitation and search. But what does he mean by "search"? We know no more than our correspondent. We can only infer, from the previous contentions upon the subject, and the decisions which the learned judge had been called upon to pronounce, that he meant something very different indeed from the mere inspection of papers to ascertain the national character of a vessel.

Undoubtedly, if Sir William Scott, after full argument and consideration, had decided against the right of visitation as now claimed, we think that no Englishman would venture to question the soundness of the decision; but to lay hold of a doubtful expression of opinion on a point not arising in the cause before the judge, and to apply it to a question which, we imagine, had never been brought before him, argues a conscious weakness on the part of those who support the American claim, and sufficiently accounts for the disinclination of our correspondent to grapple with the real question at issue, as well as the manifest soreness which pervades the preceding letter.

Our correspondent has alleged, more than once, that Mr. Stevenson has set up no claim on behalf of the United States; and, perhaps, in point of form, that statement is correct; but the ground taken by him, in his correspondence with Lord Aberdeen, and now assumed by our correspondent, amounts in substance to a claim that the American flag shall be taken as proof of nationality, and, by necessary inference, that every slaver or pirate that chooses to carry an American flag shall be free from question or examination. That any such claim as this, as absurd in its character as it would be monstrous in its consequences, can be admitted by England, is, we imagine, wholly out of the question; and we cannot believe that either the government or the people of the United States will persist in it.

In concluding this discussion with our correspondent, we cannot avoid saying, that, upon one point to which his remarks have been addressed, we were in error. Since his first letter appeared, we have taken an opportunity of reading Mr. Stevenson's letters to Lord Aberdeen with more care than we had previously bestowed upon them; and we feel bound to admit, that that perusal has removed the impression which we previously entertained, that Mr. Stevenson had avoided the real question at issue between the two countries. Being satisfied as to the injustice of our former remarks upon this point, we should have felt it necessary to say so, even if there had been no friendship subsisting between our correspondent and Mr. Stevenson; but the knowledge that there is such a friendship, renders the admission of our error more imperatively necessary.

AMERICAN MANUFACTURES.

London, June 16th, 1843.

Dear Sir:—You will have heard, by the last steamer, of the importation into this country of four hundred bales of domestics, for sale, on account of one of the Lowell manufactories, and of the sensation produced by the arrival of such a valuable consignment at the port of London. The public curiosity was greatly excited to know who in America could have ventured upon such a novel experiment: and the question was put to almost every American, "Is it decided that your country is to supply us in future with cotton goods?" All this appeared sufficiently surprising, as you may well suppose; but one of the late Boston steamers has brought us a letter, apparently the production of a Lowell manufacturer, of such an extraordinary character, I cannot forbear sending it for publication in the *Boston Post*. It should be read by every person in the country, and be carefully pondered by the next Congressional Committee on whom shall devolve the duty of preparing a new tariff for the people of the United States. It is only just that our merchants, once engaged in the foreign trade, whose business has been destroyed, and that our ship owners, whose vessels are returning from Europe empty, should understand for whose benefit the tariff of 1842 has been imposed. As they have listened so often to the complaints of the manufacturers for want of patronage and protection at home, it is but right, that they should know what their language is, when they have occasion to address their correspondents abroad. It will be seen that the writer of the above-mentioned letter states, "that America will soon export largely of twist, as well as of all manufactured fabrics of yarn under Number Thirty's;" and that, "where the principal elements, entering into the cost of an article, are composed of raw cotton and power, America will compete successfully with any country in the world." Mr. Greg also declares that "he is prepared to prove that the Americans can already produce coarse domestics, drills, and everything of that kind at least one and one-half pence a pound cheaper than the English," and that "they have beaten them out of the markets of India and China already;" and this declaration the author of the letter confirms. Now I cannot but think that some persons in America, when they read this flourishing account of the condition of American manufacturers, will be surprised to hear that the supposed writer of the letter signed A. L., is the leader of that party in the United States called, *par excellence*,—"the American system party;" that he has been the chief promoter of every tariff imposing high and onerous duties which has been passed since the year 1828; and that, upon these very Middlesex cotton drills, which he informs Mr. Greg he has shipped to the Messrs. Baring Brothers in London, and for which his price in England is three and a half pence a yard, he has a protective duty of over seven cents a yard, besides the other expenses of importation, making the whole to amount to one hundred and twenty per cent.!

Are the people of America aware that they have passed a tariff imposing a duty of one hundred per cent. to protect certain corporations of manufacturers at Lowell, who, when a new tariff is about to be passed, cry aloud for further protection and higher duties, and make long and pathetic speeches upon the injustice of bringing the labor of "the wretched operatives of England," into competition with that of the young ladies who work the machinery at Lowell; but who, when they have occasion to correspond with the employer of those operatives abroad, give him to understand that, so far from needing any protection, they are able already "to compete in cheapness with any nation in the world?" One is astonished at the boldness of such an avowal, when one calls to mind the meetings assembled at Boston and elsewhere, only a year since, to protest against a reduction of the duties to the standard fixed upon by the Compromise Act of 1832; and the pertinacity with which these same manufacturers continued their exertions until Congress was induced to violate every engagement solemnly entered into in 1832, and to pass the tariff of 1842; thereby almost destroying the whole foreign trade, and in a single day annihilating the business and occupation of vast numbers of persons. It is common for Americans to descant upon the despotism of certain European governments, and yet, it is believed, there is not a dynasty in Europe which would have ventured upon such a measure as the tariff of 1842. In England certainly such a measure, producing all at once such a violent and ruinous change in the occupations of the people, would have been resisted almost to bloodshed, and the ministry attempting it would have been driven from power; but, somehow or other, the people have a way, in republican, free America, of doing the most despotic acts without shame, and with impunity.

It is consolatory to find that the writer of the letter signed A. L. believes "that the world is large enough to consume all the productions of labor under just and wise regulations." It is only to be regretted that he has omitted to state what those just and wise regulations are.

Perhaps among them may be the following, which may be found in the tariff of 1842, viz:—Giving a protection of one hundred per cent. to the manufacturers of cotton, who declare "they can compete already in price with any country in the world;" imposing a duty of thirty per cent. upon silver plate; another of twenty-five dollars a ton upon iron costing from five to six pounds sterling; another of forty dollars a ton upon hemp for the encouragement of American shipping; taxing coarse fabrics made of cotton and worsted, and such as are used by the poor, seventy per cent.; or laying a prohibitory duty on flannels to keep out the cheaper article of Europe. A person who has been instrumental in making such regulations as these, may declare his belief that "the world is large enough to consume all the productions of labor," but by his acts he proves the insincerity of his assertion, and evinces his desire that his part of the world, at any rate, shall use only the productions of his own mills. It is this grasping spirit of selfishness, which is so disgusting and reprehensible in the conduct of American manufacturers. The history of their acts would disclose a system of deception, and excessive avarice unequalled in any other country. Who can have forgotten the Harrisburg convention, and the crisis amongst the manufacturers of New England, which followed the tariff of 1828? It ruined the fortunes of many of the oldest and wealthiest families in Boston and the vicinity, and compelled some of the richest citizens to mortgage their estates acquired by almost half a century of toil in the foreign trade, to borrow money to pay instalments upon their manufacturing stock; and although we hear much said at present of the great riches of the few, who are supposed to have made fortunate investments at Lowell, none appear disposed to take a lesson of prudence from the disasters of thousands who have been the victims of the manufacturing system, and are remembered no longer.

The export of the four hundred bales of domestics seems to have inspired the author of the letter signed A. L. with excellent spirits, and, pursuing his pleasant visions of future profits, he adds, "The hard times, through which we have passed and are passing, have taxed the wits of our ingenious mechanics, and what has appeared to us a great misfortune may, in the end, prove a high advantage, by opening foreign markets for our products, which could not be the case while we were in a state of apparently the highest prosperity." The writer is supposed to refer to the years 1830 to 1837, during which period there was a national bank, and an almost unlimited issue of paper money. What a confession this, coming too from the leader of that party by which heretofore it was confidently asserted that, without a national bank and vast circulation of paper, there could be no prosperity; that our exchanges could never be regulated in any other way; and that our merchants and manufacturers would be all destroyed! What a tribute to the wisdom of General. Jackson and of the cabinet which supported him in those days of alarm and consternation, and who dared to assert that no national bank did, or ever could regulate the exchange of a great commercial country; that a vast circulation of paper does not constitute the wealth of a nation; and that the destinies of a free and powerful country like America could never depend upon the will of a money king, lodged in his marble palace in Philadelphia.

Few persons, however, in Boston, were prepared in 1836 to receive such heresies as these; and fewer still of our citizens can have forgotten the visit of President Biddle to Boston in the summer of 1834, or the day when, descending with high and lofty step from the granite temple near the head of State Street, he was conducted in triumph upon the Boston Exchange to see his vassals, resting upon the arms of two eminent merchants and manufacturers as his dexter and sinister supports. Some time after, in 1838, we were informed by this eminent financier that, without the aid of his bank and "its penitentiary notes," "the cotton and other products of America could not be wafted down the Mississippi to the Atlantic;" but what a striking falsification of this doctrine have we witnessed the present year, in the immense production of cotton and other articles in the south and west, and in their unprecedentedly early shipments at the seaports! Truly it is high time that the leader of the tariff party, and the party itself, should begin to have a doubt whether, from 1830 to 1836, we were "in a state of the highest prosperity." As the season will soon arrive when Congress will be called upon to pass a new tariff, (for the present one has been found not only unjust, but highly unproductive also,) the citizens of Boston engaged in the foreign trade, and all who are in favor of just and equitable duties, and are opposed to such a bill of abominations as the tariff of 1842, should be upon the alert, and take active measures to enlighten the minds of the legislature upon the important duty which is so soon to devolve upon them; and among other documents which they may lay before them, let them not forget the letter signed A—— L——, to R. H. Greg, of Manchester.

I am, dear sir, very respectfully,

Your friend,

M.

To Charles G. Greene, Esq.

NORCLIFFE, May 31st, 1843.

To the Editor of the Manchester Guardian :

SIR,—In the early part of the present month, four hundred bales of American cotton manufactures, consigned to Messrs. Baring Brothers, of London, arrived by the ship Niagara.

An event so remarkable in itself would possibly have passed unheard of or unheeded, but for the fortunate accident, as I esteem it, of the seizure of the said bales at the custom house, under some misapprehension as to the origin or destination of their contents; the cause of which, I believe, you correctly suggested at the time the seizure took place.

Public attention having now been directed to the circumstance by accident, it may not be without its use. I said, long ago, that nothing short of the sale of foreign goods on the Manchester Exchange would make our manufacturers believe that other nations could compete with us even in their own markets, and I trust the arrival of four hundred bales of American domestics will not be wholly without its effect in awakening them to a sense of the precarious position they at present occupy.

When I look at the probable fate of our cotton manufactures, the raw material brought from the country of our manufacturing rivals, and charged with no trifling duty before being entered for consumption, our exchanges crippled by corn laws, and our machinery now freely exported, I confess I am not without the darkest apprehensions. Under these discouraging circumstances, and I fear overwhelming difficulties, instead of combining to procure some means of escape, we are disputing amongst ourselves —workmen, masters, and the legislature—about "ten hours' bills," multiplying restrictions of every kind, and actually proposing to limit the energies of our steam engines and water-wheels, to the extent of twenty per cent. When Lord Ashley's motion comes on, for a restriction of the hours of labor in factories to ten, or, including the short time on Saturday, to nine and a half hours daily, surely this fact, of American manufactures being now imported for sale into this country, will save us from the folly of such legislation.

Being in London last week, I went to Messrs. Barings, to see the goods in question, and inquire into the circumstances of their importation.

I found them to consist of only one kind of goods, viz.: cotton drills, a stout, twilled nankeen, used for summer trousers. This article the house in which I was concerned used to manufacture largely for export; but our correspondents diminished their orders until at last they stated they could buy the article in America ten per cent. cheaper than we could afford to send them from here. These articles, and the common plain domestics, have long since replaced the English article in the markets of South America and Canton, and they are now, it seems, come to supply our own. They are on sale, either for the home or any foreign market; and, as Messrs. Baring remarked, the ten per cent. protection duty on such articles, is only equal to the duty of five-sixteenths of a penny per pound, paid by the English manufacturer on the raw material —consequently the protection under the tariff is worse than merely nominal, being also delusive.

The following letter, received from the shipper of the four hundred bales in question, an entire stranger to me, contains so much interesting matter, you will perhaps give it insertion in the *Guardian*; and also, if not trespassing too much upon your limits, the paragraph in the American newspaper, to which the writer alludes.

The information contained in them respecting the American manufactures, and in the letter to Messrs. Jones, Gibson & Ord, in the *Guardian* of this morning, stating the exports from the United States to China alone, during the present season, to amount already to two hundred and fifty thousand pounds of twist, and four hundred and twenty thousand pieces of cotton cloth, must surely tend to awaken from their apathy both our manufacturers and the government.

I am your obedient servant,

ROBERT HYDE GREG.

[*Copy.*]

BOSTON, UNITED STATES, April 29, 1843.

ROBERT HYDE GREG, Esq.

DEAR SIR,—Although a stranger, I am induced to write to you, in consequence of having read a speech of yours, delivered in Manchester, December, 1841, and which was published in the *Manchester Guardian*. That part of it relating to the cotton manufacture of this country has proved prophetic.

The views you then presented were so much in accordance with my own, and so practical in their character, that I laid the speech aside for future reference.

Early in the present month I shipped to the address of Baring Brothers, of London, a quantity of cotton drills, which forcibly brought to my mind the declarations in your speech.

I have, therefore, in justice to you, as well as to record the fact as a matter of history, published an extract from your speech, which will be found in the *Boston Advertiser*, herewith enclosed.

I am quite satisfied we shall soon become extensive exporters of twist, as well as of all manufactured fabrics of yarn under Number Thirties.

The quantity of cotton shirtings, sheetings, and drills, now exporting from this country, is much larger than at any former period; the prices have been materially reduced by the reduction in the prices of cotton and labor.

I am fully impressed with the idea that, where the principal elements entering into the cost of an article are composed of raw cotton and power, we shall compete successfully with any country in the world. You have, however, many advantages over us at present; possessing cheaper labor and capital, and more knowledge of the arts and sciences. We have compensation in part in the abundance of water power, and a soil and climate adapted to the cultivation of cotton, to an extent which can hardly be estimated. Those are natural advantages of which we cannot be deprived. Time is the only panacea for our wants in other respects.

In all the finer fabrics we shall continue to be large customers to Great Britain; and I doubt not, from this time it will be found that the exports from Great Britain to this country will increase.

Trade appears to be improving, and will, by the autumn, again flow in its natural and accustomed channels in this country.

We are literally burdened with agricultural products. The prices are very low, which necessarily reduces the value of labor, and this reduction has caused many articles to be exported the past year which have never before been sent out of the country.

I believe the world is large enough to consume all the products of labor, under just and wise regulations; and it is to be hoped that we in this country may, in a small, comparative degree, enjoy the advantages of exporting our coarse manufactures to those countries whose produce we require for the consumption of this growing Republic.

I shall be happy to furnish you with samples of our manufactures, and compare the cost of production with those of England. Meantime, pray excuse the freedom I have thus taken in addressing you, etc., etc. Yours respectfully, etc.,

A—— L——.

[*For the Boston Daily Advertiser and Patriot.*]

MR. HALE :—I send for publication in your paper an extract from the Speech of Robert H. Greg, Esq., which appeared in the *Manchester* (Eng.) *Guardian* of the 18th December, 1841. Mr. Greg presided at the great meeting of cotton manufacturers and others interested, held at Manchester on the tenth of the same month, and is himself one of the largest cotton spinners in the world. Improbable of accomplishment as the prediction contained in the following extract seemed at the time it was spoken, it has already been fulfilled. Last week, I noticed that a vessel cleared at this port for London, with four hundred bales of drillings on board, which are believed to be the first American cotton fabrics sent to Great Britain.

All the statements made by Mr. Greg are believed to be correct. The self-acting mule to which he refers has been introduced, and will doubtless be adopted throughout the country, particularly in the manufacture of fine goods. In every description of cotton and woollen goods, since December, 1841, there have been great reductions in the cost of manufacturing, and I have no doubt there will be still greater. Further improvements will be made in the preparation, as well as in the spinning and weaving of cotton, which will materially reduce the cost of production. The hard times, through which we have passed and are passing, have taxed the wits of our ingenious mechanics, and what has appeared to us a great misfortune may, in the end, prove of high advantage by opening foreign markets for our products, which could not be the case while we were in a state of apparently the highest prosperity.

"There are, in the United States, nine hundred cotton mills: a capital of ten million pounds sterling (fifty million dollars) is invested in the cotton manufacture; they have nearly forty thousand looms, and produce two hundred and fifty millions of yards in a year. And I can state, also, on the very best authority, that the Lowell mills, which consume sixty thousand bales (out of three hundred thousand, the total consumption) produce a greater quantity of yarn and cloth, by each spindle and each loom, in a given time, than is produced by any other mills in the world. They turn off fifty yards a day in all their looms at Lowell, and we all know that no English mills produce any thing like that quantity. To be sure, they work rather longer hours than we do here. They work at Lowell seventy-three hours and a half a week; in other mills in America, seventy-five hours and a half. I got a return only last week from a friend of mine who has been at Lowell, of the work performed in the last new mills which have been built there. We are familiar with the coarse drills, that we all used to make immense quantities of at one time, to supply pantaloon stuffs for the India and China markets, and now they are used all over America; and which, not very many years ago, the house in which I am concerned used to make and ship to a great extent. The new mills at Lowell produce those at three and a half pence per pound from the cotton, six cents and three quarters, (in the other mills, seven cents,) which, with the cotton six pence, brings the cost to nine and a half pence per pound for those articles. As to the advantage they have over us, I do not exaggerate when I state it at upwards of one penny per pound in cotton alone; the freight to the American mills being about half the average freight to England, and there is our duty and other expenses. In the concern in which I am interested, the extra tax paid, owing to the high price of flour, amounts to a tax of one thousand pounds a year upon our mills, as compared with their mills in America. (Hear.) Then their water power costs, at the highest rate, three pounds ten shillings per horse power ; whilst the lowest rate in this country is twelve pounds per horse power. I have not the smallest doubt, indeed, I am prepared to prove, that they can produce coarse domestics, drills, and every thing of that kind, at least one penny and a half cheaper than we can. (Hear.) They have beaten us out of the India and Chinese markets ; of course, they produce for all their own consumption, and, after a while, I have little doubt that we shall have them introduced very largely here. (Hear, hear.)

"The last thing they will do is to attack the enemy in his own camp ; but I am quite sure we shall see it by-and-by ; of that, I think there cannot be a doubt. The rate of wages is considerably higher there ; but the great obstacle to the rapid spread of production in the American mills, is the difficulty of getting mule spinners. When they get self-acting mules, that difficulty vanishes. We must make up our minds to prepare for the loss of these markets ; it is of no use to disguise the fact ; it is of no use any of us saying, 'I can hold out as long as my neighbor ; there is nothing for it but to push the weaker ones to the wall.' That is an idle and selfish way of expression, (to say no worse of it,) which I regret too many of us have been indulging in. (Hear.) Let us take care that the strong be not also pushed to the wall ; because we may depend upon it, in production, there are stronger countries than we are ; and if we are, as a country, the weaker one, we shall all go to the wall together."

FREE TRADE AND PROTECTION.

[*From the Richmond Whig.*]

RESOURCES OF VIRGINIA.—THE REVENUE QUESTION.

We invite the attention of our readers to the interesting communication of a distinguished citizen, in our columns to-day. It is a subject which comes home to the "business and bosoms" of us all—the interests and improvements of our own State. Mr. Lawrence, during his service in Congress, was most advantageously known to the whole Union by the clear-sighted sagacity and strong practical sense, which always distinguished his views of public measures. He is eminently national in his sentiments and feelings, and has ever shown himself a true friend of the South. Suggestions from so liberal and enlightened a source, naturally commend themselves to the cordial and respectful attention of Virginians. We shall have great pleasure in laying before our readers the additional communication he gives us reason to expect.

Boston, January 7, 1846.

My Dear Sir,—When you were with us the last summer, I more than half promised to make you a short visit in February, and I have not yet given up, entirely, the long anticipated pleasure of doing so.

I have not forgotten our conversation on the condition of our country generally, and more particularly the strong desire manifested by you, to improve the condition of the people of your own State. I have always entertained feelings of high regard for the "Ancient Dominion," arising, probably, from the intimate revolutionary associations between her and our "Old Bay State," as well as from my having looked upon her as the mother of many of the greatest statesmen, and purest patriots, which our country has produced.

I am not surprised that you, of Virginia, should desire to do something by which the matchless natural resources of your native State should be developed. I have thought that the State of Virginia, with its temperate climate, variety and excellence of soil, exhaustless water power, and exuberant mineral wealth, contains within herself more that is valuable for the uses of mankind, in these modern days, than any other State in our Union.

I need not say to you, that these gifts of Providence are of little consequence to your people, or to our common country, unless developed and improved, for the purposes for which they were intended. When the constitution of the United States was adopted, Virginia contained double the population of New York, and now, New York contains double the number of people in Virginia. I do not propose to inquire into the causes that have produced such a mighty change in the relative numerical condition of these two states. I do propose, however, to state to you some of the reasons why you should now set about doing something, to bring back that prosperity, which many of your people believe is forever lost.

The truth is, and not to be denied, that Nature has been profuse in her gifts, in behalf of your people, and you have done but little for yourselves. The settlement and development of the resources of the western country have brought into existence an active and effectual competition with your people in the great staples of your agricultural products, viz., wheat, Indian corn, and tobacco. Maryland and North Carolina, like yourselves, are essentially affected by competition from the same quarter; from Ohio, Kentucky, Indiana, Illinois, Missouri, Michigan, Wisconsin and Iowa. The great West is now supplying largely the New England, and other States, which are consumers of these agricultural staples, in quantity and value to a greater extent than all the foreign world besides. The internal improvements of the country already finished, have brought Boston, by steam, within the distance of four days' travel of Cincinnati, by way of Buffalo; and a contemplated railroad from Burlington, Vermont, to Ogdensburg, New York, will bring us practically yet nearer to those fertile regions of the west. The expense of transportation is essentially reduced wherever railroads or canals have been constructed; and even the Mississippi herself bears down upon her bosom the products of the west, at less than half the freight that was charged a few years ago.

Thirty years since, a few small schooners were sufficient to carry on the commerce between this city and New Orleans; now, within the last year, we have had one hundred and sixty-five arrivals from New Orleans at this port, and many of the vessels are of the largest class; ships from five hundred to seven hundred tons burden. They have brought us tobacco, Indian corn, flour, cotton, beef, pork, lard, lead, etc., amounting in the aggregate to many millions of dollars. Of the first three of these articles, which now come to us in such quantities from New Orleans, our importations in former times were almost exclusively from Virginia, North Carolina, and Maryland. Can you expect to compete, successfully, with the western regions of our country, where, without much labor, the soil produces double, and sometimes even more, to the acre than the average crops of the last mentioned states? This competition will increase, and it appears to me that the remedy for its inauspicious effects upon your welfare, is to create a market at home for your surplus agricultural products, by establishing such manufactures as may be adapted to the peculiar condition of your labor. There are two classes of labor, intelligent and unintelligent; the former is that kind of labor which requires a considerable amount of mental culture, with active physical power. This combination is capable of applying science to art, and of producing results that are difficult, and oftentimes complicated. The latter description of labor is of that character which depends principally on physical strength; this quality of labor you have in abundance; and I hope you are not without a tolerable supply of the higher class. You may, without doubt, commence the manufacture of almost every description of articles, requiring but little skill, and prosecute the work with success. Manufactures of such articles as iron, hemp, wool, cotton, leather, etc., wrought into the coarser and more common articles, would succeed.

You will find, very soon after a regular system of the division of labor shall have been introduced, that a desire for knowledge will be created; more education, more intellectual cultivation, will be desired by those engaged in the mechanical departments, and, with this eagerness for knowledge, will follow skill and cleverness in the use of tools, and then will follow the inventive power, for which our people have become so distinguished in the estimation of the world.

You cannot do anything in Virginia, that will so completely promote the introduction of railroads, as the placing of manufacturing establishments on your beautiful water-falls. The water-power on the James river, at Richmond, is unrivalled; and it seems a great waste of natural wealth, to permit it to run into the sea, having hardly touched a water-wheel. If the prominent men of Virginia, of both political parties, will give up their party warfare, and resolve themselves into a "Committee of the Whole, on the Commonwealth, to improve the state of Agriculture," by making two blades of grass grow, where there is now but one, will establish manufactures, and carry on a well-adjusted system of internal improvements, they will then have done something that will be substantial, abiding,—which will stand as memorials of their patriotic devotion to the interest of the people, through all time. Let your common school system go hand in hand with the employment of your people, you may be quite certain that the adoption of these systems at once, will aid each other.

You cannot, I should suppose, expect to develop your resources, without a general system of popular education; it is the lever to all permanent improvement. It appears to me essential to the preservation of our republican institutions, that the people of this country should be educated, and that all intellectual culture should be founded upon our holy religion: the pure precepts of the gospel are the only safe source from which we can freely draw our morality. It is essential that we should have an educated population; inasmuch as every man can exercise the right of suffrage: the elective franchise in the hands of an ignorant and debased population, would very soon place our country in a state of anarchy. We should strive to elevate the laboring, and less favored classes. In Europe, the great body of the people have nothing to do with the election of their rulers; even in England, free as she is, compared with many of the continental states, the mass of the people do not exercise the elective franchise. This is a point of primary importance; and your people may rest assured, that taxes for education, even as a matter of pecuniary gain, would greatly enhance the value of their property. I am, therefore, clear in my convictions, not only of the duty, but the expediency of introducing manufactures extensively into your state, with an expansive system of popular education, and from these movements, will soon be seen the happiest results, in a healthful prosperity, and a striking improvement in the condition of the people.

Just for a moment imagine the whole supernumerary population of Virginia, employed at a rate of wages, such as are paid in the northern and eastern states; what, think you, would be the effect? I have not a doubt that the value of land would increase within five miles around each manufacturing village, equal to the cost of all the machinery in it. The sphere of labor must be enlarged; diversified, if you would bring out the energies of your people. I yet hope to see Virginia take that place, among the old Thirteen, that seemed by Providence to be assigned to her. It can only be achieved by energy and perseverance, on the part of those who have the destinies of their fellow citizens in keeping. Let the law-makers, and those who administer them, not only speak out, but act, give an impetus to labor; let it be respectable for every man to have a vocation, and to follow it. If not for his own pecuniary profit, let him labor for character, which he is certain to obtain, if his labors benefit others. I intended to make some remarks on the recommendation of the President in his annual message, and the report of the honorable secretary of the treasury, to change our whole revenue system. The plan proposed, if carried out, has an important bearing on the subject of this letter, which is, however, already sufficiently long. Reserving, therefore, my remarks upon the last mentioned topics, for another communication,

I remain, very faithfully,

Your friend and obt. servant,

ABBOTT LAWRENCE.

To the Hon. W. C. Rives,

Castle Hill, Albemarle County, Virginia.

We cheerfully give up our own space to-day, to a second letter from the Hon. Abbott Lawrence, and feel sure that our readers will thank us for the substitution. We have taken but a mere glance at this document, but think we may safely say, it is a powerful and impressive paper—throwing much light upon subjects of particular interest to Virginia, and indeed to the whole country:

Boston, January 16th, 1846.

My Dear Sir: I stated, in my letter of the seventh, that I should write to you again, upon the subject of the entire change proposed by the President of the United States, and the Secretary of the Treasury, in our Revenue Laws. It is no other than the adoption of *ad valorem* for specific duties, and a reduction of the whole to twenty per cent.; this being the maximum at which the Secretary supposes the largest revenue can be obtained. I shall not now discuss the rates of duty that will produce the greatest amount of revenue. I will leave the Secretary to settle that question; but shall endeavor so show what the effects will be upon the country if his recommendation should be adopted by Congress. I deem the scheme proposed to Congress, in the main, a currency question, and one, if carried out, that will reach, in its operation, the occupation and business of every man in the United States.

I believe the most economical member of Congress will agree that thirty millions of dollars will be required, annually, to carry on this government, for the next five years, and that this estimate does not include large sums that may be wanted to settle our affairs with Mexico, Texas, etc.; and that this sum is to be raised from foreign importations, and the public lands. The goods, subject to duty, imported the last year, amounted, in round numbers, to ninety millions of dollars, and the goods free of duty to about twenty-five millions. I have not the returns at hand, and may not be exactly correct as to amounts; but they are near enough to illustrate my arguments: the former paid an average duty of about thirty-two per cent., creating a revenue, say of twenty-eight millions. If the revenue derived from an importation of ninety millions, gave twenty-eight millions of dollars, what amount must be imported, to produce the same sum at twenty per cent. *ad valorem?*

The answer is, one hundred and forty millions ; add to this, the free goods, about twenty-five millions, and we have an importation of one hundred and sixty-five millions of dollars. Our exports have not exceeded, nor are they likely at present to increase above one hundred and twenty millions: we then have a deficit of forty-five millions to provide for; and how is this balance to be paid? State stocks are no longer current in Europe. Even the stocks of the United States cannot be negotiated on favorable terms.

We, who are merchants, can answer this question, having often been obliged to make our remittances in coin, when our imports have exceeded our exports.

If we are obliged to import one hundred and forty millions of goods subject to duty, to meet the wants of the government, it is quite certain that the coin must be exported to meet the deficiency. If the importations fall short of one hundred and forty millions, we then have an empty treasury. In one case, the country will be made bankrupt, to fill the treasury; and, in the other, the treasury will be bankrupt, and resort to Congress for treasury notes and loans. It may be said, that our exports will increase with our imports. This supposition I think fallacious. The policy of Great Britain, and that of all Europe has been, and is likely to continue, to protect every thing produced either at home, or in their colonies. In Great Britain, the article of cotton is now admitted free, the duty having been repealed the very last year. This was owing to repeated representations of the Manchester spinners to Parliament as to the necessity of such a measure in consequence of the competition from foreign countries in the coarse fabrics manufactured from cotton produced in, and shipped from, the United States. The argument presented in the house of commons was, that the Americans had taken possession of every market, where they were admitted on the same terms, with their coarse goods. This is a true representation, and I apprehend the repeal of the duty on cotton will not enable the British manufacturer to again obtain possession of those markets, for the heavy descriptions of cotton fabrics.

What other article of importance does the government of Great Britain admit free of duty? I know of none. Cotton is admitted free of duty from necessity. How is it with tobacco? A duty is paid of twelve hundred per cent. Wheat is prohibited by the "sliding scale," and, in case of a total repeal of the corn laws, very little wheat would be shipped from this country, inasmuch as it can be laid down, in ordinary years of harvest, much cheaper from the Baltic. Beef and pork are burdened with a heavy duty. The duty and charges on a barrel of American pork laid down in Liverpool, with the commission for sales, amount to five dollars and seventy-five cents ; so that the quantity of this article shipped to England must be inconsiderable, unless the prices here should be so low as to be ruinous to the farmer.

I cannot find, in the catalogue of our strictly agricultural products, a single article that is not burdened with a high duty, in England, or other parts of Europe, if it comes in competition with their own products ; nor can I discover that there is a disposition, on the part of a single European nation, to relax their stringent system of duties on imports from this country. It is possible that Great Britain may abate her corn laws, so far as to admit Indian corn at a nominal duty. If it should be done, I have little faith in our being able to ship it to advantage. I state the fact, then, that exports will not increase in consequence of a reduction, or even a total repeal, of the present tariff. The duty in Great Britain, on all the products of the United States, received in that kingdom, including cotton, is not less than forty-eight per cent., and exclusive of cotton, three hundred per cent. ; and this, too, on raw produce generally, where the charge of freight constitutes from one-tenth to one quarter of the cost here, and this is free trade !

I hope you, of Virginia, will examine this matter, and ask yourselves where the best customers are to be found for your agricultural products. I will just state to you, here, that Massachusetts takes more flour, Indian corn, pork, and many other articles, annually, the productions of the west, as well as of Virginia, than all Europe.

The question then arises, What will be our condition after the proposed plan of low duties goes into operation ? In twenty days after the bill becomes a law, it will have reached every country in Europe with which we have trade ; the manufactories are all set in motion for the supply of the American market ; the merchandise is shipped on account of foreigners, in many cases with double invoices, one set for the custom house, and another for the sales, so that, instead of the duty amounting to twenty per cent., it will not probably exceed fifteen per cent. This has been the experience of the American importers in New York, who, previous to the passage of the tariff of 1842, had, (most of them,) abandoned the business, not being able to compete successfully with fraudulent foreigners. I will not say that all foreigners commit frauds on the revenue ;— far from it ; — but I do say, that enormous frauds have been perpetrated by foreigners, on the revenue, under *ad valorem* duties, and will be again — prostrating the business of honest foreign and American importers. In less than twelve months after the new plan shall have been in operation, this whole country will be literally surfeited with foreign merchandise ; if it be not so, the revenue will fall short of the wants of the government ; we shall then owe a debt abroad of millions of dollars, which must be paid in coin. The exchanges go up to a point that makes it profitable to ship specie ; money becomes scarce in the Atlantic cities ; yet bills on England and France do not fall ; the loans made to the south and west are called in ; demands for debts due from those sections of country, are made ; exchange cannot be obtained ; produce is purchased and shipped ; and, when it arrives at the north, it will not command the cost in the west ; a paralysis will have struck the business of the country ; produce will no longer answer to pay debts due at the north, and the next resort is to coin, which is to be collected, and sent down the Mississippi, or over the mountains, to Baltimore, Philadelphia, New York, and Boston. Western and southern credits are cut off, as the people of those sections can no longer promptly meet their engagements. The new states, and the outer circle of the Republic, are the weak points ; and the first giving way of the banks, is heard from those points, where there is the least amount of capital. We see the storm approaching, like a thunder shower in a summer's day ; we watch its progress, but cannot escape its fall. It at last reaches the great marts of trade and the exchanges, having swept everything in its course ; and the banks of the Atlantic cities, after a violent effort to maintain their credit and honor, are forced to yield to this Utopian experiment on the currency. I have no hesitation in stating that all this will take place within the space of eighteen months from the time this experimental bill goes into operation; and not a specie-paying bank doing business, will be found in the United States. Where will be the revenue which was to produce such a mighty sum under low duties? Where is the Treasury, and the Secretary, and the President, and his cabinet? The treasury is empty; the secretary is making his estimates of income for 1849, and preparing to ask Congress for a large batch of treasury notes; or, perhaps, the deficit is so large that a loan may be required. We have now come to a point of depression in the great business of the country, which has attracted the attention and anxiety of all classes of people, all having felt its blight, excepting the great capitalists and money-holders, who are reaping golden harvests by the purchase of property, which the wants of the unfortunate throw into the market at ruinous rates. It is now seen and felt from the low wages of labor, and the great number of persons unemployed, with the cries of distress from all quarters, that it is the labor and not the capital of the country that suffers by violent revulsions caused by unwise legislation. Have the people of the south and west forgotten their troubles of 1837 to 1842, to the hour of the passage of that law, which has redeemed the credit of the government, and restored prosperity to the country? I have intimated that there is less capital in the new states, than in many of the old ones; it will not be denied that the moneyed capital of this country is held in the northern and eastern states, and that the south and west are usually largely indebted to them. Now, I should be glad to be informed what benefit is to be derived by a planter in Alabama or Mississippi, or a farmer in Ohio or Illinois, by a change like that I have described; particularly, if by chance he should be in debt? Do the people of the south believe they can raise the price of cotton, or be able to negotiate loans, to prosecute the construction of their contemplated railroads? Do Ohio, Louisiana, Illinois, Michigan, believe they are to create a better market for their produce, or sooner complete the harbors, so much desired on the shores of those "inland seas," and be able to negotiate loans, and obtain subscribers to the stock of their intended railroads, by the adoption of this new system of political economy? And now, what say the great States of New York and Pennsylvania to this proposed experiment? Can they afford to try it, and are they ready? If they are, it will be adopted; if they are not, the present law will stand, and the country will repose for a while in happiness and prosperity. Any one would suppose that those states that are now just emerging from embarrassment, which at one time seemed almost sufficient to overwhelm them in ruin, would be unwilling to try an experiment, which is certain, in my judgment, to place them in a position that will be the means of destroying the fair prospects of thousands, who are resting in quiet security upon the faith of what they deem a paternal and wise government. The question of an important alteration in our revenue laws should not be kept in suspense. The treasury will feel its effects before the end of the present year. The expectation of a great reduction of duties prevents the merchants from going on with their usual business. Voyages are delayed, and orders for goods are held back, until this important question shall be settled. I say, therefore, if we are to go through this fiery ordeal, let it come at once,—we cannot probably place ourselves in a better condition than we are now, to meet the troubles that await us.

Mr. Walker proposes to substitute *ad valorem* for specific duties, in opposition to our own experience, and that of almost every other country. I have never yet found an American merchant, who has not been in favor of specific duties, wherever it can be done with convenience to the importer and the government. I confess it is a bold measure to propose a total and entire change of a revenue system, which was established with the government, and has stood the test of experience through all the trials of political parties and administrations, from General Washington to Mr. Polk. It appears more extraordinary at this time, as the country is in a high state of prosperity. The revenue is enough for all the reasonable wants of the government, and the people appear to be satisfied with their condition. The resources of the country were never developing more rapidly; the increase of our population the present year, will probably equal that of the last, which I estimate at six hundred thousand souls; our wealth, too, has been wonderfully augmented by the construction of railroads; there has been a great increase of our shipping, engaged in the domestic commerce of the country, not only by sea, but upon our rivers and great lakes;

the manufacturing interest has been largely extended; and the soil, too, has been made to produce vastly more than at any former period. The whole productive power of the country has been greater in three years, (that is, since the passage of the tariff of 1842,) than during any equal space of time in our national history. There have been three periods of universal distress throughout our land, since the peace of 1783, and, in each case, under low duties. I appeal to those who remember those periods; and to others, I refer to the annals of our country. Those periods were from 1783, (the conclusion of the revolutionary war,) to 1789; 1815 to 1824; 1837 to 1842.

I would respectfully recommend to the Secretary of the Treasury, who appears to have received new light upon the subject of our national economy, to examine the history of the legislation of Congress, at the above periods. He will find in his own department of the government, an abundance of evidence of the distress that existed under low duties, and a deranged currency.

There is a prevalent idea abroad, that the capital of the country will suffer exceedingly by a revulsion in its business, and that the tariff of 1842 has operated in favor of the capital, and not the labor of the country. There can be no doubt that capital is generally profitably and safely employed, and well paid. The profits of capital are low, when wages are low; but capital has usually had the power to take care of itself, and does not require the aid of Congress to place it in any other position, than to put the labor in motion. Congress should legislate for the labor, and the capital will take care of itself. I will give you an example of the rate of wages under low duties, and under the tariff of 1842. In 1841 and 1842, the depression, in all kinds of business, became so oppressive, that many of the manufacturing establishments in New England were closed, the operatives dismissed, the mechanical trades were still, and every resource for the laboring man seemed dried up.

In the city of Lowell, where there are more than thirty large cotton mills, from six to sixteen thousand spindles each, it was gravely considered, by the proprietors, whether the mills should be stopped. It was concluded to reduce the wages; this was done several times, until the reduction brought down the wages from about two dollars, to one dollar and fifty cents per week, exclusive of board; this operation took place upon between seven and eight thousand females; the mills run on; no sales were made of the goods; the south and west had neither money nor credit; and, finally, it was determined to hold out till Congress should act upon the tariff. The bill passed, and, of course, the mills were kept running, which would not have been the case, if the act had been rejected; and now the average wages paid at Lowell,—taking the same number of females, for the same service,—is two dollars per week, exclusive of board. Yet, Mr. Walker says, labor has fallen. Where are the wages for labor, I ask, lower than they were in 1842? Who is to be benefited by the adoption of a system that gives up everything, and gives no reasonable promise of anything?

I have succeeded, I trust, in showing that there is no probability of our exports increasing, in consequence of a reduction of the tariff, and that the products of the western states find the best market among the manufacturers at home. In regard to the southern and cotton-growing states, they are to be greatly benefited by the increase of consumption of their staples at home. No appreciable quantity can be shipped to England, if the tariff should be repealed, it being already free of duty. The establishment and successful prosecution of the spinning of cotton, in this country, has enabled the planters to obtain, for several years past at least, an additional cent per pound on the whole crop, and, perhaps, even more. The Americans are the greatest spinners of that article in the world, the British excepted. This competition has kept the price from falling to a ruinous point, on several occasions, and it has been acknowledged, by many of the most intelligent planters in the south. Our consumption reached, the last year, one hundred and seventy-six millions of pounds, which is equal to the whole crop of the Union, in 1825, and equal to the whole consumption of Great Britain, in 1826. This is a striking fact, and one that should be remembered by the planters.

The history of the production and manufacture of cotton is so extraordinary, that I propose to send to you some statistics on the subject, furnished me by a friend. I hope you will not deem me over-sanguine when I tell you it is my belief that the consumption of cotton in this country will double in eight or nine years, and that it will reach four hundred millions of pounds in 1856; and further, that we are not only destined to be the greatest cotton-growers, but the most extensive cotton-spinners in the world. We have all the elements among ourselves to make us so. The manufacture of cotton is probably in its infancy; but a moderate portion of mankind have yet been clothed with this healthful and cheap article. Nothing can stop the progress of this manufacture, but some suicidal legislation, that will prostrate the currency of the country, and deprive the people of the means of consuming. There can be no legislation that will break down the manufacture of cotton and wool, excepting through the operations of the currency. We may be disturbed by low duties; the finer descriptions of cotton and woollens, printed goods, and worsted fabrics, would be seriously affected by low *ad valorem* duties; but the coarser fabrics, such as are generally consumed by the great body of the people, will be made here under any and all circumstances. If we have competition from abroad, the labor must and will come down; this has been often tested, and our experience establishes the fact.

In Virginia and other southern states, and even at the west, many persons have believed that the protective system was made by and for New England, and that New England, and particularly Massachusetts, could not thrive without it. Now this is an error; the south and west began the system of high protective duties, for the purpose of creating a market for their produce, (although the principle of discrimination was recognized and established when the first tariff was enacted.) It is not true, that we are more dependent on a protective tariff, than the middle, western, or southern states. Those states that possess the smallest amount of capital, are the most benefited by a protective tariff. We have in New England a great productive power; in Massachusetts far greater than any other State, in proportion to population. We have a hardy, industrious, and highly intelligent population, with a perseverance that seldom tires, and we have also acquired a considerable amount of skill, which is increasing every day; besides, we have already accomplished a magnificent system of intercommunication between all parts of this section of the country by railroads; this is the best kind of productive power, having reduced the rate of carriage to a wonderful extent; this being done, we have money enough remaining, to keep all our labor employed, and prosecute our foreign and domestic commerce, without being in debt beyond the limits of our own state. Now I ask, how we shall stand, compared with Pennsylvania, Ohio, Alabama, Georgia, or Louisiana, when the day of financial trial shall come. I do not deny we shall suffer; but as it has been in times past, we shall go into, and come out of the troubles far stronger than any other state out of New England. It is not my purpose to present to you the balance-sheet of Massachusetts, but it is due to her character and her dignity that she should stand before you in her true position. I have never advocated a protective tariff for my own or the New England States exclusively; nor have those gentlemen with whom I have been associated in this cause, at any time, entertained a narrow or sectional view of the question. We have believed it to be for the interest of the whole country, that its labor should be protected; and so far as I have had to do with the adjustment of those difficult combinations embraced in a tariff bill, I have endeavored to take care that the interests of all the states were protected, whether they were large or small. I say now to you, and it should be said in Congress and to the country, that Massachusetts asks no exclusive legislation. If Pennsylvania, New York, and Ohio, the three great states, with Kentucky, Georgia, Missouri, Alabama, and Louisiana, wish to try an experiment on iron, coal, hemp, cotton bagging, sugar, etc., etc., I am ready as one citizen of Massachusetts to meet it, and await in patient submission the result, which I doubt not will be found, within eighteen months, in the realization of all I have predicted. I say, again, I would not, if I could, have a tariff made for Massachusetts alone. If, however, there should be a new one, let our interests, with those of every other in the Union, share that protection to which we are all entitled, and of which we claim our full share. I can, with confidence, assure you, that we shall go upward and onward. We will work. If twelve hours' labor in the twenty-four will not sustain us, we can, and will work fourteen; and, at the same time, feel that Congress cannot take the sinews from our arms, or rob us of the intelligence acquired from our system of public schools, established by the foresight and wisdom of our fathers.

At the risk of writing a long letter, I cannot forbear alluding to the fact, that the habitual agitation of this question of the tariff has worked, in the main, to the advantage of New England.

We were, previous to the war of 1812, an agricultural and navigating people. The American system was forced upon us, and done for the purpose of creating a home market for the products of the soil of the south and west; we resisted the adoption of a system, which we honestly believed would greatly injure our navigation, and drive us from our accustomed employments, into a business we did not understand. We came into it, however, reluctantly, and soon learned, that, with the transfer of our capital, we acquired skill and knowledge in the use of it, and that so far from our foreign commerce being diminished, it was increased, and that our domestic tonnage and commerce were very soon more than quadrupled. The illustrations were so striking in every department of labor, that those who, fifteen years ago, were the strongest opponents among us, have given up their theories, and acknowledged that the revelations are such as to satisfy the most sceptical. We have gone forward steadily, till many descriptions of manufactures are as well settled in New England, as the raising of potatoes. Our experience has given us skill, and of course we have confidence in our own resources that does not exist elsewhere.

When I converse with gentlemen from the south and west respecting the establishment of manufactures, they reply that they should long ago have engaged in it, but the repeal of the tariff, the action of the government, prevented them. Now you cannot blame us, if this constant agitation of the tariff question has tended to give New England, not a monopoly, but advantages which she has not been instrumental in bringing about. I have no doubt we have been gainers on the whole by these agitations, yet we have at times been great sufferers. I wish those states that have withheld their energies from entering upon these industrial pursuits, to examine this matter,—and, if I am right, to take an observation and a new departure. We have no jealousy whatever concerning the establishment of manufactories in all parts of the country; on the contrary, I believe those gentlemen from the south and west who have been here, will bear witness to the desire, on the part of the people who are engaged in manufactures, to impart all the information in their power. There is room for us all. When the southern and western states shall manufacture their own clothing, we shall have become extensive exporters of the variety of manufactures produced here. We have the ships, and the men to navigate them. We shall pursue an extensive foreign commerce with manufactures, and bring home the produce of other countries, such as coffee, tea, etc., and pay for the produce of the south and west, with foreign luxuries, and necessaries of life. It has often been said here by us who advocate protection to American labor, that, in wearing British cottons, woollens, etc., we are consuming British wheat, beef, pork, etc. I am happy to find authority of the highest respectability for this opinion, in the person of one of the most eminent merchants, as well as one of the best and most honorable men in England, Mr. William Brown, of Liverpool—lately the free trade candidate for Parliament from the county of Lancaster. In a letter to John Rolfe, Esq., a landholder, upon the advantages of free trade, he says: "You next allude to the league wishing to injure you. I presume it will not be denied, that all interests in the kingdom are so linked together, that none of them can suffer without the others being injured. We must sink or swim together! Paradoxical as it may appear, I think Great Britain is the largest grain-exporting country in the world, although it is impossible to estimate accurately, what quantity of grain, etc., is consumed in preparing £50,000,000 value of exports, by which you are so greatly benefited. It is placed in the laboratory of that wonderful intellectual machine, man, which gives him the physical power, aided by steam, of converting it into broadcloth, calico, hardware, etc., and in these shapes your wheats find their way to every country in the world."

I thank Mr. Brown for the clear statement he has presented, of the importance of a home market, and commend this extract from his letter to the consideration of every farmer in the United States; it is perfectly sound, and applies with particular force to our present condition. To place the people in a condition of permanent and solid prosperity, you must encourage home industry, by obtaining the greatest amount of production; this can only be obtained by diversifying labor, which will bring with it high wages; and unless the labor is well paid, our country cannot prosper. Agriculture, the foundation of all wealth, depends on production, and a market for those products. The encouragement of agriculture, in the establishment of manufactures, if maintained, will be certain to secure a market.

I ask the farmer to look for a moment at the following statement. American flour in Cuba pays a duty of about ten dollars per barrel : in Rio Janeiro, five to six dollars ; and in many other ports, the duties vary from fifty to one hundred and fifty per cent.; in return, we take coffee, most of which we pay for in coin, free of duty—and this is free trade. We have, too, treaties of reciprocity with foreign countries ; and, among others, Great Britain, (not including her colonies,) by which her ships are admitted into our ports on the same terms as our own ; they come freighted with her minerals and manufactures, which are sold here, and take in return a variety of articles, the produce of the United States, such as timber, lumber, fish, etc., touch at New Brunswick, or some other colony, and go home, free of duty. We have, too, triangular voyages made from England to Jamaica, and other British islands, with cargoes, and thence to the southern states, where they load with cotton, tobacco, and other produce for England : this, too, is called free trade. I will not pursue this branch of the subject, but give you a fact. Not long since, the foreign carrying trade was nearly all in our own hands ; now the reciprocity system, not including the colonies of foreign nations, gives to foreigners more than one-third of all the carrying trade of the United States ! ! I cannot believe the time is far distant when the government of the United States will protect, as it ought, the foreign navigating interest of this great country. If we would have American seamen to man our navy, the mercantile marine must be protected in the carrying of our own productions. One more fact, and I will close these long, and, I fear you will think, desultory remarks. Some years since, a few bales of American coarse cottons were sent from this country to Hindostan, as a commercial experiment ; the superiority of the frabric, and the material out of which it was made, gradually brought the goods into notice and use in that country, and the annual exportation from the United States increased from a few bales up to three and four thousand per annum. The British manufacturers were much annoyed at this interference, and it is presumed that it was through their influence that the East India

Company (the government of that country) have repeatedly augmented the discriminating duty on these goods, (which are called drillings,) for the purpose of protecting their own manufactures against those of the United States. Prior to 1836, the duty was five per cent. in favor of British goods; in that year, it was increased to eight and a half per cent.; a few years after augmented to ten and a half per cent.; and even this rate of differential duty proved insufficient to keep out the Americans, who drove a profitable trade, notwithstanding the great difference against them.

And now, within a few months, the East India Company have been compelled again to increase the discriminating duty to fifteen per cent., in order to exclude our goods altogether; and this difference, will, without doubt, accomplish the object. These facts are deserving of a passing remark, as illustrative of the energies and resources of the United States. As late as the declaration of the last war in 1812, this country imported almost all its coarse cotton fabrics from Hindostan, whence they came literally by ship loads, and were paid for almost altogether in coin. No country seemed to be more abundant in means necessary to supply such goods cheaply, than Hindostan: its soil furnished an abundance of cotton, which, though not of equal quality to that of the United States, was much less in price, and labor was cheaper than in any country in the world. Cotton spinning machinery was available through the medium of British capital, and the manufacturers received a protection of ten and one-half per cent., against foreign interference. No country seemed more secure from foreign competition in these goods, than Hindostan, and least of all was there fear of competition from the United States; a country fifteen thousand miles distant, where a day's labor will earn about twenty-five pounds of good rice, while, in Hindostan, it obtains less than ten pounds of very inferior rice. But the American planter furnished a better raw cotton; the manufacturer, a better and cheaper fabric; the ship owner, a speedy and cheaper conveyance. Their united efforts drove the British manufacturer of these coarse goods from the largest British colonial market, and which the American would now be in possession of, but for the interposition of the East India Company, with another protective duty to sustain their manufactories. I have no fault to find with the course pursued by the British in these regulations. I have introduced these facts, to exhibit to you the transcendent folly of attempting a system of low duties and free trade, where it is all on one side. I have not yet known the British government to reduce the duties to a point, that has reached a single important interest. Their free trade and low duties never apply to any article that seriously competes with their own labor, nor are they likely to adopt such measures. The free trade of the political economists of Great Britain is a transcendental philosophy, which is not likely to be adopted by any government on the face of the globe, unless it be the Chinese, and we have already the earnest of the effect of low duties on the internal condition of that country. The trade of that empire is fast approaching to barter; the precious metals having been drained, to pay for the foreign products introduced into it.

I am aware that I have written a long letter, but I could not well abridge, consistently, with glancing at many topics in which I take a deep interest. The subject is boundless, and I would cheerfully carry out, by illustrations and examples, many of the points upon which I have touched, but I forbear for the present. When I have the pleasure to meet you, we can discuss all these questions, embracing not only the present condition, but the future prospects and destiny of our beloved country, for which I entertain the strongest attachment. Our strength and glory is in upholding and maintaining the Union.

I shall send, in a few days, statistics, furnished me by a friend, who is intelligent, careful and accurate in these matters, and who holds himself responsible for all that will be stated.

I pray you, my dear sir, to accept the assurances with which I remain, most faithfully, your friend and obedient servant,

ABBOTT LAWRENCE.

To the Hon. William C. Rives,
Castle Hill, Albemarle County, Virginia.

WEST ROXBURY, 16th February, 1846.

DEAR SIR,—I send you, this morning, three communications, containing some comments on two letters of the Honorable Abbott Lawrence, addressed to Mr. Rives, of Virginia, which were recently published in the Richmond *Daily Whig*, and also in the Boston *Daily Advertiser*.

They were first offered to the editors of the first-named journal, but, not having heard from them in reply, in the time specified, I had a personal interview, on Saturday last, with Nathan Hale, Esq., editor of the Boston *Daily Advertiser*, and desired him to give them a place in the columns of his paper. This request, Mr. Hale thought proper to decline. They are now offered, for insertion, in the Boston *Post*.

I remain, dear sir, very respectfully,
your friend and obedient servant,
S. D. BRADFORD.

C. G. GREENE, Esq.,
Editor of the Boston Post.

WEST ROXBURY, (near Boston.)
February 5th, 1846.

DEAR SIR,—I have read with attention the two letters recently addressed by you to your friend, Mr. Rives, of Virginia, and being unable to admit many of your premises, or, having admitted them, being compelled to draw from them opposite conclusions, I avail myself of the earliest opportunity in my power to address you upon the various subjects brought under consideration. This is of the greater importance, because, looking at the time you have chosen to reappear before the public; the channel of commmunication you have selected, as well as the nature of the arguments you have used, no one can doubt that your object is to act upon the Congress now assembled at Washington, and to do what you can to prevent any change or reduction in the tariff of 1842. This is all fair, and was to be expected. We all like to have our own way, and, when one is doing well, and engaged in a highly prosperous business, it cannot be supposed he would desire a change.

I do not propose to say anything on the subject of your first letter, devoted almost exclusively to the suggestion of a plan for restoring the State of Virginia to her former riches and magnificence, because my opinion of it will be easily deduced from the general remarks I shall offer upon your second letter. No one can wonder that you should propose, for adoption by Virginia, a scheme which you have found to answer so admirably for yourself, and the other manufacturers, with whom you are connected. Whether, however, you have not acted, as some doctors do, who, having confidence in only one medicine, propose it as the panacea for all kinds of diseases, however different in character, may admit of some doubt. Leaving then this point unsettled, I pass directly to the topics discussed in your second letter.

From the intimation given near the close of your first communication, I had made up my mind that your second would be devoted to break down, demolish, and overthrow the report of Mr. Walker, Secretary of the Treasury; nor could I wonder that you should desire to do so. This public document had attracted universal attention, not only in America, but in Europe also, especially in England, where it had been hailed as the olive branch of peace, and had rendered almost acceptable to that proud nation the high and lofty pretensions of the President's message. It had been mentioned as a most extraordinary state paper by the Governor of Massachusetts in his annual message. It had charged upon the protective system, as sustained by the tariff of 1842, the greatest injustice and inequality. It had attempted to show how it enriched the few at the expense of the many; how the highest rates of duty were paid upon the articles consumed principally by the poorer classes; how oppressive it was to our commerce and navigating interest; and unjust also towards the agriculturists and planters, in limiting their markets. Mr. Walker had estimated the sum of extra taxation imposed in this manner upon the country for the particular benefit of the manufacturers, as amounting to fifty-four millions of dollars per annum; being equal to double the amount of the revenue of the whole United States. These are high charges, and ought to be disproved, if they can be. I hope, however, that you will pardon my freedom of speech, and impute it only to my regard for the truth, when I assure you that I have been unable to find in your letter the refutation of any one of the charges above enumerated.

You commence by saying that the proposal to change or reduce the tariff of 1842, is a "question of currency," and, having stated the amount of revenue likely to be wanted for the next three years, (equal to thirty millions a year,) you assume it cannot be raised by the rates of duty likely to be recommended by Mr. Walker, (viz., about twenty per cent. *ad valorem*,) without an importation of one hundred and sixty-five millions a year. You then describe the disastrous effects of over-importation, the drain of our coin to pay our foreign debts, the probable suspension again of specie payments by our banks, and the general, if not universal, prostration of the commerce, occupations, and prosperity of the country. We all remember the fearful convulsions in the trade of the country, which have happened so often ever since the peace of 1815; and, had you assumed, as a caption to your letter, the following: "Remarks on the Ruinous

Consequences of Over-banking, and of Excessive Issues of Paper Money;" or had you taken the still shorter one of "A Defence of the Sub-treasury System," I should have said you had made a good argument, and that the verdict ought to be given in your favor. But, when you attribute all these disastrous panics and revulsions to a certain ordinance called a tariff, and to "low duties," I perceive at once you have fallen into an error, very common in practice, but often very fatal in its consequences, of considering certain occurrences, because they happen to be cotemporary, as causes and effects. "There have been three periods," you remark, "of universal distress throughout our land since the peace of 1783; and in each case under low duties. Those periods were from 1783 to 1789—1815 to 1824—and 1837 to 1842."

Respecting the first-named period, you, as well as myself, must have reference only "to the annals of our country." No doubt the country was distressed, and this was to be expected at the conclusion of a long and disastrous war, which was carried on by the colonies, consisting of thirteen distinct States, refusing "to form a union for the benefit of all;" owing a vast debt incurred during the revolutionary struggle; without credit, and almost without hope; but how that distress could have been alleviated by imposing a high tariff of duties upon this poor and miserable nation, deprived of the means of payment, I am unable to comprehend. Your remark, as respects this first period, of course has reference to the tariffs established by the different States themselves, as our present United States Government dates only from 1789.

As respects your second period, 1815 to 1824, I must express my surprise how you can call that a period of low duties under the tariff of 1816. If you will refer to the debates of that time, you will find it was considered as imposing very high duties. This was the tariff, into which was introduced, for the first time in our country, that legislative puzzle called "*minimums*," which used to perplex us so much in casting the duties on our importations. It may be called a happy invention of the government for taxing an article seventy-five per cent. on its cost under a pretended duty of twenty-five per cent. *ad valorem*. It was found to succeed, that is, to create a revenue; and was at a later period extended to woollen goods as you may remember, in the celebrated tariff of Henry Clay in 1828, which soon after produced such a frightful revulsion in the business of the country, and caused the rebellion in South Carolina.

With regard to the third period you have named, from 1837 to 1842, the duties, although on the leading articles of importation much above a revenue standard, were no doubt considerably lower than those imposed by the tariff of 1828; and let me remind you what was accomplished during the existence of the tariff then in being, which commenced in 1832. General Jackson completed the payment of the public debt, amounting at the conclusion of the war to one hundred and fifty-eight millions of dollars; and besides providing for all the annual expenses of the government, amounting to an average of nineteen millions per annum, actually paid back to the different States the sum of thirty-seven millions, being the surplus then on hand in the public treasury. Such results as these are unparalleled in the history of our own or any other country. If from 1837 to 1842 the last half of the ten years, during which the tariff of 1832 existed, there were violent revulsions in the trade of the country, the true cause of them may undoubtedly be found in the previously inflated condition of the currency.

I do not intend to deny, nor to extenuate in any way, the frightful crisis which took place from 1837 to 1842, commencing in the spring of the first-named year, when our whole paper money system, having been somewhat convulsed and shaken from the date of the famous specie circular of the eleventh of July, 1836, gave way, and sank into chaos; when some of the richest and most extensive manufacturers in Boston are said to have had a meeting to deliberate whether they should stop payment, or compel the banks to do so; and which ended in the surrender of the last named, in defiance, as Mr. J. Q. Adams justly said at the time, "of every principle of honor and justice." We all remember those times "which tried men's souls," and their pockets too; but if you attribute them to the tariff, you deceive yourself. They were produced by our system of banking, and abuse of paper money; and although at present the mountain appears to stand so strong that nothing can move it, yet its foundation rests on paper as much as ever; and what happened in 1837 may occur again under similar circumstances at any time. Every reflecting mind must see the subject in this light; and this fact, coupled with another, viz., that property, which rests on the continuance of high protective duties, can never be depended upon, is the reason why some of the Lowell shares in companies, which make a profit of thirty per cent. per annum, have been sold at par or under, and can even now be had at thirty per cent. advance. Call to mind for a moment two facts which illustrate the frightfully inflated state of the currency during the time now under consideration. In 1833, the foreign importations amounted to one hundred and eight millions. In 1836, they rose to one hundred and ninety millions. In 1833, the sales of the public lands were five millions. In 1836, they were twenty-five millions; and had not General Jackson, with an energy which never faltered, and a vigilance which never slept, promptly issued his specie circular, (so much abused and misrepresented in Boston,) the whole public domain would have been soon in the hands of reckless speculators. In 1838, when the paper money system had fallen into a state of collapse, the sales of the public lands amounted to less than two millions. No country in modern times has probably suffered so much from paper money as our own, except perhaps China some time ago, before America had any trade with her. If you happen to own, or have access to a certain book on China, written by an author named Claproth, you may find there a full account of what that country endured, strikingly similar to what has occurred in our own. The emperor finally abolished the use of paper money altogether, to save the empire from entire destruction.

Convinced, as I think you must be, of the fatal consequences of paper money, and filling, as you have at times, a place in the legislative halls of our country, I have looked with aching eyes to see you attempt some remedy for so great an evil. Year after year I have waited to see you use your powerful influence to have some measures adopted to increase our specie basis, to do away with the circulation of small notes, and to subject our eight or nine hundred banking corporations to some more stringent and necessary regulations, in order to prevent the recurrence of such a frightful revulsion, as you predict will happen again, should the present tariff be reduced.

There is no country in the world which has the means of giving itself a better currency than our own. There is no empire or kingdom in Europe, where it is so bad. I have seen it recently stated that there is one State (Michigan) in which every bank has failed, that has been established there since its admission into the Union.

Another gentleman in Boston occupies a position somewhat similar to yours, the Hon. Nathan Appleton, of whom I have also at times had some hope, as he has, during, I believe, almost every crisis we have had since the war, written a very sound and sensible letter upon the currency; but I cannot call to mind any effort of his when in public life to carry his views into effect. This gentleman, also, during the discussion of most of the tariffs which have passed, has published communications upon the impolicy of having very high duties, and yet he held up his hand in Congress in favor of the tariff of 1842, which was carried by a majority of only one vote, which led some one to remark that "Mr. Appleton was the gentleman, who always wrote right, but voted wrong." I do not intend to speak invidiously of a gentleman so much esteemed as Mr. Appleton, for whose opinions the public have so much respect. I only regret that, when in his sound judgment he had decided against a measure as injurious or impolitic, he should, under any circumstances, have been induced to give it his support. From able communications of Mr. Appleton before the public, I conclude he must have considered many of the duties imposed by the tariff of 1842 as too high.

To return to your prediction that, under the tariff to be submitted by Mr. Walker, it will require an annual importation of one hundred and sixty-five millions to raise a revenue of thirty millions, it might be sufficient to reply that as yet the financial scheme of Mr. Walker has not been published, nor definitely decided upon at Washington. It will be in time to show its fallacy, when we are in actual possession of it. Without any great stretch of the imagination, I can conceive of a plan, by which the required revenue may be obtained without increasing the importations a single dollar beyond the amount received last year. The amount, you say, imported in 1845, was one hundred and fifteen millions, of which ninety millions were subject to an average duty of thirty-two per cent. This, you think, may be reduced to twenty per cent. That would produce a deficiency of ten million eight hundred thousand dollars. Now it is well known that the annual consumption of tea in this country is about sixteen million of pounds, and of coffee about one hundred millions, which are now free from duty. Lay an average duty on tea of thirty-seven cents per pound, and on coffee a duty of five cents, and you have the deficiency made good, and a surplus of one hundred and twenty thousand dollars. This you may consider a bold proceeding, but I would remind you that, up to the twentieth of May, 1830, there was a duty on coffee of five cents per pound, of which, even then, when the price was double what it is at present, I do not remember to have heard any great complaints; whereas now, on account of the low price of the article abroad, the consumer here, after paying a duty of five cents, could be supplied at the cost of twelve and a half to fifteen cents. The duty on tea also, you may remember, was at one time very high, amounting to from twelve to fifty cents per pound.

Be pleased to understand that I do not admit that there would be the deficit you name under any modification of the tariff, which Mr. Walker would be likely to propose On the contrary, I am confident that, on many articles of import, the revenue would be increased by reducing the duty, because, as the secretary very justly remarks, "many of the duties imposed by the tariff of 1842 are becoming dead letters, except for the purpose of prohibition, and if not reduced will ultimately compel their advocates to resort to direct taxation to support the government." I am against exorbitant rates of duty altogether, and would therefore avoid, if I could, imposing so high a rate upon coffee and tea. I have merely named these two articles to prove to you that, were it necessary, we could make up the deficit you have so confidently predicted, by imposing on two articles only a rate of duty which, although very heavy on the cost of those commodities, would, after all, be scarcely felt by the consumers. If they pay already fifty-four millions per annum for the exclusive benefit of the manufacturers alone, not one dollar of which ever reaches the public treasury, they could well afford to exchange this enormous burthen for the tax I have proposed on tea and coffee, and would make a saving of more than forty millions.

I need not remind you of the inevitable result, which always follows the reduction of duty upon a commodity. Look at the wool trade in England. Prior to 1824, the duty on wool was sixpence sterling per pound, and the imports about ten millions of pounds. In 1825, that free trader, Mr. Huskisson reduced it to one penny. The consequence was, that the very next year, the imports amounted to forty-two million, eight hundred and thirty-seven thousand, eight hundred and sixty-one pounds. The farmers in England, who had "slumbered so long under the tree of protection," like our farmers in 1828, 1832, and 1842, cried out they should be ruined. Now listen for a moment to the remarks of the talented author of the article upon the woollen trade of Great Britain in the last edition of the Encyclopædia Britannica. "The reduction" says he, "has produced the most beneficial effects, not merely on manufactures, but also on the steady price of English wools, which have been much higher on the average since the reduction than they were before, although we have become importers to the extent of half the whole quantity we consumed when Mr. Vansittart imposed the tax of sixpence per pound in 1819." I hope the agriculturists of America will read and ponder upon this when the manufacturers would attempt to persuade them that they can flourish only "whilst slumbering under the tree of protection."

"We, the manufacturers," you say, "have no jealousy

whatever concerning the establishment of manufactories in all parts of the country," and you have recommended this plan to Virginia. Why, then, have you such a jealousy of foreign manufactures that you would have them prohibited, or subject to such exorbitant duties? There are some manufacturing establishments at the south already; and I have been informed that they, finding it difficult to compete with the manufacturers of New England, are desirous of being protected against the Yankees. This might have been anticipated; for, the purpose of protection being to sustain an interest which cannot support itself, the principle is the same in both cases.

In my next letter, I shall offer some remarks upon what you have alleged as to the illiberality of England in refusing to take our products, and upon the great increase in our shipping and general prosperity, which I shall attempt to show we are in possession of, not in consequence of our high protecting duties, but in spite of them. I may also submit some observations on other topics of your communication, which do not occur to me at the present moment.

I remain very truly,

Your friend and obedient servant,

S. D. BRADFORD.

To the Hon. ABBOTT LAWRENCE, Boston.

WEST ROXBURY, (near Boston,)

February, 7th, 1846.

DEAR SIR,—I promised, in my last communication, to offer some remarks in the present upon what you have alleged respecting the illiberality of England in her commercial dealings with us; upon the great increase in our shipping and general prosperity; and perhaps, also, upon some other topics discussed in your letter. In order to decide the first point, no method can be so fair as to compare the amount we import from England with the amount which she imports from America. In a word, we must cipher a little, in order to settle the matter; as you have done to ascertain how large our importations would have to be, in case the present tariff should be reduced.

I have not before me the official returns of our imports and exports for the last year, but I have those of 1838, which probably will do just as well; as if any material change has since occurred, it will most likely show a relative increase of our exports to Great Britain.

I find, then, that, in 1838, our total of exports amounted to	$108,486,616
Of this amount, England took	50,445,076
Scotland,	1,695,978
Ireland,	38,555
The British West Indies, Gibraltar, Malta, British East Indies, British American Colonies, Cape of Good Hope, Australia, Honduras, and British Guiana,	6,663,802
Making a grand total of	$58,843,412

It will be seen, by this, that Great Britain furnished a market for more than one-half of our exports to all parts of the world; and, on cotton, which constituted, in that year, sixty per cent. of our total exportations, the duty imposed was only two shillings and eleven pence, or seventy cents per hundred weight, equal to about eight or nine per cent. on the cost of the article during that year; not seventy-five to one hundred per cent., which we were exacting at the time on many kinds of her coarse cotton manufactures. Our imports during the same year from Great Britain and her possessions abroad, before enumerated, amounted to forty-nine million, fifty-one thousand, one hundred and eighty dollars, and the greater part of them were subject to very high rates of duty, varying from ten to one hundred per cent.; as any one may see by turning to the tariff of 1832.

During this year, you perceive the exports exceeded the imports by the sum of nine million, seven hundred and ninety-two thousand, two hundred and thirty-two dollars; but, on reference to the official value of imports and exports during the year ending thirtieth of June, 1844, I find our exports to Great Britain and her foreign possessions amounted to sixty-one million, seven hundred and twenty-one thousand, eight hundred and seventy-six dollars, whilst our imports from these countries amounted to only forty-five million, four hundred and fifty-nine thousand, one hundred and twenty-two dollars; showing a balance against Great Britain of sixteen million, two hundred and sixty-two thousand, seven hundred and fifty-four dollars in a single year! Surely, if such a result be a proof of illiberality, I hope we may continue to have many such, not only from Great Britain, but from all the other countries in the world.

I find, also, on turning to the annual circular of Messrs. Colin Campbell & Son, of Liverpool, that the total import of cotton into the United Kingdom in 1845, was one million eight hundred and fifty-six thousand, eight hundred and sixty-five bales, of which one million, five hundred thousand, three hundred and sixty-nine bales were from America; and that this amount exceeded that of 1844, by two hundred and fifty-two thousand, six hundred and eighty-four bales; equal to more than half of all the cotton consumed in the United States, according to your own estimate. How can you expect the intelligent planters of South Carolina, and of the other cotton-growing states, to be content with the narrow-contracted market you have offered them, when they have before them such a fact as this; when they see that single illiberal nation, called Great Britain, has taken, in one year, very nearly two-thirds of all the cotton produced in the country?

I do not find that you are contented with the home market for the sale of your manufactures. On the contrary, it would seem, by your account, that you have invaded with them South America, India, China, and have even sent a few hundred bales of "cotton drills" to London, in order that you might "beard the lion in his den;" writing to your friend, Mr. Greg, late member of Parliament for Manchester, at the same time saying that you were quite satisfied "the Americans would soon become extensive exporters of twist, as well as of all manufactured fabrics of yarn under Number Thirties," and that, "where the principal elements entering into the cost of an article are composed of raw cotton and power, America will compete successfully with any country in the world," whilst, at the same time, such cotton drills were subject to a duty of seventy-five to one hundred per cent. in this country, not one fraction of which are you willing to relinquish. The letter to Mr. Greg, in which you made the above statement, was published both in England and America.

You have informed Mr. Rives how you, or some of your friends, have been treated by the East India Company, (at Calcutta, I suppose,) "having increased the discriminating duty on some coarse cottons, (Suffolk drills, I have understood they are called,) for the purpose of protecting their own manufactures against those of the United States." You add,—"you have no fault to find with the British, in these regulations;" nor could you, with any propriety, do so, knowing the tariff of 1842, which you are so desirous to perpetuate, affords you a protection, as I have before observed, on a similar article of British manufacture, of more than four times the amount.

I do not think, however, that you more than half like this fiscal regulation after all, or you would not have devoted so much of your letter to a statement of it. You should remember it is one of the legitimate consequences of the protective system, and from this example you may be able to form some conception how the manufacturers of Europe felt when they received the news of the passage of the tariff of 1842. I should be reluctant to repeat the execrations I heard some of them utter, especially those who had shipped their property to our shores upon the faith of the American government, that a duty only of twenty per cent. should be exacted; whereas that actually demanded, and paid also, amounted, in many instances, to more than one hundred per cent. They called it a legislative fraud.

I cannot say I think you have spoken with justice or candor of the motives which actuated the British government in the total repeal of the duty on cotton. The struggle was long and animated, and finally terminated victoriously for the manufacturers, in consequence of the untiring exertions of those free traders in Manchester and the vicinity, whose system of political economy you characterize as a "transcendental philosophy," fit only for adoption by the Celestials of China, I suppose, whose commerce you represent as having been revolutionized by this novel fallacy called free trade. "It is fast approaching," you say, "to barter, the precious metals having been drained to pay for foreign productions." Probably a large proportion of these "products" consisted of Lowell cottons. Indeed, we all know this to be the fact; and how can you, of all men in the world, complain of this? In what other way do you expect to find a vent for the manufactures, in which are to be consumed "the four hundred millions of pounds of cotton," which you say will be required in 1856? "But a moderate portion of mankind," say you, "have as yet been clothed with this cheap and healthful article." Free trade, according to your account, is fast producing this desirable result. If the manufacturers or merchants have found their recent shipments less profitable than before, it arises probably from their having sent too many goods. You and I recollect very well when the Chinese would take nothing from us but specie: and the fitting out of half a dozen Chinamen by the late Theodore Lyman, and the present T. H. Perkins, and Bryant & Sturgis, produced a revulsion in the money market of the country, similar to that which occurs now in London, when there is a bad harvest, and the Bank of England is called upon to furnish gold to pay for foreign corn. What has saved us from this revulsion now but free trade, according to your own account?

The true reason why the British government did not abandon the duty on cotton sooner, was, that they deemed it absolutely necessary to enable them to maintain the public faith. It amounted to about three millions of dollars, and being obliged to raise two hundred and fifty millions per annum, to pay the expenses of the government and the interest of the national debt, they could not then see any way to do without it. It was, however, finally relinquished; government at the time remarking to the deputation which waited upon them, they regretted not having it in their power to repeal some other taxes on commodities connected with the prosperity of British manufactures.

In speaking of the increase of our shipping, I am in some doubt whether you have referred to our foreign or domestic tonnage, or to both. That the first should have greatly increased was to have been expected, from the great addition to our population, and from the vast increase of our productions. I am, however, wholly unable to see any connection between this increase and the protective system. On the contrary, I believe it would have been vastly greater without it. I will give you my reasons. I find, on reference to the statistics of our country, that, as long ago as the year 1807, when our population was only six and a half millions, the foreign exports amounted to the astounding sum of one hundred and eight millions, and our imports to one hundred and thirty-eight millions; whereas, for the year ending thirtieth June, 1844, when our population was estimated at about twenty millions, the exports were only one hundred and eleven millions, and the imports one hundred and eight millions, exactly what the exports amounted to thirty-seven years before! The duties at that time, too, (1807,) were very low. Surely there must be a cause for such stupendous effects, and here again you must pardon me if I can find it only in free trade.

The fact is, our government, at that period, was administered upon wise and elevated principles. Our legislators were followers of the maxims laid down with so much force and illustrated in such beautiful language in the third book of Telemachus, where Narbal explains to him the way in which Tyre had become such a rich and commercial city; for I can assure you that this "transcendental philosophy," as you call it, is as old as the seventeenth century, and was proclaimed in France during the reign of Louis XIV. by Fenelon. "Soyez constant," says he, "dans les régles du commerce;" which may be fairly translated "alter your tariff as seldom as possible." Mr. Walker says ours has been changed thirty times since 1789.

It was under the wise and paternal administrations which ruled and watched over the welfare of our country from 1789 to 1807, that so many of the citizens of Boston, Salem, and other towns acquired those large fortunes, which made the names of Gray, Thorndike, Peabody, Lyman, Perkins, and several others, famous all over the world. In 1807 came the embargo; the non-intercourse followed; in 1816, the tariff. These gentlemen seldom made any great voyages afterwards. The evidence is perfectly satisfactory to my mind that our tonnage, especially that engaged in the foreign trade, is nothing like what it would have been, had it not been crippled and crushed by the protective system. Look at the public documents, and see what a tale they unfold. Since 1815 we have had five tariffs, viz: In 1816, 1824, 1828, 1832, and 1842. All of them, except that of 1832, called the "Compromise Act," have raised the duties, especially that in 1828. Now let us see the changes in our tonnage at or near the above named periods:

	Tons.
In 1815 the tonnage registered, enrolled and licensed was	1,368,127
1818	1,225,184
1828	1,741,391
1829	1,260,797
1830	1,192,776

In 1832, as I have already said, was passed the Compromise Act reducing the rates of duty.

Let us now see how the account stands.

In 1832 the tonnage was	1,439,450
In 1833	1,601,149

and it went on increasing every year until 1837, when it reached 1,896,685 tons.

I remember it was stated in 1828, the year in which you took such an active part in the famous Harrisburg Convention to stimulate the government to pass the tariff of that year, that, in the great commercial city of New York, there could not be found a ship upon the stocks in all the numerous ship-yards there; and that to every part of the Union, where vessels are constructed, countermands had been sent in cases where any were building. This statement may not have been true to the letter, but the falling off of the tonnage in a single year to the extent of four hundred and eighty thousand five hundred and ninety-four tons, (a circumstance almost incredible, if it were not proved by the public documents,) gives to it a sufficient confirmation.

I hope, however, that portion of our nation connected with the building or navigating of vessels, will remember what happened in 1829, when they are called upon to give their votes for candidates, who support high protective duties.

Your statements respecting the tonnage are so extraordinary, I apprehend the printer of your letter must have fallen into a great error.

Speaking of your commencement in manufacturing you say—"We (meaning, I suppose, the manufacturers of Lowell and other parts of Massachusetts,) came into it, however, reluctantly, and soon learned that with the transfer of our capital we acquired skill and knowledge in the use of it, and that so far from our foreign commerce being diminished, it was increased, and that our domestic tonnage and commerce were very soon quadrupled."

I do not know the exact period from which you date, but presume you refer to 1828, when you first engaged in domestic manufactures. The American Almanac states the amount of tonnage for that year to have been one million seven hundred and forty-one thousand three hundred and ninety-one tons, and on the thirtieth of June, 1844, two million two hundred and eighty thousand and ninety-five tons, an increase of only thirty-one per cent. in sixteen years; whereas, according to your statement, it ought to have been seven millions!

I infer, from your remarks upon our navigating interest, that you disapprove of what you call "the reciprocity system," which allows foreign vessels to enter our ports upon the same conditions accorded to American ships entering the ports of foreign nations. If these reciprocity treaties are of a comparatively recent date, commencing, I believe, from 1815, the reason may be found in the illiberal and unwise legislation of other countries. From what we know of the enlightened policy of Washington, Hamilton, Madison, and nearly all our great statesmen, it may be inferred they would have approved of the "reciprocity," which you would discard. Indeed, the first treaty of the kind was made with England by Mr. Madison, and is dated third of July, 1815.

Thus we perceive that Great Britain, the most commercial and enlightened nation in Europe, adopted it first; the Netherlands followed next. Later, came Denmark and Prussia. You think this system does not work well. "Not long since the foreign carrying trade," say you, "was nearly all in our own hands. Now the reciprocity system, not including the colonies of foreign nations, gives to foreigners more than one-third of all the carrying trade of the United States." Probably you have particular reference to those cheaply navigated vessels from Bremen, Hamburg, and Sweden, which are so fast driving our merchant ships from the ocean. Would you know how this has come to pass? Turn to the debates of Congress, and you will find an admirable speech of Mr. Webster's, to which I had the pleasure of listening in the House of Representatives at Washington, in 1824, when he was the champion of free trade, and the inflexible opponent of the protective system.

He was giving his reasons for opposing the high duties on iron, hemp, canvas, and the other articles entering into the construction of a ship, in answer to the arguments of Henry Clay and others; when he made an estimate of what the extra cost of a vessel would be, if Congress should sanction the rates then proposed, amounting, if I remember rightly, upon a ship of the usual demensions, from four to six thousand dollars. He spoke of the madness and folly of such a tax, and predicted that it would ruin our ship-owners, and that foreigners would take away our carrying trade. Time has proved the truth of Mr. Webster's predictions, and so it has of all the principles he laid down in the famous Faneuil Hall resolutions, sustained by him with so much power and eloquence in 1820.

Mr. Webster and yourself were both, at that period, the advocates of free trade and low duties. Of late years, at any rate since 1828, you have sustained the protective system with all your energies and power. The question is often asked how all the opinions upon political economy, which you and Mr. Webster must be presumed to have adopted after long and mature consideration, could all at once have become so changed; how you could have been induced to abandon the great and immutable truths so firmly established by such great men as Adam Smith, Ricardo, and Brougham, and become the disciples of the doctrines of the late Judge Baldwin and Henry Clay.

Be assured you cannot retain the foreign carrying trade, and a high protective tariff at the same time. To compete successfully with the cheap vessels of Bremen, Sweden, Hamburg, and other places in Europe, you must enact laws to favor the navigating interest, not to oppress it by excessive taxation. Hamburg and Bremen, you know, are free Hanseatic cities. Commerce requires freedom. It cannot live without it. Look at Rotterdam and Amsterdam, if you wish to see the effects of high protective duties. Hamburg is now what Tyre once was. Its population, at the time I was there, in 1840, was estimated at one hundred and twenty-five thousand. The import and export trade amounted to seventy millions of dollars per annum; and what think you was the duty paid on this sum? It amounted to only one hundred and fifty thousand dollars, about equal to what is paid at New York on the arrival of a Liverpool or Havre packet.

Do you wonder that we should hear the exclamation made every day how New York is falling off in the increase of its commerce and riches compared to what they might have been under a more enlightened and liberal policy? And yet, after all, there is something so deceptive in the name of "protecting home industry," that many of the friends of the protective system may be found amongst the most active merchants in that city. I am not quite certain that the citizens of New York could not afford to have a fire every year nearly as destructive as that of July last, if, by that means, they could be relieved from the incubus of the protective system.

There are a few other statements made in your letter of the sixteenth January, which I am unwilling should pass without comment; but my remarks upon these must be deferred for my third and concluding communication.

I remain, very truly,

Your friend and ob't serv't,

S. D. BRADFORD.

To the Hon. ABBOTT LAWRENCE, Boston.

WEST ROXBURY, (near Boston.)
February 10th, 1846.

DEAR SIR,—In your letter to Mr. Rives, of the sixteenth of January, in speaking of Mr. Walker's report, you say—"it is no other than the adoption of *ad valorem* for specific duties, and a reduction of the whole to twenty per cent." In another part of your letter you call it "a total and entire change of a revenue system, which was established with the government, and has stood the test of experience through all the trials of political parties and administrations from General Washington to Mr. Polk."

Now I would appeal to you, as a candid inquirer after truth, whether the above be a fair representation of the case. How can Mr. Walker's plan be called "an entire change," when the *ad valorem* system is as old as the American government; and when even last year, the revenue arising from *ad valorem* duties exceeded that realized from specific duties; although the average of *ad valorem* duties was twenty-three per cent., and the average of specific duties forty-one per cent.? If you had said that the adoption of specific duties, now so much in favor with the protectionists, because they cut off importations, was an innovation upon the system of revenue which has usually been adopted, it would have received the general assent of your readers.

The first tariff established by the administration of Washington is now before me. It is dated 20th July, 1790. The duties imposed by it are in general *ad valorem;* and the rate on woollens, cottons, silks, linens, and upon fabrics of a mixed character, is only twelve and a half per cent. *ad valorem.* These five descriptions of goods must then, as since that period, have constituted the principal value of our imports. There were a few commodities on which was imposed a duty of fifteen per cent. *ad valorem;* and four articles were doomed to pay twenty per cent., viz: coaches or chariots, girandoles, glass and looking-glasses, being no doubt considered luxuries, and therefore subjected to a higher duty, agreeably to the principle recognized in Mr. Walker's last report. There are also specific duties on liquors, teas, coffee, and some other commodities, such as have usually been taxed in this way. It was under this tariff that our Republic made such rapid advances, and our merchants acquired such large fortunes. Our ships were upon every sea.

You dwell upon the frauds which have been committed upon the revenue heretofore, and which you think will be again; but you do not even allude to the smuggling, which exorbitant duties are sure to produce in every country which adopts them. You must have read of the effects they have produced in Spain, and some other countries in Europe. The estimate has been made that three-fourths of the whole foreign trade of Spain is in the hands of smugglers. Mr. McCulloch, so frequently quoted by Sir Robert Peel as an authority, writing upon smuggling, remarks—"It does not originate in any depravity inherent in man, but in the folly and ignorance of legislators. To create, by means of high duties, an overwhelming temptation to indulge in crime, and then to punish men for indulging in it, is a proceeding subversive of every principle of justice. The true way to put down smuggling is to render it unprofitable."

Is this sound doctrine, or is it false? Let it be adopted in the next tariff, and you will have very little cause in future to complain of "fraudulent foreigners," or double invoices. The protectionist and the smuggler have a close affinity. The one produces the other. Lord John Russell recently said in Parliament, that "protection was the bane of agriculture." It is equally true that smuggling is the bane of protection. The government may commission thousands of custom-house officers; may line our coast with troops; may establish coast guards from Massachusetts to Florida—but smuggling and defrauding the revenue will continue so long as the duties are prohibitive, or exorbitantly high.

I do not think you are quite just towards our southern brethren in the account you give of the origin of what you call the "American system," which you say was "forced upon the north, and done for the purpose of creating a home market for the products of the soil of the south and west." At the assembling of the Congress which passed the tariff of 1816, the public debt of the

United States—principally incurred in the war against Great Britain, which ended in 1815—amounted to one hundred and fifty-eight millions of dollars. Nearly all the banks in the Union had suspended specie payments. The government was without credit, and almost without revenue. During the war, a new interest had grown up, viz.: the manufacturing; and when the Secretary of the Treasury was about to prepare his report, or to bring in his budget, he was beset on the one hand by the manufacturers, and on the other by the merchants engaged in the foreign trade, who, notwithstanding all their losses by the embargo, non-intercourse, and war, continued even then to retain a good part of those riches they had before acquired under that system of free trade and low duties which I attempted to describe in my last communication. These were the parties whose interests had to be considered by Congress, in enacting a new tariff. The high-minded and patriotic statesmen of the south, J. C. Calhoun, William Lowndes, and others from that section of the country, came forward, as they had always done before, and responded to the necessities and wants of the nation. Their means were the least considerable. They had suffered incredible hardships and losses during the war, but they said the honor of the country must be preserved, and they passed the tariff of 1816; not so much, as you seem to suppose, to create a home market, as to sustain the credit of the country, and to liquidate the enormous debt which then oppressed it.

That novel experiment, called "the minimums," was at this time introduced, because the people of this country being then principally clothed in cotton fabrics imported from India, it did not occur to the wisdom of Congress that the revenue then wanted (about twenty-three millions) could be raised in any other way. Such, I believe, is to be a true account of the introduction of what you call "the American system." You would date its birth from 1816; I, from 1828. You would attribute its paternity to J. C. Calhoun or William Lowndes; I would say it was unlawfully begotten by Henry Clay.

There is one portion of your letter in which I fully concur. I allude to that part in which, speaking of protection, you remark that "New England, and particularly Massachusetts, could thrive without it." There can be no doubt of this, for it is confirmed by the experience of all those countries in Europe, which have avoided the protective system.

In what parts of the old world have manufactures most flourished since the peace of 1815? The answer is, in Switzerland and Saxony, where there is no protective duty whatever. The manufactures of Switzerland can only be said to have been established since 1813; about the time we began to manufacture by power in the United States; and now they enter into competition with those of Great Britain in the markets of the East, and are sent to America and Brazil in large quantities.

As respects Saxony, her woollen, cotton, and linen manufactures have reached a degree of perfection and cheapness unequalled upon the continent of Europe. In the manufacture of cotton hosiery, she has deprived Great Britain of nearly all her foreign markets; and the beaux of Broadway, who, when you were engaged in the importing business, used to appear clad in one of Thomas Shepherd's best, are now clad in superfine from Saxony.

In Austria, on the contrary, where the protective system has always prevailed, the manufacturers are in a state of bare existence. In Great Britain, the same results have been witnessed in the silk trade. It was, until 1824, a monopoly. French silks were prohibited, but the trade of Spitalfields presented only a succession of the most ruinous bankruptcies, until 1824, when Mr. Huskinson reduced the duty on raw silk to three pence per pound, and permitted French manufactured silks to be admitted for home consumption, at a duty of thirty per cent. The usual effects soon followed. The silk trade revived at once, and in nine years afterwards, (1833,) had more than doubled. "To the prohibitive system," said Mr. Huskinson, "it was to be attributed that, in silk only, in the whole range of manufactures, are we left behind our neighbors." From the above remarks, you will perceive that, in my opinion, low duties are most favorable, even for the manufacturers themselves.

You have made a strong and animated appeal to the people of Pennsylvania, Ohio, and other states, to alarm their fears for the safety of the protection of their "iron, coal, hemp, cotton bagging, sugar, etc., etc." No one can mistake the object of this. You would have them to understand, I suppose, that if they fail in their duty of protecting the cottons and woolens of New England, they can no longer expect the aid of this section of the country, in protecting the manufactures or productions in which they are interested. If, however, those states are ready to try "the experiment," you add that "you, as a citizen of Massachusetts, are ready to meet the result, which you doubt not will be found within eighteen months in the realization of all you have predicted." You then add—"We will work; if twelve hours labor in the twenty-four will not sustain us, we can and will work fourteen."

I would be the last person to doubt the energy or perseverance of New England, but I may perhaps be permitted to suggest that, in my opinion, the plan you have proposed for meeting the frightful revulsion you predict, in "the failure of all the banks," "the drain of our coin," "the surfeit of foreign goods," etc., appears a most extraordinary one. The very nature of the crisis anticipated supposes an almost total cessation of business transactions. I have witnessed in Europe, in 1819, and in 1837 to 1842, the most disastrous crises amongst the manufacturers, and the method they adopted to save themselves from ruin, was to shorten the hours of labor, instead of increasing them. Sometimes they have been compelled to dismiss all their operatives, and shut up their mills.

And now, as respects the selfish and unaccommodating disposition of Europe in general. "You cannot discover," you say, "that there is a disposition, on the part of a single European nation, to relax their stringent system of duties on imports from this country." If this anti-commercial spirit really exists, how was our distinguished and talented ambassador at Berlin, Mr. Wheaton, able to negotiate the Zollverein treaty? and by whom was this first-born of free trade and reciprocity strangled in the Senate of the United States? by the manufacturers, or by the advocates of a more liberal system of legislation? We all know that the manufacturing interest opposed this treaty, as it probably will all others, founded upon a reciprocal reduction of our own and foreign tariffs to a revenue standard.

Has Sir Robert Peel made no reduction in the English tariff upon various articles produced in this country? Has his recent resignation nothing to do with an attempt on his part to greatly reduce, or repeal altogether the duty on corn? We shall soon see. Would it not be something for our grain-producing states to have their breadstuffs admitted, duty free, into a country containing twenty-seven millions of people, estimated to consume sixty millions of quarters, or four hundred and eighty millions of bushels of corn per annum? I use the word corn as it is understood in England, representing wheat, and other descriptions of grain.

But how can we expect foreign nations to make us any concessions, when we refuse to make any to them? You are aware that most of the governments of Europe are despotisms. The people have no concern in making the tariffs or the laws. In England, where the people are daily acquiring more power, they are making unheard-of exertions in favor of free trade. I need not remind you what have been the herculean labors of C. P. Villiers, Richard Cobden, J. B. Smith, John Bright, and a host of others, in the cause of free trade; nor what they have accomplished. All Europe is looking on with amazement and admiration. Their ranks have been recently increased by the addition of Lord John Russell, Lord Morpeth, and Mr. Labouchere; and it is supposed Sir Robert Peel himself is only waiting a convenient opportunity to follow suit. Such changes are remarkable, and foreshadow what may be expected in future.

You say, "I state the fact, then, that exports will not increase, in consequence of a reduction, or even a total repeal of the present tariff." I only state my opinion that your prediction will prove false. Already I have shown what was the result in England, with regard to the silk trade. Not only was the home consumption, but the export also, doubled in nine years after the reduction in the duty. This view of the subject is confirmed not only by the experience of our own country, but by the history of other nations.

You have remarked that "but a moderate portion of mankind have yet been clothed with the healthful and cheap article of cotton," and hence you have predicted that the consumption of that article in this country will have reached four hundred millions of pounds in 1856, a considerable part of which will have to be exported.

I, on the other hand, would remind you, that but "a moderate portion" of the people of Great Britain are fed with corn and butcher's meat; and that, in Ireland alone, we are assured by a strong protectionist in the British Parliament, "there are five millions of people who rejoice on potatoes." All these people are in want of the bread-stuffs and provisions, which can be supplied in such vast abundance by our brethren in the west; and how can you venture to predict that they cannot compete with foreign nations in their productions, as you say you have done with your cotton manufactures? Free trade has already obtained the total repeal of the duty on raw cotton. The next steamer may bring us the news of the total repeal of the duty on bread-stuffs; and who can doubt that ere long there will be a total repeal of the provision laws? *

It may be considered as almost certain, especially if we will reduce our tariff to a revenue standard, as recommended by Mr. Walker.

Let this be once done, so that we may import freely the productions of other nations, and instead of our having to intercede with the governments of those countries, their own people would do the work for us, as soon as they began to experience the difficulty of getting back their returns. This is the plan recommended by the first political economists of Great Britain, who are now perfectly satisfied that their country has become great and powerful, and acquired its great preëminence in manufactures, not in consequence of protection, but in spite of it.

Go from one end of Europe to the other, as I have done, and hear the opinion the wisest statesmen and most intelligent merchants express of American legislation, especially as respects our commercial policy, and our paper

* This third letter to Mr. Lawrence was handed to the Editors of the *Post* on the 18th of February, for insertion the next day. Late on the evening of the same day, the Cunard Steamer Cambria arrived at Boston, in fourteen days from Liverpool, with the tidings that, on the 27th of January, Sir Robert Peel had brought a bill into Parliament, repealing not only the corn, but the provision laws also; so that the same number of the *Post* that contained the prediction concerning those laws, comprised a copy of the bill which had been introduced for their repeal. This bill was soon after passed by Parliament; has not been essentially altered since; and under it the exports of Great Britain have increased from forty-seven millions of pounds sterling in 1846, to about one hundred and twenty-seven millions in 1857.

money currency. You will find it anything but flattering. But you are satisfied with the protective system, and its "illustrations," you inform Mr. Rives, "are so striking in every department of labor, that those who, fifteen years ago, were the strongest opponents among us, have given up their theories, and acknowledge that the revelations are such as to satisfy the most sceptical."

You refer, I presume, especially to certain citizens of Boston, who, having been free traders in 1831, are now protectionists; and what you state is, unfortunately, too true. We all remember Irving's amusing story of Rip-Van-Winkle, who, having had a sleep of twenty years in the Kaatskill mountains, when he returned to his native village on the Hudson, was so changed that no one knew him, and that "troops of strange children ran at his heels, hooting after him." This must have been a great alteration indeed. But if those free traders just mentioned, will only refer to the principles they advocated once, or go back to the famous Faneuil Hall resolutions, to which you yourself were a party, and compare them with the doctrines they advocate now, they will find the change quite as great as was that of Rip-Van-Winkle. Rip imputed his metamorphose to a certain intoxicating draught. "That flagon last night," said Rip, "has addled my poor head sadly." Perhaps those *ci-devant* free-traders, but now protectionists, have had their "poor heads addled," by extravagant dividends of twenty to thirty per cent. per annum.

But there are many exceptions to your remark, even in Boston. I have not changed; and the more I compare the condition of my own country with that of others in which I have travelled or resided, the more I am convinced of the injurious effects of the protective system. There was a period when our opinions were the same, and we acted in concert. You and I began life nearly at the same time.

We launched our barks upon the wide and uncertain ocean of commerce, it might be said, on the same day. For many years we sailed along, almost always in sight of one another. The best and kindest feelings always prevailed between us. We felt there was sufficient room for all. Some time about 1828, you decided, to use a simile of your own, to "take an observation and a new departure." In process of time you have become, *par excellence*, the great manufacturer, whilst I may be said only to have contributed probably a larger sum to the public treasury, during the twenty-nine years I have been in business, than any individual of the same age in the United States. The foundation, then, of your fortune was laid in Leeds, Huddersfield, and Bradford in Wiltshire, and not in Lowell. If you are indebted for the larger part of it to the carding, roving, spinning, and weaving of cotton, you owe a respectable portion of it to the scribbling, scouring, slubbing, and teasing of wool. I have no fault to find on this account with you. I would on no account speak invidiously of one for whom I entertain the most friendly feelings, and whose energy and enterprise I so much admire; nor would I be personal in my remarks. My objections are to the system itself, and to the policy of the government, which has disfigured this young republic of ours, by clothing it with the cast-off garments of Europe, in the shape of protection and monopoly.

Do what you will, you cannot destroy free trade, nor retard its progress much longer. Its course is "upward and onward." It is being adopted by the nation which General Cass informs us "possesses already one-seventh of the whole earth, and whose government rules over one-eighth of all the inhabitants of the globe." It has recently overthrown the strongest, and, in my opinion, the best ministry which has existed in England for a long time, because they hesitated to repeal the corn law.

It will overthrow the next probably, unless they will agree to remove the restrictions on provisions, and also on tea, coffee, and sugar. It is destined to change the fiscal regulations of the whole world. The opinion is becoming almost universal, that, when Great Britain shall adopt a scale of duties, founded on a true revenue principle, the tariffs of all other nations will soon fall before it. It does not ask whether the industrious but suffering operative dwells in the mountains of Switzerland, or upon the steppes of Russia. Its philanthropy is expansive. It embraces the whole world. It assists the deserving, and relieves the wants of the suffering, wherever they may be found. It is the herald of peace and civilization. Free trade may be compared to an Alpine plant. It is healthy and hardy, and survives the concussions of the severest tempests, for it depends on itself alone for support. Protection is a hot-house plant, always kept alive at a great expense, often sickly, and requiring constant attention. What wise legislator would hesitate to which he should give the preference?

I remain, very truly,
Your friend and ob't serv't,
S. D. BRADFORD.

To the Hon. ABBOTT LAWRENCE, Boston.

PROCEEDINGS OF THE FANEUIL HALL MEETING,

IN THE YEAR 1820.

THE famous Faneuil Hall resolutions, of 1820, having been alluded to in one of the letters forming a part of the present correspondence, and so many years having elapsed since their first publication, it has been deemed proper to have them annexed to the present publication. They are now, therefore, given with a part of "the record" of the different meetings of the merchants which preceded them.

At a numerous meeting of the merchants and others, interested in the prosperity of the commerce and agriculture of the State of Massachusetts and of the United States, convened at Concert Hall, in the town of Boston, the 17th day of August, 1820, to take into consideration a communication from the Chamber of Commerce, of Philadelphia,—

The Hon. WILLIAM GRAY in the chair, WILLIAM FOSTER, Jr., Secretary,—

Voted, That the Hon. WILLIAM GRAY, JOHN PARKER, Esq., and WILLIAM STURGIS, Esq., be a committee of nomination to designate and to fix the number of a committee.

Voted, On the report of the committee of nomination, that the following persons be a committee:

WILLIAM GRAY,
JAMES PERKINS,
JOHN DORR,
NATHANIEL GODDARD,
BENJAMIN RICH,
ISRAEL THORNDIKE, JR.,
WILLIAM SHIMMIN,
THOMAS W. WARD,
WILLIAM HARRIS,
DANIEL WEBSTER,
NATHAN APPLETON,
ABBOTT LAWRENCE,
JOSEPH SEWALL,
JONATHAN PHILLIPS,
LOT WHEELWRIGHT,
CALEB LORING,
SAMUEL A. WELLES,
GEORGE BOND,
GEORGE HALLET,
SAMUEL GARDNER,
JOSIAH KNAPP,
ISAAC WINSLOW,
WINSLOW LEWIS,
THOMAS WIGGLESWORTH,
JOHN COTTON,
JOHN PARKER,
WILLIAM STURGIS.

Voted, That a committee of twenty-eight be appointed to consider what measures are proper to be pursued, in order to avert the calamity which must eventually flow from the passage of the tariff bill, referred to the ensuing session of Congress; and this committee be invested with plenary powers to carry into effect such measures as may by them be deemed most expedient on the occasion.

Voted, That this meeting be adjourned to the first Monday in October next, then to meet at Faneuil Hall, at eleven o'clock, A. M., for the purpose of receiving the report of their committee, and adopting such further measures as the meeting may think expedient.

Provided, That this committee be authorized to call the meeting together at an earlier period, if they should think it necessary.

Signed, WILLIAM FOSTER, Jr., Sec'y.

Mr. WEBSTER having been the first named upon a committee subsequently appointed "to prepare and publish an address," is understood to have been the author of the address, which may be found in the papers of the day, and also of the following resolutions:

[*From the N. E. Palladium and Commercial Advertiser.*]

GENERAL MEETING.

YESTERDAY, an adjourned meeting on the subject of the proposed tariff, was held at Faneuil Hall, Hon. WILLIAM GRAY, Chairman, and WILLIAM FOSTER, Jr., Secretary.

A long and interesting report was read from the respectable committee appointed at a former meeting, which concluded with the following resolves :

Resolved,

1st. That we have regarded with pleasure the establishment and success of manufactures among us, and consider their growth, when natural and spontaneous, and not the effect of a system of bounties and protection, as an evidence of general wealth and prosperity.

2d. That, relying on the ingenuity, enterprise, and skill of our fellow citizens, we believe that all manufactures adapted to our characters and circumstances will be introduced, and extended, as soon and as fast as will promote the public interest, without any further protection than they now receive.

3d. That no objection ought ever to be made to any amount of taxes equally apportioned, and imposed for the purpose of raising revenue necessary for the support of government; but that taxes imposed on the people for the sole benefit of any one class of men are equally inconsistent with the principles of our constitution, and with sound policy.

4th. That the supposition that, until the proposed tariff, or some similar measures be adopted, we are, and shall be dependent on foreigners for the means of subsistence and defence, is, in our opinion, altogether fallacious and fanciful, and derogatory to the character of the nation.

5th. That high bounties on such domestic manufactures as are principally benefited by that tariff, favor great capitalists rather than personal industry, or the owners of small capitals, and, therefore, that we do not perceive its tendency to promote national industry.

6th. That we are equally incapable of discovering its beneficial effects on agriculture, since the obvious consequence of its adoption would be, that the farmer must give more than he now does for all he buys, and receive less for all he sells.

7th. That the imposition of duties, which are enormous, and deemed by a large portion of the people to be unequal and unjust, is dangerous, as it encourages the practice of smuggling.

8th. That, in our opinion, the proposed tariff and the principles on which it is avowedly founded, would, if adopted, have a tendency, however different may be the notions of those who recommend them, to diminish the industry, impede the prosperity, and corrupt the morals of the people.

James T. Austin, Esq., and the Hon. Daniel Webster addressed their fellow citizens in favor of the report and resolves in speeches which were distinguished for closeness of argument, variety of illustrations, and abundance of fact.

The report was then accepted, and the resolves recommended by the committee, unanimously passed.

A vote of thanks to the Hon. Mr. Otis, of the Senate, and to those members from this state, in the House of Representatives of the United States, who opposed the new tariff, was unanimously agreed to.

The report, constituting the preamble to the above resolutions, is too long for insertion this day, forming twenty-three manuscript pages. It is to be printed in a pamphlet.

NAOMI;

OR, BOSTON TWO HUNDRED YEARS AGO.

THIS is the title of a book recently published, and understood to have been written by a lady belonging to Boston or its vicinity. It is intended to portray the manners, feelings, and customs of the above-named city, in or about the year 1660; especially the intolerance of its people towards the Quakers; whose persecution at that early period of our history, and by persons, too, who assigned, as their principal reason for coming to this western wilderness, (as it was truly called in those days,) the desire of escaping from the persecution of Europe, and of worshipping God according to the dictates of their conscience, has always been considered so disgraceful in the conduct of the early Puritans.

The writer is evidently one, who has acquired many of the graces of composition, especially in describing natural scenery, and the effects produced on external nature by the revolution of the seasons. The book also gives evidence of a familiar acquaintance with the early history of our ancestors, and of the characteristics by which they were most distinguished. It has been often said, that, in the composition of a letter or work of any kind, the most difficult part was the commencement; but the writer of this pleasant book cannot have found it so, as the two first chapters, giving an account of Naomi's arrival and settlement at the house of her step-father, "on the south side of what is now called Washington street," are written with an ease and elegance, and the semblance of one relating an undoubted historical fact, which have, it is believed, been seldom surpassed. The characters of Naomi, of Faith, of Mr. Aldersay, Herbert, the reverend Mr. Wilson, the reverend John Norton, and last, though not least, of Sambo, all claim the attention of the reader, and will reward a careful perusal.

Some persons, perhaps, especially the young and inexperienced, having read the book, will lay it down and exclaim, Could the inhabitants of Boston have ever been the hypocritical, illiberal, exclusive, aristocratic and intolerant people they are represented to have been by the writer of Naomi? Could they have ever proscribed their fellow citizens, of unblemished character and excellent life, merely because they differed with them upon the subjects of religion and politics? Can it be that the great and eminent men there were ever like Mr. Aldersay, "a zealous church member," "a magistrate," "a keen detector of heresy of opinion," "having the outside demeanor of sanctification," and yet stained with "those mean and grovelling propensities which are honored because wealth and luxury attend them;" and who, under the garb of humility, "carried an expression upon his brow that ever said, There is between us an immeasurable gulf; stand thou aside, I am holier than thou?" But, however bold the assertion may appear to some, it is believed that there is the most undoubted evidence to prove that what Boston was in 1660, it continues to be in 1848, and that the same exclusive and uncharitable feelings continue to fill the hearts of the people, and to control their conduct. No doubt some will smile at this—that any one should venture to affirm that the capital of the Bay State is essentially now the same it was in 1660. To such may be addressed the words of Horace:

> "Quid rides? mutato tempore, de te
> Fabula narratur."

It may be true that this spirit does not exhibit itself under the same form. Time and circumstances may have changed the objects, against which it is directed. It is impossible, for instance, to persecute the Quakers, because it is not known that a single member of that drab-coated sect can now be found within the precincts of the tri-mountain city. It would be also a fruitless undertaking to attempt to drive out or banish the Roman Catholics, the Calvinists, Episcopalians, or the Unitarians, because each denomination has become formidable by its numbers, its wealth, and its power. All this may be admitted readily; but it does not prove that the spirit which animated the Reverend John Norton in 1660, has ceased to exist; or that Christian charity and love have taken the places of exclusiveness and uncharitableness. In confirmation of this opinion may be adduced the severe and unhallowed zeal which is weekly, if not daily, displayed in the religious publications of Boston; even such as hold the highest place in the estimation of the rival sects which divide the community; the *Recorder*, the *Christian Observatory*, and the *Christian Register;* which word Christian, however, must not be understood, it is presumed, in its literal sense. The writer of *Naomi* has furnished us with a short extract from one of the addresses of the Reverend John Norton in 1660, where "he paused in his sermon, and said, in a stern voice, 'What do you here, children of the devil, daughters of blasphemies, and inheritors of lies?'" but there is reason to fear that few of the sermons of that exemplary divine have come down to posterity. It may be doubted, however, whether they would have contained any thing more bitter, more unchristian, or more severe, than four articles which may be found, not in a religious publication of 1660, but in the *Christian Register*, dated the 15th January, 1848, and published at Boston, under the motto of "Liberty, Holiness, Love," and to which it is hoped the reader of this may have time and inclination to refer. Two of the articles are copied from the *Recorder* and *Christian Observatory*, and the remaining two are editorial on the part of the *Register*. No unprejudiced person can read these ebullitions of religious hatred and priestly spite without admiring, and feeling grateful also to the founders of our republic for having withheld from the clergy, as a body, all semblance of religious or political power; and no one, who has well considered the lessons taught by history, can doubt that, if we have any religious freedom at present, we owe it not to any increase of charity on the part of the clergy since the time of Naomi, in 1660, but to other circumstances altogether.

In this connection one need only to refer to the violent language and proceedings of Unitarians as respects slavery and the Mexican war, and to the recreant spirit they have recently manifested in yielding to the dictation of their brethren in England, and sending a memorial to Congress requesting our legislators to withdraw our troops from the soil of "our sister republic," "offering the amplest atonement in our power for the wrongs we have done her," and thus disgracing the name of our country; although the Honorable Reverdy Johnson, of Maryland, one of the senate, a distinguished lawyer and whig, and an opponent of the present administration, declared himself, only a few days since, from his seat in the senate chamber, in the following words: "The war is just, because Mexico commenced it. It does exist by her act; and so help me God, but for this conviction, as I reverence truth and detest falsehood, I would never have voted for the act of the 15th of May, 1846."

It is quite a work of supererogation on the part of our

wealthy men, giving and bequeathing their money to build up a sect, the spiritual guides of which have thus abused the functions of their sacred office. It was announced only in the January number of the *Christian Examiner*, (the words of one of its editors are here quoted,) that "at the last annual meeting of the British and Foreign Unitarian Association, in London, a warm discussion arose in consequence of a passage in the report of the committee, alluding, in friendly terms, to an invitation which had been sent from this city, (Boston,) to our English brethren to attend our anniversary meetings. The invitation proceeded from a few individuals, but was unhappily supposed to have emanated from the American Unitarian Association, which had committed the offence of including a slaveholder in the number of its vice-presidents." It is well known what exertions the Unitarians are making to increase the number of their converts in the southern states, where their peculiar belief is considered as amongst the deadly sins; and where, having gained over the distinguished jurist, Judge Wayne, of Georgia, they were probably anxious to stimulate his zeal in the cause by conferring upon him the honor of being enrolled amongst their vice-presidents; and this is understood to have been the cause of the severe reprimand they have received at the meeting in London. From this it may be inferred that the spirit of exclusiveness is not confined to Boston, but has crossed the Atlantic. It remains to be seen what order will be taken in relation to this proceeding. It is hoped that there will be more firmness and consistency displayed than there has seemed, at any rate, to have been exhibited in relation to some matters nearer home. No one, it is presumed, can have forgotten the violent discussions and recriminations with which the religious journals and papers were filled, about three years since, when the true faith was supposed to have been attacked. The preachers of the day rushed to their pulpits to denounce the heresy, with all the vehemence, if not with the eloquence of Cicero, when he ascended the forum to denounce the conspiracy of Catiline. It seemed almost a sin, for a season, to preach upon any other topic; as, in the time of Naomi, every faithful servant of the Lord was expected to cry out against the Quakers. Recently, however, no more is heard of the heresy; although it has never been announced that the heretic has recanted. Then the heresy emanated from a hamlet near Boston. Since then, its supporters have erected a public altar in the holy city. One or two other societies have been formed, where similar opinions are advocated; and of a class of twelve students, who graduated in July last at the Divinity School of Harvard University, fully one half are suspected of favoring the proscribed doctrines.

But too much time has probably been already devoted to what may be considered only one view of the subject. An exclusive disposition has many ways of exhibiting itself besides as relates to religion; but, in other respects, there is great reason to fear that Boston now is essentially the same it used to be. Even that eminent divine and distinguished philanthropist, the late Dr. Channing, a year or two before his death, when addressing his fellow citizens, pronounced these words: "Shall I say a word of evil of this good city of Boston? Among all its virtues, it does not abound in a tolerant spirit. The yoke of opinion is a heavy one, often crushing individuality of judgment and action. No city in the world is governed so little by a police, and so much by mutual inspection, and what is called public sentiment." And, at a later period, in speaking to a friend and brother, in allusion to the same subject, he used these remarkable words, as true now as in 1660: "No man, Mr. ———, can draw a long breath in Boston." That record stands, and cannot be blotted out.

If reference be had to the state of political feeling in Boston, its intolerance would probably appear incredible to one who had never lived there. The late prime minister of France, M. Thiers, in his celebrated History of the French Revolution, in allusion to the hatred which the Spaniards entertained towards Napoleon and the French nation, when that country was invaded by the imperial troops, recites a part of a catechism, which the Spanish priests were accustomed to teach the people, especially the junior part of the population, of which the following is a literal translation:

"Who art thou? A Spaniard, by the grace of God. Who is the enemy of our happiness? The Emperor of the French. How many natures has he? Two; the one human, the other diabolical. How many emperors have the French? One true one in three deceptive persons. What are they called? Napoleon, Murat, and Manuel Godoï. Which of them is the most wicked? They are all equally bad. Of whom was Napoleon born? Of sin. Murat? Of Napoleon. And Godoï? Of the fornication of the two. Is there any sin in killing a Frenchman? No! my father, the way to gain heaven is to kill those heretical dogs."

Now it would not be, perhaps, accurate to say that in Boston there is a precise form of questions which the candidate for the favor and good will of the people is called upon to answer; but yet it may be truly asserted that he is obliged to submit to an ordeal equally inquisitorial; and the catechism by which he may be said to be examined, runs thus:

"Who is your father? Do you belong to a high or a low family? Are you acquainted with any of our prominent people? What is your religion; but above all, what are your politics? Are you a true whig? Do you hate and detest democracy and the vulgar locos? Are you in favor of an United States Bank, having a large capital to lend to the manufacturers, and which shall issue notes having the 'odor of nationality?' Do you wish your country to incur a heavy national debt, the interest upon which will be so great as to compel the country to impose high taxes upon foreign imports? Is it your opinion that the most effectual way to raise a large revenue is to lay prohibitory duties?" If the candidate can answer these questions in the affirmative, all other considerations are of trivial importance, and he receives a free pass.

The political course pursued by the people of Boston, has been a most unfortunate and peculiar one ever since the commencement of the government in 1789. Guided by a sordid spirit of selfishness, they have opposed every enlightened plan, by which our greatest statesmen have attempted to extend the limits of the United States since the adoption of the constitution; beginning with the acquisition of Louisiana, and ending with that of Texas. If their counsels had prevailed, the noble river of the Mississippi would, at this moment, have been under the jurisdiction of France. It was with reference to this magnificent purchase by that great man, Thomas Jefferson, that a member of the French chamber of deputies, in 1835, during the discussion upon the payment of the indemnity demanded with so much determination by that distinguished patriot, President Jackson, gave, as a reason for his refusal to vote the money, that "he, for one, had never forgiven America for having acquired for so inconsiderable a sum the finest, most fertile, and most valuable region of the globe." Yet the people of Boston denounced Mr. Jefferson and the democratic party which enabled him, against the votes of the federalists, (so called at that time) to acquire this right arm of our confederacy; and, at a later date, they opposed with violence the war with Great Britain, so ably advocated in those days by Henry Clay, who declared in Congress that Josiah Quincy, the representative of Boston, and the apologist of Great Britain, "had soiled the carpet on which he stood." Some years after this, on the receipt of the news of the lamented death of Jefferson, Daniel Webster pronounced an eulogy upon the patriot and philosopher, and the people applauded it; thus confirming the truth of a remark, made so long since by Dr. Franklin, that "whatever one might think of America as a country to live in, it was certainly the finest one to die in upon the globe; as no sooner was a man dead than all the papers announced what a good father, brother, son, or patriot he was." Mr. Webster, not long ago, in a speech he delivered at Philadelphia, pronounced a similar eulogy upon General Jackson, calling him a patriot and benefactor to his country, or using words to that effect. Such is the power of truth; and sooner or later its voice will be heard.

About the same time, however, at a meeting of the common council of Boston, on the 19th June, 1845, S. Abbot Lawrence, having moved the passage of an order "to devise such measures as may be suitable to mark the respect of the city government for the memory of General Andrew Jackson, late President of the United States," it is stated, in the journals of the day, that a "considerable debate arose;" and the result was, that twelve persons were found who actually voted against the passage of the order. Those persons were Messrs. Brown, Cook, Demerest, Gibson, Green, Hayden, Hooper, Littlehale, Sampson, Seaver, Thayer, and Williams. It is only necessary to name them. All comment would be quite superfluous.

It may also be mentioned, that, whenever a new state has applied for admission to the Union, the people of Boston have always received her with coldness and reluctance, not as one having a right to become one of the family, but as an unwelcome step-sister, whose admission would diminish the amount of the inheritance.

It would be an easy task to trace the workings of this same exclusive spirit in various other ways; particularly in the division it has made of the people into numerous cliques, each jealous of the other, and separated by lines of demarcation, which it would be impossible to define by any rules or principles recognized by any other city in the world. No person who has watched the way in which they imitate the manners and customs of the privileged classes in Europe, and especially of England, can doubt for a moment that, should the various orders of nobility be introduced here, as they exist on the other side of the Atlantic, there would be a multitude of candidates for the prizes, ready to cry,

> " Good-morrow to my sovereign king and queen,
> And princely peers; a happy time of day ! "

It is not deemed expedient, however, to pursue the subject at present; especially as, from some intimations in Naomi, there is reason to believe that the intolerance of the literary emporium, which has thus been so imperfectly alluded to, has not escaped the notice of the writer of that work; and that one of the objects in publishing it may have been to rebuke it. On this account, it is sincerely hoped that the same lady will direct her attention to the subject, as the readers of Naomi feel assured that one who has so well described what Boston was in 1660, could not fail in giving to the public a true and interesting picture of what it is in 1848.

PILGRIMENSIS.

HONORABLE BENJAMIN F. BUTLER,

OF NEW YORK.

A LECTURE was delivered at the Temple in Boston, on Wednesday evening week, by the above-named gentleman, before the Mercantile Library Association. It occupied an hour and a half, and was listened to by a numerous auditory with profound attention and delight. Such of the persons present as were personally acquainted with the learned and accomplished lecturer, who possessed a knowledge of the exalted place he holds as a member of the New York bar, or who remembered the distinguished talents he displayed as a statesman, when connected with the administration of President Van Buren, were fully prepared to expect a performance of great brilliancy and power; and yet, it may be truly affirmed, that even their anticipations were more than realized. The subject, most happily chosen by Mr. Butler, was " The Anti-Federalists of the Olden Time," which must be understood, however, to refer to a part only of the eminent patriots and sages, who were members of the convention which assembled in Philadelphia in 1787, for forming the present constitution of the United States. It was well known, the lecturer remarked, that great diversity of opinion existed in the convention, upon the various provisions proposed to be introduced into that instrument, and that many of the delegates had received the most stringent instructions from their constituents, in relation to the votes they might be called upon to give. Such instructions might always be considered as imperative and obligatory upon the representative, whenever the action upon a measure is final and irrevocable; but, in the assembly at Philadelphia, the members were called upon to pass upon an instrument which was to be afterwards laid before the people for their acceptance or rejection, on which account, there is reason to believe, that several ventured to give their assent to it, contrary to the directions they had received from their constituents. The people were much attached to the constitution of 1778, under which they were then living; and the prevailing opinion was, not that a new one would be proposed, but that the old one would be new modelled, and invested with enlarged powers. When, therefore, it was decided by the majority of the convention to adopt an entirely new constitution, some of the delegates felt that they had not permission or power to give their assent, particularly as, in their opinion, it was wanting some of the safeguards of civil liberty, which they considered as of vital importance, and especially as it contained no provision for the freedom of religion, of speech, or of the press; and had altogether omitted that stipulation so dear, from that day to this, to the heart of every anti-federalist, that "the powers not delegated to the United States by the constitution, nor prohibited by it to the states, are reserved to the states respectively, or to the people." Indeed, it did not contain a bill of rights. Even Hamilton, who labored so strenuously, and in connection with Messrs. Madison and Jay, wrote so much and so powerfully to render the constitution palatable to the people, in the eighty-fourth number of the *Federalist*, (particularly mentioned by Mr. Butler,) admitted those defects, which it was impossible to conceal; adding, in his forcible language, "I never expect to see a perfect work from imperfect man." Under these circumstances, fourteen members actually withdrew from the convention, and refused to sanction the new constitution by their signatures. This number comprised many of the most eminent patriots and statesmen of the day, constituting, in fact, the founders of the anti-federal party, which has existed in the United States from 1787 to the present time; and it is only necessary, said Mr. Butler, to study the records and proceedings of those days with impartiality and care, to be convinced, not only of the unsullied purity of the lives, and of the patriotism, which actuated the conduct of the anti-federalists, but also to be carried to the conclusion, that, but for their exertions in the cause, the constitution could have never been adopted, and that thus our glorious Union might have never been formed.

In nearly all the thirteen states of the old confederacy, the new constitution, when proposed to the people in their conventions for adoption, was received with coldness and distrust, especially in Massachusetts, which, at that early period of our history, possessed such a controlling influence, and was so looked up to by her sister states, many of which refused to act definitively, until they had received the decision of Massachusetts. When the convention assembled at Boston, it was soon found that the friends of adoption were in a hopeless minority; and, after a protracted discussion, the vote was about to pass in the negative, when John Hancock came to the rescue, and, by a fortunate suggestion, understood, however, to have been previously agreed upon by himself and the other leaders of the anti-federalists, saved this palladium of American freedom and happiness. Mr. Hancock readily admitted the various defects of the instrument, which had also been pointed out by Elbridge Gerry, and other patriots in the convention, but suggested it would be best to adopt it notwithstanding, with the addition, however, of certain amendments, securing those great principles of civil and religious liberty, which have been already mentioned. His proposition was seconded by Samuel Adams, and thus, through the interposition of these two anti-federalists, the constitution was adopted by a small majority. It was soon afterwards accepted by New Hampshire, which had been apparently waiting the action of Massachusetts, but with the same condition, as respected the amendments, which were to be recommended for adoption to the first Congress, which should be assembled under the new act of Union. The great state of New York soon followed New Hampshire, but not until after long and laborious discussions, in which the two Clintons took part against the adoption, as the instrument then stood, and which was finally carried by a majority of only three votes. It was even proposed, by some of the leading politicians of the day, in New York, to invite the other states to call a new general convention, which suggestion, had it succeeded, must have proved fatal to the constitution which we now possess. The leader of the opposition in Virginia was the celebrated Patrick Henry, whose eloquence, during the debates upon the subject, is said to have been never surpassed, if indeed, it had been ever equalled. It is asserted by his biographer, that he even surpassed himself; and the lecturer mentioned that Mr. Wirt had stated that Henry, upon this occasion, availed himself one day of a violent storm of thunder and lightning, which occurred during the description he was giving of the ruin which would fall upon the country, if the constitution should be adopted as it then was, in a manner, and with a power so terrific that the members of the convention could not endure it, but actually arose from their seats before the regular hour of adjournment, and left, in a body, the house where they had been assembled. Edmund Randolph was another of the distinguished patriots in Virginia, who spoke and voted on the same side with Patrick Henry.

At length, however, an anti-federalist, who had heretofore opposed the adoption of the instrument as it was, proposed a similar expedient to that which had proved so successful in Massachusetts, and thus, gaining the support of the majority of his party, was able to secure the adoption of the constitution in the Old Dominion. Mr. Jefferson was in Paris at the time, but was kept advised of the proceedings of his friends in Virginia, and approved the amendments, without which it was his decided opinion the constitution ought not to be accepted by his native state. Some letters of his have been published, confirming this view of the subject. It might almost appear, said Mr. Butler, to be an act of the retributive justice of heaven that two citizens of Boston, John Hancock and Samuel Adams, whom George III. had denounced as traitors, should have had the glory and honor of acting so conspicuous a part in the establishment of a constitution under which the United States have become so great and powerful. The lecturer then gave a most interesting account of the proceedings of the several conventions in the other states, and displayed a knowledge of the transactions of those days, which to some persons might appear almost incredible, unless the lecturer had devoted his whole life to the consideration of the subject.

In this part of his address, he paused to bestow a beautiful and well merited eulogium upon Washington, and dwelt, for a moment, upon the "almost superhuman wisdom" of the Father of his Country, in the selection of the members of his first cabinet. He said it was worth a journey to Boston at any time, to have an opportunity of contemplating the character of Washington in this new point of view, which had not, so far as he could judge, been duly appreciated by others. Sensible that the new constitution was received with distrust by many of the states, and that certain of its provisions were not approved by some of the best men in the nation, Washington had a proper regard to this feeling, and called to his councils Thomas Jefferson and Edmund Randolph, one as Secretary of State, and the other as Attorney-General, both anti-federalists, and known to be opposed to the adoption of the constitution without the amendments. Such a course could not fail to conciliate the favor of the opposition.

In speaking of Washington, Mr. Butler was more animated than ever. There was a beauty, as well as a force in his language, which his hearers will not soon forget. It was easy to perceive that he had not studied the eloquent productions of Patrick Henry in vain. As an additional proof how highly esteemed and beloved were the anti-federalists of those days, mention was made by Mr. Butler, of the high offices of power and trust conferred upon them by the people. John Hancock, Samuel Adams, and Elbridge Gerry were chosen governors of Massachusetts, and the latter, in 1813, was elected Vice-President of the United States. The two Clintons, in New York, were also elected governors of the state. In Virginia, the three individuals who were amongst the most active in opposition to the constitution, were James Monroe, afterwards President of the United States, and Messrs. Harrison and Tyler, whose sons, some years later, were also honored with the highest place in the gift of the people. It had not always been the custom, Mr. Butler remarked, to speak of these great and eminent men, as they deserve; and even the anti-federalists of the present day, the descendants of such virtuous and patriotic ancestors, did not seem always to duly appreciate the wisdom, patriotism, and goodness, which distinguished their lives and characters. He earnestly hoped, therefore, that they would all read the proceedings of the convention in Philadelphia, which were not published till 1819, and of the state conventions, that they might realize, as they should, to whom they are in truth indebted, for the glorious constitution under which we live, and have acquired so high a rank among the nations of the earth. Mr. Butler concluded his lecture at nine o'clock, and took his leave amidst loud, hearty, and prolonged plaudits.

It was gratifying to witness such a full attendance on the part of the young men of Boston, who are destined soon to mark the future character of the city. All attempts to change the views of the members of the Hartford Convention, or Essex junto, by any arguments or proofs, however incontrovertible, would be a hopeless undertaking; but, fortunately for the fame of the capital of Massachusetts, its political reputation will hereafter depend upon another, and, we trust, a different race of persons.

UN' AUDITORE.

GENERAL JACKSON AND THEODORE PARKER.

[THE following interesting correspondence puts to rest the charge lately brought against General Jackson, of having been a "slave dealer," in the sense intended by Mr. Parker. The friends of the noble old general will feel grateful to Mr. Bradford for his prompt exposure and effectual refutation of the misstatement contained in Mr. Parker's address.—*Boston Post.*]

WEST ROXBURY, (near Boston,)
8th June, 1848.

SIR,—In reading a letter of yours "to the people of the United States, touching the matter of slavery," published at Boston during the last winter, my attention was particularly drawn to a statement made by you upon the fortieth page, in the following words: "General Jackson was a dealer in slaves, and, so late as 1811, bought a coffle, and drove them to Louisiana for sale." The statement upon its very front seemed to me improbable; and desirous to defend the character of my lamented friend against such a charge, if it could be done, I addressed a letter, on the 11th of February last, to Francis P. Blair, Esq., of Silver Spring, near Washington, D. C., mentioning the statement you had made, and requesting him to furnish me with such evidence of the truth or error of the same, as might be in his power. Mr. Blair, you may perhaps remember, was for many years the editor of the *Washington Globe.* He was the intimate and faithful friend of General Jackson, who, prior to his decease, gave him his papers, and left it in charge to him "to take care of his character when dead."

Upon receiving my letter, Mr. Blair immediately wrote to Andrew Jackson, the adopted son of the late President Jackson, with the above extract, and requesting him to communicate with me or with himself upon the subject. That gentleman, indignant at the charge, did not hesitate a moment to give it a positive denial; and being then at a distance from home, (at Memphis,) promised upon his return to furnish such evidence as should remove all doubt upon the question. He accordingly, on reaching Nashville, called upon his neighbors, who had known the general before and after the year 1811, and they have furnished him with the following statements, which will be published in the *Boston Post*, together with this explanatory communication to you. I have understood that your letter containing the charge has been extensively read; on which account it seemed to me only just and proper that these communications containing its refutation should have such a circulation, as it might be in my power to give them. To my mind they are perfectly conclusive; and, therefore, unless I am deceived, you will see at once the error into which you have fallen, in having made so grave a charge against the character of one, who will live forever in the grateful remembrance and admiration of his country. Assertions of this kind, in derogation of the reputation of the good and great, may answer for the World's Convention at Exeter Hall, and escape contradiction; but, when an author undertakes, as you have done, to write and publish an elaborate letter, addressed "to the people of the United States," he should carefully examine the testimony upon which his statements are made, and have always in remembrance those lines of the poet Burns:

"If there 's a hole in a' your coats,
I rede you tent it :
A chiel's amang you taking notes,
And, faith, he 'll prent it."

If you are in possession of any evidence to sustain the allegation that General Jackson was a slave-dealer, you will, of course, now have an opportunity of informing the public what it is.

It has been the fortune of but few persons to contend with such injustice and detraction as General Jackson encountered, during the eight years he was President; but, even prior to his decease, most of the unjust charges, which various persons had made against him, had been retracted by their authors; the Senate of the United States had expunged from their journal, the celebrated resolution of Mr Clay, alleging that he had violated the constitution by the removal of the public deposits, and he had, in a good measure, realized the exalted praise which will be awarded him by the pen of the impartial historian. Mr. Webster, even, who opposed him for so many years in the Congress of the United States, has since availed himself of more than one occasion, to do justice to his memory; and, in his speech at Philadelphia, reported in the *Boston Daily Advertiser*, of the 7th December, 1846, in speaking of him, made use of the following remarkable words: "He was a man of sense, and a man of strong character. I believe that his aims were all for the happiness and glory of his country. I thought, to be sure, that, to extend and perfect that glory, he did exercise a little more power than he was constitutionally in possession of; but candor compels me to say, that I ever thought he meant well, and while, to a certain extent, he sought his own glory and renown, that he connected the glory and renown of his country."

On this account, the charge you have made now, seemed to me gratuitous and uncalled for, by the subject under consideration. You may be of opinion that he had his imperfections; but yet, I cannot doubt, that you have the greatest veneration for the public and private life of General Jackson. It was my fortune to be educated amongst those who were accustomed to speak evil of him; but when I became personally acquainted with him, and could appreciate all the excellencies of his character, I found him to be a hero, a patriot, and a Christian. About the year 1828, I happened to read, in a newspaper, a letter of his to Mr. Monroe, written during the darkest period of the war with England, which commenced in the summer of 1812. General Hull had surrendered, with his army, at Detroit; the city of Washington had been entered by the British troops, and the public buildings had been burnt. In this dilemma, not knowing which way to turn, Mr. Monroe, who was the Secretary of State, and, I believe, also acting Secretary of War, wrote to General Jackson, then living in a distant state, for counsel and advice. The letter was a private one, and the writer had no reason to suppose that it would ever be made public. General Jackson replied to it at once, and, amongst other lessons of wisdom which he gave, expressed himself, as nearly as I can remember, in the following words: "In times like the present, when our country is in danger, all party distinctions must be forgotten. The crisis is such as to demand the greatest talents, and the most exalted patriotism. In all your future appointments, let the only inquiry be, Is the candidate capable, is he patriotic, is he fit for the station?"

I laid down the paper, and I said, The writer of this may not be a Greek, or Roman, but I have read the annals of Greece and Rome in vain, if a nobler sentiment, if a more exalted love of country, can be found in them. Some time after, I made his personal acquaintance, and, as his public measures seemed to me the most conducive to the greatness and best interests of my country, I gave them, at all times, my most cordial support.

A few years only have passed away since General Jackson occupied the presidential chair, yet, the great principles, which he proclaimed with such intuitive wisdom, have already become the settled policy of the nation.

As respects the character of the testimony sent me by Mr. Jackson, nothing need be said. The names of the gentlemen who have thus joined in vindicating the reputation of their venerated fellow citizen, are well known to the country, and require no endorsement of mine.

The letter from Major Thomas Claiborne, mentioned in Mr. Jackson's letter of 23d April, not having been yet received, it has been decided to publish the other communications without further delay.

I remain, sir, truly your most ob't servant,

S. D. BRADFORD.

To Rev. Theodore Parker, Boston.

Silver Spring, (near Washington City,)
Feb. 23, 1848.

Dear Sir,—The kind interest you have always taken in the honest fame of General Jackson, is in good keeping with your own high character. Allow me to thank you for the present instance of it. It evinces how well he placed his confidence in regarding you as a friend, on whom he might fix his strong attachment.

On the reception of your letter, I enclosed it to Andrew Jackson, and desired him to obtain from the general's old neighbors a contradiction of the story, which I knew must be false. He was not at home, but replies from Memphis, Tennessee, and contradicts, absolutely, the charge as quoted in your letter from the statement of the traducer. He says: "You are at liberty to state to Mr. Bradford, that my lamented father was never engaged in the slave trade, as can be proved by highly respectable citizens of Nashville and its neighborhood, well acquainted with all the transactions before and after 1811, the period assigned for his participation in this traffic. Their testimony I will get, and forward, as soon as I return home."

Supposing that the author of the accusation could not invent such a calumny without being the dupe of some misrepresentation, the letter suggests that "the reverend gentleman may have been imposed upon by some false relation of an occurrence, in which General Jackson was engaged a few years anterior to 1811, touching some slaves in the low country, the property of a Mr. Coleman. This gentleman came to Nashville, introduced to the good offices of the general as a man of fortune, high standing, great enterprise, and public spirit. He was plausible and ingratiating, and gained confidence by entering largely and successfully into the western trade. The extent of his business, and his apparent means commanded, as they required, large credits. In the course of his negotiations with the banks, among others he involved General Jackson to a considerable amount, as an endorser. Thus sustained, after having pushed his speculations in tobacco, cotton, and other produce, he undertook himself to become a planter; he bought slaves in Virginia, and settled plantations in Louisiana and Mississippi. In this career he broke, and left General Jackson to pay a large amount of his debts. The general, with his characteristic energy, immediately mounted his horse, and hastened to the low country to secure himself, in some degree, out of the wreck of the estate there. He found some negroes, which he secured and brought home with him, travelling along with them through the wilderness and Indian nations. The Indian agent, Dinsmore, who lived in the Choctaw country, was in the habit of extorting considerable sums for safe passports, through the terror of the tribes he controlled, from emigrants and other travellers. When such were without money, he detained them, and made them work for a passage. The general resolved to put an end to this abuse. At the head of his negroes he marched through the agency and the surrounding Indians with a countenance that defied Dinsmore, who, in this instance, waived his demands. But General Jackson was not satisfied with immunity in his own case. He wrote to Mr. Madison, and had Dinsmore dismissed.

"From this narrative, you will perceive that my father, so far from selling the negroes in the slave market, where he might have turned them to the best account, saved them from this fate at considerable hazard to himself. Others of Coleman's negroes might have been sold there to discharge his obligations, and probably out of this the misrepresentations in regard to my father may have sprung."

In this, you have, my dear sir, a sufficient reply to the imputation which you have had the goodness to bring to my notice.

With great respect, I am, dear sir, yours, etc.,

F. P. BLAIR.

To S. D. Bradford, Esq.

Silver Spring, May 4, 1848.

My Dear Sir,—I received yesterday the enclosed letters from Andrew Jackson, and hasten to transmit them to you, trusting that your generous feeling will at once employ them to clear up the unjust aspersions cast by Mr. Parker on General Jackson's character. Probably it would be well, in any communication you make to the public press, to connect, with the letters sent now, a portion of Mr. Jackson's former letter, the substance of which I gave in my letter to you. This would show that the matter commanded early attention, and was only deferred by Mr. Jackson's absence from home. I leave it, however, altogether to your management, and shall only repeat my thanks for your kind interposition, with my entire confidence in the prudence with which it will be directed.

Yours truly,

F. P. BLAIR.

To S. D. Bradford, Esq.

Nashville, April 23, 1848.

Dear Sir,—Enclosed I forward you a statement of Major W. B. Lewis, also Judge Balch's, on the subject of the slander against my venerated father, and which you will please forward to Mr. Bradford, and in a few days our friend, Major Thomas Claiborne, will write Mr. B. a full statement of facts, etc., and if that will not answer for the reverend gentleman, we can get the statements of at least fifty old settlers here to the facts, etc., that my father was never considered a slave-dealer in the sense intended to be applied to him. To be sure he occasionally bought a few for his own use, but never sold any; nor did he ever traffic any in that way. What he had, and what he kept, loved him like children, and were treated as such, etc. If at any time you or friend Bradford wish any information on the subject, please address me, and it shall be punctually attended to.

Respectfully, your friend and ob't servant,

A. JACKSON.

F. P. Blair, Esq.

Nashville, April 24, 1848.

Dear Sir,—I have read an extract from a pamphlet recently published by the Rev. Theodore Parker, in which he charges that General Andrew Jackson was a negro trader, and that, "as late as 1811, he drove a coffle of slaves to New Orleans, where they were sold on his account."

I became a resident of the immediate vicinity of Nashville in 1812. In 1813, General Jackson and myself were qualified as executors of the last will and testament of a gentleman who died, leaving a large estate, which was involved in difficulties. We were then brought into intimate private relations. It was well known to the people here generally, that General Jackson made a journey by land to Natchez, in 1811—that he went there to secure himself from injury, in consequence of being bound as surety for some persons, whose names I do not now remember—that he indemnified himself by purchasing from those persons a parcel of slaves, which he brought to Tennessee and placed on his own plantation, where the survivors and the descendants of those who have died, now are.

That I might be satisfied of the correctness of my recollection of this ancient transaction, I have conversed with a person of this city, who became a resident of it in 1809, and who differed politically with General Jackson. He will testify to the truth of all that I have here stated. This gentleman is known to maintain the highest character for veracity.

I have no doubt that the reverend divine has published to the world a vile and atrocious calumny, to injure the character of your honored and deeply lamented father.

Very respectfully, your obedient servant,

ALFRED BALCH.

To A. JACKSON, Esq., Hermitage.

FAIRFIELD, April 20, 1848.

DEAR SIR,—I have just received your note enclosing a letter from Mr. Bradford, of Roxbury, together with an extract from a pamphlet written by Theodore Parker, who charges General Jackson with having been engaged in the slave trade, and "that, as late as 1811, he drove a coffle of slaves to New Orleans, where they were sold on his account."

Supposing, from my long acquaintance with the general, and intimate knowledge of his business transactions generally, that I would be likely to know the truth or falsity of this charge against your deceased father, you ask me if there is any foundation for it. In answer I say, Not the slightest. He never was engaged at any time in the "slave trade." I have had no opportunity, since the receipt of your note, of conversing with any of the early settlers of this country, but I feel confident that there is not one of them, who would not testify to the correctness of this assertion.

The general did go down to the lower Mississippi in 1811, as alleged; but Mr. Parker is altogether mistaken in regard to the object of his visit to that country. It was not for the purpose of selling slaves, but to secure a debt, for which he had become responsible; and, to effect this, he was necessarily compelled to take a parcel of negroes. But, instead of selling them there, where they would have commanded the highest prices, he brought them home with him, and put them on his own plantation, where they remain to this day; or such of them, at least, as are still living.

No, sir; your father was no trafficker in slaves. He occasionally bought a few for the use of his own estate, but I never knew him, in my life, to sell any. The reverend abolitionist, therefore, has done great injustice to the memory of your illustrious father, in charging him with having been engaged, at any period of his life in the slave trade. I am, dear sir, very truly yours,

W. B. LEWIS.

To ANDREW JACKSON, Esq., Hermitage.

LETTER TO THE HON. H. G. OTIS.

West Roxbury, (near Boston,)
October 30th, 1848.

Sir,—Upon a recent occasion you have thought proper to address a long and elaborate letter to "the People of Massachusetts," touching the pending election for President of the United States. I have bestowed upon that communication all the time and consideration which are due to the subject discussed, and to the distinguished source from which it emanated, and, although but an humble individual, and without any of the testimonials of public favor which have marked your career, yet, as one of the people to whom your letter was addressed, I venture to offer some obvious remarks upon some of the topics to which you have invited the public attention. Referring to "your personal friend, but political antagonist," Mr. Van Buren, and his present position before the country, you say "you have scarcely recovered from the astonishment and perplexity excited by his course;" and yet, I am sure your astonishment could not have equalled mine, when, upon taking up the *Boston Daily Advertiser*, I found you had enlisted as a volunteer under the standard of General Taylor, a southerner, a slave-holder, a military chieftain, a person whom you have never seen, with whom you havé no personal acquaintance, and of whom you can know absolutely nothing, as respects his qualifications for the presidency, except upon the report of others. It is the peculiar property of military achievements, to dazzle and bewilder; and it would be very easy to mention instances, in which young and inexperienced persons, under the influence of this feeling, have left friends and home to seek their fortunes in the tented field; but, from those who have reached your matured years, one looks for caution, and a thorough examination of the credentials of such as would claim confidence and credit. If you had volunteered a letter in favor of Mr. Clay, the champion of Prohibitory Duties, the advocate of a National Bank, the opposer of the Sub-treasury system, it would have excited the surprise of no one. It would have corresponded with the opinions and sentiments which you have always been understood to entertain, and which, so far as you have had the opportunity, you have always maintained and supported. In the case of General Taylor, however, you have no evidence whatever that he would be in favor of one of the above-named measures; and as they are all diametrically opposed to the sentiments of the people amongst whom "he has lived, and moved, and had his being," there is a strong probability that not one of them would receive his favor. He has said already, to his supporters, "You must take me on your own responsibility"—"I will not be the candidate of a party; nor will I be the exponent of your party principles; nor look to the doctrines of your party as the rule of my actions." He has positively declined to give his opinion on any one question except the practical use of the veto power; refused to be governed by the action of the Philadelphia Convention, and would have accepted a nomination from the Convention assembled at Baltimore, and have become the candidate of the Democratic party. He has never filled a civil station; has publicly declared that he has never sufficiently considered the leading questions, which divide the public mind, to give an opinion upon them; and has no experience of public affairs, except as a military commander.

All these things were known to the Whig delegates at Philadelphia, and yet they nominated him, as Mr. Webster has honestly and truly declared, on account of his "availability." "The nomination," says Mr. Webster, in his speech at Marshfield, "is not satisfactory to the Whigs of Massachusetts, and it would be idle to conceal the fact. General Taylor was nominated exactly for this reason: that, believing him to be a Whig, they thought he could be more easily chosen than any other Whig. That is the whole of it;" and in another place he adds, "There is no man who is more firmly of opinion than myself, that such a nomination was not fit to make." Such are the views of Mr. Webster, of whom you have spoken in such terms of panegyric, and who has returned the compliment by saying, in a more recent speech, that your letter "exhibits the vigor of youth, and the wisdom of age." Surely, he must have forgotten, at Abington, on the 9th of October, the sentiments he expressed at Marshfield on the 1st of September; for few things can be found to differ more than Mr. Webster's first speech, and your letter. Mr. Webster would have General Taylor supported, if at all, upon the principle of "availability;" you, on the other hand, would claim the suffrages of the people for him on account of his own intrinsic merit; and, in your ardor for his cause, have compared him to the great Duke of Marlborough and the Duke of Wellington. He must be a bold man, who would deny the transcendent talents of either of those great generals. Their military achievements can be never forgotten; and yet, few persons would venture, probably, to propose them as models for the presidency of the American republic. However brilliant may have been the victories gained by Marlborough, the fact is no longer attempted to be concealed, that a long and most burthensome war was continued against France, for sake of the spoils and plunder, which were wanted to satisfy the cupidity of the Duchess of Marlborough; and a spirited writer in France, M. Scribe, in the amusing historical comedy of the Verre d' Eau, has ably shown that, however great may have been the duke in the field, there was a greater (his wife,) in the court at home; and that if the duchess had not spilt the glass of water upon the dress of Queen Ann, which occasioned a quarrel, and a change of ministers, the war might have been continued for an indefinite period. Of the Duke of Wellington, as a civilian and minister, it is praise enough to say that, not originating, but yielding his assent to the various wise and useful reform measures proposed by Sir Robert Peel, he has clearly proved, by his example, how much better it is sometimes to follow than to lead. Of Napoleon and Washington, whose examples you have also cited as proofs that General Taylor ought to be the next President, little need be said. The sounds of the Te Deums, which were chanted in Boston, for the downfall of the first, as "the greatest of tyrants and usurpers," can almost even now be heard. As respects General Washington, he had been engaged in the councils of his country from the commencement of the troubles with Great Britain; he had been a member of the Continental Congress, and was as much admired for his wisdom and prudence in debate, as for his courage and conduct in war. That the negative of all this is true as respects General Taylor, has been proved already, and is denied by none.

In reading your panegyric of these eminent military men, the mind is involuntarily carried a few years back to 1828, when the people of the United States, mindful of his past sacrifices and unwearied labors for the happiness of his country, were about to elevate General Jackson to the presidency. It was declared by the party to which you belong, to be a "precedent fraught with the greatest danger to the republic, to elevate a military chieftain to the presidency." The history of Greece and Rome was searched through to find instances confirmatory of the assertion. It was said that General Jackson would declare war against England, and that he had not the qualifications for filling the office it was proposed to give him. The people, however, often wiser than those who would be their leaders, heeded not these vaticinations of the Whigs, and raised him to the place, which he dignified so much during the eight years he filled it. Time would fail me should I attempt to recite the noble and disinterested actions which distinguished his previous life: his labors as a judge, a senator, and a leader in the long and bloody wars against the Indians, in which he ruined a constitution, once one of the firmest, by enduring hardships and privations of the severest kind. All those noble deeds and sacrifices are part and parcel of the history of our country, and can never be blotted out; and this is an account of the patriot and sage whose administration, in your letter to the people of Massachusetts, you have thought proper to assail; and which you say "you regard as the fountain of all subsequent abuses." What those abuses are, must be a matter of conjecture, as you have not named them. His use of the veto is probably one; although this same power was exercised twice by General Washington, six times by Mr. Madison, and once by Mr. Monroe, at periods in the history of our country when our legislation, as all must admit, was, comparatively speaking, pure and disinterested. General Jackson was president eight years, during a period of great political excitement, and exercised the veto power only three times oftener than Mr. Madison. But if the administration of General Jackson be, as you now assert, "the fountain of all subsequent abuses," why did you oppose the measures of Mr. Jefferson, and his successor, Mr. Madison, from 1801 to 1817? why, in almost every instance, did you denounce the plans from year to year submitted by those patriots for the good of their country, and do your utmost, by the pen and the tongue, to drive them from power? Surely those abuses must have had a much earlier origin in your opinion; as the contrary supposition would go to prove that your only object, prior to 1829, in opposing the measures of the Anti-Federalists, was to gain for yourself and friends their places of emolument and power.

I have already stated the surprise I felt, at your coming out in favor of General Taylor; but the feeling I entertain on account of the attack you have made upon the administration of General Jackson, is one of regret, not on his, but on your account. It evinces a bad taste, and a want of a just appreciation of the admiration entertained for him by his countrymen in all sections of the country, and by people of both political parties. Even Mr. Webster, as if conscience-stricken for his opposition to him for so many years in the senate, has availed himself of more than one opportunity of doing justice to his memory in the midst of his countrymen. Comparisons, they say, are odious; and yet, sometimes they are apposite and useful. Let, then, the parallel be drawn between what you have done for your country, and General Jackson. I have already mentioned his toils and sacrifices in the Indian wars. One other achievement of his, the defence of New Orleans, and final defeat and dispersion of the British army on the memorable 8th of January, 1815, shall suffice. It is admitted by all, that but for the unparalleled exertions and great skill of General Jackson, that important city would have fallen under the dominion of the enemy.

Permit me to inquire, what were you, sir, doing for the safety and preservation of your country, in December, 1814, and January, 1815? According to a letter of yours, printed by your authority, in 1814, you, and eleven other citizens of Massachusetts, in secret conclave, assembled at Hartford, on the 15th of December, 1814, and remained in deliberation till the 5th of January, 1815, plotting, as was reported at the time, and has, in the opinion of many persons, been never refuted since, a dissolution of the Union! I do not assert this, but I have before me, a letter of the late John Quincy Adams, addressed to you and others, and dated the 30th of December, 1828, in which he reiterates a statement he had previously made to certain members of Congress, and adds, "it was in those letters of 1808, and 1809, that I mentioned the design of certain leaders of the Federal party, to effect a dissolution of the Union, and the establishment of a Northern Confederacy. This design had been formed in the winter of 1803, and 1804, immediately after, and as a consequence of the acquisition of Louisiana." In another part of the letter, he adds, "That project, I repeat, had gone to the length of fixing upon a military leader for its execution, and, although the circumstances of the times never admitted of its execution, nor even of its full development, I had yet no doubt in 1808 and 1809, and have no doubt at this time, that it is the key to all the great movements of those leaders of the Federal party of New England, from that time forward, till its final catastrophe in the Hartford Convention." I hope you will not think me unreasonable, in saying that you ought to vindicate your name against such a charge, before you venture to designate General Jackson, an "Iron-willed oppressor." You will, doubtless, remember this remarkable letter of Mr. Adams, which he addressed to you and twelve other gentlemen, of Boston and Salem, in 1828, from the presidential chair, and in answer to one from you and others, in consequence of an article Mr. Adams was understood to have caused to be inserted in the *National Intelligencer* of the 21st of October, 1828. The ostensible object of the letter was to inquire "who were the persons designated as the leaders of the party prevailing in Massachusetts, in 1808, whose object was, and has been for several years, as Mr. Adams had asserted, a dissolution of the Union;" and, secondly, "the whole evidence on which that charge was founded." It must have excited a smile upon the face of Mr. Adams, the inquiry by you, who were the persons designated as the leaders of the party prevailing in Massachusetts in 1808, "whose object he asserted to be the dissolution of the Union?" Mr. Adams, in his reply, remarked that "your avowed object was controversy," and in confirmation of that, he reminded you that, in the statement of the charge to Mr. Jefferson and others, he had asserted "that, although he knew it from unequivocal evidence, yet it was not provable in a court of law." You perceive how he connected the proceedings of 1803 and 1804 with those of the Hartford Convention in 1814. He never retracted the charge; and concluded his memorable letter in these words: "It is not improbable that, at some future day, a sense of solemn duty to my country may require of me to disclose the evidence, which I do possess, and for which you call. But of that day, the selection must be of my own judgment, and it may be delayed till I myself shall have gone to answer for the testimony I may bear before the tribunal of your God and mine. Should such disclosure of names even then be made by me, it will, if possible, be made with such reserve, as tenderness to the feelings of the living, and the families and friends of the dead may admonish." These are words of fearful import, especially when one considers by whom they were uttered. Some persons will be unable to resist the conclusion that Mr. Adams' celebrated journal must have contained some entries confirmatory of what he had stated. More than eight months, however, have elapsed, since Mr. Adams has gone, to use his own words, "to answer for the testimony he bore, before the tribunal of his God and yours," and yet, it has never been stated that you have called upon

28

his son and executor, to disclose the evidence, for which the public has been waiting so long, and which must contain the proofs of your innocence or guilt. Nay, Mr. Adams has ordered, in his will, a fire-proof building to be constructed at Quincy, to contain, I suppose, the evidence to which he had referred, in his letter of 1828. It must be in the possession of his son, Charles Francis Adams, if in existence, and should be produced, not only for your sake, but for that, also, of your native state. Furthermore, it will be remembered, that, in March last, certain citizens of Boston, to illustrate the decease of Mr. Adams, like the ancient Greek inhabitants of what was once called Parthenope, (now Naples,) erected, at the Revere House, a "mensa," or eating-table, whereon a Silicernium, or funeral repast, was served. The only difference was, that amongst the Greeks, the worth of the deceased was extolled previous to the repast; but in Boston, after due justice had been done to the viands. At this funeral feast, according to the journals, you attended, and took an active part. The circumstance need only be mentioned. All comment would be quite superfluous.

I am aware, that the paternity of the Hartford Convention, has been, by you, ascribed to another; and that, in 1824, you wrote and published a series of letters in its justification. But few persons, there is reason to think, were convinced by the arguments adduced at the time; and a lapse of twenty-four years has added nothing to their force. The secret conclave at Hartford, cannot, under the most favorable construction, be viewed in any other light than a bold attempt to intimidate the national government, and to compel it to make peace with the enemy, on such terms as might be offered. The recent assemblies in Ireland, of the Repealers, and in England, of the Chartists, have attempted to produce the same result but by different means; and every arrival from England, is bringing us account of the trial and conviction of the leaders.

But I return to your support of General Taylor, and, with a few more observations, I will conclude. It seemed probable, from the first, that some powerful motive must have actuated you to advocate, as you have done, the claims of General Taylor; and some persons have supposed you must have had a sight of his mysterious letter to Mr. Lawrence, to which he alluded in Faneuil Hall, and also in Vermont; and that it must have promised, in the event of his election, a restoration of the Tariff of 1842. Since, however, the speech of Mr. Webster, on the 24th of October, in Boston, all doubt upon the subject is over, as that gentleman plainly tells us, that the Whigs must strive to elect General Taylor, because then they will be able to re-establish the high tariff of 1842. Mr. Webster complains that "it is difficult to borrow money now;" and thinks the sub-treasury act should be repealed; although this measure has been daily gaining converts, even in the ranks of those who once opposed it so much; and, amongst others, Albert Gallatin, a Whig, and claimed by his party, to be the greatest financier in the country, in his letter, dated the first of February last, upon the expenses of the war, makes use of these words: "It is true, that the sub-treasury act is an experiment, which no one state has attempted to try for itself. But I wish it may have fair play; for I am clearly of opinion that it is equally necessary for the government, for the public at large, and for the banks themselves, that they should never be permitted to use the public moneys, for the purpose of increasing their discounts." According to Mr. Webster, however, and the Whigs, the sub-treasury act must be repealed, and the whole fiscal concerns of the country be revolutionized; and then, they predict, money will be abundant. In other words, all their zeal for electing General Taylor, and all this profession of patriotism, resolves itself into an affair of dollars and cents.

I will not trespass longer, upon your time and patience.

I have endeavored to express myself with measure and moderation, without forgetting what is due to you, or to my own self-respect. Should you think I have been dazzled with the splendor of military glory, in defending the administration of General Jackson, I may, perhaps, be permitted to remark, that you have been betrayed into the same weakness, in blazoning the merits of General Taylor. I would not, willingly, say anything to give offence, nor, on any account, be personal. I have spoken only of events and public measures, which are recorded in the archives of our native state. You have shown, in the case of Mr. Van Buren, that there is no necessary opposition between being a "personal friend and political antagonist;" and I have never failed, at any time, to duly appreciate that rare combination of talents, so remarkably exhibited in your case, which have enabled you to become so distinguished as a finished orator, an able advocate, a learned judge, and eminent senator. Some of our countrymen, with qualifications inferior to yours, have attained the highest offices in the gift of the nation; but their idea of patriotism embraced the whole United States. They would not "give up to a party, what was meant for mankind;" and a membership with the Essex Junto, or the Hartford Convention, they would have considered as an offence against their country. Is there not some reason to suppose, that, could you be permitted to live your long and eventful life over again, you would avoid the errors which have been pointed out? May we not, at any rate, hope that your example will be heeded by the young men of our country; and that they will learn from it that lesson which it is so eminently adapted to teach?

I remain, sir, very respectfully,

Your most ob't servant,

S. D. BRADFORD.

To the Hon. H. G. OTIS, Boston.

LETTERS TO THE HON. WILLIAM M. MEREDITH.

West Roxbury, (near Boston,)
February 1st., 1850.

Dear Sir,—I send you, to-day, some letters addressed to Mr. Meredith, Secretary of the Treasury, of which I ask the insertion in your paper. They were written, with the exception of a few trifling additions, in November last, several weeks before Mr. Meredith's report was published. So accurately had public rumor foreshadowed the policy which such a document, emanating from such a quarter, was likely to recommend, that I have had occasion to alter only one paragraph, in which I had taken it for granted, that the secretary would propose an increase of the duty upon iron and coal, distinctly and by themselves. Forgetting, for a moment, the profession to which he recently belonged, and that a lawyer is like a pilot, who often takes an oblique course to reach a point of land, which he could never fetch by sailing upon a straight and direct line, I had supposed that Mr. Meredith would place the two favorite articles of his native state, in the foremost rank, as every one knows they must have occupied the first place in his thoughts. I could not have anticipated, at the time, that not only the report itself, but the subsequent proceedings of the secretary, in conducting the business of his office, would have called forth such a host of critics and commentators in the papers of New York, and of nearly every other city in the Union, writing over every variety of signature except their own. It did not seem to me that the moment had arrived for publishing the letters, because congress, ever since the session commenced, having been occupied with only two things—the choice of a speaker and the slavery question—no one appeared ready for a discussion upon the tariff.

The consequence probably is, that some of my remarks and statements may have been anticipated by the writers I have just named, and a further delay may increase the difficulty. On this account, and that the public may not be more wearied than is necessary, in reading discussions upon a subject so threadbare, and upon which so little of novelty can be expected, (though so important, that it should be well understood,) I send you the letters for publication in your valuable journal, without further delay.

I have made no comment on that part of Mr. Meredith's report, which recommends an increase of duty on cottons and woollens. I have not seen an account of any convention of the cotton or woollen manufacturers, to request of the government more protection; and most of them are either so prosperous already, or have such a brilliant future before them, that I cannot persuade myself they intend making any appeal to the sympathy, or the justice of congress, this year, at any rate. Should they do so, it will be time to examine their claims, after they shall have been presented. But if our manufacturers are prosperous, it would be the grossest flattery to assert that they have improved, as they should have done, and as the manufacturers of other countries have done. The duties now paid are too high to expect much improvement; and the manufacturers "slumber too soundly under the tree of protection," to attempt making the finer fabrics of cotton. They continue to manufacture, principally, coarse, grey sheetings, or printing cloths. They have gone largely into the former, since the passage of the tariff of 1846 ; and should it be necessary hereafter to publish an account of all the investments they have made, in land, water privileges, mills, and machinery, since that date, it would, if I mistake not, unfold a tale of which your distant readers have a very imperfect conception.

I remain, dear sir, very truly,
Your friend and ob't servant,
S. D. BRADFORD.

To the Editor of the Boston Post.

West Roxbury, (near Boston,)
February 1st., 1850.

Sir,—I have not the pleasure of your personal acquaintance, and yet, I shall offer no apology for addressing to you the observations I may deem it my duty to make, upon the late treasury report, which, in obedience to custom and the law, you have recently prepared, and laid before congress. The occasion is one of the greatest national importance, and concerns the interest and welfare, of every individual in the country. The subjects discussed, and the recommendations offered, affect deeply our national growth, our wealth, and our prosperity. The person, therefore, who fills the office which you hold, should not belong to any particular clique, political, mineral, or metallic, but should possess those high and eminent qualifications, which distinguish the patriot and statesman. The successor of Hamilton, Gallatin, Woodbury, and Walker, should be one animated by the same elevated spirit, and having always near his heart, not the particular exclusive interest of the state, to which he happens to belong, but the general welfare and prosperity of the whole nation. On a review of your report, it is painful to remark the want of all these essential qualifications. We look for wise, and well-considered counsels from the Secretary of the Treasury of the United States, but we find only the unwise and inconsiderate recommendations of the agent, or attorney, of the iron masters, and owners of coal mines in Pennsylvania. It is true, you have, nowhere in your report, devoted a distinct paragraph to recommending an increase of duty upon iron or coal by themselves The practice of your profession had, no doubt, taught you that, being a native of Pennsylvania, you would be more likely to obtain your object by placing those articles in juxtaposition with sugar and other commodities.

> "Cosi all'egro fanciul porgiamo aspersi
> Di soavi licor gli orli del vaso :"

The most casual reader, however, cannot fail to have remarked that iron and coal are always uppermost in your thoughts, and that, on these articles especially, you would have the duty increased. Indeed, we all know that, ever since March last, the protectionist journals through the whole land, have spoken of the assembling of congress, as if its principal business would be to give additional protection to iron and coal.

The position, in which you have placed yourself, is the more painful to contemplate, because having, before your acceptance of office, belonged to a liberal profession, in which you had acquired an ample independence, and never having had occasion to serve that apprenticeship of servility, deceit, and tergiversation, which constitute the preliminary education of so many American politicians, the public had expected better things of you—your friends, and those too, who differed with you in politics, were willing to forget those memorable words of Junius, who, in addressing another distinguished member of your profession, remarked, "that the indiscriminate defence of right and wrong contracts the understanding, while it corrupts the heart; that subtlety is soon mistaken for wisdom, and impunity for virtue; and that if there be any instances upon record, (as some there are, undoubtedly,) of genius and morality united in a lawyer, they are distinguished by their singularity, and operate as exceptions." If I were personally unfriendly to you, if I had any private antipathies to gratify, I would dwell upon the elevated standing you recently occupied at the bar. I would speak of the reputation for candor and independence conceded to you by the other members of the profession, and by the public at large. I would repeat the vaticinations of some of your friends, that having accepted office without solicitation or pledges of any kind, you would act up to the principles laid down by the President himself, (and which he has so flagrantly violated,) when he said to the Whigs, "You must take me on your own responsibility. I will not be the candidate of a party, nor will I be the exponent of your party principles." But although actuated by no unfriendly feelings, I would not fail to do what I can to expose the injurious effects of the policy you have recommended, before it shall be adopted by congress, and receive the sanction of the laws.

> "The evil that men do lives after them ;
> The good is oft interred with their bones."

As you had accepted the office of a cabinet minister from a President who had publicly declared he had never sufficiently considered the leading questions which divide the public mind, to give an opinion upon them ; and who had never any experience in public affairs except as a military commander, the eyes of the whole country were turned upon you as the Mentor, whose duty as well as whose pleasure it would be to enlighten the ignorance, to guide the inexperience, and to direct the public measures of your neophyte. It was taken for granted that you had been an observer of the events which have been passing of late years in Europe, especially in England; where a nation, once amongst the most restrictive in its commercial laws and regulations, had, upon conviction of their impolicy, cast aside the rags of protection, abandoning them to the Russians, and other uncivilized hordes, and inviting all other nations to join them in an unbounded freedom of trade and commerce. It was deemed impossible that the wise and far-sighted measures of Mr. Walker, which have filled his country with such unexampled prosperity, and secured for their distinguished author a world-wide reputation, could have escaped your observation; and it was hoped that you would have had the good sense and humility to have imitated the example of one of the most illustrious of our patriots and statesmen, (Mr. Van Buren,) and have publicly declared that you considered it "glory enough to follow in the footsteps of your illustrious predecessor." Such were the anticipations of many, both Whigs and Democrats, at the time it was announced that General Taylor had offered you a seat in the cabinet. How these expectations have been disappointed is the subject of daily remark, and is known to all. In mentioning, as I have, your immediate predecessor, (Mr. Walker,) and the happy effects of his measures upon the welfare and prosperity of the country, I do not speak as a personal friend or partisan, but express only the sentiments and convictions of the candid and intelligent of both political parties. The just and judicious tariff, which he prepared and recommended to the adoption of congress; the life, energy, and order which he infused into his department of the government; the valuable statistics which he caused to be collected to guide the legislature in their action upon the difficult questions of finance and revenue; the introduction of the warehouse system, and, above all, the distinguished and unrivalled ability, by which he sustained the credit of the country and supplied the means for conducting a foreign and expensive war, (negotiating most of the public loans at a premium,) have extorted the admiration of those who differed most with the secretary in a political point of view, and can never be forgotten by the nation. The merchants of New York, of both political parties, testified their approbation by tendering him a public dinner; and, whatever part of the country he visited, he was received as a public benefactor.

Such are a few of the measures of that minister and statesman, whose revenue system you would subvert and destroy by recommending a new and different tariff; by dismissing from the public service without the least cause of complaint most of the collectors, public appraisers, and other officials, in whom he reposed the greatest confidence; and by every other method in your power; and all this, too, by the most reckless violation of the pledges voluntarily given by the President, your superior, who, in his inaugural address, declared, "So far as it is possible to be informed, I shall make honesty, capacity, and fidelity, indispensable prerequisites to the bestowal of office; and the absence of either of those qualities shall be deemed sufficient cause for removal." Of course, then, the thousands, who have been removed under the most proscriptive administration, which has existed since the commencement of the government, have all fallen under one of these categories, and are deemed unworthy to serve their country longer.

> "Credat Judæus Appella,
> Non ego."

But you assign what some persons may consider satisfactory reasons for these changes, and you assert that the imposts on some articles, especially iron, coal, woollens, cottons, etc., are too low and variable; that specific are to be preferred to *ad valorem* duties; and that, in adjusting the same, protection should be afforded to such domestic manufactures as require it. You have not ventured to designate the amount of protection, and, unlike some protectionists, who would destroy our foreign trade and commerce altogether, you intimate that, "if required, you will hereafter present a plan in detail." Fearing, probably, that you might alarm your patient by practising upon the Allopathic system, you have adopted the Homœopathic, and recommend only "unknown and indefinite portions" of protection for the body politic. By this you betray the weakness of your cause, and give occasion to your opponents to doubt if you have confidence in your own specifics; for surely, if a little protection be such a good thing, a great deal could not fail to be much better; and a total prohibition of importations, as was recommended some years since by a distinguished manufacturer and protectionist in Boston, Mr. Brown, would be best of all.

Mr. Baldwin, in 1824, and Mr. Clay, in 1828, had no scruples of this kind, and some of the duties then recommended were prohibitory, as they intended they should be. The duty on bar and rolled iron, for instance, by the tariff of 1828, was twenty-two and thirty-seven dollars per ton. The legislation upon this article, (iron,) has been of a character truly unique. The duty upon it has been changed by nearly every tariff adopted by congress, and the same individuals have sometimes voted for raising it, and at other times for lowering it, actuated by motives, which all may easily imagine, but which need not now be characterized. When, for instance, in 1824, it was proposed in congress, to raise the duty on this article from fifteen to twenty-two and a half dollars a ton, Mr.

Webster inveighed against it with all the power of his arguments and eloquence. "The present duty," he said, "on the imported article, is fifteen dollars a ton; and as this duty causes, of course, an equivalent augmentation of the price of the home manufacture, the whole increase of price is equal to seven hundred and fifty thousand dollars annually. This sum we pay on a raw material, and on an absolute necessary of life. The bill proposes to raise the duty from fifteen to twenty-two and a half dollars a ton, which would be equal to one million one hundred and twenty-five thousand dollars, on the whole annual consumption; so that, suppose the point of prohibition which is aimed at by some gentlemen to be attained, the consumers of the article would pay this last mentioned sum every year to the producers of it, over and above the price at which they could supply themselves with the same article from other sources. There would be no mitigation to this burthen, except from the prospect, (whatever that might be,) that iron would fall in value by domestic competition, after the importation should be prohibited. It will be easy, I think, to shew that it cannot fall, and supposing for the present that it shall not, the result will be, that we shall pay, annually, a sum of one million one hundred and twenty-five thousand dollars, constantly augmented, too, by increased consumption of the article, to support a business which will not support itself. It is of no consequence to the argument that this sum is expended at home; so it would be, if we taxed the people to support any other useless and expensive establishment; to build another capitol, for example, or to incur an unnecessary expense of any sort." "These are sound principles," says a distinguished writer upon political economy, Henry Lee, Esq. "They may be denied, renounced, and even assailed, by those who once maintained them, but they cannot be subverted. Talents and ingenuity can do much. They can, when misapplied, as they too often are, mislead the selfish and the ignorant; but they cannot unsettle or overturn those original and self-evident principles which lie at the foundation of truth and justice." These memorable words of Mr. Webster, were addressed, twenty-six years ago, to the assembled wisdom of the nation, and they will favorably compare with any thing which can be found in the profound works of Adam Smith, Ricardo, McCulloch, or any other writer on political economy. They were, no doubt, at the time, the sincere convictions of Mr. Webster's mind, fixed there by extensive reading, reflection, and observation. They are a complete refutation of the sophisms daily advanced by manufacturers, essayists, politicians, and others in our midst, and should, it seems to me, have been well considered by you, before you decided to recommend an increase of the duty upon iron.

The further consideration of this subject will be continued in my next communication.

I remain, very respectfully,

Your most ob't servant,

S. D. BRADFORD.

To the Hon. WILLIAM M. MEREDITH,
Secretary of the Treasury, Washington, D. C.

WEST ROXBURY, (near Boston,)
February 2d, 1850.

SIR,—Mr. Webster, when he made the speech, from which my last communication contained an extract, had been, for several years, a member of congress, had placed himself in the foremost rank of statesmen, and his arguments urged, at that time, against protective and prohibitory duties, have lost none of their force by lapse of years. I cannot help thinking they are his real opinions now; and I am not without a hope that he may yet declare them to be so. He has an illustrious example in Sir Robert Peel, who, having been a member of parliament for over thirty years, and having always sustained protective and prohibitory duties on corn, and nearly all other articles of import, had the magnanimity, at the age of fifty-eight, to make an honest confession of his error, and to become a leader in the cause of free trade. He made one of his last great speeches in parliament, holding in his hand a volume of Adam Smith, and recommending it as a text-book, for the study and guidance of all statesmen. I am not willing to believe that Mr. Webster is second in magnanimity to his illustrious cotemporary on the other side of the Atlantic. I do not forget his votes in congress since 1824, nor his elaborate speech in Faneuil Hall, in October, 1848, against the sub-treasury, and the tariff of 1846; nor his plea for the iron masters of Pennsylvania, in which, however, he omitted to mention what rate of duty he would consider sufficient on iron; but on that point, we may probably expect him to define his position during the present session of congress. Let every traveller over our six thousand miles of railroads, ponder these calculations of Mr. Webster, made in 1824, and ask himself to whom he is indebted for the facility he possesses of safe and rapid locomotion, and of the transportation of commodities at the moderate price which he is called upon to pay. Surely, not to the manufacturers of domestic railroad iron; for they, before the passage of the tariff of 1846, and the fall of the metal in England and Wales, had fixed their price at seventy dollars a ton; whereas, the article can now be had for forty dollars. Take, for instance, the railroad now in process of construction from New York to Albany, by the Hudson river, estimated to require eighteen thousand tons of rails. The difference between the domestic price some time since, and the foreign value now, being thirty dollars per ton, would amount to the sum of five hundred and forty thousand dollars on that enterprise.

That you should have proposed, in your report, to impose a duty upon some of the articles which are now free, to provide a larger revenue, might, perhaps, have been expected; but that you should have recommended an addition to that on iron and coal, may well excite our special wonder. Who does not know that this commodity, (iron,) is absolutely essential for the machines of manufacturers, for all the implements of agriculture, and all the tools of the mechanic arts? It is largely used, also, in the manufacture of nails, in which we had arrived, many years ago, to such a degree of excellence, that they had become an article of export, and a single firm, in a neighboring county, manufactured of them, forty-five thousand casks a year, as long ago as 1832. That the manufacturers of cottons, woollens, machinery, etc., should favor an increase of duty on iron or coal, can only be accounted for, by supposing that they have received pledges from the owners of those articles, that they will vote for representatives, who will use their influence to increase the duty on the commodities in which they are interested. It is recorded, that "the annual consumption of coal at Lowell only, was, several years ago, (1843,) six hundred thousand bushels;" and in another statistical account of the same place, compiled some years since, it is stated "that the Locks and Canal Company there, employ five hundred laborers, and, sometimes, twice as many, and manufacture, annually, one thousand two hundred and twenty-five tons of wrought iron." How can they expect to supply the home demand with cottons and woollens, and to be able to export the former with a profit, having to pay for iron the price set upon it by the iron masters, seventy dollars a ton, whilst the same article is used by their competitors, the British, at thirty dollars a ton? Our ships, too, which have to meet such a sharp rivalry, not only with those of Great Britain, but with the cheaper and inferior vessels of Bremen, Hamburg, Sweden, and Norway, in what way can we so effectually enhance their cost, as by adding to the price of iron? Mr. Webster, in 1824, computed the value of that metal used in the construction of a ship of the ordinary dimensions, at from four thousand to six thousand dollars.

The annual production of iron in the United States, is now estimated at eight hundred thousand tons. The importation varies from year to year, according to circumstances. It may amount, the present year, to three hundred thousand tons. The annual consumption of this country is, by some very intelligent iron masters, estimated as high as one million of tons; and by others, at somewhat less. The correct amount must, of course, be conjectural only; but all agree it is very great, is yearly increasing almost beyond computation, under the present moderate cost and duty, and is constantly entering more and more into the construction of dwelling-houses, warehouses, bridges, etc., where its high price once precluded its being used. The import of iron into the port of New York, from the 1st of March to the 1st of September, 1849, is stated, by that valuable commercial paper, the *New York Journal of Commerce*, to have been one hundred and twelve thousand and ten tons, valued at a cost of four million, one hundred and fifty-five thousand, four hundred and eighty dollars, and fifty-eight cents. The price having fallen to a low figure in England, on account of the deranged state of commercial affairs since 1847, and the railroad panic, which has caused the suspension or abandonment of so many railways, the American manufacturers have found it impossible to realize the price, which, at one time, they had expected to obtain, and attribute their disappointment to the tariff of 1846, which imposes a duty on iron of thirty per cent. The actual duty, paid since 1846, is estimated at about nine dollars a ton; whereas, had it been fifteen dollars, it is alleged, by some persons, that they might have continued the business, and have received a fair compensation. It is presumed that this calculation must have been made when the price of bar iron in England was nine pounds a ton. The price recently paid having been five pounds, sixteen shillings, eleven pence, it could be imported to cost only forty-eight dollars, under a duty of fifteen dollars, so that the iron masters could scarcely expect consumers to pay the price required two years ago—seventy dollars a ton. It is a recorded fact, that the Hudson River Railroad Company, of New York, contracted with a company in New Jersey, in August, 1847, for six thousand tons of rails, at sixty-seven dollars, fifty cents, on which they afterwards paid a considerable sum as an indemnity, for having a part of the order cancelled after the fall of the metal abroad.

If, under these circumstances, some of the iron masters of Pennsylvania, or other states, have been obliged to limit their production, or where the capital employed had been borrowed, they have been compelled, in some instances, to discontinue their operations altogether, the occurrence need not excite any surprise, as the same thing is constantly happening in England and Wales, into which coun tries the usual annual amount of iron, imported principally from Sweden, and paying a duty of thirty shillings sterling a ton, is only about twenty thousand tons; so that the iron masters may be said to have the almost entire supply of the home market. Digging for gold, silver, copper, or lead, has always been amongst the most hazardous and uncertain of human pursuits. The most frightful revulsions often occur amongst persons engaged in that kind of business. At one time, they make money very fast, and then lose it again as rapidly as it had been made. It was stated in England, in 1839, that, out of the several large companies engaged, in 1837, in working the Cornwall copper mines, (the produce of which was at that time about one million, five hundred thousand pounds sterling per annum,) nearly every one was in difficulty, and a pecuniary crisis during that year.

Such was the depression in iron of all kinds in 1843, and so low was the price in consequence of the inability of the iron masters to hold their stocks, that the Messrs. Rothschild, of London, were said to have purchased a large quantity of pig iron in the Clyde at thirty shillings sterling a ton. It was worth, a short time previous, four pounds; and it sold in 1825 at from twelve to thirteen pounds a ton! It is absurd to assert that protecting the article would prevent these fearful fluctuations. It would be far more likely to increase them. The most severe crisis our cotton and woollen manufacturers ever passed through, was after the passage of the high and impolitic tariff of 1828, the paternity of which has generally been ascribed to Henry Clay. Some of the wealthiest families in New England, especially in Boston, who, stimulated by the unwise policy of the government, had entered largely into the business, were reduced to absolute want; and some of our richest capitalists to a state of the most unenviable embarrassment.

The iron masters here, then, must do as those engaged in the same business do in England and Wales, when the price of the metal is low, introduce improved and cheaper methods of manufacturing it, extinguish such blasts as are not wanted, and more than supply the demand, and wait for that improvement which is sure to come soon, and will give them employment again. Calling upon the government to lay new burdens on one class of the people for the benefit of another, "to support a business (to use Mr. Webster's expressive words) which will not support itself," would be neither just nor expedient, and in the end would prove injurious to the manufacturers themselves. This is proved by the history of similar attempts in England and in other countries.

Some facts, which I have to adduce in confirmation of this assertion, and some further observations upon iron in general, will form the subject of my next communication.

I remain, very respectfully,

Your most obedient servant,

S. D. BRADFORD.

To the Hon. WILLIAM M. MEREDITH,
Secretary of the Treasury, Washington, D. C.

WEST ROXBURY, (near Boston,)
February 4th, 1850.

SIR,—I promised in my last letter to adduce some facts to prove that high protective or prohibitory duties are injurious to the manufacturers themselves, and also to offer some further remarks upon the subject of iron.

Let us look, then, at the example of England, which for so many centuries pursued a restrictive and prohibitory policy. In 1840, the House of Commons appointed a committee comprising the names of some of the most eminent statesmen in the kingdom, to thoroughly investigate the restrictive system. Amongst a great number of witnesses who were called, was Mr. William Leaf, an extensive silk merchant in London, who, in speaking of the silk trade, thus testified: "When I first knew Manchester, which was about the year 1816 or 1817, there was but one silk manufacturer there, and he upon a very small scale, and even up to the year 1825, when the reduction on silk took place, there were but ten silk manufacturers in Manchester. I estimated the whole return of Manchester in silk goods then at four hundred and fifty thousand pounds, and now (1840) the return in goods, entirely silk, is from one million six hundred thousand pounds, to one million eight hundred thousand pounds per annum." He added, "The distress, which so frequently visited Spitalfields, during the term of prohibition, has never returned to the same extent since French goods were introduced. Though silk is at this moment higher than it has been for the last ten years, yet goods range now from twenty to thirty per cent. lower than they did in 1825 and 1826, arising entirely from improved modes of manufacture, stimulated by the competition arising from a freer state of trade."

And upon the same occasion, the late James Deacon Hume, on being asked if it was his opinion "that protection is always imposed at the expense of the consumer," answered "I think that is manifest. I have always considered that the increase of price in consequence of protection amounted to a tax. I pay it with regret, because it does not go to the revenue of the country. I must be taxed a second time for the state. It is tempting parties to embark in a trade by a fictitious support, which, in the end, may prove a fallacious one. I have often wondered how any rulers could consent to incur the responsibility of such a policy." The authority of Mr. Hume, as a sound political economist, and, what some persons may value much more, as one who had had the largest experience, having been in the British customs thirty-eight years, and for eleven years a member of the board of trade, acting as the very high priest of monopoly and protection, at a time when the duties were nearly all protective or prohibitory, may be considered, I think, as beyond appeal; and I would venture to recommend his reasonings and statements upon the subject now under consideration, (should they have escaped your notice,) to your particular and careful attention. He is often quoted as an authority by Sir Robert Peel; and most of the changes recommended by him in the British tariff in 1840, have been since adopted, and have produced the most beneficial effects.

But to return to the subject of iron. Many persons, I apprehend, are not aware how heavy the duty and charges upon it are already, amounting to fifty-seven and a half per cent. *ad valorem;* so that a ton of iron, costing in England five pounds sixteen shillings and eleven pence, cannot be landed in this country under forty dollars and ninety-two cents. Some manufacturers, it is said, have admitted that these charges are high enough, but demand that the duty should be specific so as always to remain the same, or should be regulated by a sliding scale. Thus far, however, I have seen no good reason assigned for the adoption of either plan. The *ad valorem* system has many and great advantages over all others, on which account it was adopted by Mr. Hamilton at the commencement of our republic, and has been continued ever since. The protectionists themselves, whatever they may allege against it now, must have approved the system highly, when they arranged the tariff of 1842, (of which they always speak in such terms of panegyric,) as out of a revenue of one hundred and two millions of dollars collected under it, sixty millions were levied upon the *ad valorem* principle.

As respects adopting a sliding scale, that has become a by-word. It sounds harshly to the ears. It was in England a weapon taken from the armory of want and starvation, to compel the poor to buy dear bread, or none at all.

Let it not be introduced into this land of plenty, to enhance the price of iron, or any other necessary of life. Why should the government become the makers of sliding scales, or of any other contrivances to guard the iron master's against those fluctuations in trade, to which they are subject in common with the agriculturist, the merchant, and the manufacturers of other articles? The constitution authorizes congress "to lay and collect taxes, duties, imposts, and excises" for revenue, and not for protection. If by impolitic laws it compels one individual to purchase of another a domestic production at a higher price than he could procure one of foreign manufacture of the same quality, is not the buyer impoverished to the extent of the difference in the price, and is the country made richer for it? This and similar questions have been often asked, and it is time they should receive a satisfactory answer.

But it seems that the iron masters did not think it expedient to await the assembling of congress; and the Philadelphia papers announced, in November last, that at a meeting of the iron masters of Pennsylvania, assembled at Pittsburgh, the following resolution was proposed and adopted:

Resolved, That it is the sense of this convention, at the present state of the foreign market, that it will require a duty of ten dollars a ton on pig iron, and twenty dollars per ton on common bar, and a corresponding increase on all other iron and manufactures of iron, in proportion to cost of make, to protect the American market.

The present cost of pig iron in England and Wales being two pounds, eleven shillings, sixpence, or eleven dollars, forty-four one-hundredths, the duty called for amounts to about eighty-seven and a half per cent. on the value abroad; and if there be added to this the other expenses of importation, premium on exchange, freight, insurance, etc., amounting to twenty-seven and a half per cent. more, the whole protection claimed is one hundred and fifteen per cent.! The present cost of bar iron being five pounds, sixteen shillings, eleven pence, or twenty-five dollars, ninety-seven one-hundredths, the duty asked for is equal to about seventy-seven per cent. on the foreign value, or adding the other expenses of importation, equal to a protective duty of one hundred and four and a half per cent.!

No one can accuse these Pennsylvania gentlemen of excessive modesty in the call they have made for legislative aid; but I have deemed this meeting worthy of particular mention, on account of the remarkable similarity of the proceedings at Pittsburg, in 1849, to those which took place at Harrisburg, in the same state, in August, 1827. Every one may not remember the famous convention which assembled there, to stimulate the government to enact the tariff of 1828. Thirteen states were represented by delegates. Messrs. H. Niles, from Maryland, C. J. Ingersoll, T. Ewing, and J. Tallmadge were of the number. They assembled in the "splendid hall" of the state; and after having made the protestations of patriotism and duty to their constituents, and "the American system," usual in similar assemblies, called together to overawe the government, they proceeded to business. Mr. H. Niles, of Maryland, was selected to prepare "an address to the people of the United States," in which he made the following declaration, in the spirit of which our legislators have since made so many unjust and prohibitory laws. "The constitution of the United States," he said, "was made for the farmers, manufacturers, and mechanics; not for the merchants; the last being only a small number of the whole!"

This new method of expounding the constitution by the gentlemen from Maryland, may possibly surprise some persons not so well versed in the study of that instrument. It would probably have produced quite a sensation in

1787, when the convention assembled in Philadelphia, to form a constitution, were about to adopt the eighth section of article first, "to regulate commerce with foreign nations, and among the several states," had some member risen in his place and opposed it, alleging that "the constitution was not to be made for the merchants, they being only a small portion of the whole." Another member charged with making a report upon "the British trade and prohibitory laws," in speaking of the corn laws and other prohibitory imposts of England, said, "Were the British ports now open to the reception of our grain at a fair rate of duty, the fee of Pennsylvania would be worth a hundred millions of dollars more than it now is, and her one million, two hundred thousand freemen would rejoice, whilst the sweat poured down their manly brows, in the fatness of their fields, the capacity of their barns, and just reward of their honest and honorable labor. We do not speak without thought, for if by the increased demand abroad the price of flour should be advanced, as it certainly would be, that advance would be obtained on all the surplus products of all farmers, whether for foreign or domestic use." These are sound free trade doctrines, and would, no doubt, receive the full concurrence of Mr. Cobden or Mr. Walker. But if the fee of Pennsylvania would have been worth in 1827 a hundred millions of dollars more, "if the British would have opened their ports to our grain at a fair rate of duty," what, it may be inquired, may the value be now, in the opinion of the same honorable member, and of the protectionists in general, when not only our grain and cotton, but most of our provisions also, are admitted without any duty whatever? Is it generous, is it honest, under such circumstances, to call upon the government to increase the duty upon any article produced by Great Britain, beyond the rate required to raise the revenue necessary for the support of government, and the gradual extinction of the national debt?

But what especially deserves our notice in the proceedings of the convention of 1827, is the resolution offered and adopted upon iron, which recommended an increase of the duty from eighteen dollars to twenty-two dollars and a half a ton, "which would really have the effect, it was said, to furnish the article cheaper to the consumer, because the home market would be secured for the home supply." As the price of bar iron in Great Britain at that time (1827,) was nine pounds, ten shillings, instead of five pounds, sixteen shillings, and eleven pence, its present value, the duty then asked for was only about fifty per cent. instead of seventy-seven, the rate now required. What a comment do these proceedings offer upon the allegations so often made by the protectionists, that "by the aid of a protecting duty to sustain and encourage the first attempts of an infant manufacture, the assistance of the government will soon cease to be required, and that competition amongst the manufacturers themselves will insure at all times an ample supply of a superior quality, and at a reduced price!"

Does not this seem to prove that protected manufacturers are like spoiled children—never satisfied with any given quantity of kindness, but always clamoring for more? In the latter, as in the former case, the only expedient method of proceeding, is to act with firmness and decision, and to all unreasonable requests to return a prompt and peremptory answer in the negative. This will be the duty of the Congress now assembled at Washington; and the people, their constituents, will not fail to watch their proceedings with vigilance.

In my next communication, I propose to point out the

causes which have produced the present depression in the iron business, and to conclude the observations I have to offer upon the proposal to increase the duty on iron.

I remain, very respectfully,

Your most obedient servant,

S. D. BRADFORD.

To the Hon. WILLIAM M. MEREDITH,
Secretary of the Treasury, Washington, D. C.

WEST ROXBURY, (near Boston,)
February 5th, 1850.

SIR,—I proceed now to state the causes which have, in my opinion, produced the present depression in the iron trade; and I would remark that if, as is asserted by some persons, the business be in a very unsatisfactory condition, so that some masters have curtailed their operations, and others, who depended upon borrowed capital, possessed fewer local advantages, or did not avail themselves of the best and most scientific methods of manufacturing, have been compelled to abandon their works altogether, it requires no great wisdom to assign the cause. It has in fact been assigned in 1847, by the iron masters themselves, and is contained in two words, protection and overproduction, caused by the tariff of 1842, which it is now attempted to restore. I have before me a pamphlet entitled "Pennsylvania, the Pioneer of Internal Improvement. The coal and iron trade, embracing statistics of Pennsylvania; a series of articles published in the Philadelphia Commercial List, in 1847, prepared by C. G. Childs, editor." This pamphlet contains an account of several conventions of the iron masters from 1830, and ends with that called "The Committee of the Iron and Coal Association of the State of Pennsylvania, which met in Philadelphia on the ninth January, 1846;" from whose report it appears that up to 1842 the charcoal furnaces in Pennsylvania amounted to two hundred and six, producing

		173,369	tons.
The anthracite amounted to seven, producing 16,487 tons, together, say		189,856	"
New charcoal furnaces since, 67, producing		75,200	"
New anthracite, 36, producing		103,000	"
Total, 316 furnaces, producing		368,056	"
Increase on old furnaces,	37,971		"
" on new "	178,200		"
	216,171		"

more than one hundred per cent. since the bill of 1842, and requiring a capital of fourteen million, six hundred and sixty-nine thousand, eight hundred and eighteen dollars, in the rude state of the metal, and of twenty million, two hundred and one thousand, four hundred dollars, in its converted state. These figures are taken from the pamphlet itself.

What bill, it may be asked, could have produced such an extraordinary increase as the above, in four years and three months, in a country where the population requires twenty-three years to double its numbers? The answer is, the tariff of 1842, which laid a duty of seventeen dollars a ton on iron in bars, not rolled, of twenty-five dollars on iron rolled and railroad iron, and of nine dollars on pig iron.

In 1830, the production of iron in the United States was estimated at only one hundred and sixty-three thousand, five hundred and forty-two tons, whereas, here in a single state, we find an increase of two hundred and sixteen thousand, one hundred and seventy-one tons in four years and three months!

Well might the editor of the pamphlet exclaim, after

giving the above statements, and alluding particularly to the anthracite furnaces, "the increase of this branch of the iron trade in this state, (Pennsylvania,) has no parallel in history." Who can wonder that the iron masters, having doubled their production in the time mentioned, under the influence of the vicious and impolitic stimulus furnished by the government, should, in some instances find themselves embarrassed, and in want of sufficient customers to take off this extraordinary supply? No doubt in some cases the loss of capital will be heavy, as must always happen when a revulsion comes in a business which has been pushed beyond its natural capacity and bounds, by what is called "the fostering care of government." Let it be a warning to our legislators, in all coming time, never to fall into the same lamentable error again.

The sum, then, of the whole matter is this: It having been ascertained, from an inspection of the invoices, that the average cost of common bar iron, imported into New York, from the 1st of March to the 1st of September, 1849, was five pounds, sixteen shillings, and eleven pence, and the duty and expense of importation being fifty-seven and a half per cent. *ad valorem*, the article can be laid down in any of our Atlantic cities at a cost of forty dollars and ninety-two cents. The iron masters, in their convention at Pittsburg, require a duty of twenty dollars per ton, which would enhance the cost to fifty-three dollars for the imported, and also fix the value of the domestic article at the same, or a higher price. If, then, the annual consumption be eight hundred thousand tons, as has been estimated by some of the most extensive manufacturers themselves, and the demand of the iron masters having been granted, the people shall be called upon to pay even fifty-three dollars per ton for what they could otherwise have obtained for forty dollars and ninety-two cents, the difference would amount to nine million, six hundred and sixty-four thousand dollars per annum. If the manufacturers could obtain sixty-seven dollars and fifty cents, the price asked, and obtained, too, in August, 1847, it would amount to twenty-one million, two hundred and sixty-four thousand dollars.

Not one dollar of this large sum would go into the public treasury, but into the pockets of the iron masters, and would thus be a tax upon the farmers, merchants, and other consumers of iron, amounting to about a third of the annual revenue of the United States. Can it be possible that any respectable number of senators or representatives in congress, will be found to vote for such an unjust and unnecessary burden? We all remember what an outcry was made when Mr. Walker, to sustain the credit of the country during an expensive foreign war, called for a duty of three millions only, on tea and coffee, especially by our brethren in the west. Will they ever consent to lay this heavy duty on iron imported principally from the country which has now become the best customer for their breadstuffs and provisions?

Formerly, the city of Boston alone imported from Sweden fifteen thousand to seventeen thousand tons of iron per annum. The importations at present amount to only about three thousand tons. Our annual importations from Russia amounted, a few years since, to seven thousand tons, whereas, in 1848, they were only one thousand tons, and last year, were only six hundred tons.

In 1826, the whole exports of the products of the United States, as stated in 1827, by Mr. H. Niles, of Maryland, amounted to only twenty million, four hundred and thirteen thousand, two hundred and sixteen dollars, of which, eighteen million, six hundred and four thousand, and ninety-four dollars was in cotton and tobacco, leaving for all the rest, only one million, eight hundred and nine thousand, one hundred and twelve dollars. In 1848, not 1847, the year of famine, (as it is called by the protectionists,) Great Britain took from us in domestic exports, cotton, rice, tobacco, breadstuffs, provisions, etc., of the value of sixty-four million, two hundred and twenty-two thousand, two hundred and sixty-eight dollars, exclusive of specie. During this same year, ending June 30th, 1848, our exports of breadstuffs and provisions only, amounted to the sum of thirty-seven million, four hundred and seventy-two thousand, seven hundred and fifty-one dollars, being more than double the average annual export under the tariff of 1842. Our tonnage increased, during the same time, from two million, eight hundred and thirty-nine thousand, and forty-six, to three million, one hundred and fifty thousand, five hundred and two tons. The total revenue was thirty-one million, seven hundred and fifty-seven thousand, seventy dollars, and ninety-six cents, being more, by nearly eight millions, than the annual average of the revenue during the tariff of 1842.

It had been predicted in 1846, by the protectionists, that, "in case our imports should amount to one hundred and forty millions of dollars, under Mr. Walker's proposed tariff, our coin would have to be exported to meet the deficiency; that, if they should fall short of that sum, we should have an empty treasury, and that our exports would not increase with our imports." Time has shown the fallacy of all these predictions, our imports having been, during the year ending 30th June, 1848, one hundred and fifty-four million, nine hundred and seventy-seven thousand, eight hundred and seventy-six dollars, and our exports one hundred and fifty-four million, thirty-two thousand, one hundred and thirty-one dollars. The treasury, in the mean time, instead of being empty, was always well supplied, and the demands upon it met with the greatest promptitude; the government having, in June, negotiated a loan of sixteen millions of dollars, at a premium of nearly half a million, at the moment of the termination of a long and expensive war, leaving a national debt of sixty-five millions of dollars. Had not the tariff of 1842 been repealed, there is good reason to believe that the public debt, in October, 1848, would have amounted to ninety-three millions of dollars.

If any occurrences of a similar character can be found in the previous history of our country, during the days of protective or prohibitory duties, I have been unable to find the page where they are recorded. Our intelligent brethren of the south and the west cannot have failed to have noticed all these evidences of prosperity and national advancement since 1846, and to have connected them with the changes then made in our commercial policy. Any attempt to restore a different policy, which has been tried and found wanting, cannot and will not succeed.

The iron masters, if they were wise and far-sighted, would not desire to disturb the tariff of 1846, and to produce another inflation of the business, such as has occurred since 1842. One of their own number has recently stated, in a letter published in the Philadelphia and Washington papers, "that the profits are now fully equal to those of any other kind of business;" and he computes the cost of manufacturing pig iron in Pennsylvania, with anthracite coal, at from twelve to fifteen dollars a ton; whereas the cost of a ton of the same imported into New York or Philadelphia, he estimates at twenty-one dollars and ninety cents. "The business is now," he says, "overdone, but the demand is gradually growing upon the supply, and if the tariff is let alone, the business will, in another year, be healthful and prosperous." This prediction may or may not be fulfilled in the time mentioned; but that the iron business, "if left alone," will presently become profitable and prosperous again, cannot be doubted by any one, who has watched its course either in Great Britain or this country; and no person will deny that immense fortunes were made by the iron masters many years since, when the duty was seven and a half to fifteen per cent., and long before the process of manufacturing by anthracite coal had been introduced. That dates only from 1840.

The annual production of iron in England and Wales is estimated in your report at one million, two hundred thousand tons. You have not given the authority upon which this statement is made; but, if it be correct, those countries must have sadly retrograded in the production of the metal, for, when Sir John Guest was called, in 1840, before a committee of the House of Commons, to give his evidence upon the article, he stated "that the produce of iron in those countries had been raised from one hundred and twenty-five thousand tons, in 1796, to more than one million, five hundred thousand tons, in 1839." This extract I have made from a copy of the parliamentary papers, and I am the more particular in calling your attention to it, as otherwise the estimate I have given of the American production, eight hundred thousand to one million of tons, might appear extravagant. Sir John Guest, at the time he gave this evidence, was proprietor of one of four iron establishments in South Wales, which produced above one quarter of the whole amount of iron manufactured in the empire. If it were necessary to assign any further reasons why the duty on iron should not be increased, it might be added that the money derived from it is wanted to meet the current expenses of government, and pay the interest upon the national debt. After the passage of the tariff of 1842, raising the duty, the revenue derived from iron and manufactures of iron, from October, 1842, to 30th June, 1843, amounted to only nine hundred, two thousand, and fifty-four dollars, and eighty-three cents. The next year it reached the sum of two million, four hundred and seventy-seven thousand, three hundred and forty-two dollars, and thirty-five cents, but under the reduced tariff of Mr. Walker, during the year ending the 30th June, 1848, it amounted to the enhanced sum of three million, seven hundred and thirty-six thousand, two hundred and twenty-three dollars, and twenty cents; and during the year ending the 30th June, 1850, it will probably reach the sum of five millions of dollars. The fact that the way to augment the amount of revenue derived from an article is to lower the duty to a revenue standard, and not to increase it, so as to make it protective or prohibitory, is too well established now to require further argument; and yet in your report, surrounded as you are on every side with the evidences of the truth of this proposition, you have recommended raising the duties to obtain more revenue. Of all the positions assumed by you, this, if I mistake not, will be considered the most extraordinary, unsound, and paradoxical. One would have supposed that the state of the post office receipts, since the rates have been reduced, not only in Great Britain but in the United States also, as exhibited in the postmaster general's report, might have furnished you with a safe and useful guide in preparing a programme for a tariff of duties upon imports.

It cannot be denied, that the theory of monopoly and protection, under whatever aspect the subject may be viewed, is founded upon scarcity as its principal support. It is a system which looks upon plenty and abundance, not as blessings to be desired, but as a calamity to be deprecated and avoided. It is akin to the error which induces the workmen in times of manufacturing distress, to band together and break the machinery in the factories and workshops, because it increases the quantity of manufactures, and, as they ignorantly suppose, lowers the wages of labor. The protectionist papers, in announcing the arrival of several packets from Liverpool or Havre, at New York, with woollens, cottons, linens, and silks, for the supply of our wants, are accustomed to speak of our being "inundated with goods," as if some destructive river had broken through its boundaries, or what they call, at New Orleans, a crevasse, had taken place.

The American Congress, ever since 1816, with one or two short intervals, have been passing laws to sustain this fallacy; for high tariffs can only accomplish their work by enhancing the price of commodities in one mode or another. The legislators, the manufacturers, the politicians, who cater for the taste of the multitude, and traffic in patriotism by professions of their devotion to what they call "the American system," all sustain the sophism that scarcity is to be desired. They seem unconscious that man is a being who consumes, as well as produces, and that if, as a seller, his interest be promoted by having the article he deals in, dear and scarce, yet, as a buyer, a cheap market and abundance are what he most desires. The iron masters would have a monopoly of iron; the owner of coal mines one of coal; and the manufacturer of cottons, woollens, etc., would have foreign importations prohibited, to give him "the supply of the home market." The consumer, on the other hand, desires that all these articles may be abundant, and that he may supply his wants at the most moderate prices. Surely, then, when the government interposes its authority, and passes laws in favor of one class, and that consisting of the smaller number, against the rights and interests of the other classes, which compose the majority, it seems to me to exercise a power which may be usurped by a despot, but should never be conferred by the suffrages of a free and intelligent community upon their rulers. These truths would appear to be simple and obvious enough, and yet, how little have they been heeded, until recently, by governments and legislators! Even now we find persons amongst us of talents and education, and filling an elevated rank in society, who continue to speak of what they sneeringly call "free trade," as "an abstraction," "a dream," "a chimera," which it is impossible, were it desirable, to reduce to practice, whilst daily experience teaches us that every one is, in fact, a free trader, so far as his actions can prove him to be so; as no person ever knowingly goes to a dear shop to purchase what he wants, but always to that which can supply him with the best article at the lowest price. All commerce is conducted on this principle, and ever must be. It is only after some men have become interested in a manufactory, that they begin to protest against using foreign productions, and "employing the pauper labor of Europe," and talk loud about "philanthropy" and the "home market," "patriotism" and rich dividends of eighteen per cent. per annum.

These remarks upon free trade and protection, are not made with any unfriendly feelings towards the iron masters of Pennsylvania, or the manufacturers of New England. I am perfectly aware how unwelcome such observations will be to the great majority of the people of Boston and its vicinity, where a most bigoted and illiberal spirit prevails on subjects of this character, so that to him who entertains and openly professes such opinions, may be literally applied the words of the Latin satirist,

> "Non uxor salvum te vult, non filius; omnes
> Vicini oderunt, noti, pueri atque puellæ."

They may appear futile and unpalatable to you also, since you have become a member of General Taylor's cabinet; but the principles I have endeavored to establish, I believe to be founded upon truth and justice, and that, sooner or later, they will be adopted by those who deserve the name of statesmen, everywhere.

The last steamer only from Liverpool, brought the announcement that the President of the French nation was about to have "his tariff of duties revised with reference to some important reductions;" "that the Dutch, encouraged by the example of the English, were about to take measures to repeal their navigation laws;" and last, though not least, that "the representative of her majesty, Queen Victoria, at St. Petersburgh, had opened negotiations with the minister of the Emperor Nicholas, with the view of increasing the commercial relations between the two nations." It is added that "a considerable change is contemplated in the import duties on articles of British manufacture, and in cotton, especially, a great though gradual *ad valorem* reduction will be made." By this you will perceive that you have lost already your most faithful and trustworthy ally, the Emperor of all the Russias, in sustaining longer the restrictive system which you are endeavoring to restore. But I am not sure that even this will have any effect in inducing you to retrace your steps; for it is impossible not to draw the inference, both from your report and your treasury circulars since, that you do not expect to continue in the service of the nation long, when you probably intend to return to Philadelphia, and "order your buggy for the home circuit again."

It will not answer longer to assert that free trade must fail unless adopted by the nations in general. The contrary of this has been proved by the example of Great Britain, which has, ever since 1842, been fighting the hostile tariffs of other countries by free imports, and always gaining the victory. For six years before 1842, the year in which the English tariff began to be modified, the annual exports of the United Kingdom, being British produce and manufactures, amounted to forty-nine million, two hundred and ninety-six thousand, eight hundred and ninety-five pounds, whereas the annual exports during the six succeeding years, have been found to be fifty-six million, seven hundred and forty-two thousand, two hundred and ninety-seven pounds.

Such results as these offer very little inducement to return to monopoly or protection; and, although the Duke of Richmond, Earl Stanhope, Col. Sibthorpe, or Mr. Disraeli, in their present agitation of the subject of free trade and protection, may receive the support of needy noblemen or landlords, whose estates are heavily mortgaged, and who cannot or will not reduce their rents, they will receive very little sympathy from the people at large. These gentlemen complain bitterly of the present price of wheat, forty shillings and ninepence sterling a quarter, and impute it to the repeal of the corn laws. They have probably forgotten that the price, in 1835, was only thirty-six shillings, when the corn laws, enacted expressly to raise the price of food and land, were in full operation, and the cry of agricultural distress was heard from one end of England to the other.

I have already alluded to the specific duties, which you so much approve; but, upon that part of your report, in which you recommend that "the *ad valorem* duties shall be levied on the market value in the principal markets of our country at the time of arrival," I do not design at present to say a single word. The suggestion is so "childish," (to borrow a word from the *London Times*, in their review of your report,) and, I will add, so utterly impracticable too, that I incur no risk in asserting that no committee of Congress will be found to entertain such a proposition for a moment.

I will here conclude what I had proposed to say upon the increase of duty, which you have recommended on iron, by which you will perceive, I trust, that if I would oppose an increase of duties in general, it is because I believe such an augmentation would be unjust to the people at large, and, if rightly understood, unfavorable to the best interests of the manufacturers themselves. This opinion, if I am not deceived, is daily acquiring advocates, not only in our halls of legislation, but amongst the people themselves; and therefore, whenever the subject of repealing the tariff of 1846 shall come before Congress, I shall confidently expect to see the project rejected by a large and decisive vote. The country, it seems to me, is ready for the question now; nor will the friends of free trade and of a liberal commercial system shrink from the trial, let it come when it may.

I remain, very respectfully,
Your most obedient servant,
S. D. BRADFORD.

To the Hon. WILLIAM M. MEREDITH,
Secretary of the Treasury, Washington, D. C.

WEST ROXBURY, (near Boston,)
February 6th, 1850.

SIR,—In several former communications, I have taken occasion to address you upon the subject of iron; and if I have felt constrained to expresss my sentiments freely upon the increase of duty, which you have thought it expedient to recommend upon that article, the addition, you would have imposed upon coal may be considered perhaps even more surprising and objectionable.

The remarks heretofore made upon the former, as an essential necessary of life, of almost universal use, and vast consumption, apply perhaps with still greater force to the latter.

The history of the coal trade is of too recent date, and too familiar to almost every one, to require more than a passing notice. Anthracite coal was first used in this country upon tide-water in 1820, and the total quantity dug from the mines and sent to market in that year amounted to only three hundred and sixty-five tons. For a long time, the difficulty of kindling it prevented its coming into general use. After, however, this obstacle had been overcome, the consumption increased at a rapid pace for several years. In 1821, it nearly trebled, having reached one thousand and seventy-three tons. In 1822, the quantity received in Philadelphia from the various mines in Pennsylvania amounted to two thousand two hundred and forty tons; and it went on increasing from year to year at a rate never probably conceived of in any other country, until, in 1846, the last year of the tariff of 1842, (under which the duty on imported coal was one dollar and seventy-five cents a ton,) it amounted to two million, seventy-seven thousand, two hundred and eighty tons.

In 1847, the first year of Mr. Walker's tariff, which reduced the duty from one dollar and seventy-five cents a ton, to thirty per cent. *ad valorem*, (equal to an average of about sixty cents a ton upon the several costs and qualities imported,) the quantity received from the mines at Philadelphia reached the unprecedented amount of two million, six hundred and fifteen thousand, six hundred and thirty tons, and in 1848 it was still larger. So immense had the trade become, that in 1846 the total number of clearances from the port of Philadelphia of vessels or boats loaded with anthracite coal, amounted to eight thousand nine hundred and fifty-three, carrying one million, sixty-five thousand, two hundred and twenty-eight tons; in addition to the quantity shipped in boats from the Lehigh mines. The article has come into extensive use for domestic purposes, for producing steam in manufactories, for propelling steamboats and railway locomotives, and since 1840 for the manufacture of iron.

One company alone in Philadelphia, the Reading Railroad, has already expended the vast sum of sixteen millions of dollars, in conveying part of the above mentioned quantity from the mines in the interior of Pennsylvania to tide-water, at or near Philadelphia.

Having glanced thus at the origin and rapid increase of the coal trade in Pennsylvania, I proceed to inquire what may be the foreign competition, with which it has to contend, of which such severe complaints are made by the protectionists. On reference to official documents, I find the rivalry to be with Great Britain and Nova Scotia, and that the total amount of coal imported amounted in

1842 to	141,526 tons.
1843 "	41,163 "
1844 "	87,073 "
1845 "	85,771 "
1846 "	156,853 "
	511,860 "

making the average annual importation, for the term of five consecutive years, one hundred and two thousand, three hundred and seventy-three tons, equal to less than one-fifth of the increase of Pennsylvania coal in a single year from 1846 to 1847, and amounting to about the quantity brought from the interior to Philadelphia in a single month by the Reading Railway. The above statements are given principally upon the authority of the pamphlet before mentioned, by C. G. Childs, editor. The quantity imported during the year ending the 30th June, 1849, is understood to have been one hundred and ninety-eight thousand two hundred and thirteen tons, and the present year will probably show an increase upon even this amount.

The truth is, there is an increase since 1846, in the importation of almost every article, which conduces to the comfort and well-being of the community, as well as an increase in the exports of our surplus products; which the advocates of free trade predicted would take place from the beginning. The effects produced by our present liberal tariff, are being more and more developed daily, and are visible in the unexampled prosperity of the country in all its diversified pursuits. The people were never before so abundantly fed, so comfortably clad, nor so well employed, at good wages too.

Who can have forgotten, soon after the passage of Mr. Clay's impolitic and prohibitory tariff of 1828, the prostrate condition of our foreign commerce, the numerous bankruptcies amongst the manufacturers, for whose special benefit it had been made, and the general derangement of commercial affairs? Our numerous shipyards were deserted, and the operatives without employment. Our exports of domestic produce from 1828 to 1832, the year of the compromise, averaged only fifty-eight million, forty-nine thousand, two hundred and eighty-one dollars per annum. The average, from 1832 to 1837, under the reduced duties of the compromise act, was ninety-one million, two thousand, four hundred and seven dollars.

What a change do we witness now! A short time since a statement was made of the number of vessels which had been built in New York, and launched, or were then upon the stocks in 1849, and they consisted of eight steamships, eighteen steamboats, twenty-five ships, three barks, four schooners, six ferryboats, and three sloops, say sixty-seven vessels, having a tonnage of sixty-three thousand, six hundred and seventy-five tons. In Massachusetts, and especially in Maine also, the shipbuilders, it is believed, were never so full of orders. In the small village of Medford, five miles from Boston, containing, in 1840, only two thousand, four hundred and seventy-eight inhabitants, there were built and launched last year, twenty-one vessels, most of them large ships, of admirable workmanship and beauty of proportion, having a tonnage of thirteen thousand, two hundred and fifty tons. In the district of Bath, in Maine, there were also built in 1849, forty-four vessels, and the tonnage was twenty-two thousand, two hundred and sixty-three tons. So certain is it that a nation has only to establish wise and liberal regulations amongst its own people and with foreign nations, and navigation and commerce are sure to flourish there. The greater freedom they have the better, and above all, let the custom house regulations be simple, uniform, and changed as seldom as possible. "*Le commerce*," says a celebrated French author, "*est comme certaines sources ; si vous voulez detourner leur cours, vous les faites tarir.*"

In watching the wonderful progress of our country since 1837, every candid observer must have perceived, I think, that the two great measures, to which we owe not only our prosperity but our stability also, are the tariff of 1846, and the sub-treasury act. For the first we are indebted to the clear judgment and unwearied perseverance of Mr. Walker, never forgetting the patriotic and intrepid conduct of the vice president, Mr. Dallas, in giving the casting vote; and for the latter to the wisdom and patriotism of Mr. Van Buren. Let our gratitude be in proportion to the value of the benefits conferred.

But let us inquire in what respects the owners of coal mines in Newcastle, England, or Nova Scotia, have any particular advantages over those of Pennsylvania, that the latter should be deemed entitled to any special protection by government. The invoices and documents before me, are not of a character to authorize any such addition of duty as probably will be asked for, nor indeed any increase at all. The cost price of a ton of Newcastle coal, landed at Boston, New York, or Philadelphia, is about seven dollars and thirty cents, and of Sydney, four dollars to four dollars and twenty-five cents. This supposes the shipment to be made at the most favorable season of the year, and at a reasonable rate of freight.

The cost of anthracite in the above named cities is about four dollars and seventy-five cents to five dollars; four dollars and fifty cents to four dollars and seventy-five cents; and two dollars and seventy-five cents to three dollars and thirty cents; by which it will be seen that the Newcastle costs the consumers nearly double the price of the domestic article, and that the price of Nova Scotia coal is nearly the same as that of anthracite. Why, under these circumstances, should more duty be asked for, except to give the coal-owners in Pennsylvania a monopoly, and thus enable them to compel the consumers to pay them an enhanced rate?

Thus far, my remarks have related principally to anthracite coal found in Pennsylvania; but mines of bituminous have been discovered in Cumberland, in the state of Maryland, and are now coming into use, especially on board steamers engaged in long voyages, where the best article is required, and it is said to be superior for that purpose to any found even in South Wales. The owners, it is alleged, offer now to deliver it at Boston or New York, at six dollars and twenty-five cents per ton; and, next year, when a certain canal is finished, expect to deliver it at five dollars a ton. As coal wanted for similar purposes cannot be imported from South Wales, for less than six dollars to six dollars and twenty-five cents the ton, why should the duty on foreign coal be increased?

The statement, which has sometimes been made, that the present duty is only about forty-five cents a ton, would appear to be incorrect. The custom house returns show it to be about sixty cents on the whole average annual quantity imported. It is very evident that the coal business in Pennsylvania, is progressing with a speed never before equalled, and it would no doubt be greater still if capital could be had to multiply the means of transportation from the mines to tide-water. The city of Boston is said to have lent some millions of dollars to promote this object. London, New York, and other cities, have done their part; but yet capital is said to be wanted. The consumption of coal in Great Britain was estimated, in 1840, at fifteen millions of tons; but the increase since must have been vast, and almost beyond belief.

But what further aggravates the unreasonableness of demanding a high protective or prohibitory duty upon foreign coal, is that it is a different article from the anthracite, is used for purposes for which the latter would not be equally fit, and that to prevent its importation would be, for the present, at any rate, to deprive the country of the privilege of using it. Should the owners of the Cumberland mines be ever able to supply the demand, and the quality prove as good as is anticipated, as the price is so low, the coal of Great Britain or Nova Scotia may soon cease to be wanted; but let us not, in the mean time, be left to the tender mercies of the owners of the mines in Pennsylvania.

Besides, to some persons, the use of anthracite coal is exceedingly unpleasant, if not intolerable; and why should they be deprived of the bituminous, or have to purchase it at a price unnecessarily increased by the interference of government, not for the sake of an increased revenue, but to enhance the profits of certain owners of mines in Pennsylvania? Such a proposal should receive no countenance in the national legislature; and should the attempt be made by interested parties to induce congress to increase the duty on this essential article, I trust it will be rejected with a unanimity and promptitude, which will prevent any future enterprise of the same kind.

There are other recommendations in your report, of which it would be easy to show the inexpediency or entire impracticability, as must be obvious to every experienced merchant. It does not, however, seem advisable to discuss their merits or demerits at the present time, when there appears no reason to suppose that any committee can be found in congress to recommend any material changes in a tariff, (much less its repeal,) which has so approved itself to the great majority of the people, and so admirably answered the purposes of those who framed it, and caused it to be adopted. In conclusion, then, it only remains for me to add once more that

I remain, very respectfully,

Your most obedient servant,

S. D. BRADFORD.

To the Hon. WILLIAM M. MEREDITH,
Secretary of the Treasury, Washington, D. C.

THE LATE CAPTAIN BURSLEY.

Lost at sea, off the coast of Ireland, on the 13th of January last, Ira Bursley, master of the New York packet ship Hottinguer.

The account of the wreck of the Hottinguer, and the circumstances under which the life of her heroic commander was sacrificed to his zealous desire to discharge his duty, have been already given in the public journals, and need not be repeated here; but justice and gratitude both demand that when such a person is numbered among the dead, the event should be suitably noticed, and some mention be made of the many uncommon and estimable qualities which distinguished him. The announcement of his loss will have caused many a heart to ache, and many a tear to fall amongst a very numerous circle of acquaintances and friends, beside those who were connected with him by the ties of relationship. He belonged to a class of men, who, for nautical skill, intrepid courage in the hour of danger, and gentlemanly conduct always, have never been surpassed, and of which America may justly be proud. Their superiority has been universally admitted, and has called forth the admiration and encomiums of travellers from every clime.

Since the introduction of steamers, which have now in a great measure monopolized the passengers who once depended upon our packet ships, less is heard of these American shipmasters; but all who used to cross the Atlantic before the steamers had commenced their career, can never forget how much they owe to them during a service of more than twenty years. Those can best appreciate these advantages and privileges, who have been so unfortunate as to have had occasion to make voyages under a foreign flag.

Captain Bursley was a native of Barnstable, Cape Cod, a section of our state to which we are indebted not only for so many of our enterprising and excellent shipmasters, but also for some of our most distinguished and wealthiest merchants. He came to Boston at a very tender age, absolutely without any pecuniary means, but he brought with him what is incomparably more valuable, a character for industry, sobriety, and good conduct, and immediately entered upon that career, for which probably the place of his nativity upon the seashore had given him a preference, under the care and guidance of one of our most skilful navigators, as well as most successful merchants, Daniel C. Bacon, Esq.

He rose rapidly in his profession, and became master of a vessel at an unusually early age. At a later date, he commanded, for several years, one of the ships which belonged to the Liverpool and Boston line of packets, and never can the writer forget his departure one day during that period from the end of the Long wharf in the packet ship Dover, for Liverpool. The wind being perfectly fair, and the heavens bright and clear in the month of October, that graceful vessel started upon her voyage with an unusual speed, and bounded over the waves like some beautiful bird winging its way over the waters. Captain Bursley had taken his station far aft in the vessel, upon the part called the hurricane house. He was in the prime of life, full of health and vigor, and so majestic appeared his noble figure, more like that of the Apollo of the Vatican than of any one else, that it seemed impossible to withdraw one's eyes from him, and the writer stood gazing and watching him sailing over the sea, until distance concealed him from his view. It was not Apollo, however, as he is sometimes described, the mere representation of personal beauty, but Apollo, as he is portrayed in the classics, having just defeated the giant Tityus, or slain the serpent Python. The writer has been affected in a similar manner whilst standing before some of the chef d'œuvres of Grecian art in Rome or Florence; but never before by looking upon any living man.

The soul, the spirit within, was worthy of the form which contained it. No dangers could appal him; no difficulty cause him to hesitate or falter. He had a sound judgment, and never decided rashly; but, when he had marked out his course, no obstacle could turn him aside. Had he belonged to the navy, and, in some engagement with the foe, received a mortal wound, his last words would have been those of the immortal Lawrence, "Don't give up the ship!" Had he belonged to the army, and been left behind, as Marshal Ney was by Napoleon, in the retreat from Moscow, in a hostile country, surrounded by a victorious army, with thousands of his own soldiers daily falling victims to famine and cold, he would never have abandoned his flag, or his companions in arms, but would have reached Smolensk with that part of his division, which had survived the sufferings of that dreadful march, as did the great marshal; of whom history relates that, "when at two leagues distance, Napoleon heard that Ney was coming, he leaped for joy, shouted aloud, and exclaimed, 'I have saved my eagles, then. I would have given three hundred millions of my treasure to save the life of such a man.'"

The same historian, the Count Segur, his companion in arms, in speaking of Marshal Ney, adds, "that so simple and unpretending was he in his disposition and manners, that, had it not been for the signs of astonishment and admiration which he could not help observing in the eyes the gestures, and the acclamations of his companions in glory, he would have remained unconscious of his having performed a sublime action."

No words could better describe the modest, unaffected manners of him whose loss is so deeply deplored, and who has been so suddenly taken away.

Much as he valued his home, (and few men had more reason to love their homes,) and dear to him as were the relations of wife and children, in the hour of danger he seemed only to think of what he owed to his character as a commander, to his passengers and crew, the owners of the vessel and cargo, and the underwriters. Who can have forgotten his noble conduct during the great gale in Liverpool, on the 7th January, 1839, when the English coast, for miles below that town, was strewed with wrecks, and three New York packets were stranded; the wind raging furiously, his noble ship, the Cambridge, swinging to and fro, having already dragged her anchors, and being only within a few feet of the granite dock walls, (against which it was expected every moment she would strike and go to pieces,) he hoisted a placard upon the stern of his vessel, on which were inscribed, in large characters, these words:

"One thousand pounds for any one who will bring me a steamer to take my ship into the stream."

Three brave fellows procured a rope, dashed into a boat, and attempted to carry it on board, but were immediately overwhelmed in the boiling surge, and drowned. The escape was a narrow one; but the ship was saved with a cargo valued at three hundred thousand dollars; and the brave captain arrived safe at New York to carry out the first news of the gale, and of the loss of that excellent man, Captain Smith, (who commanded one of those packets already named, and who lost his life in attempting to save her;) and to receive the congratulations of his friends and the thanks of the underwriters. No doubt he looked for a similar result upon the recent emergency, which has proved so fatal to his hopes.

It would seem that his judgment and skill were equal to his heroism and intrepidity; for when the tide arose the vessel floated from off the Blackwater bank, on which she first struck, and would perhaps have been saved, had not she struck a second time upon the Arklow bank, upon which she foundered. It must be remembered that he had sent his passengers and half of his crew ashore the day before, and therefore had only a part of his men on board. Probably the rudder had become deranged, so that the ship would not steer. The writer was on board his ship, the Hottinguer, during a tempest by night, when "the waters of the great deep seemed to be breaking up," the waves roaring like some famished wild beast impatient for its prey; the thunder rolling, the lightning flashing, and he stood gazing upon the fearless commander with wonder and admiration, as he passed with rapid step from one part of the vessel to another, giving a word of command here, and another of encouragement there, whilst all around him were momently expecting shipwreck, and he himself was as calm and composed as upon some quiet Sabbath morning in the country in the season of summer. In seasons of great danger, like that now described, he seemed more like some Grecian or Roman Deity, Jupiter or Neptune, than a man. Many other instances might be mentioned of his presence of mind and fearless conduct.

In all his dealings with others he was systematic, exact, prompt, and honorable; as a shipmaster and navigator, he may have had equals, but, it is believed, no superior. It is not remembered that during the more than thirty years he was a master he ever lost a ship, or met with any serious disaster previous to that which terminated his life.

To admit that such a man had faults, would be only to say that he was human. The writer would be amongst the last to admit the validity of the maxim which directs us to say "*nihil nisi bonum de mortuis;*" but it may be asserted with the strictest truth, that not many instances can be found of men, who had fewer failings or so many amiable traits of character; and it was these qualities which rendered him such a valued and agreeable companion whilst living, and will preserve his memory fresh and green in the hearts of his relatives and friends, now that he is no more with them.

It is not denied that he sometimes gave way to sudden bursts of passion, and this might have been expected; for there is a beautiful harmony, consistency, and proportion in the works of nature, and men endowed with rare talents and uncommon physical power, have often passions graduated by the same scale.

But whenever he yielded to feelings of this nature, reason almost instantly resumed its empire, and he lost no time in making a full and generous reparation. He has been known, in a moment of excitement, on account of some omission or mistake committed by one of his crew, to strike him, and, immediately after, taking from his pocket a considerable sum of money, hand it to him, make an apology, and desire him to think no more of it. He said to the writer one day, "I know I sometimes give way to my temper, but I never harbor any bad feelings towards any one a moment afterwards. I strive very hard to correct this fault. I have many blessings, and have been a successful man, and I endeavor to be a good citizen, a good neighbor, and to contribute my share to supply the wants of those who have need of my assistance."

It would be easy to mention many instances in confirmation of the sincerity and truth of this declaration, but here let this imperfect account of him be concluded.

He has gone from us, no more to be seen by mortal eyes. His pleasant and encouraging voice will no more be heard. His requiem will be chanted only by the surges of the broad Atlantic. His body, if not recovered, is under or upon the sea, his favorite element; but his soul has gone to God, who gave it.

S. D. B.

SPEECH AT DEDHAM.

West Roxbury, (near Boston,)
October 1st, 1850.

Dear Sir,—In the report of the fair and cattle-show at Dedham, on the 25th ultimo, which was published in your paper on the 27th of September, it is stated that "S. D. Bradford, Esq., of Roxbury, quietly worked in some free trade philosophy as an antidote to some strong tariff suggestions, which had fallen from some of the speakers who had preceded him."

From this some persons, I regret to say, have drawn an inference that I made an unjustifiable use of an occasion devoted exclusively to the subject of agriculture, to introduce certain opinions of my own, upon free trade, which are supposed not to accord with the general sentiments of the people of Norfolk county. I should have considered it most impolitic and improper, upon such an occasion, to have entered upon the discussion of politics, free trade, protection, or any other subject upon which the public are much divided; and that I avoided falling into that error will, I am sure, be evident to any one who takes sufficient interest in the subject to read the speech I delivered, of which I now send you a corrected copy, having, however, added a few paragraphs which were omitted in the delivery, for want of time. Should you find room for it in the columns of the *Post*, it will confer a favor on,

Dear sir, your friend, and
Most obedient servant,
S. D. BRADFORD.

Charles G. Green, Esq.,
Editor Boston Post.

REMARKS OF S. D. BRADFORD,

AT THE CATTLE-SHOW, AND FAIR OF THE NORFOLK AGRICULTURAL SOCIETY, AT DEDHAM, SEPTEMBER 25TH, 1850.

BEING called upon by the president, the Hon. Marshall P. Wilder, Mr. Bradford rose and said:

MR. PRESIDENT, LADIES, AND GENTLEMEN,—In rising to answer the call which has been made upon me by our worthy president, and to return thanks for the honor conferred, I have not the vanity to suppose that I shall be able to offer any suggestions which may have the charm of novelty, or prove of beneficial consequence to the interests of this society. I see around me a large number of farmers belonging not only to this, but to other counties in the state, and some also from other states of our Union, distinguished not only for a knowledge of the theory, but the practice also of agriculture; and should I attempt to lay down any new rules, or prescribe any new methods for the management of their farms, I feel confident I should soon discover upon their countenances a certain smile, such as I have sometimes seen upon those of some experienced tars at sea, when some unfortunate novice has essayed for the first time to go aloft. As I do not wish to have my feet tied, I will get to the land as fast as possible. My course of life, as all who know me are aware, has been for the most part through a path very remote from that of agriculture. It is true that during my wanderings and travels through nearly every country of Europe, for a period of time almost equal to a third of my life, my attention has often been called to that subject. It could not be otherwise. The first exclamation a stranger makes in passing through the cultivated fields of England, of parts of Scotland, Italy, Holland, or Belgium, is, what wonders have been effected by agriculture in those countries! What a garden the labor and skill of man have made of soils once considered worthless or indomitable! Even in Russia, the traveller may find at Tsarsköe-Selo, near St. Petersburg, lawns, which for smoothness will compare with those of England; gardens filled with the choicest fruits and flowers, and a collection of farm animals selected from the best breeds of Europe. No person can have visited, I think, the model farm and school of Fellenberg, at Hofwyl, near Bern, in Switzerland, in sight of the Alps, pushing their summits almost to heaven, covered with eternal ice and snow, without being filled with admiration at what agriculture has achieved, not only there, but through a great part of the whole canton of Bern, under a most inhospitable climate. There not only

"Winter lingers in the lap of May,"

but the inhabitants have only three or four months, in which to prepare and plant their lands, and to reap the harvests. I retain a pleasant recollection of these and other places; but the estate which has left the deepest and most lasting impression upon my mind is that of the late Thomas William Coke, of Holkham, county of Norfolk, England, with whom I had the privilege of passing some days in 1835, being indebted, for his acquaintance, to a letter of introduction from the late General Jackson, at that time President of the United States.

As the life of that great and remarkable man is connected, not only with the history of agriculture, but with that also of my country, and, as I do not remember to have seen any book containing an account of what he did for America in its colonial state, I will, with your permission, recount some particulars, not only of the estate, but also of the life of this, the greatest agriculturalist which England has produced.

His estate consisted of forty thousand acres, all in a condition of the highest and most perfect cultivation. He retained for his own use about seventeen hundred acres, and leased the remainder, on a term of twenty-one years, to his tenants, some of whom had acquired fortunes of forty to sixty thousand pounds sterling, kept packs of fox-hounds, and enjoyed not only the necessaries, but the luxuries of life. He had four hundred head of cattle, all of the North Devon breed, which he preferred to all others; four thousand sheep, and sixty working horses. At the time I speak of, he had four hundred acres devoted to the production of turnips, and seventy-five to that of mangel-wurtzel. The game killed annually upon the estate, consisting of pheasants, partridges, woodcocks, snipes, hares, and rabbits, amounted to forty thousand in number. He had a chaplain who, in addition to his usual official duties, kept an exact account of all the game killed upon the estate during the sporting season. The damage done annually to the crops by the rabbits was estimated at five thousand pounds sterling. The usual course of his crops was, first turnips, next barley, thirdly clover, and fourthly wheat; and the production of the latter was generally equal to sixty bushels to the acre; although when he first took possession of the estate, rye was almost the only crop attempted, and his neighbors told him the land was too poor to grow wheat. The usual rent he obtained was at the rate of twenty-five shillings sterling, equal to about six dollars of our money, per acre. He had a magnificent park, of ten miles in circumference, containing three thousand five hundred acres; the choicest of the trees having been planted by his own hand. His income was estimated at sixty to seventy thousand pounds sterling per annum.

At the date of my visit, he was in his eighty-second

year. By his first wife, whom he married in 1775, he had three daughters, but no son. He married secondly, in 1822, Lady Anne Amelia Keppel, daughter of his particular friend, the late Earl of Albemarle, the bride being in her nineteenth, and the bridegroom in his sixty-ninth year; a difference of just half a century. By her, he had five sons and a daughter. The youngest child was only a few days old at the date of my visit. His oldest son is now a member of the house of lords, and his second a member of the house of commons. Both are gentlemen of great worth of character, and do honor to the family from which they descended. Lady Anne was distinguished for her various accomplishments,—for beauty, but above all for domestic virtues. She, as well as Mr. Coke, was almost adored by the tenants, whom she always visited in times of sickness, and administered to their wants. Their children were educated in the vicinity, at schools under her particular care and inspection.

Mr. Coke was over fifty years a member of parliament, took a deep interest in the contest between the mother country and the colonies, and, because he favored the latter, was called for many years the American rebel. It was this intrepid and independent farmer who had the courage, first of all, to rise in parliament and offer the celebrated resolution, that, "The American colonies, now the United States of America, are and ought to be declared free and independent." He did this in concert with another friend of America, Charles James Fox, who promised to second the motion, and to advocate it by a speech. It was adopted by only one vote. Those who are familiar with English history at that period, may easily imagine what a sensation the passage of such a resolution must have produced. It required some intrepidity in those days to be a patriot and politician, and oppose the king and his ministers. An active opponent of the government was in danger of being sent to the tower and tried for treason, a crime very imperfectly defined at that epoch.

The king, George III., had said that he would insult publicly, any member of parliament, who should dare to bring to the throne an address containing the resolution I have named. Mr. Coke, on hearing this, presented it to his majesty clad in the suit of clothes he was accustomed to wear during a fox-chase, instead of those in which he usually appeared in parliament, but the king took good care not to insult him, and received him with all those marks of respect due to his character and rank.

It was this same independent farmer, also, who first ventured, in 1782, to offer another celebrated resolution in the house of commons, viz., "That this house is thoroughly corrupt, and ought to be reformed." It was made at periods afterwards, for half a century, ineffectually, however; for the reform bill was finally passed in 1832, just fifty years, by the records of the house, from the day on which Mr. Coke first made the motion I have recited! Many here present may probably remember the commotion it produced in England, and that a hundred thousand men were said to be in readiness, at or near Birmingham, to have marched upon London, if the house of lords had rejected it.

Mr. Coke, having now carried his favorite measure for reforming parliament, retired from public life, and seldom took an active part in politics afterwards. He had refused a title from seven prime ministers of England, including the celebrated Lord North, and declared to me, in 1835, his determination never to be ennobled. In 1836, however, he received a visit from the Princess Victoria, now Queen of England; and the king, William IV., being unwell at the time, some one remarked at the table one day, that the princess would probably be soon called to ascend the throne; upon which the princess declared that whenever that event should occur, the first title she should confer would be upon her worthy host; and that, coming from a lady, he could not and must not refuse it. The queen was proclaimed on the 20th of June, 1837, and, on the 12th of August following, the great Norfolk farmer was ennobled by her majesty, under the name and title of Earl of Leicester, and Viscount Coke.

Mr. Coke was born on the 6th of May, 1753. Six villages in the vicinity annually celebrated his birth-day, by dinners and festive games. He died in August, 1843, at the good old age of ninety. The American Congress was in session at the time, and I could have wished that they had adopted measures to express the nation's sense of his great worth, and its gratitude for what he did for our country. I regret, however, to say that in the hurry and turmoil of politics this sacred duty was omitted; and but few Americans, I apprehend, have any adequate knowledge of the history of this eminent patriot and unrivalled farmer, of whom I have attempted to give some particulars in so imperfect a manner.

But to speak of persons and things nearer home. The time was, when the name of a farmer (in this country) seemed to signify some one who was obliged to labor daily for his bread. It sometimes also seemed to imply a want of information or refinement. Farmers were sometimes called clod-hoppers, although it is difficult to see how any of us would be able to hop long without them. That day has passed away, and agriculture now numbers amongst its votaries the most accomplished gentlemen, the profoundest scholars, and the most distinguished statesmen. The great Washington himself was a skilful agriculturist, and found time, during the most critical periods of the revolutionary war, to prepare and transmit to his overseer in Virginia weekly directions for the management of his farm. The distinguished gentleman who recently represented this state in the senate of the United States, Mr. Webster, has also found time, amidst his arduous engagements, for the pursuit of agriculture; and if we may credit only a part of the accounts which every now and then find their way into the public journals respecting his farm at Marshfield, it will sustain a comparison, in point of cultivation, with the estates of some of the great landed proprietors in England. He told you himself, in this town last year, that "he had turnips there which he was willing to compare with any farmer in Yorkshire." He urged, you may remember, the importance of cultivating this root, and added that without it Great Britain would be unable to feed her sixty or seventy millions of sheep and her fat cattle, or to pay the interest on the national debt.

I have mentioned already that the late Mr. Coke devoted four hundred and seventy-five acres to the culture of this root and mangel-wurtzel, which seems to confirm the opinion expressed by Mr. Webster. A single acre of land in Ayrshire, in Scotland, has been made to produce sixty tons of turnips, without the tops. The land always remembers a kindness done it, and if well fed, will feed us in return. "It is never"—as a politician once said to me, (who had been recently deserted by his friends and lost his election,) as we were inspecting a field of his which had been highly manured and was covered with an abundant crop,—"the land is never ungrateful."

We are all accustomed to hear of the vast exports of Great Britain—the country upon which the sun is said never to set. They amounted, during her former restrictive system, to fifty-five millions of pounds sterling, equal to two hundred and seventy-five millions of dollars. Since the repeal of the corn laws and the changes made in the English tariff by that great and good man, the late Sir Robert Peel, they are eight millions of pounds sterling more. The tears are scarcely dry which England has shed over the grave of that distinguished statesman, patriot, and philanthropist. All classes in Great Britain feel that the country, by his death, has sustained an irreparable loss.

In my opinion, America, and I will add, the whole world, has the strongest and most powerful reasons also to lament his death. I have always considered his life as the best guarantee we could have for continued peace and amity between Great Britain and the United States. One city after another in his native land is taking measures to honor his memory, and the poor and laboring classes are about to erect a monument to him by subscriptions of a penny each. They feel that they have lost their best friend. On this monument it has been proposed to inscribe the concluding words of Sir Robert's celebrated speech, delivered in 1846, as he was about to resign the seals of office into the hands of the queen. They are so beautiful, so modest, and so prophetic, too, that, with your leave, I will recite them to you. "Recollect," as some one has well said, "they were delivered at the moment of his severest trial, when he was about to close his official career; after speaking of the ties of party, which he had severed forever; of the political friendships he had converted into bitter enmities; of the floodgates of calumny he had let loose upon himself—after recounting, mournfully, but without repining, the sacrifices he had made, he turned for sympathy and justice to the mass of the people, and closed with the following words:"

"It may be that I shall leave a name sometimes remembered with expressions of good will in the abodes of those whose lot it is to labor, and earn their daily bread by the sweat of their brow, when they shall recruit their exhausted strength with abundant and untaxed food, the sweeter because it is no longer leavened by a sense of injustice."

Well, Mr. President, great as those exports of England are, amounting last year to sixty-three millions of pounds sterling, equal to about three hundred and fifteen millions of dollars of our currency, I remember that in a speech made a few years since by a distinguished scholar, who, at that time, represented this country at the court of St. James, he stated that the grass crop of Great Britain only, had been estimated as of greater value than the whole of her foreign exports; and he added that he was satisfied with the evidence on which this statement had been made. We are too much accustomed, I fear, to over-estimate the amount of our foreign imports, and to undervalue that of our home production. The former varies from one hundred and twenty-five millions of dollars, to one hundred and fifty millions of dollars per annum; whereas, the aggregate of the products of the labor and capital of the United States amounted, in 1847, according to the report of the patent office, to one billion, seven hundred and thirty-eight million, seven hundred and seventy-nine thousand, nine hundred and seventy-five dollars.

There is another aspect, Mr. President, in which agriculture may be considered, in some respects, the most important of all. I refer to its conservative influence in sustaining civil governments. Deprived of this I am convinced that no government could long subsist in any country. Look at the revolutions which have taken place in France since 1793, and have crimsoned the fields of that fine country with blood! Where did they originate, and where were they all concocted? In the country, amongst the farmers, or in the cul-de-sacs—the crowded courts, and the loathsome cellars of Paris? This has become so evident now that I will venture the opinion that no government, republic or monarchy, can be established in France, which shall have any considerable duration until the seat of the government is removed from its present position. The prophetic wisdom of the founders of our republic foresaw this difficulty, as may be ascertained by a perusal of the debates in convention, and on that account they resolved to erect the capitol not at Philadelphia or Baltimore, but at Washington, in an agricultural district.

The oldest republic in the world is that of San Marino, near the Adriatic, in Italy, surrounded by despotism and oppression. It dates from the fourth century. It has maintained its liberty, laws, and territory, for thirteen hundred years. It was respected by Napoleon in the height of his power; and he received a deputation from it at Milan with the most distinguished honors. It is said to be almost without criminals or poor-rates. There has not been an execution there for a hundred and fifty years. I remember having visited it in 1837, and after inspecting its public buildings, to have called at the house of the jailer to inquire how many prisoners there were under his care. The door was opened by an interesting young woman, who, holding the keys in her hand, stated that the prison was at present without an occupant. She added that the doors of the cells were all open, and I could inspect them for my own satisfaction, should it be my wish to do so. This republic consists wholly of agriculturalists.

I need not tell you how conducive agriculture is to health and vigor of body, and peace and tranquillity of mind. It is also most favorable to the growth of the domestic virtues. No one, I think, can have owned a farm, especially if it happen to have been that upon which he was born, and where his parents have always resided, without having felt that there was one spot on earth which claimed his attachment, and which he could call by the endearing name of home. Such an one is always prepared to exclaim, with the Latin poet:

"O Melibœe, Deus nobis hæc otia fecit."

He can truly realize not only the poetry, but the truth also, of those beautiful lines of the great English poet:

"'Tis sweet to hear the watch-dog's honest bark,
Bay deep-mouthed welcome as we draw near home;
'Tis sweet to know there is an eye will mark
Our coming, and look brighter when we come;
'Tis sweet to be awakened by the lark,
Or lull'd by falling waters; sweet the hum
Of bees, the voice of girls, the song of birds,
The lisp of children, and their earliest words."

Ladies and gentlemen, I will not detain you longer. I thank you sincerely for the great attention with which you have listened to me. I congratulate you upon the success which has attended this society thus far, and I see no reason to doubt that its future career will realize the most sanguine expectations of its patrons and friends.

I give you in conclusion—Prosperity and success to the Norfolk Agricultural Society.

DECLENSION OF OFFICE.

[WE are very sorry to announce that Samuel D. Bradford, Esq., declines being a candidate for congress in the eighth district. His letter to this effect will be found below. It was sent to the committee appointed to inform him of his nomination on the day of its date; but its publication has been delayed until now, in hopes that he might be induced to withdraw it. Notwithstanding, however, pressing solicitations to allow his name to be presented for the suffrages of his fellow citizens, he feels compelled to adhere to his first resolution. Mr. Bradford is so admirably qualified for the position which his friends desire to see him occupy, by education, talents, experience, integrity, and general popularity, that it is truly a misfortune to the cause of liberal principles and enlightened legislation, that circumstances compel him to decline the prominent attitude a large portion of the freemen of his district are anxious he should fill.—*Boston Post.*]

WEST ROXBURY, (near Boston,)
October 16th, 1850.

GENTLEMEN,—I have had the honor to receive your communication, dated the 11th instant, informing me that I have been nominated by the convention assembled at Dedham on the 8th of October, as a candidate to represent the eighth district in the Congress of the United States.

My grateful acknowledgments are due to the gentlemen of the convention, for this unexpected testimonial of their confidence and favor, which I shall never cease duly to appreciate and value most highly; and the first impulse of my heart would be to make almost any personal sacrifice to comply with their wishes. I know it is sometimes said that the honor of having a place in the national councils is not now what it once was, and that it has ceased to be the object of a worthy ambition. This opinion has no doubt some advocates, and, if it be founded in truth, it furnishes the strongest reason why every true patriot should take the front rank in our popular elections, and do all in his power to restore the former high character of our national legislature. Let it be granted that we have witnessed of late less moderation of language, or dignity and propriety of manners, than prevailed there formerly, and yet it ought, I think, to be considered a distinction which any citizen, however elevated, may justly prize, to have a seat in those halls of legislation which have been dignified by the presence of the most eminent patriots and statesmen, who have illustrated and adorned the annals of our country. When, therefore, I announce to you my intention to decline the nomination so kindly offered, it is not because I do not value the honor you would confer upon me, nor because I do not feel grateful for the preference you have given me; especially when it is remembered that so much of my life has been passed abroad; that, since my return, I have had the pleasure of making the acquaintance of but a very limited number of the electors; and have never, upon any occasion, taken a part in a political meeting of any kind. Do not infer from this, that I have been indifferent to the success or progress of those noble principles of liberty which, first proclaimed by Hampden and Sidney in England, and afterwards by Franklin, Jefferson, and other illustrious patriots in this country, constitute the political creed of the great Democratic party. What American but must have been proud of the triumphs achieved by it since 1801?

To whom, but the anti-federalists, are we indebted for the acquisition of Louisiana and Florida; the demolition of that political monster, the United States Bank; the introduction and successful working of the sub-treasury system, reforming and improving our currency; the repeal of the unjust and unconstitutional bankrupt act; and the passage of the tariff of 1846, not for protection, but for revenue, as was contemplated by the constitution of the United States? What party in any country can justly claim to have been the authors of so many great and important measures, all conducing to the prosperity and happiness of the people? Nor have the people been ungrateful; for, with the exception of four years and a month, the government of the United States has been in the hands of this same Democratic party from 1801 to 1849, and, for aught I know, would have continued there till 1949, had it always remained united as formerly. Surely its principles must be founded in truth and justice, to have taken such deep root in the American heart, and to have controlled the action of the government for so many years. In fact, they control it now, for the position of parties in this country, at present, is unprecedented. The government is nominally in the hands of the Whigs, and yet, after a struggle of seven long months, the late president, with all his personal popularity, (the usual attendant upon military success,) and his whole cabinet, were not able to carry a single measure of their own. Every important act which has been passed since the decease of Gen. Taylor, has been either a democratic measure, or the administration has been indebted for its passage to the favor and coöperation of the Democratic party.

An anomaly of this kind could not have occurred in England, for, there, the cabinet would have been compelled to resign their places of emolument and power into other hands; but the complacency of our constitution permits to the holder a continuance of office, after the people have repudiated his measures. It would, however, be surprising if the electors should permit this state of things to be prolonged for a single day after the time prescribed for its termination by the constitution and the laws.

Having declined to be a candidate for the suffrages of

my fellow citizens, it might appear presumptuous on my part, to volunteer any opinion upon the great and delicate political questions which have recently so agitated the public mind. I cannot, however, refrain from the expression of the deep regret I feel for the unhappy division, which one of those questions has, to some extent, produced in the ranks of our party. It seems to me as unnecessary as it is unfortunate and impolitic. In England, we have frequently witnessed the permission of what are called "open questions," even amongst the members of the same cabinet, consisting of only a few persons, upon whose united decisions the fate of that great monarchy depends. Even in the house of commons, members of the same cabinet are sometimes found voting against one another, and yet the action of the government is unimpeded and without interruption. Why, then, should not some open questions be permitted amongst those who advocate our cause, consisting of so many millions of persons, without preventing their harmonious action upon the great and leading questions, concerning which they all agree? Without union and harmony, nothing valuable can be accomplished. "United we stand; divided we fall." There are good men and bad men belonging to every party; and whilst all classes reprobate the political agitator, who violently denounces such as differ from him for the sake of acquiring an unenviable political notoriety, or the emoluments of office, ought we not at the same time to exercise a Christian charity towards those who honestly entertain opinions upon some collateral subjects different from our own? It is this union of action only which will restore to our ancient county of Norfolk the high position it once occupied, and which was the subject of so much pride to every patriot living within its borders. To mention only one instance. Its former representative in Congress, the late Ebenezer Seaver, of Roxbury, heedless of the floodgates of calumny which he let loose upon himself, had the independence and moral courage, in 1812, to give his vote in favor of that war which the federalists opposed with so much violence, but which, every one now sees, was demanded by every sentiment of patriotism and duty, and which raised our country to such a high position amongst the nations of the earth.

But to return to the subject of your communication. In declining, as I now do, the nomination so kindly and unanimously offered to represent in congress my native county, to which I am attached by so many and such strong ties, it is quite unnecessary that I should mention the various and cogent reasons which have conduced to this decision. I have always, heretofore, upon every suitable occasion, declared my preference for continuing to occupy the place I now hold, that of a private citizen; and if any one had announced to me his intention of nominating me previous to the meeting at Dedham, I should have declined the proposed honor in advance. You have done me the favor to speak, in your communication, of "my support of Jeffersonian democratic principles," and I can assure you, that my devotion to them was never greater than at the present moment. If I mistake not very much the signs of the times, they are destined to be soon in the ascendant again. I shall continue to support and advocate them so long as I believe them conducive to the honor, the integrity, and the happiness of our common country.

Returning to you and those other members of the convention whom you represent, my sincere thanks for this proof of esteem and confidence.

I remain, very respectfully,
Your fellow citizen, and
Most obedient servant,
S. D. BRADFORD.

To EDWARD CASNEAU, Esq., President.
W. G. LEWIS, Esq.
JOHN GREEN, Esq. } Secretaries.
JOSEPH BARNEY, Esq.

MEETING AT FANEUIL HALL.

Mr. Chairman and Fellow Citizens,—I hold in my hand a note from the committee of arrangements of this meeting, which I received yesterday, inviting me "to meet them punctually at four o'clock at Faneuil Hall, and to make a short address." I have interpreted this to mean that if it would not exceed fifteen minutes, you would listen to me, and I will endeavor not to exceed the time mentioned.

In rising to address you upon this important occasion, I feel oppressed by a sense of the responsibility I have assumed, and must throw myself entirely upon your candor and kindness. After the profound, spirited, and eloquent addresses to which you have listened, from the learned and talented gentlemen who have preceded me, it would be presumptuous on my part to enter upon a constitutional argument, or to attempt more than a glance at the interesting subjects which have been discussed. I am proud to say that I belong to the great Democratic party, but I have not come here to-day as a Democrat or a Whig, or as belonging to any party organization whatever, but as an American citizen, to take part and act in concert with good and true men, of any and every party, to sustain the Union, the Constitution and the Laws. I rejoice to see before me such a large number of my fellow citizens, who, having left their usual engagements and pursuits, have come forward and filled this vast hall to overflowing. It cannot be any ordinary occasion which has produced such a gathering as this. It reminds one of days gone by, when our country being engaged in a disastrous war with Great Britain, and the ships of the enemy almost within our harbor, the people were accustomed to come up here to take counsel together for the safety and welfare of the republic. The country, thank God, is not attacked by any foreign foe. We are at peace with all the world, so far as our foreign relations are concerned; but unhappily we have an enemy within and in our very midst, that has destroyed the peace and happiness of more nations than foreign war, pestilence, or famine; and that is the spirit of disunion and insubordination to the laws.

The country is prosperous beyond all former precedent, labor is well paid, the people are employed, our commerce is upon every sea, we have passed the Rocky mountains, and acquired a vast empire upon the shores of the Pacific. All Europe is looking upon our progress and growth, our institutions and laws, with admiration and envy; and yet, strange to say, there are persons amongst us, and I regret to add, American citizens too, who seem to place no value upon all these blessings, and who are doing all they can to destroy our glorious Union, to which we are indebted for all these privileges.

They would enter the temple of Liberty raised by the hands of our forefathers, after so many years of labor and sacrifice, throw down the pillars which support it, and scatter the broken fragments to the winds.

And why, permit me to ask, must the constitution, the charter of our liberties, the work of Washington, Franklin, Adams, Jefferson, and of the other illustrious statesmen and sages who formed it, be destroyed? The answer is, because according to them it contains an article opposed to what is called, in the cant of the day, "the higher law," which forbids, they allege, the restoration, to his master and owner, of a fugitive slave. We have been living under this article of the constitution, and under the law of 1793 made to enforce it, and signed by Washington, fifty-seven years, and, until very recently, have heard of no complaint against it; but now, all at once, the cry is raised by some persons, that it is unconstitutional and must be resisted, even unto blood, and to the dissolution of the Union. Where, let me inquire, have these fanatics, with such tender consciences, been living during all this long period? Have they, like Rip Van Winkle, been asleep in the Kaatskill mountains, not twenty, but fifty-seven years, and have they just awoke on the eve of the recent elections? I have remarked, on former occasions, that the qualms of their consciences have been periodical, as Kean, the actor, once said, the taste for Shakspeare was in Boston; and that they were always most distressing a short time previous to the second Monday in November.

But have they read the fugitive slave bill of the last session, and compared it with that of 1793? If they will do so, they will find it rather a recognition of an old law, with the addition of certain needful amendments, than a new one. It was not passed hastily, as some have asserted, but was discussed in the senate during four long summer days from the 19th to the 23d August, section by section, and received the sanction of some of the greatest and best men in the nation. The yeas and nays were many times called for, and the latter seldom exceeded eleven, whilst the former were double or treble that number. The opposition to it, in the senate, so far as one can judge by a report of the speeches, (I do not say it invidiously,) was feeble and inefficient. The impression left upon the mind of the reader is, that the gentlemen who spoke against it were acting under a restraint, perhaps imposed by the legislatures of the states to which they belonged.

"But no individual in the senate," to use the words of Mr. Clay, "was hardy enough to maintain that a fugitive slave ought not to be returned to his owner and lawful master."

Should any one be of opinion that parts of the fugitive slave bill of 1850 are more stringent than that of 1793, he should remember its enactment would not have been called for, had the old law been enforced in accordance with its true spirit, and as Washington, who signed it, intended it should be. Do you, can you believe, for a moment, that it would have been sustained by Mr. Clay, General Cass, Mr. Foote, and by the other distinguished statesmen in the senate who advocated it, had they believed it unconstitutional or unjust? Who does not know that the law of 1793 has been pronounced constitutional by Chief Justice Taney, by Mr. Justice Story, and by many other profound jurists who might be named; and, as respects the bill of 1850, Mr. Webster, who long since was proclaimed the "Defender of the Constitution," and has now acquired, and justly too, the honorable title of "Champion of the Union," has not only declared it to be constitutional, but has also said "that no one, whose opinion was worth regarding, has pronounced it otherwise." The same opinion has been given by the distinguished counsellor, Mr. Curtis, to whom we have all had the pleasure of listening this evening, and who, every citizen of Boston knows, holds the very first place in his profession here. He must be a bold man who would venture to oppose his individual opinion to such authority as this. But, then, the objection is made that, if the fugitive slave bill be constitutional, it is, after all, opposed to what is called the "higher law." This phrase, "higher law," perverted, as it has been by fanatics, is fast becoming a by-word. Its real meaning is nullification, repudiation, or abolitionism; and we all know what these words mean. But may not a law be too high?

I remember to have seen in a conspicuous place in Florence, in Italy, an elevated column surmounted by a figure of Justice with the scales; and I also remember, that a citizen of Florence passing by, and seeing a foreigner gazing at it, is said to have remarked to him, that "Justice was so high in Florence, that no one could reach it." The same charge, I strongly suspect, may be made against "the higher law" of the nullifiers and abolitionists. It is above justice, for it refuses to return the property of our brethren of the south, when found within our precincts. Well! what then, fellow-citizens, is to be done in this crisis of our public affairs? Does any one believe that the south will continue to remain in the Union, unless the fugitive bill be carried into effect according to its true spirit? Can we expect it; or should we respect our brethren in the south were they to remain indifferent spectators of the violation of the law? It must, then, be carried into effect; peaceably if we can, forcibly if we must; or the Union will be dissolved, and the nation will be plunged into all the horrors of anarchy, and probably of civil war. Can it be that we have those amongst us, and American citizens too, who would raise their parricidal hands against the blessed Union, the work of our forefathers, and the foundation of that noble structure erected upon it, the United States of America? It is difficult to realize it, or, at any rate, that they can be found in Massachusetts, the state which struck the first blow for liberty and independence in 1775. But if it be otherwise, and the spirit of disunion and fanaticism cannot be extinguished in any other way, we all remember what was done in 1833, by that hero, patriot, and statesman, President Jackson, during a crisis in some respects resembling the present, and how nobly the country supported him, both Whigs and Democrats. The proclamation he issued will never be forgotten by Americans, and will ever hold a high, if not the highest, place in the archives of the nation. But he was prepared and determined, too, to execute the law by the other means, had that appeal proved insufficient. Let the memorable words which he used then, "The Union; it must be preserved," be our watchword now; and let us frown indignantly upon every one, (whatever may be the party name under which he may range himself,) who would lay his sacrilegious hands upon the ark of our safety, the union of the states. Let us no longer inquire so much of candidates for office, Are you Whigs or Democrats; are you for protection or free trade; for a large expenditure of the public money for internal improvements, or a small one; but rather let us put these questions to them: Are you for obeying the laws of your country, or for breaking them; are you in favor of jeopardizing the Union by a further agitation of the slavery question; or will you do all you can to give peace and quiet to this distracted country, of which it stands so much in need? Let us support them, or otherwise, according to the answer they may give.

In this way only, may we still preserve our glorious and once-happy Union, and hand it down with all its blessings to succeeding generations.

LETTER TO THE LEGISLATURE.

West Roxbury, (near Boston,)
January 7th, 1851.

Gentlemen,—I am not one of your number, and occupy only the place of a private citizen, and yet I will offer no apology for addressing you at the present crisis. It is enough that I am one of the great Democratic party, whose principles I have always supported, and to whose conduct of our public affairs, during the various trials through which it has heretofore been called to pass, I have looked back with pride and satisfaction. It dates from the commencement of the government; has been the object of unceasing opposition and attack from 1789 to the present day, but has been nearly always in the ascendant, and has deserved and received the cordial support of the people. I have always hoped and believed that its future career would fulfil all the bright promises of the past. Judge, then, of my surprise and dismay on seeing, in a morning paper to-day, the following announcement:

"The Negotiations.—The Democrats and Free Soilers held meetings in the State House last evening, and mutually ratified the terms agreed upon by the conferees, viz: giving to the Democrats, the Governor, Lieutenant Governor, State Treasurer, five Councillors, and the United States Senator for the short term: giving to the Free Soilers the Senator for the long term, Secretary of the Commonwealth, the State Auditor, four Councillors, and the

Sergent-at-Arms. In the reports, no names of candidates were mentioned; but Charles Sumner will certainly be proposed by the Free Soilers as the candidate for the long term in the Senate."

In other words, we see it here announced that "the Democratic party is to be abolitionized, and merged into that of the Free Soilers," and the consideration too "is nominated in the bond," viz., one governor, one lieutenant governor, one state treasurer, five councillors, and a United States senator for the short term!

These are the gilded baubles which the Free Soilers are holding up before your eyes to seduce you from your allegiance, crying out, "Come buy, come buy." They have probably ticketed each of the offices, like other articles for sale in the shop windows. Surely it was not without reason that John Randolph, in writing to a friend, in 1815, remarked: "I am more and more convinced that, with a few exceptions, this world of ours is a vast madhouse."

It is not even pretended, by any one entitled to any credit, that the coalition entered into in the autumn, in certain counties, between the Democrats and Free Soilers, was to have any relation except to state offices and state concerns; and yet, here we see it announced that, at such a crisis as this, a red-hot Abolitionist is to be sent, like a fire-brand, for six years, into the senate chamber of the United States, and by the aid of Democratic votes!

Gentlemen, I have a personal acquaintance with but very few of your members, but it seems to me impossible to realize that you have entered into such a monstrous agreement as this. Had I supposed such an agreement possible, I would have addressed you at an earlier period. If it be not too late, I conjure you to stop short upon the abyss which is yawning before you—to consider your position, standing, as you do, upon the very brink of political annihilation, and to retrace your steps. It will be soon too late; for, when the act is once consummated, you may call yourselves Democrats, but all who deserve the name will repudiate you throughout our wide-extended Union; and the Free Soilers even will look upon you with contempt and derision. Already, even before you met or counselled together, they have almost exhausted their voluminous dictionary of vituperative terms in characterizing you as "villains," "liars," "slave-catchers," and "friends to the Union," which they have done all in their power to destroy; and when you have deserted your principles, and voted with them in the choice of a senator, they will say, with justice, that you have deserved the charges made.

Can you, for the sake of a little brief authority, and a few paltry offices, which may be holden by you, for only a year at farthest, consent to place yourselves in such a position as this? If you hesitate, turn to the records of the past, so full of political tergiversation and corruption. Read the history of William Pulteney, the patriotic Whig, in the time of George I., and Sir Robert Walpole, who, for so many years, opposed the corruptions of the court and ministry, but who, in an evil moment, accepted a peerage, and, from that day, sank into insignificance and contempt. "So mortified was he," remarks a faithful historian of that period, "that he is said, in the agony of his shame and disgust, to have trampled the patent of his peerage under his feet." And, be assured, if you give your votes for Charles Sumner, or any other Free Soiler, Abolitionist, or Disunionist, the day will come when you would rejoice to obliterate the memory of the transaction, and when you will be ready to trample under your feet also the record of such a proceeding.

How can you, not only as democrats, but as philanthropists and as friends of the slave, do any act to increase the power and influence of that party, by whose assumed regard for that unfortunate race their emancipation has been put back a century, or certainly a generation, and can probably be never accomplished so long as their violence continues? It is a true maxim, and has been exemplified in the pretended regard for the slaves in this country, that "men are never made so ridiculous by the qualties they possess as by those they affect to have." We all know how to estimate that sensibility for the wrongs of the African race, which begins generally upon the hustings, becomes more and more noisy in the halls of legislation, but ceases all at once on the acquisition of office. How can you avoid seeing that, if you give your vote for an Abolitionist, as a United States senator, you abandon and prove false to all the pledges you have given in various conventions for so many years, and do all you can for the repeal of those compromise measures to which the good faith of the nation is engaged, and without which, probably, the Union would have been dissolved?

You have, no doubt, seen the letter recently addressed, by a leading member of the Free Soil party, Mr. Palfrey, to that section of the legislature, and I commend it to your careful perusal. It seems to me to express the sentiments of an honest man, who appears to feel that those whom he has addressed are in great danger, and, on this account, he points out the only course they can pursue to preserve their integrity and honor. It remains to be seen how far they will follow it. "Whatever you do," says Mr. Palfrey, "do not vote for Mr. Boutwell for governor, who would do nothing for freedom. In my opinion, you have as good a chance of choosing both officers, governor and senator, as of choosing either one in the way proposed, perhaps a much better chance."

He recommends, you perceive, what has been called sometimes "a masterly inactivity," and, if ever such a policy was wise and expedient, it is upon the present occasion. No man can withhold his vote too long when, by casting it, he abandons his principles, and sacrifices his honor.

But it may be asked, on your part, what is to be done? Are we not bound to organize the government, and to place Mr. Boutwell in the chair of state designed for him by the votes of thirty-six thousand freemen? In answer to this I would say, Better never have another governor than violate your principles, and bring disgrace upon the party to which you profess to belong, and which has guarded the fortunes of our country so gloriously for so many years; and this, be assured, must be the feeling of every honest man of every party. On the present, as on every occasion, a straight course is not only the best and most politic, but the only one to follow. If this be not evident to every one now, it soon will be.

I have not intended, gentlemen, to give offence to any one by the way I have spoken of the Abolitionists or Free Soilers, whom I look upon as the same, for they are now everywhere considered as identical. I have spoken freely, but I believe also justly, of them; or perhaps I should add, of those who direct their movements; for I own, gentlemen, that there are good as well as bad men of every political denomination. When, however, I see one of their leaders, Mr. Giddings (their apostle, as he is sometimes called by them,) rise in his place in congress, as he did at the commencement of the present session, and compare our present distinguished secretary of state, Daniel Webster, who has devoted a long life to the service of his country, to Dr. Webster, the murderer, I blush for my country; and I am prepared to say and to maintain that any party which sustains such leaders, and advocates such principles, is deserving of the execration of every American citizen.

Gentlemen, I have written in great haste, and may have said some things I ought not to have said; but I am told that every moment is precious, and that the question may be decided in the legislature to-day or to-morrow; or that it is perhaps decided now. Do not imagine, for a moment, that this is a question which concerns only our native state; for it embraces the whole country, and will decide the character of the whole national Democracy. In conclusion, I will only add that the eyes of the whole nation are fixed upon you, and that to your hands are committed the future destinies of the Democratic party. Pardon, I pray you, the freedom with which I have addressed you; it is no time for soft words when the character and integrity of that party are at stake. Reflect long and well before you give the decisive, I hope it may not prove the fatal, vote; and I feel assured that the decision will be such as will preserve your honor, that of the commonwealth to which you belong, and the blessed Union itself.

I remain, gentlemen, with sincere respect,

Your fellow citizen and obedient servant,

S. D. BRADFORD.

To the DEMOCRATIC MEMBERS
of the Legislature of Massachusetts.

ADDRESS AND RESOLUTIONS,

ADOPTED BY THE DEMOCRATS OF NORFOLK COUNTY.

Committee on the Address,—Samuel D. Bradford, West Roxbury; Nathaniel R. Childs, Dorchester; Ezra Wilkinson, Dedham.

Committee on Resolutions. — A. Loring Cushing, Dorchester; Caleb Stetson, Braintree; William W. Comstock, Wrentham.

ADDRESS.

Fellow Citizens,—The duty has been assigned to us of preparing an address to accompany the report of the proceedings of the convention assembled at Dedham on the 14th of October. It is a task which, at such a period as this, few persons would probably have desired, but which should not, in our opinion, be declined.

The time has evidently arrived when at least a respectable number of the Democrats of Massachusetts, dissatisfied, if not utterly disgusted, with the proceedings of a portion of the Democratic party in the legislature during last winter and spring, have resolved to remain merely lookers on no longer, but to take a more active part, and to do what they can to place that party once more upon the platform of the Union, the constitution, and the laws.

It will not be necessary, nor is it deemed expedient, to enter, at any great length, into the detail of those proceedings, which have gained, for our state and county, such an unenviable reputation. The history of them will not be forgotten soon, and is one which every true patriot would blot out from the record if he could. The highest offices in the commonwealth put up for competition, and bargained for like other merchandise on sale in the very capitol of the state; Democrats, Free Soilers, and Abolitionists, all holding sessions at the same time, and sending and receiving delegations from one another, to agree upon the prices which should be paid; resolutions introduced into the senate, (and passed, too, by that body,) by the member for Middlesex, (who long since expressed the hope "that he might live and die in the faith of the Hartford Convention,") which it would seem could have had no object or intent but to irritate and offend our brethren in the south, "to characterize parties by geographical discriminations," and to produce "those jealousies and heart-burnings," against which Washington warned us in his Farewell Address: the time and money of the people wasted in electioneering and intrigue; dissensions and recrimination between members of the same party; and last, though not least, the election of one as United States senator, who had always acted in concert with Whigs, Free Soilers, and Abolitionists, who, in a volume of his published addresses and speeches, has inserted one delivered in Faneuil Hall, on the 3d October, 1850, in which, denouncing the President of the United States for having signed the fugitive slave bill, he remarked, "There are depths of infamy, as there are heights of fame;" and added, "Better for him had he never been born; better for his memory, and for the good name of his children, had he never been president." These, fellow citizens, are some of the fruits of the far-famed coalition (so called) of last year. If they be such as you approve, and as, in your opinion, do credit to the state, you will enter into it again in November next. If, on the contrary, you consider them as disgraceful, and would put the seal of your condemnation upon such proceedings, you will condemn and avoid such an unnatural union, and will cast your votes for such candidates only as deserve your confidence and support. The portrait here presented is no production of fancy or the imagination. The charges here made are not denied by the parties themselves. Some of them have been defended upon various, but, to our minds, frivolous excuses; but, of the traffic in offices, we are not aware that any defence has been attempted by any person of character or respectability. Nor can this excite any surprise amongst those at any rate, who can call to mind a similar charge, in 1825, against Mr. Clay, of having promised to Mr. Adams the vote of Kentucky on condition that Mr. Adams would, if elected, make him his secretary of state; which, up to that time, had almost invariably proved the next step to the presidency. Who, that was living then, can have forgotten the burst of indignation, which the very suspicion of such a bargain (for, it is believed, it was never proved,) produced from Maine to Georgia; or who can doubt that, but for that imputation and the change of his politics, this eloquent statesman of the west, who, for so many years, was the leader of the Democratic party in congress, and who has since held the same place amongst the Whigs, would long since have reached the highest honor in the gift of the nation? His rejection, under the circumstances, is creditable to the people of the United States, and evinces a regard for principle which we should do well to imitate; as all must admit that a candidate for that high office should be, "like Cæsar's wife, not only pure, but above suspicion." Can we wonder, then, at the astonishment produced by this wholesale auction of offices in January last, or that it was unequivocally condemned in every state of the Union?

If, then, Massachusetts has been thus disgraced, and her good name brought into question, what advantages, it may be asked, social, political, or physical, has she received from the coalition? Mention has been made by the Free

Soil press of three, the secret ballot, the homestead exemption bill, and the general corporation law. These, of course, are new measures and untried experiments, the value of which can only be proved by time and experience. It is hoped they will be found to work well, and to promote the good of the people; but, whatever may be their operation, they sink into utter insignificance in comparison with the question of sustaining the honor and former high character of the state. In the mean time, it is a subject of the deepest regret and mortification to your committee, and, as we believe, to a large majority of the people of Massachusetts, that the choice of United States senator for six long years has fallen upon a Whig and Abolitionist, who has publicly denounced a law of congress, as unconstitutional and unjust, which was enacted to preserve the Union at the moment of its greatest danger, and who, comparing it to the stamp act of 1765, expressed the hope "that the parallel might be continued until it should produce the same burst of public feeling against any action under it, which glowed in the breasts of our fathers against the former law." How speedily the wishes of Mr. Sumner were realized by the disgraceful proceedings in Boston, where the officers of the court were resisted and overcome; where the majesty of justice and law was openly insulted and violated under the very eyes of the judge, and the prisoner assisted in making his escape, you all have witnessed, and will no doubt long remember. The rebellion of Daniel Shays, in 1786, which alarmed so much the early guardians of our republic, was an offence of a venial character compared to this. He only sent a message to the judges of the supreme court in session at Springfield, ordering them not to open the court, or indict the rebels. The Free Soilers and Abolitionists at Boston burst open the doors of the court house, and liberated the prisoner.

The history of this fugitive slave bill, and the opposition which has been made to it, are amongst the most extraordinary events of the day. Prior to 1850, the country had been living under a similar law for fifty-seven years, and before the organization of the Abolition party, it had always been carried into effect when cases arose under it, without complaint from any quarter. It was passed during the administration of Washington, received his signature, and was approved by the country. In August, 1850, a similar bill was passed by the national legislature, which might be characterized as rather an old law than a new one—having, however, certain amendments, which had become necessary on account of certain enactments by two or three state legislatures, which had impaired the effect of the former law. It was considered by competent judges more favorable to the slave than the law of 1793, had been pronounced constitutional by every distinguished jurist whose attention had been called to it, passed both the senate and house of representatives by large majorities, after a protracted debate in the former of three days, and seemed, at the time, to be satisfactory to both of the great political parties in Congress. Shortly after, however, an agitation was commenced against it of the most violent and determined character, and combinations were formed for resisting it, even to violence and bloodshed. A large meeting was convened at Faneuil Hall on the 3d of October last, where violent speeches were made, and resolutions adopted, which, by some persons, were declared to involve the crime of treason—and the agitation has been continued ever since, in different parts of the country, attended, in some cases, with loss of life, and the most flagrant violations of the laws of the land. The chief, if not the sole participators in these acts of violence and resistance to the constituted authorities have been Free Soilers and Abolitionists, or persons influenced by them to commit these outrages. The cause or excuse generally assigned has been compassion for the slave, and a regard to what has been called "the higher law." How far these motives have influenced the actors, you can all determine for yourselves; but it is certain that, until lately, some of the leaders were never suspected of having an extraordinary degree of philanthropy, and have been petitioners for offices, which require a solemn oath that "they will, to the best of their ability, preserve, protect, and defend the constitution of the United States."

Indeed, the organization, if not the very name of the Free Soil party, dates only from 1848, the year in which it made so formidable a demonstration at Buffalo. It had its origin in disappointed ambition, and a desire to prevent the election of General Cass to the presidency. It succeeded in accomplishing its object, and there its career should have ended. Without doubt it would have terminated there, had it not been sustained by disappointed Whigs and Democrats, who have since kept it alive to advance their own selfish purposes and designs. It has found a new and powerful ally in the coalition of last winter, and how much it values the alliance, and feels its dependence upon it, is proved by the imploring and beseeching manner in which it begs the Democrats to continue the unequal and nefarious connection. Prior to the copartnership, the Democrats who ventured to advocate the execution of the fugitive slave bill, were called, by the leading organs of the Free Soil press, "abandoned scoundrels," "slave-catchers," "voluntary serfs and minions of the slave power," "dupes and doughfaces," "hirelings and mercenary traitors." The public were cautioned against all association with them, and their presence was declared to be "a defilement."

What a change do we witness now, upon the eve of

another election, on the part of the same Free Soilers! Our ears are dulcified by the soft sounds of "charity," and "Christian forgiveness." In one of their leading journals, we were reminded, only a few days ago, of the necessity of "generous concession," "candor," and "a little worldly wisdom." "Agreeing," says this exponent of Free Soil principles before alluded to, "what is to be done, it is perfectly immaterial who does it. Extremists must moderate their views somewhat; they must remember that honesty is not a plant of peculiar local or individual growth, but is to some extent indigenous to all minds. Free Soilers cannot be expected to vote for men who have labored, in season and out of season, to ridicule and reproach them; nor can Democrats vote for Free Soilers who, in all uncharitableness, have pronounced them 'to be almost if not altogether accursed.' Such men should tarry in the shade awhile, and divest themselves of their censoriousness and undue heat."

Such, fellow citizens, are the instructions which your newly acquired allies, the Free Soilers, would lay down for your guidance on the second Monday of November next. Surely you will say of the writer of these instructions, as Othello said of Iago,

> "This fellow 's of exceeding honesty,
> And knows all qualities, with a learned spirit
> Of human dealings;"

and, if we mistake not, you will be of the opinion that such rules "are more honored in the breach than the observance."

It requires but a plain statement of facts to perceive what deception has been practised upon you from the commencement. It has been repeatedly asserted by some of the most truthful and respectable individuals composing the Democratic party, that it was fully agreed and perfectly understood between the members of the two parties, who entered into the coalition at first, that it should be confined strictly and solely to state affairs and politics, and should not be extended to national concerns at all. Now be pleased to compare this statement with that of a writer in the *Commonwealth* journal, who addressed a letter to the editors of that paper, on the 30th of January last, over the initials of H. W., understood to have been those of the Honorable Henry Wilson, late president of the senate.

In that communication, General Wilson remarks: "The Free Soil committee proposed to concede the governor to the Democrats, on condition that the United States senator should be conceded to Free Soilers. The committee stated that the Free Soil party went into the late election for the purpose of securing the senator. The Free Soilers had avowed this in their journals before the people. This was the motive that induced them to form the union with the Democracy for the choice of senators and representatives!" If this statement be correct, those Democrats who entered into the coalition in November last, have been grossly deceived, and should they consent to continue it, would seem to verify those lines of Hudibras,

> "Doubtless the pleasure is as great,
> Of being cheated as to cheat."

To mention another instance of want of sincerity, if not of honesty, on the part of the Free Soilers: The reputed author of the Whig State Address, Mr. Everett, has stated, "that, of the Free Soil party, one half at least must be supposed to have been originally Whigs, and to concur with the mass of the Whig party in their views of general political questions." This estimate must be supposed to be correct upon the principle that every shepherd is supposed to know his own sheep better than a stranger. Yet the reason the Free Soilers allege for having left the

Whigs, is "their subserviency to the slave power," and "their having deserted the ground upon which, it is asserted, they once stood;" and this is the principal, if if not the sole cause we have seen assigned; and, to remedy this difficulty, they have united with the Democratic party, which advocated the annexation of Texas, voted for the war with Mexico, and against the Wilmot proviso, and heretofore have always been charged, by the Free Soilers and Abolitionists, as the chief supporters of slavery! One of their pleas for this is, that they sympathize with the Democrats "in desiring certain state reforms," which, however, are of a character which they had heretofore opposed from the beginning. Mr. Palfrey, too, the present candidate for governor, in his letter to the Free Soil members of the legislature, dated the sixth of January last, stated that he should have voted for Mr. Winthrop for speaker of the congress house of representatives, had he not considered him "as wanting in his attachment for freedom." Do not suppose, then, that, in voting with Free Soilers, you are promoting the cause of a party having any fixed and defined principles of their own. That would be to commit a great error.

If the Free Soilers do sympathize so warmly with the Democrats, and approve so highly "the state reforms" already achieved, and others understood to be in contemplation, why have they not declared, in advance, their intention to vote for our present justly popular chief magistrate on the second Monday of November, instead of enacting the pitiful farce of holding a state convention at Worcester, for nominating a gentleman for governor, who, they knew, could never be elected by the people, and whom they doubtless intend to desert upon the first opportunity when, it having been decided that there is no choice by the people, the election will devolve upon the legislature, when they probably intend to vote for Governor Boutwell again. That would have been the honest course, and one which would have commended itself to men of honest minds. It may, perhaps, excite the wonder of some persons that any respectable gentleman can be found who will permit "his name to be associated (to use the words of the candidate of the Free Soilers) with the votes they are about to cast."

It cannot, it is hoped, be necessary to enlarge upon these topics to open the eyes of all true Democrats to the real character of the persons with whom they have been acting in concert. Let any one ask himself the questions,—Why should such a coalition be continued? Is there any union of opinion or sympathy of feeling between Democrats and Free Soilers? Has not each party repeatedly expressed the detestation it has of the principles and sentiments entertained by the other? Has not Free Soilism now, whatever it may have been once, become identified with Abolitionism and resistance to the laws? Is it not sectional, whereas Democracy is and always has been national, in the most enlarged sense of the word?

Turn to the resolutions adopted by the Democratic convention, assembled at Worcester on the 20th August. Do they not sustain the Union, the constitution, and the compromise measures, including the fugitive slave bill, all of which the Free Soilers have denounced? What question, except that of obedience to this bill, is now a subject of much discussion or interest, either in the halls of legislation, or at public meetings of any kind? And not without good cause; for any person of observation or reflection must perceive that on its just and faithful execution the Union itself depends.

At no former period were so many of our brethren in the south anxiously watching the proceedings of the people of Massachusetts, and one may not fear to venture the assertion that the success or defeat of the disunionists in South Carolina, Georgia, and Mississippi, depends on the execution or defeat of the fugitive slave bill in this and the other free states of the republic. In the selection of candidates, therefore, to represent you in the legislature or in a national convention, it is of vital importance that you should select such persons as will sustain "the compromise measures as they are, and will oppose all agitation of the questions settled by them." Will you continue to act another year with those who have deceived you, have compromised the good character of the commonwealth, and openly advocated resistance to the laws? Why, fellow citizens, we may take an example of what we ought to do, even from one of the leaders of the Free Soil party itself, the learned gentleman who has been nominated for the office of governor for the ensuing year. In the letter, to which we have already referred, when he perceived that the members of his party were about to join a coalition with the Democrats, which his conscience told him could not be honestly done, he urgently besought them not to vote for Mr. Boutwell, "who," he said, "would do nothing for freedom." In the same spirit we would say to you, with all due respect, Do not on any account vote for a Free Soiler or Abolitionist, who will be certain to do all he can to agitate the people to resist the laws, to sow dissension and discord between the free and the slave states, and, if his object cannot be accomplished in any other way, to dissolve the Union.

Do not hesitate to strike off the names of all such persons from the votes you may give on the second Monday of November next.

Be assured the longer you continue the connection the deeper the moral and political corruption will sink into your souls. Every patriot must grieve to perceive to what a degree it has tainted the public sentiment already.

Surely there was great truth as well as pertinent metaphor in those words of Bishop Watson after D'Alembert, when speaking of court favors, and the corrupting influence of the emoluments of office, he remarked, that "the highest officers in church and state resemble a pyramid, whose top is accessible to only two sorts of animals, eagles and reptiles. My pinions," he added, "were not strong enough to pounce upon its top, and I scorned by creeping to ascend its summit." If our politicians would be governed by this honorable and independent spirit, we should not be soon called upon to wipe off the disgrace of another coalition.

We have thus endeavored, fellow citizens, to give you a plain, unvarnished history of the past, that you may be able to act understandingly for the future. It has not been our intention to speak with harshness, but with moderation and truth. We have no personal injuries to redress, no private animosities to gratify. Our hopes and aspirations begin and end in the honor, the integrity, and the success of the great national Democratic party, which is connected with so many glorious reminiscences of the past, and encouraged by so many animating hopes for the future, if it prove true to its principles, and to the cause of liberty and truth. On no account would we attempt to influence you by dictation, or by any other unworthy means. The issue is in your hands, where we cheerfully leave it. Look back to the unworthy expedients which have been adopted to place you in the position you now hold, and forward to the consequences, should the coalition be longer continued.

Remember that "the constitution is the object of our reverence, the bond of our Union, our defence in danger, the source of our prosperity in peace," and that Free Soilism resists its injunctions and violates its laws. Remember, too, the exalted attitude exhibited by Norfolk, during the memorable contest with England in 1812; and whatever may be the course pursued by other sections of the state, let there be one spot, at any rate, uncontaminated by the slime of coalition, and which is true to the principles of '76 and '98.

Recollect that the vote you will soon be called upon to give, concerns not only the honor and integrity of our county, but of our state and of our common country; and that you cannot be Democrats and Free Soilers at the same time.

Reflect seriously upon these things, and we feel assured that your decision will be just, and will do credit to yourselves, and to our ancient county and commonwealth.

RESOLUTIONS.

1. *Resolved,* That the great objects of the Democratic party are, and ever have been, from the date of its origin, the preservation, unimpaired, of the great republican principles expressed in our constitution, and from time to time embodied in it, by virtue of, and according to, its own provisions—the faithful performance of all compacts and agreements therein contained or entered into under it—the determined and honest support of every law constitutionally enacted, without distinction, so long as it remains a law, and its continuance as a law, so long as the constitution requires it—security to the rights and liberties of all by a strict construction of the constitution, and, above all, the continuance of peace, good fellowship, and prosperity within our borders, by opposing all interference on the part of one state with another; it is not by any new test that therefore opposition to the new compromise measures is considered a departure from the Democratic platform, but by an application of old principles to a new emergency.

2. *Resolved,* That the obligation to deliver up fugitives from service, upon claim, to whom such service may be due, is fully recognized by the constitution of the United States, and consequently

an unconditional repeal of the present fugitive slave law, leaving no law enforcing such constitutional obligation, is a violation of the constitution itself, being a refusal to carry out and fulfil its plainest requirements by the only means through which such obligation can be enforced—a substitution of anarchy and confusion for law and order, and an act of treachery to our sister states—that, therefore, the Free Soil party, organized to effect such a repeal of the fugitive slave law, is, so far, a party arrayed against the constitution, the laws under the same, and the peace and good order of the Union.

3. *Resolved*, That the principles of the Whig party of to-day, manifested in opposition to all reforms with reference to the substantial good of the whole, and in favor of special legislation only for the benefit of the few—in their general distrust of the people, and in their attempt to enslave domestic labor, under the specious cry of protection against foreign labor, are the same against which the Democracy of the country have been called upon to defend our institutions and the rights of all under them, from their very origin in our earlier times "that tried men's souls"—in the foreign war of 1812, in the almost civil war during the administration of the illustrious Jackson, and in their base treachery to our noble soldiery while fighting our country's battles in the wilds of Mexico.

4. *Resolved*, That a coalition with any party, having objects to accomplish, and with views antagonistic to our own, for any political purpose, is utterly inconsistent with a strict fidelity to the principles we profess, as it cannot be effected without giving strength to the party with which such a coalition may be formed; thereby aiding and encouraging enemies to the cause of true republicanism—weakening our influence for good—paralyzing our efforts, and spreading distrust and confusion throughout the great national Democratic party.

5. *Resolved*, That we most heartily approve of the reformatory measures of the last session of our state legislature, as emphatically Democratic in their character—in the general banking law, and the act relating to joint stock companies, giving to all equally, as a right, what heretofore has been granted to a few only as a privilege—in the secret ballot act, protecting from insulting espionage the exercise of a freeman's most sacred right, the right to vote uninfluenced but by his just sense of duty to himself, his country, and his Maker

—to vote in secret, as he worships in secret,—in the act relating to insolvent corporations, bringing them more directly within the reach of the law and their creditors—in the homestead exemption act, securing to all a home, a haven of rest at the close of the voyage of life—and especially, in the act relating to a revision of the constitution by the people, that it may more fully harmonize with the progress and spirit of the age;—and being determined to advance to other and even more salutary reforms, we cordially invite the coöperation of all friends of Democratic equality to join us in the cause of the people.

6. *Resolved*, That, having entire confidence in the integrity, ability, and nationality of George S. Boutwell and Henry W. Cushman, we most cordially respond to their nominations for governor and lieutenant governor of this commonwealth; and we here pledge ourselves to use every honest endeavor to reinstate them in those offices which they have adorned by a strict and faithful discharge of their respective duties.

DEMOCRATIC RATIFICATION MEETING.

REGULAR TOASTS.

1. Franklin Pierce and William R. King — They deserve, and will receive the support of the Democracy of the Union, in November next. Nine cheers.

2. Democracy and the Union — one and inseparable! who ever knew a Democrat hostile to the Union? Music.

3. The Democracy of the town of Randolph — always on hand when true men are to be supported — and just measures to be sustained. Nine cheers.

4. The Whig candidate for the Presidency — selected for his availability — the Democracy of the Union, by the election of Franklin Pierce, will render availability unavailable. Three cheers.

5. The Press — The watchmen on the watch tower — They proclaim that the fires burn brightly in the Democratic wigwam. Three cheers.

6. Disaffection to the Union — known only among the opponents of Democracy. Six cheers.

7. The election in November — the Democracy of the nation is united — victory is certain! Six cheers.

8. The Democratic platform — it places the Democratic party on the high national and patriotic ground, for which it has ever been distinguished. Nine cheers.

9. The memory of General Jackson — "He lives forever in the voice of fame." Music — Dirge.

10. General Scott — Fired with indignation, he took a hasty plate of soup. Three cheers.

11. The sages and the heroes of the Revolution — the Democracy will secure the fruits of their wisdom and their valor. Six cheers.

12. The most impudent man living — The Massachusetts Democrat who carps at the Democratic platform. Nine cheers.

13. The Democracy of the eighth district — they will give a good account of themselves in November next. Nine cheers.

After the dinner, the following sentiment was proposed by Arthur W. Austin, Esq., one of the vice presidents:

The late Democratic convention at Baltimore — it made no mistakes.

To which the Hon. Samuel D. Bradford responded in the following speech:

SPEECH OF S. D. BRADFORD, ESQ.

Gentlemen,—In rising to address you upon this occasion, I feel it is one of the most interesting and joyful upon which we have ever assembled. You did me the honor, in October last, to elect me your delegate to the Baltimore convention, and inclination as well as custom prompt me to come before you this day, and give an account of the manner in which the trust committed to me has been discharged. That convention met by appointment on the first Tuesday of June, and on the fifth of June made the nominations which have been announced; and we have come up here to-day, as I understand it, to express our opinion upon the same, and, if we approve, to ratify them. For the first time in the history of our republic, the nomination has fallen upon a Democrat who is a native and resident of New England; and, what is equally worthy of note, his name was first proposed to the convention by Virginia, the venerable mother of states, statesmen, and heroes, and the native state of Washington. Yes, gentlemen, it was the noble state of Virginia which first cast its vote for our honored nominee, and we are assured by the nominee himself that "the delegation from New Hampshire, with all the glow of state pride, and all the warmth of personal regard, would not have submitted his name to the convention, nor would they have cast a vote for him under any circumstances other than those which occurred." No occasion, it seems to me, then, could be more interesting than this, or awaken in our hearts more lively sentiments of patriotism, of friendship for our brethren of the south, and of love of our blessed and happy Union. It was peculiarly gratifying at a period like this to receive such a mark of confidence and regard from a sister state, possessing as she does so many great and distinguished statesmen of her own. It produced the happiest effect in the convention, and mainly contributed to the fortunate result which we have recently witnessed. May I not, then, gentlemen, express the hope that the proceedings of the convention have met your entire approbation, and that you are ready to ratify and confirm them? If any dependence can be placed upon the public press, it seems to me they have received the unanimous approbation of the whole Democratic party from Maine to Georgia. At all events, I may venture to say that your delegate, as well as his substitute, the Hon. Bradford L. Wales, who was also present at Baltimore, were very desirous of meeting your wishes, and acted in the manner which they deemed best for the interest of the great republican party, without favor or partiality. It was not, of course, entirely a question of who was the best man; but we had to consider who was fit for the office, and who, also, could command two-thirds of all the votes. If I consented to accept the appointment of your delegate with reluctance at first, candor requires me to confess that I have been well rewarded for any time or attention I may have devoted to it, and that the proceedings, especially of the last day, were interesting in the highest degree, and will be long remembered. It was gratifying to witness the perfect harmony and courtesy which prevailed from first to last.

I do not remember to have heard a disparaging remark made by any one during the five days we were in session; and those discordant words, Freesoiler and Abolitionist, only once grated upon my ears. But what, most of all, excited my admiration, was the kind spirit and generosity displayed by the several delegations on the last day of the session, in giving up their favorite candidates, (to whom some of them had unalterably adhered during more than forty ballotings, and upon whom all their future hopes of political advancement might be supposed to depend,) and, for the sake of harmony and union, casting their votes for a candidate who was personally unknown to most of them, and whose good qualities could only be confirmed to them by the report of others—thus laying down all their personal predilections and preferences on the altar of patriotism.

It was a noble spectacle—one which could be witnessed only in our beloved country—and I may add, I believe, without exaggeration, only in a Democratic convention. Virginia first set the example, which was soon followed by all her sister states, and with a cheerfulness and alacrity which I shall never forget.

The name of our distinguished nominee was received with a welcome, and seemed to inspire a confidence and joy which I cannot express. A short time before, after three whole days of balloting, without any result, we felt as if unanimity in the selection of a candidate was impossible, and that, perhaps, we might be compelled to return home, leaving our work undone. But the name of Franklin Pierce, as soon as it was proposed, seemed to act like a charm, and all our difficulties were overcome in a moment. The delegates rose and felicitated one another, as if they had escaped from some great and common danger. Joy beamed on every countenance; congratulation was upon every tongue. It would not, perhaps, be quite true to say that the joy experienced, was wholly without any emotion of regret, for no doubt the thoughts of some would turn to the other candidates, whose hopes had been disappointed, and many probably regretted that they had only one such high distinction to confer.

Amongst the candidates, first and foremost, was the distinguished statesman and diplomatist, General Cass, who with such singular ability succeeded in preventing

France from becoming a party in 1842, to the quintuple treaty, which was designed to institute an odious and vexatious police over the freedom of the seas. Next came James Buchanan, the favorite son of the Keystone state, of incorruptible integrity, of great experience and wisdom in council, who had served his country faithfully and long, and was admirably qualified for any appointment, however high. There was Governor Marcy, too, the favorite adopted son of the Empire State, always a great favorite with all true Democrats, never swerving in his principles or friendships, and whose administrative talent, as secretary, contributed so largely to the brilliant victories and triumphant success of the Mexican war; and then came Stephen A. Douglass, a native of the Green Mountains of Vermont, but now from Illinois, who has been called "the young giant of the west," because, I suppose, he has grown so rapidly in favor, and exhibited such sagacity and ability in the councils of the nation, that at the convention ninety-two delegates cast for him their votes, and pronounced him fit to be the successor of Washington, Jefferson, and the other great men who have filled the presidential chair. Besides these, there were others, whom time will not permit me to name, but who had "many times and oft," exhibited proofs of their devotion to their country. Well have these statesmen and patriots proved that our estimate of them was not too high, by the noble and generous manner in which they have come forward and pledged their support to the nominations which have been made. Need I say to you, gentlemen, that I sustained the nomination of Franklin Pierce, and that, for the first time during forty-nine ballotings, the Massachusetts delegates were unanimous in awarding to him the vote of the state? Need I add that I approve the nomination, that I rejoice in it, and that it deserves and shall receive all the support which it may be in my power to give it? I like it, because it promises us an honest and economical administration of the government, a strict construction of the constitution, and a just and equitable execution of the laws. I like it, because, should our nominee be chosen president, his high character will enable him to form a cabinet of the ablest and best men in the nation.

We shall have no omnibus internal improvement and river and harbor bills, but every expenditure of the public money will be regulated by justice and the constitution. I like the nomination, because, beyond all others which could have been made, it unites the Democratic party throughout the country; abolishes those abominable nick-names of barn-burners and the like, and produces harmony and peace even in the Empire State. In confirmation of this, already has John Van Buren, the leader of the Free Soil party, at the ratification meeting on the 9th of June, in New York, come back to the Democratic fold, given in his adhesion to our nominees, and promised to support them "most cheerfully;" and if we may judge by the warmth of the expressions he used, no Swiss soldier, after a four years' service under a foreign flag, ever returned more delighted to his native mountains, or listened once more with greater joy to the favorite national song of the Ranz des Vaches. I like it, because, under the administration of our nominee, I feel a perfect assurance that peace will be cultivated, and a liberal intercourse encouraged with all nations, and our glorious Union be defended against its enemies, be they foreign or domestic. I am certain, also, that our nominee will be true to the platform of principles which has been established at Baltimore, and which was received with such unanimity and favor by the convention. Finally, I like the nomination because it has fallen upon one who is a wise legislator, a brave soldier, and an honest man, universally respected and admired by all who have the pleasure of knowing him.

I am no political partisan nor man-worshipper, and never will be. I shall not, in my ardor to promote the election of General Pierce, ascribe to him the wisdom of Solomon, nor shall I assert, that, as a military man, he is equal to Marshal Turenne. His best eulogium is a recital of the actions of his past life, with which probably all of you are by this time familiar, in which case I am sure you cannot wonder at the enthusiasm with which his name was received by the convention. Although admirably qualified to fill any office, however high, such was his modesty, we find he positively declined to be nominated as governor of New Hampshire, refused the appointment of attorney-general tendered him by his personal friend, President Polk, and prevented the legislature of his native state from nominating him for the presidency, an office so much sought for by all, and which some one has called "the highest upon earth."

Such conduct reminds one of the innate modesty of Washington, who, after all the brilliant victories he had gained over the French in 1759, returned to Virginia to receive a vote of thanks from the House of Burgesses, and of whom it is related that, "when the speaker, obeying the resolve of the house, gave him the thanks of Virginia for his services to his country, the young man, taken by surprise, hesitated for words as he rose to reply, "Sit down," rejoined the speaker, "your modesty is equal to your valor, and that surpasses the power of any language I possess." I will only detain you, gentlemen, to dwell for a moment upon the conduct of General Pierce in Mexico. Those who have read his life will have observed that when, in 1846, he declined a seat in the cabinet of President Polk, he told him "that, when he resigned his seat in the senate in 1842, he did it with the fixed intention never again to be voluntarily separated from his family for any considerable length of time, except at the call of his country in the time of war; a very singular resolution for a civilian to make who had never mixed in any way in the din and bustle of war, and who was pursuing his profession in the quiet town of Concord; and it proves his intense love for his country. Soon after, in the midst of the contest with Mexico, the president sent a requisition for a battalion of volunteers to New Hampshire, upon which General Pierce enrolled as a private, and was drilled in the ranks. The brave Ransom, who afterwards fell in Mexico, was of this regiment; and General Pierce wrote to the president, and requested him to appoint Colonel Ransom to the command; but the president decided otherwise, and appointed our illustrious nominee brigadier-general. Through his exertions, the battalion was soon raised, and he and his "cheerful lads" (as he afterwards called them) embarked for Vera Cruz, and, as soon as he was able, he pushed forward for the interior, and joined General Scott. He took an active part in the several brilliant actions which followed, at the head of his regiment. Wherever the danger was the greatest, there he and his brave soldiers were to be found. In one attack, having fallen from his horse, like Antæus, he rose again, but not the stronger for the fall; for he was seriously injured; but he mounted another horse, refused to leave the field, and, except on one occasion, when sickness confined him to his bed, he continued to battle for his country until the flag, with the stars and stripes, was seen floating over the walls of the city of the Montezumas.

The war being ended, he resigned his commission, was complimented by the warmest declarations of approbation from his brother officers, and especially from the commander-in-chief, General Scott, and returned to his native state, New Hampshire, there to receive the thanks of his grateful countrymen, having nobly fulfilled the pledge which he gave, when taking leave of some friends in Boston,—"I will come back with honor, or I will not come back."

Gentlemen, can you conceive of any conduct more patriotic, more heroic, than this? It was well and truly said by Mr. Buchanan, in his admirable letter, which was recently published, upon the qualifications of our nominees, "that General Pierce's military services in Mexico constitute a beautiful episode in his life." Had he been a graduate of West Point, or belonged to the regular army, as was the case with General Scott, his conduct would not have excited any surprise, for he would have done only what the government had called upon him to do; but, situated as he was, to become thus a volunteer, to break away from all the cords and ties which bound his heart so firmly to his family, and abandon a lucrative profession in which he held the very first place—all these things prove the patriotism and heroism of our illustrious nominee. The convention were aware of these things, and, as a proof of their gratitude, they nominated him for the presidency. The nation, in November next, will ratify that choice, and elevate him to the high place he so well deserves.

You may have seen, perhaps, that some of the Whig papers have recently indulged in a good deal of pleasantry concerning General Pierce's fall from his horse in Mexico. I am sorry to expose the ignorance of these writers, but as they may have recurrence to the same subject again, it may perhaps be as well to recommend to them now to read Froissart, before they indite any more articles on that topic, and they will find that the rules of chivalry required one of two things of a true knight before he could be admitted "to all the honors," viz., "a fall from his horse, or to receive a wound," and it is well known that, at the famous battle of Cressy, Edward III. refused to send succors to the Black Prince "until he should hear he was wounded or dismounted," being determined, as the historian adds, "that he should, on that memorable day, have full opportunity to win his spurs."

Gentlemen, I will detain you no longer upon the personal qualifications of our candidate for president. I fear I may have dwelt upon them too long already. They speak for themselves; and Shakspeare also says:

> ——————'t is very silly
> To gild refined gold, or paint the lily.

Of the qualifications of the gentleman who is the nominee for the vice-presidency, Colonel W. R. King, of Alabama, it seems quite a work of supererogation that I should say a single word. A person who has been in the national councils over thirty years; who, as long ago as 1812, gave his vote for Mr. Madison's war; who has served his country as ambassador abroad with such distinguished ability, and whom the senate of the United States, as if anticipating the verdict of the people, have long since chosen to preside over their deliberations, requires no eulogium from me. With great force has Mr. Buchanan said of him, in the letter before mentioned, that "he is one of the purest, the best, and most sound-judging statesmen he has ever known; a firm, enlightened, unwavering democrat, an amiable, honorable, and benevolent gentleman." The delegates at Baltimore seized with avidity the opportunity afforded them of testifying their gratitude and admiration of one who had done so much for his country, and been always such a consistent politician; and his nomination was unanimously agreed upon, as soon as his name was proposed to the convention. Gentlemen, I have not yet mentioned the platform which was established at Baltimore, and yet no one can place too high a value upon that part of our work. To have left it undone would have implied, in my opinion, a great want of firmness, if not of principle, on the part of the convention. I know how often it has been said, in certain quarters, that the Baltimore platform of 1848 was wide enough, large enough, strong enough, and comprehensive enough; and no doubt it was for the year in which it was made, as an almanac is always supposed to be good for the year for which it was calculated, but not for another.

Since 1848, however, certain important acts, called the compromise measures, have been passed by congress, and violently opposed in some sections of the country by persons calling themselves Democrats; by some of whom they have even been called unconstitutional. It was quite necessary and fit, therefore, that the great Democratic party, in council assembled, should declare their opinion upon these measures, and pass the resolves which were adopted.

On the first test in the committee on resolutions, all but four of the states came upon the platform at once, and it was adopted with a unanimity seldom witnessed in such an assembly. We have now a rule and standard by which we can measure any one who professes to be a Democrat, whilst at the same time he is something else, and this has been wanted by us all. But it has been asserted by some persons, that we require no platform or declaration of principles whatever. The founders of our republic were not of this opinion, when, on the 4th of July, 1776, they prepared and adopted that immortal document called the Declaration of American Independence. Not require any declaration of principles! Why, principles make the Christian; principles make the statesman and patriot; principles make the Democrat; principles make the honest man; and it is the want of principles which makes some men what they are. But why do certain persons, calling themselves Democrats, object to the platform of 1852, which has been called the "Democratic creed?" They never objected to that of 1848. They even commend it now. Perhaps it forbids some sin they are accustomed to commit. It is related of some clergymen, who were once discussing the propriety of religious creeds, that one of them remarked, when asked his opinion, that he supposed "almost any one would be willing to lengthen his creed if he could only shorten the commandments." Probably the Democratic creed of 1852 contains some commandment which those gentlemen are in the habit of violating.

But, gentlemen, if any one disapproves the platform established at Baltimore on the 5th of June, or refuses to stand upon it, be assured he is no true Democrat, by whatever name he may be designated. He has not learnt the first duty of a good citizen, obedience to the laws of his country.

Gentlemen, I highly approve the recommendation of General Cass, in his ratification speech at Washington, as to the manner in which the approaching campaign should be conducted, and I hesitate to say a single word concerning the Whig party, because it is at present in such a delicate and critical position. I regret the division amongst the Whigs. I had hoped that they might have met us on the second of November next, with banners flying, and full ranks, that we might, for once, have had a regular Waterloo day. I regret that they should, for the third time, have been so regardless of the welfare of their country, as to nominate another "military chieftain" for president, which, in 1828, on the nomination of General Jackson, they declared "to be a precedent, which augured the speedy dissolution of our glorious Union, and the extinction of our liberty and independence." I regret it, on another account, because for the sake of the friends of Mr. Webster, if not on his own account, I had hoped he might have received the Whig nomination at Baltimore;

he who has defended so nobly the Union, as to have acquired and merited, too, the name of its champion; whose fame has become the property of the nation, and who has displayed such amazing talents in the forum, in the senate, and, indeed, in every station which he has been called upon to fill, that we hear him daily spoken of as the greatest statesman of the age. I knew the Whigs owed him a debt of gratitude so vast they never could pay him if they would, but until recently I never even suspected they would not if they could.

Before I sit down, I would make a special appeal to my brother farmers, who have favored us with their company to-day, and also to those who may have been prevented from coming, and I would bespeak their aid and assistance in the coming contest; for I feel that without them, little would be accomplished. I fear we do not realize as we should how much we are indebted to them, and how much we depend on the honest labor of their hands.

Truly has the poet said of them—

> "Princes and lords may flourish or may fade,
> A breath can make them, as a breath has made;
> But a bold yeomanry, their country's pride,
> When once destroyed, can never be supplied."

When I reflect upon their vast number and great strength, though they are so still and quiet, and compare them with our politicians, who, though really small in number, are so boisterous and noisy, I am reminded of a comparison of Mr. Burke's, when speaking of some agitators in England, during the French revolution, he said, "Because half a dozen grasshoppers under a fern, make a whole field ring with their importunate clink, whilst hundreds of noble cattle, under the British oak, chew the cud and are silent, we must not suppose they are the only tenants of the field."

If you, brother farmers, will, on the second of November next, promise me to give the long pull, the strong pull, and the pull altogether, our success, I think, may be considered as certain.

Well, then, fellow-citizens and fellow-townsmen of the eighth district, whom I am happy to meet in such numbers on this occasion, we behold the campaign fairly opened, and we have chosen for our standard-bearers Pierce and King; and let me ask you, could the choice have fallen on two statesmen and patriots more worthy of our confidence, or who would carry it higher? Who would hesitate to enlist under such a flag? On it are inscribed, "The Constitution, Union, Liberty, Independence."

We have opposed to us, General Scott and Mr. Graham. The former, we are told, "was never beaten;" and I may add, that our champion, too, was never beaten, and, in my opinion, never will be.

In the same way you may remember they had a warrior amongst the ancient Greeks, Achilles, the bravest of them all, who was declared "invulnerable," and Vulcan made for him a suit of armor which nothing could pierce; but this proved to be a mistake, for when Thetis plunged him into the river Styx, she held him by the heel, which failed to acquire this quality of invulnerability, and he was afterwards killed by Paris, whilst he was soliciting the hand of a lady in the temple of Minerva.

Who knows, gentlemen, that General Scott has not some place about him, in the heel or somewhere behind, which is also vulnerable? for we all remember what a dread he has always had "of being taken in the rear."

But let him engage in combat with our champion when he will, I predict he will find out the unguarded place, if he has one, and that the hero of Lundy's Lane will not have the good fortune to escape, as he did at Queenstown, with being only taken prisoner.

I thank you profoundly, gentlemen, for the kind and flattering attention with which you have listened to me. I could not even hope to reward your attention, by relating anything new, after the full, accurate, and highly graphic account of the proceedings at Baltimore, by the Hon. Mr. Hallet, published a few days since, and who, I had hoped, would have been present here to-day. As regards that convention, he could truly say not "*quorum pars magna fui*," but "*quorum pars maxima fui*," and well has he described the proceedings. Once more, gentlemen, accept the tender of my sincere thanks, and in due time may we all meet here again to ratify, confirm, and celebrate, not the nomination, but the election, of Pierce and King!

HON. DAVID HENSHAW.

THE great heart of the nation has not ceased to throb from the severe and sudden shock it received from the death of the exalted leader of the Whig party, Mr. Webster, when it is violently agitated and grieved again by the announcement that the great, the good, and the distinguished leader of the Democratic party, David Henshaw, is also numbered with the dead! The tears of the nation for the loss of the former are not yet dry; the habiliments of mourning, with which our public and many of our private buildings were shrouded, have not been removed, when we are called upon to shed fresh tears over the tomb of another patriot and statesman, no less venerated and beloved. It was only yesterday that the papers announced that the Hon. David Henshaw died on the 11th instant, at Leicester, his native place, at the age of sixty-one years, having been born on the 2d of April, 1791; admired, beloved, and revered by all who knew him. Like the illustrious defender of the constitution, he died in the town and upon the spot which he had chosen as the place of his retreat, upon his retirement from the more active duties of life, and surrounded by those relatives and friends who were so dear to him whilst living, and who will never cease to venerate his memory now that he is dead. A distinguished statesman, General Pierce, in giving utterance to his grief upon the decease of Mr. Webster, after mentioning the great men who have recently been called to "pass through the dark valley"—Wright, Woodbury, Calhoun, and Clay—has feelingly asked, "who are to take their places in the perils through which our country may be called to pass?" In the same spirit would we inquire who, in future, is to counsel and guide the Democratic party in Massachusetts? In whom can they confide at all times of difficulty or danger as in him whose loss we are called upon to deplore?

Should any one hereafter attempt to write his life, it would involve the history of the party for the last twenty-five years; for no important movement has been made without his concurrence, and the most important measures which have been adopted were many of them suggested by him. General Jackson, at an early period, discovered the incorruptible integrity, fidelity, and talents, which distinguished him, and appointed him collector of Boston and Charlestown—a post he held for so many years with such honor to himself, and such universal approbation on the part of the merchants of both political parties. Indeed, his administration of that office is often spoken of now, after a lapse of so many years, as a model for imitation.

By President Tyler he was appointed secretary of the navy, which place, however, he did not hold long, on account of a combination of circumstances existing at the time, such as, it is believed, never existed before, and, it is hoped, for the honor of the nation, will never exist again; but he held it long enough to display a skill and an administrative capacity such as astonished persons who were strangers to Mr. Henshaw, but which only confirmed the predictions of his friends. It is scarcely a week since meeting, in the street in Boston, a venerable and distinguished officer of the navy, he remarked, whilst speaking of Mr. Henshaw, "We never had such an admirable secretary before, and I doubt if we ever shall have again;" and this was the opinion of the whole nation.

Convinced, early in life, of the truth of democratic principles, he advocated them fearlessly, and with an ability seldom equalled. Although not educated for any of the learned professions, so called, there was no question of morals, jurisprudence, or equity, which he shrank from discussing, and with an ability seldom if ever surpassed. Upon several occasions, he wrote upon some of the most intricate and difficult questions which can exercise the understanding. The points he attempted to establish on political questions were almost always opposed to the opinions generally received in Boston; but few, if any, persons ever ventured to reply; and it is not remembered that he ever had occasion to resort to a rejoinder.

He had a great original mind, formed and adapted to consider and weigh questions of mighty import; and it is not doubted that, had he been educated for the bar, he would have left a name second to none in the brilliant galaxy of American jurists. He was a diligent reader; but, what is far more uncommon, he was a profound thinker also, and was never satisfied with any present attainments. His books were his great solace under the pain and confinement of the complaint (the gout) with which he was so seriously afflicted for so many years, and which he endured with a patience and resignation which excited the admiration of all his friends.

Of his patriotism, it is impossible to speak in terms of too exalted praise. He thought no sacrifice too great to promote the glory, the prosperity, and the happiness of his country, and he took a deep interest in all the great public measures of the last twenty-five years. He was an uncompromising defender of the principles of Jefferson, Jackson, and of the other fathers of our republic, at a time when a defender of these measures required some courage, patience, and Christian fortitude. He never waited to see whether a great public measure would probably be popular or otherwise; but, if he approved it, and believed it would promote the good of the country, he advocated it without fear or hesitation. He sustained two administrations in their refusal to re-charter the United States Bank. He advocated powerfully the sub-treasury system, at one time so denounced as pernicious if not impracticable, but now admitted, by both political parties, as a wise and salutary regulation, and as the guardian and preserver of our moneyed institutions, instead of their destroyer. Free trade found in him a most constant and able advocate and defender; but, at the same time, no one took a livelier interest in the prosperity of our home manufactures, which, however, he believed, would be injured rather than benefited, by high protective duties. In his devotion to the Union, which he considered always as the foundation stone of our greatness and happiness as a nation, he was second to none, and availed himself of every proper occasion to impress a love of it upon the hearts of the people.

To say that such a man was permitted to remain at all in private life, and that the people of his native state did not invite and urge him at all times to accept the highest and most important offices in their gift, is only to admit that the people do not always reward great talents and exemplary public and private worth as they deserve. Office, however, could confer no real distinction on such a man, although the public service may be greatly injured by being entrusted to less able and deserving hands.

There was no situation, however high, not even the highest, to which Mr. Henshaw would not have brought talents, zeal, and ability, equal to any emergency which could have arisen. No subject, however difficult or abstruse, seemed too high for his comprehension; and he possessed a power of investigation and analysis such as falls to the lot of very few persons.

To describe the domestic life and character of our

departed friend would be to present a portrait of all the virtues which are most esteemed amongst men. The goodness of his heart was as great as the power of his understanding. Benevolent to a degree seldom witnessed, he was never so happy as when he could do a kindness to another. Hospitable in the largest sense of the word, he was always gratified when he could receive and entertain strangers or friends. He had a wise and sensible appreciation of money, avoiding equally avarice and prodigality, and this is no small praise; for, as a distinguished English author has said, "a right measure and manner in getting, saving, spending, giving, taking, lending, borrowing, and bequeathing, would almost argue a perfect man." In all these respects, the example of Mr. Henshaw was one to be imitated and followed.

But it has pleased our heavenly Father to call him out of this world, and we shall no more look upon his noble and benevolent countenance. A few short weeks only have elapsed since he returned from Europe, where he had been passing two or three months for the benefit of his health; and it was our happiness to congratulate him on the improvement which had taken place, and which filled us with the hope that he might live many years. Little did we anticipate that, when he left Boston for Leicester, it was to be for the last time. If, however, the decree had gone forth that he was to die so soon, it is some consolation to reflect that he died where he did, upon the site of that old Indian fort upon his paternal estate, in the arms of his nearest and dearest relatives; and in the vicinity of those respected neighbors and friends who valued him so highly, and who now so deeply lament his loss. At one time, we had great fears he might pass away in a foreign land, in the midst of strangers. We may, therefore, apply to him the words of Tacitus, in lamenting the death of his father-in-law, the distinguished

Roman general, Agricola: "*Tu vero felix, non vitæ tantum claritate, sed etiam opportunitate mortis. Admiratione te potius, temporalibus laudibus, et, si natura suppeditet, simitudine decoremus.*"

FUNERAL OF HON. DAVID HENSHAW.

LEICESTER, Nov. 16th, 1852.

Having seen in your paper the obituary notices of the great statesman and philanthropist, David Henshaw, whose death we have so recently been called upon to mourn, your readers, or, at any rate, some of them, may, perhaps, feel an interest in reading a brief account of his funeral, which took place to-day in this, his native town. It was an occasion which has made a deep impression upon the minds of all present, and which will be long remembered.

The directors of the Worcester railway, with which Mr. Henshaw was connected for so many years, and of which it may in fact be said, he was one of the principal founders, seized the opportunity to place a special train at the service of such persons in Boston and its vicinity, as might desire to pay the homage of their respect to the memory of the deceased; and Mr. Twitchell, the attentive and courteous superintendent, accompanied the train to Worcester, and then proceeded to Leicester in one of the numerous carriages which had been ordered for the occasion. The directors of the company also attended the funeral, and the arrangements were all well made, and executed in the most prompt and most effectual manner.

The engine employed, said to be the most powerful one on the line, was called David Henshaw, and was draped with the habiliments of mourning. The train left Boston at half past eight o'clock, A. M. On reaching Framingham, half way, it was joined by several families, who had been waiting its arrival there; and on reaching the terminus at Worcester, at ten o'clock, it was almost surrounded by the carriages which had been ordered to convey the passengers to the late residence of the deceased, distant about six miles. The morning was bright, clear, and cold; the ground under the trees by the roadside was strewed with fading or dead leaves, so emblematic of the season of the year; and the funeral cortege, on being formed in a long, straight line, presented a sight most imposing, and such as is not often seen in this part of the country.

The gathering about the terminus, the array of vehicles, the quiet, dejected aspect of the people—everything indicated that some important but painful occurence had taken place.

On arrival at the late residence of Mr. Henshaw, almost the first object seen was the metallic case or coffin containing his body, placed upon a support upon the lawn, opposite the principal entrance to the house, as was done at the funeral of Mr. Webster, at Marshfield; and there the company had an opportunity of gazing, for the last time, upon the mild and benevolent countenance of their departed friend. It was as placid, composed, and peaceful, as if he had only just fallen asleep. A procession was soon formed, and moved in the direction of the church, distant about a mile. As it passed over the hills and through the valleys of this beautiful town, not a person was seen at work in the fields; the plough was laid aside; the sound of the anvil was nowhere to be heard; the shops were closed, and hung with black, and on reaching the church it was shrouded in mourning. In a few minutes it was filled to overflowing, and the solemn religious services commenced, being performed by the Rev. Dr. Nelson, assisted by his colleague, Rev. Mr. Dennison. They consisted of two prayers, the singing of the two hymns, commencing "God moves in a mysterious way," and "Whilst Thee I seek, protecting Power," and a short, but appropriate eulogy upon the life and qualities of the deceased, by the Rev. Dr. Nelson, in which he spoke of the most salient points in the character of Mr. Henshaw; his incorruptible integrity; his indomitable energy; his untiring industry; of the able manner in which he filled so many important places; of his unwearied exertions in the introduction, progress, and perfection of railways, and of his unbounded charity and benevolence. He alluded to the recent death of the other distinguished statesmen, Calhoun, Clay, and Webster, and said that we must now add that of David Henshaw, which proved that

"Death loves a shining mark."

The speaker was evidently aware of the irreparable loss sustained by the town, by the state, and by the nation; but yet it might not be quite true to say that he comprehended fully the genius and mental powers of Mr. Henshaw, in all their grandeur and extent; and possibly this arose from the very circumstance of his nearness to him; as great men, like lofty mountains, require to be viewed from a distance, fully to comprehend their vast majesty and height. The mind of Mr. Henshaw was like the wonderful productions of some of the old masters in painting, which, every time you look at them, display some new beauty and power. Like an autumnal landscape, as the sun strikes upon it first, in its full effulgence, and then, after passing through a cloud, some new phase of beauty and variety is every moment presented to the view. Dr. Nelson spoke also of the great antiquity, as well as of the elevated character of Mr. Henshaw's ancestry, (higher even than any one suspected until reference had been had to the Herald's College in London, by a relative,) and of the important part they acted in the early history of

New England; and he stated that, although Mr. Henshaw was one of nine brothers and sisters, the circle had never before been broken by death since 1801, a period of over half a century, a circumstance which he believed to be almost without a parallel.

He made some very pertinent and useful remarks on the manner in which the deceased passed his evenings when an apprentice in Boston; reading and studying useful books, instead of wasting the seed-time of life, and he expressed a hope that his example might be followed by the young men of the present day. He did not speak, but others have spoken, of his great love of children, of his delight in the society of intelligent and educated ladies, and of his kindness in aiding so many young men by his useful counsels, and in other ways; services which no one perhaps has rendered more freely; and to which so many persons are ready to bear witness.

Such is a brief outline of the character of this great man, as portrayed by Dr. Nelson, and "O! how devoutly to be wished it is" that all our distinguished public men were like Mr. Henshaw, morally virtuous and good as well as intellectually great; that they could feel and realize that a country can be progressive without, at the same time, becoming aggressive; that fidelity to treaties, to truth, justice, and the laws of God, is the best and only foundation on which the liberties of a nation can permanently rest; and that even the suspicion that a nation would take by violence the property of another, especially should it be a weaker power, must tarnish its reputation, and effectually destroy its moral influence forever! Let all our public men adhere to principle, and "do justly." Then may ours indeed be called, with truth, "the model republic," and we may expect soon to realize the beautiful vision of the Hon. R. J. Walker, in his recent letter to Arthur Davies, Esq., of London, in having "our confederacy embrace the whole earth, with one untaxed and unrestricted commerce, one language, and one Christianity, all enlightened, educated, and trained in moral, scientific, political, and religious culture—each state, as under our Union, taking charge of its own local concerns, and the general government exercising but few powers under specific provisions. Such a government would present incalculable advantages for the advancement of the human race."

But to return to the obsequies. The services in the church having been concluded, the procession was again formed, and followed the body, which had been replaced upon the hearse, to the new cemetery called the Pine Grove, where it was deposited in the receiving tomb, from which it will be removed to-morrow to the family tomb in the burial-ground of Leicester, from which, in due time, it will be taken to a new tomb about to be constructed by the surviving relatives of Mr. Henshaw, in the Pine Grove Cemetery, whose beautiful grounds are being laid out like those of Mount Auburn or Forest Hill, near Boston.

Mr. Henshaw's farm consists of about three hundred acres, and the land, in general, is of excellent quality. Amongst the persons present were His Excellency Governor Boutwell, Hon. Albert Smith, of Maine, Hon. B. F. Hallett, Hon. Isaac Emery, Major Grafton, several members of the governor's council, and many others too numerous to mention. The pall-bearers were eight neighbors of Mr. Henshaw, all belonging to Leicester.

Thus ended a day which will be long remembered in Leicester, as that devoted to the funeral of its most beloved, most liberal, and most distinguished citizen; a statesman, philanthropist, and patriot, such as would do honor to any town, or any country. It remains to be seen if the Democrats, no, not the Democrats, (for Mr. Henshaw, like Mr. Webster, cannot be said to have belonged to any party, but to the nation,) but the Whigs, and, in short, all who love their country and the Union, will be content to rest here. Mr. Henshaw was eminently the friend of the laborer and the poor; and, should an appeal be made to the masses, as was done in England, when she lost that great and good man, Sir Robert Peel, it could not fail to be followed by a like result; for the masses never desert such a man, and are always true to his memory; and if this be the monumental age, and if great excellences and distinguished public services are to be marked and commemorated by marble, granite, or bronze, let it be remembered that, amongst the arches or columns to be erected, David Henshaw, the originator of the printed vote, merits, and ought to have, one of the tallest and most magnificent.

"PLORATOR."

To the Editors of the Boston Post.

CHARACTER OF MRS. SUSANNAH BILLINGS.

Died, in West Roxbury, on Saturday, the second of April, 1853, Susannah Billings, aged eighty-two years.

It was an observation of that great man, Lord Bacon, "I have often thought of death, and I find it the least of all evils." And so might any one say, whose life had been beautiful and blameless, like that of our departed friend, whose loss we have so recently had occasion to deplore. A character so adorned with all the Christian graces is not often found. It is pleasant, as well as useful, to dwell for a moment upon such an example.

Mrs. Billings belonged to an ancient and most respectable family of Roxbury, consisting of four sons and seven daughters, all of whom are now deceased, except one. The last brother, who died but a short time since, was Daniel Weld, for so many years a devoted member of Hollis Street Church in Boston, and upon whose life and character the Rev. Thomas Starr King pronounced a warm, but well deserved eulogy, on the ninteenth of September last, which was published. The brothers were all distinguished for enterprise, industry, and the strictest integrity; and the sisters for those social, amiable, and domestic qualities which endear the wife and mother, and render home what it always should be. Their devotion to the cause of religion was constant and unwavering; and "their good works were known unto all men."

The object of this notice was singularly endowed with

all those Christian virtues, which inspire us with love and admiration. United early in life to one who was a model of everything which is excellent and praise-worthy in the human character, and blessed with children affectionate as they were dutiful, almost the first affliction which arrested the even course of her happiness, was occasioned by the death of her esteemed and beloved consort, who died on the twentieth of August, 1829, at the age of sixty-four years. This must always be a bereavement of the most painful character to a loving and affectionate wife; and life can never be again what it was before. Then, more than ever, is she dependent upon the sympathy, kindness, and devotion of her children. In this respect, Mrs. Billings was truly blessed; and if, from her happy abode in heaven, she be cognizant of what is passing upon earth, we may easily imagine her saying, to each of her children,

> Ah! weep not—it shall be
> An after thought to cheer thee,
> That while mine eyes could see,
> And while mine ears could hear thee—
>
> Thy voice and smile were still
> The spells on which I doated,
> And thou, through good and ill,
> To me and mine devoted.

It would be grateful to specify and dwell upon the various excellences which marked the character of the deceased; but to such as enjoyed the privilege of her acquaintance it is unnecessary, as they are engraved already too deeply upon the memory ever to be effaced. Benevolence, or a desire to make others happy, was the predominant sentiment which directed and controlled all her actions.

Few persons were so free from selfishness. Her generosity had not the irregularity or impetuosity of the torrent, but, like some gentle fountain, was never failing, and always equable in its course. The kindness of her heart was such as to be ever moved by a tale of suffering and distress, and she always relieved it when she could. She was a kind neighbor and a faithful friend. So unfailing was she in performing all the duties of her station, that her example diffused a wholesome influence upon all around her. Her approbation was esteemed a test of worthiness and good conduct. The young looked up to and reverenced her. The middle-aged could conceive of nothing more beautiful than an old age like hers. In her religion she was full of faith; and she trusted implicitly in the promises of the Savior, which were her best solace in all the trials of life; but she was liberal towards those who entertained different sentiments from her own, and believed in the efficacy and indispensable necessity of good works, without which she conceived there could be no true discipleship. She was a communicant of the church, and so long as her health permitted, was a constant and devout attendant upon the ministrations of the sanctuary. Nothing could exceed the interest she took in the parish to which she belonged, or her kindness and consideration for the ministers, who, during her protracted residence in Roxbury, were her spiritual guides. If the fathers live no longer to testify to this, yet some of their children survive:

> "And the tear that they shed, though in secret it rolls,
> Shall long keep her memory green in their souls."

We might speak also of her fine person, (the beauty and comeliness of which even extreme old age had but little impaired,) and of her benignant and pleasant countenance, which was a true index of her mind.

The closing scene of the life we have so imperfectly described, was worthy of its previous stages. Although her last illness continued for a month, during part of which time her sufferings were intense, arising from that severe and painful complaint, inflammatory rheumatism, not a word of impatience or complaint escaped her lips. Instead of saying, " How long wilt thou forget me, oh Lord?" her ejaculations were, "I will love thee, O Lord, my strength." "The Lord is my rock, and my fortress, and my deliverer." "A father of the fatherless, and a judge of the widows, is God in his holy habitation."

A part of the time it appeared as if her thoughts were wholly withdrawn from earth, and rested amongst the blessed spirits of heaven; and she seemed listening to those beautiful words in Revelation, "And he said to me, These are they which came out of great tribulation, and have washed their robes, and made them white in the blood of the Lamb. Therefore are they before the throne of God, and serve him day and night in his temple; and he that sitteth on the throne shall dwell among them. They shall hunger no more, neither thirst any more; neither shall the sun light on them, nor any heat. For the Lamb, which is in the midst of the throne, shall feed them, and shall lead them unto living fountains of waters, and God shall wipe away all tears from their eyes."

Many days previous to her decease, she had taken an affectionate and most affecting leave of her children and her grand-children, like one about to commence a long journey; and she died surrounded by the former, upon the arm of one of whom she rested at the moment of death. She had been her staff and constant attendant in life, and became her support when her spirit took its flight to God who gave it.

It may be deemed perhaps superfluous to add, that by the decease of one of such uncommon excellence and worth, her relatives and friends, the town where she resided, the poor whom she assisted, the young whom she counselled and advised, and the religious society to which she belonged, have sustained a heavy loss. If, however, we continue to think of her as we ought; to follow her example; and to reverence her memory as it deserves, may we not say, "She is not dead, but sleepeth?"

May we not realize the truth as well as the poetry of these lines?

"'T is said, that when life is ended here,
The spirit is borne to a distant sphere;
That it visits its earthly home no more,
Nor looks on the haunts it loved before.

'T is a cruel creed, believe it not!
Death to the good is a milder lot.
They are here—they are here—that harmless pair,
In the yellow sunshine and flowing air,
They watch, and wait, and linger around,
Till the day when their bodies shall leave the ground."

FUNERAL OF PRESIDENT BATES.

DUDLEY, Mass., Jan. 19, 1854.

As you will have seen in so many papers obituary notices of that excellent and distinguished divine, the Rev. Dr. Bates, who died at this place on the 14th instant, at the age of seventy-eight years, some of your readers, who have known him, may feel an interest in reading a short, imperfect account of his funeral, which took place on Tuesday, the 17th instant. It was an occasion full of the most painful interest for those who were present; and cannot fail to excite a corresponding feeling in the hearts of many relatives and friends in various sections of our extended country. Few persons were so distinguished as the deceased in the various situations he has filled, or were so extensively known, not only in New England, but in places far removed from that which gave him birth. The day was cold and severe. A piercing wind, which seemed to come from regions of frost and ice, the ground covered by a slight coating of snow, the trees deprived of their foliage, and waving to and fro under the influence of the current of air, reminded us all that we were in the midst of a New England winter.

As this romantic town is made up of lofty hills and valleys, one might almost imagine himself in parts of North or South Wales. It is most pleasantly situated, and stands on the Quinnebaug and French rivers. It was a favorite spot with Dr. Bates and his family, and he had become much attached to the people, by whom he was almost idolized.

It was evident, early in the day, that some severe loss had fallen upon the town. The cessation from labor, the walking to and fro of the people, seemingly without any fixed purpose, their quiet but dejected looks, everything indicated that some important but painful occurrence had taken place. At noon arrived the carriages from Webster, distant three miles, and bringing the railway passengers from Boston and the intermediate towns, who had left their homes and usual occupations, to pay this last tribute of respect and love to their departed friend. The church bell commenced to ring soon after; an appropriate and fervent prayer was made at the parsonage by the Rev. Mr. Bardwell, of Oxford, and the body was then removed to the meeting-house, parts of which were draped in the habiliments of mourning, and which was crowded by an audience such as is seldom seen on such a day in a country town.

The services commenced at about two o'clock, with the reading of the hymn:

> "There is an hour of peaceful rest,
> To mourning wanderers given."

The Rev. L. Griggs, of Millbury, then made a prayer. This was followed by another hymn:

> "There is a land of pure delight,
> Where saints immortal reign."

The Rev. William B. Sprague, D. D., of Albany, then delivered the funeral discourse, which, for beauty of language, discrimination of character, and true eloquence, has been seldom if ever surpassed, and which will be long remembered. The sentiment was taken from the third chapter of Isaiah, first and second verses:

"For behold the Lord, the Lord of hosts, doth take away from Jerusalem, and from Judah, the stay and the staff, the whole stay of bread, and the whole stay of water. The mighty man, and the man of war, the judge, and the prophet, and the prudent, and the ancient."

The three last characteristics of "the prophet," "the prudent," and "the ancient," were those upon which Dr. Sprague particularly dwelt in illustrating the character of Dr. Bates. He gave a succinct but most interesting account of his life; spoke of his having been the classmate of that distinguished and almost angelic divine, the Rev. Mr. Buckminster, at Harvard College, and attaining the first honor on graduating; of his settlement at Dedham, near Boston, in 1803; of his unwearied labors to build up the University at Middlebury, Vermont, during the twenty-one years he was its president; of his appointment as chaplain to Congress by the recommendation of the late Silas Wright and other friends; and finally, of his settlement at Dudley, in 1843, when he had reached his sixty-seventh year; an instance of so late a settlement in the Christian ministry, that it is believed to have no precedent in the history of New England churches. He paid a just and well merited compliment to the people of Dudley, who, deviating from the usual custom of selecting the young and inexperienced as pastors, could discern and knew how to appreciate those uncommon qualities which he possessed as a religious teacher and pastor; and to which, it is believed, very few could lay claim in an equal degree.

He dwelt on the logical accuracy of his mind, his love of investigation, and his determination to sound the depths of every subject to which he turned his attention; adding that all the faculties of his mind were so highly cultivated, so nicely balanced, and in such harmony with one another, it was difficult to say for which he was most distinguished.

Finally, he addressed the mourners with a pathos, a

tenderness, and propriety, which would not suffer in comparison with the most successful efforts of Bossuet or Massillon. He mentioned that Dr. Bates, some years since, had requested him to perform this last melancholy duty in case he should survive him, and had given him the leading particulars of his life. In this he displayed the same judgment and discrimination which so distinguished him upon other occasions.

Horace, in his ode "*Ad Lollium*," has said:

> "Vixere fortes ante Agamemnona
> Multi; sed omnes illacrimabiles
> Urgentur ignotique longa
> Nocte, carent quia *vate sacro*."

I rejoice that this cannot be said of our departed friend, and no one could look upon Dr. Sprague during the delivery of his discourse without being reminded of another ode of Horace to Virgil, where he says:

> "Multis, ille bonis flebilis occidit
> Nulli flebilior quam *mihi*."

But it is unnecessary to dwell longer upon the discourse of Dr. Sprague, as it will, of course, be published, be widely circulated, and read by the numerous relatives and friends of Dr. Bates. The opinion was expressed by every one, that, while it extolled so highly the various excellences and virtues which distinguished the character of the deceased, it had not over-estimated them in the least, but had done justice to them with great discrimination, and truth, and feeling.

The services in the church were closed by singing the hymn:

> "When I can read my title clear,
> To mansions in the skies."

and by the benediction.

A procession was then formed, which followed the body

from the church to Webster, where, at half-past six o'clock, P. M., it was taken on board a railway car, and conveyed to Worcester, from which it was next day carried to Middlebury, Vt., there to be interred by the side of his first wife and three of his children, whom he had survived. It was attended by three of his mourning and affectionate sons, and by a deputation from the church and parish of Dudley.

Thus ended a day which will be long remembered by the people of this town as that which dissolved forever in this world their connection with one who, as a husband, a father, a citizen, a pastor, and a man, was beloved, esteemed, and venerated by all who knew him. He has been taken from us by the decree of a wise and just, but merciful Providence, in the fulness of his intellectual and physical powers; for, though aged in years, there were scarcely any marks or evidences of age about him; and every day he lived, and every literary effort he made, seemed to add to his reputation for wisdom, learning, and goodness. Those, however, (and they are many,) who have been his pupils, and listened to his words of wisdom and instruction; those who have been benefited by his counsels and example, or encouraged by his always cheerful advice; his bereaved consort, the object of his constant solicitude and care; his sons and daughters, whom he loved so tenderly, and whose affection and kindness in return have been so exemplary; in a word, every one here and elsewhere, who enjoyed the privilege of his acquaintance, will never forget the Christian philanthropist whom they have lost.

"And the night dew that falls, though in silence it weeps,
Shall brighten with verdure the grave where he sleeps,
And the tear that we shed, though in secret it rolls,
Shall long keep his memory green in our souls."

S. D. B.

To the Editor of the Boston Daily Advertiser.

[*From the New York Herald of October 3d,* 1854.]

THE SCHUYLER SWINDLE.

MEETING OF THE STOCKHOLDERS OF THE NEW YORK AND NEW HAVEN RAILROAD.

AN EXCITING FIGHT BETWEEN MASSACHUSETTS, CONNECTICUT, AND WALL STREET. THE POLICE CALLED IN TO SUSTAIN THE CHAIR.

NEW YORK, October 3d, 1854.

A SPECIAL meeting of the stockholders of the New York and New Haven Railroad, was held yesterday morning, at 11 o'clock, at the Apollo Rooms, in accordance with the notice previously published. The meeting was well attended, there being present about four hundred stockholders.

W. W. Boardman was called to the chair.

Upon taking the chair, he addressed the meeting, and said the over-issues of Robert Schuyler demanded action. A great fraud had been perpetrated, and somebody must be the loser. There were two parties assembled there—the holders of the good and of the bad stock. The directors, he said, had carefully prepared a report for the stockholders, which he would now lay before them. "Gentlemen," said he, "what is your pleasure? Shall the report be now read?"

Several Voices. "Yes," "yes."

Chairman. "The secretary will now read the report."

As soon as the reading of the report was finished, a gentleman, dressed in a blue coat, with brass buttons, and looking very much like the late Daniel Webster, arose, and began to speak. It was evident his bearing and appearance impressed every one present with the idea that he was some gentleman of importance who stood before them; and immediately there were cries of "name," "name."

Chairman. "Mr. Bradford, of Roxbury, (Massachusetts,) gentlemen."

Several Voices. "Take the stand." "Take the platform." "Let us all hear."

Chairman. "Keep order, gentlemen, and you shall all hear." "Mr. Bradford, will you come to the stand?"

Mr. Bradford, in obedience to the call, then mounted the platform, and spoke as follows:

Mr. President and Gentlemen,—Being the holder of a considerable amount of stock in the New York and New Haven Railroad from its commencement; having bought it as an investment of capital only, and having never purchased or sold a share since I became one of the original subscribers; having been intrusted also with a large number of proxies by shareholders residing in Boston and its vicinity, I hope I may not be considered as making an unreasonable demand upon your time or patience, by offering a few observations upon the business which has called us here to-day. A fraud has been committed by one "who (we are told in the report which has been read) had sustained the highest reputation for intelligence and integrity, and was particularly distinguished for his experience and skill in the construction and management of railroads," of such a stupendous character as to be almost, if not quite, without a parallel in the history of the past, or in the experience of any one living. The sum of two millions of dollars, or about that amount, has been obtained by fraud, by Robert Schuyler, late President of the New York and New Haven Railroad; and we have been called here (many of us from our distant homes) to see what order we will take in this emergency. Various plans have been proposed, by the public press and by individuals, and some of the holders of the fraudulent certificates have, as might have been expected, expressed the confident opinion, that this company is bound to assume those certificates which have been fraudulently issued, and amounting to nearly two millions of dollars. On the other hand, the directors, a few days ago, have published their report, in which they have abstained from expressing any opinion upon the liability of the company, but have laid before you the opinion of high and eminent counsel in New York, who declare that the corporation is free from all liability.

I have read with care that opinion of the learned counsel, which, I may add, has only confirmed the conclusion which I had previously formed; and unless I am greatly deceived, it will be triumphantly sustained by the stockholders assembled here to day.

What I, as an individual, may think upon the subject, may be quite immaterial; but I have had many opportunities of hearing the opinions of able lawyers, learned judges, and distinguished counsellors in my own state, (Massachusetts,) and I have not yet met with the first man, who expressed the opinion that the corporation is liable. Indeed, I apprehend that, if the fact could be ascertained, the same opinion would be found to prevail generally throughout the community. We must all regret the heavy loss which is likely to fall upon some persons who are the innocent holders of the fraudulent certificates, and who lay so much stress upon the acts of an agent as binding his employers, reminding us of that principle of law "*qui facit per alium facit per se,*" forgetting, however, altogether, that other useful caution, "*caveat emptor.*" It seems, however, almost incredible, that any disinterested person should expect this company to make good to the holders of the spurious shares the loss they may have sustained; as every one must see that, were they disposed to do so, they have not the power without violating the charter, and the rights of such shareholders as might refuse their consent; besides establishing a principle which would be fatal to the safety and security of every kind of incorporated property. No doubt, Mr. President, many gentlemen here present, like myself, are owners of property in incorporated companies; but let it once be settled that an agent or officer, whom we appoint to do certain acts permitted by the charter, can do any other he pleases, in violation of that instrument, and by an act of fraud annihilate the property he was chosen to guard and protect, who, permit me to inquire, under such circumstances, would continue to hold property so situated? I would not for one; and all such investments would soon have few if any advocates.

A corporation is, as it has been defined, "a society." It consists of many persons or partners, who unite for the general good of all concerned. Every holder of shares in the New York and New Haven Railroad, is the partner, in this sense, of all others holding shares. Now, Mr. President, let me inquire of any merchant here present how he would act in a case which I will suppose to happen. I will suppose him to be a special partner in what is called a limited copartnership, under the revised statutes of New York, and to have furnished all the capital agreed upon. He lives, perhaps, at a distance from the city, like many of the stockholders in this company, but occasionally visits New York; and, in going to his counting-room some morning, finds it full of new and strange faces. He calls one of his original general partners aside, and inquires who they are, and receives for answer, that he, the general partner, wanting to raise a certain sum of money to pay his private debts, had, for a valuable consideration, (but in violation of the articles of copartnership,) admitted several new special partners into the concern. Let me next inquire, what course would probably be taken by the original special partner under these circumstances? Would he assume the new special spurious partners, or would he inform them of the error they had made, demand their withdrawal, and, on receiving their refusal, call in the police?

It is easy to answer a question of this kind, because no one feels any pecuniary interest in it; but this is precisely the case of the holders of the fraudulent certificates in this company, who demand of the original stockholders to assume the same. To such a proposition I feel assured you will never agree, but will reject it with unanimity.

I am aware that such a decision may lead to litigation, and that it has been announced already that "the Board of Brokers in New York, have had a meeting, and appointed several members of the board a committee to defend the rights of the members in the matter of the New York and New Haven Railroad Company, and to fight the case with the funds of the Board, by employing counsel, and taking other needful measures." It has also been announced, that they have employed Charles O'Connor. But who 's afraid, Mr. President? We live, I hope, in a land of law; and the greatest eloquence and most profound learning must, and I trust will, yield to justice. I, for one, do not fear the result; and I do not think you need have any serious apprehensions. I cannot see why the Board of Brokers have any special reason to complain. I hope I have as much respect for them as I ought to have, but they must forgive me if I look to another and a different quarter, to learn the rules of morality, truth, and justice.

It is not true that this company have repudiated, or intend to repudiate, any debt they owe. They repudiate only the fraud of Robert Schuyler. They acknowledge the validity of all acts of his which he did by their authority; but they never empowered him to do what they could not do themselves, or, *colore officii*, to cheat and defraud the public to raise money to pay his private debts. For such he is answerable, but not the company.

I come here, gentlemen, the representative of nearly all the stock in this road owned in Boston and its vicinity, which, unsolicited on my part, has been committed to my care. All the gentlemen who have given me their proxies, (and more high-minded or upright men can nowhere be found,) have instructed me to vote against the assumption of those spurious certificates, and I shall do so, not only in obedience to their requests, but also in obedience to my own sense of what is just and right.

We are a peaceful corporation, and would prefer to be at peace (to use the words of General Taylor) "with all the world, and the rest of mankind." Our desire is peace; but, should the holders of the spurious stock pursue us through the law, we will, I trust, be found ready to defend our rights; and, in the language of Lord John Russell on the Turkish war, "May God defend the right."

[Reported for the New York Journal of Commerce.]

MEETING OF THE NEW YORK & NEW HAVEN RAILROAD STOCKHOLDERS.

GREAT GATHERING IN BREWSTER'S HALL, NEW HAVEN.

THE SPEECHES AND THE RESOLUTIONS.

THE long-talked-of meeting of the stockholders, and others interested in the affairs of the New York and New Haven Railroad Company was held in Brewster's Hall, New Haven, yesterday, pursuant to the following notice:

NOTICE is hereby given, that a special meeting of the stockholders of the New York and New Haven Railroad Company will he held at Brewster's Hall, in the city of New Haven, on Wednesday, the eighth day of November next, at eleven o'clock, forenoon, to take such order as they may deem expedient, upon the issues of fraudulent certificates of stock by Robert Schuyler, late President and Transfer Agent of the Company, and to transact any other business that may come properly before said meeting.

WILLIAM W. BOARDMAN, President *pro tempore.*

NEW YORK, October 15.

Immediately on the arrival of the eleven o'clock train from New York, the hall became pretty well filled, and the Hon. William W. BOARDMAN took the chair. There was a large delegation present from New York, and several persons from Boston, Providence, and Philadelphia. We saw one solitary lady in the audience, who appeared to take a deep interest in the proceedings. Mr. E. S. Abernethy, the Secretary, having read the above call, Mr. Robinson, of Philadelphia, rose and said:

Mr. President,—It is very clear that, before we get through this day's work, there will be occasion to take a scale vote, and I therefore hope a committee may be appointed to decide upon this question, and decide what is good and what is bogus stock. I therefore beg leave to offer the following resolution:

Resolved, That a committee of two be appointed to ascertain what stockholders are present in person, and by proxy; and to act as judges of the vote, in the event of a scale vote being called for.

Mr. Homer, of Boston, and Mr. Brown, of Providence, were appointed said committee, when

Mr. S. D. BRADFORD, of Boston, rose and said:

Mr. Chairman: The Committee of Investigation are ready to present their report, prepared at the request of the meeting held in New York on the 3d of October.

Mr. BRADFORD, as chairman of this committee, now read the following

REPORT.

AT a meeting of the stockholders of the New York and New Haven Railroad, held at the Apollo Rooms, Broadway, New York, on the third day of October, 1854, it was voted:

Whereas it is believed, by the shareholders of the New York and New Haven Railroad Company, that, owing to the manner in which its affairs have hitherto been conducted, the earnings of the road have been less than they should be; and that a road which has the capacity of becoming one of the most profitable in the Union, has, for a considerable time, made no return whatever to the holders of the shares; therefore

Resolved, That a Committee, consisting of — persons, be chosen from among its shareholders, to investigate and review the proceedings of its managers and employés, from its commencement to the present time, and see if any favoritism has been used in the giving out of contracts, or making purchases on account of the road; if all its income has been duly accounted for, and appropriated to legitimate purposes; if suitable and capable employés have been engaged by its managers to perform the various duties devolved upon them; and to report, at a future meeting of the shareholders, the result of said investigations; making, at that time, a full disclosure of all proceedings which may have come under their inspection, by reason of which the shareholders have suffered any damage or loss, or have a claim upon any person or persons, for injuries received, or for acts in violation of the charter.

Voted, That S. D. Bradford, of West Roxbury, Massachusetts; Charles G. Griswold, of Lyme, Connecticut; Eli A. Elliott, of Clinton, Connecticut; H. G. Dyar, and Philip Dater of New York; be appointed the committee under the preceding vote."

The committee, to whom the investigation of the affairs of the New York and New Haven Railroad was thus delegated, beg leave respectfully to report, that, as the committee was directed "to investigate and review the proceedings of the managers and employés of the New York and New Haven Railway from its commencement to the present time," a period of eight years, it became apparent at once that to accomplish such a work in a satisfactory manner would require much time and labor, and incur considerable expense. Those who are conversant with such investigations must be aware that there are many perplexities to be disentangled; that to seek is not always to find; that one inquiry often leads to another, and that success is not easily attained. In confirmation of this, it may not be out of place to state that a similar investigation of the affairs of another railroad, under a resolution very much like the one already cited, was ordered about two years ago in another state, (Vermont,) on the 5th of May, 1852, but the report of the committee, consisting of three gentlemen, distinguished, perhaps, beyond all others for their skill and knowledge of railroad affairs, was not made until the 1st of July, 1853, and at an expense of fifteen thousand dollars, which had been provided for by the vote ordering the inquiry to be made. They were also fully empowered to employ such means, and to hire such assistance, as they might think necessary.

Your committee sought personal interviews not only with gentlemen who had performed a similar service, but with experienced accountants also most accustomed to such examinations, but no one named less than six months as the period which such an investigation as is called for by the resolutions would require. It is true that your committee were ordered to report at "a future meeting," and not on the second Wednesday of November; but it seemed nevertheless the wish and expectation, at the meeting at the Apollo Rooms, that they should be prepared to report on that day, and they very much regret that it has been found impracticable to do so. It was admitted, on all hands, that the time would not permit such an examination to be made as the occasion seemed to demand, and that an imperfect or incorrect report would be unsatisfactory, and without any beneficial result.

Under these circumstances, your committee, after much anxious consultation and reflection, came to the conclusion that to proceed with the investigation would be doing injustice, not only to themselves, but also to the best interests of the company, and they trust the course pursued will be approved by the stockholders.

Your committee conclude by requesting that they may be discharged from the trust which was committed to their hands on the 3d of October last. Mr. Dater, of New York, having declined to act upon the committee, his name is not appended to this report.

S. D. BRADFORD,
CHARLES G. GRISWOLD,
ELI A. ELLIOT,
H. G. DYAR.

New Haven, November 6, 1854.

After Mr. Bradford had read the report, he said:

MR. BRADFORD'S SPEECH.

MR. CHAIRMAN,—Having, upon a former occasion, expressed my opinion upon the course which, as stockholders of the New York and New Haven Railway, we ought to take, and that we are not liable on account of the fraud committed by Robert Schuyler, I would ask your indulgence for a short time only, whilst I offer a few observations upon the position in which we find ourselves placed at the present time.

You must be all aware that, since our last meeting, high legal advice has been taken by the holders of the fraudulent certificates, and that several learned counsellors in New York have given an opinion in favor of the liability of the company. This is a fact which is not to be concealed, and which, I presume, no one present has any disposition to deny; but still, Mr. Chairman, I cannot perceive any particular reason for apprehension on this account. I know not why it is so, but such opinions do not alarm people now as they once did. It was remarked by Junius, (an acute observer of men and manners) nearly a hundred years ago, in speaking of lawyers, "That the indiscriminate defence of right and wrong contracts the understanding, whilst it corrupts the heart; and that, if there be any instances upon record (as some there are undoubtedly) of genius and morality united in a lawyer, they are distinguished by their singularity, and operate as exceptions."

I am not sure, Mr. Chairman, that I would be willing to go quite so far as this, and I am very desirous to do full justice to the high character and standing of the learned gentlemen employed by the holders of the fraudulent certificates; nor would I undervalue their power because they are opposed to us; but yet I must confess that, whilst I was reading their elaborate opinion, I could not help thinking that, had they in the first instance been engaged by the holders of the original and true shares, these ingenious gentlemen would have made a much more powerful argument for our side, and for a very good reason, too—because I believe it to be the right one. It has been said, (though I will not vouch for the truth of the statement,) that it is the custom for the lawyers in New York to give an opinion in favor of the wishes of the persons who consult them. If that be so, the matter is explained at once. No doubt you all remember the story of the advocate, who, having made a learned and eloquent speech against his own side by mistake, as soon as he had discovered his error, making a long pause, said, "Gentlemen of the jury, such are the arguments which will no doubt be made by my opponent. Now you will please listen to me whilst I lay before you my side of the case."

I stated, you may remember, at our last meeting, that I had nowhere met with a judge or lawyer in Boston or its vicinity, who had expressed an opinion that the company are liable; and you will no doubt recollect how that statement was commented upon, and has since furnished the subject for so many communications for the press. I repeat, however, that statement here to-day; and have heard of no change since our last meeting. I have met with no one ready to maintain the doctrine of unlimited power in a transfer agent, as laid down by Judge Bronson and others; nor do I believe it will be sustained by the courts of law. Why, such a latitudinarian principle would jeopardize, or wholly destroy, the security of all kinds of incorporated or other, property intrusted to the care of directors or agents. The treasurer of the United States might defraud the government of all the money in the sub-treasury in a single day. A person having millions of property holden in this way, might go to bed as rich as Crœsus, and wake up next morning as poor as Lazarus. And yet we are gravely told that, if we deny this unlimited power to a transfer agent, no one will invest any longer in our railway, or other incorporated companies. But who, let me inquire, would ever invest in them at all hereafter, if the principle be once admitted that property in them can be rendered valueless, nay, annihilated, by the fraud of one of the officers or employés of such a company? Mr. O'Connor informs us that if we will assume the fraudulent shares, the capital stock of the company will be depreciated only forty per cent. Of course, had Mr. Schuyler issued fifty thousand instead of twenty thousand shares, it would, by the same arithmetic, have been annihilated, or rendered worthless.

But these certificates, we are told by the learned counsellors, passing from hand to hand, are very convenient, and if we deny the transfer agent the power of doing as he likes, and issuing as many as he pleases, it will greatly and injuriously retard the present expeditious mode of doing business, and incommode the Stock Exchange. Well, Mr. Chairman, suppose this be admitted, what then? When we lend our money on mortgage, we require the registry of deeds to be searched to ascertain that the property is unincumbered; and we require, also, to have a certificate from some able lawyer that the title is good; and in some places in my native state, when a person lends money to a town, he requires not only the note of the town treasurer, but also a copy of the vote of the town authorizing him to borrow the money. Why, let me ask, should we not use as much caution when we invest our money in railway or other incorporated companies, or lend it upon a hypothecation of their shares? Can any one doubt that this stupendous fraud of Robert Schuyler will introduce new safe-guards in the transfer of stocks of every kind? I shall be very much mistaken if it does not.

Those of you who have carefully read the opinions of the counsel in favor of the liability of the company, cannot, I think, have failed to remark that the principal reasons assigned by them are, first, that the power of the transfer agent is unlimited; and, secondly, that a person buying shares or lending money upon them had no access to the books of the company, and could not, therefore, ascertain whether he had over-issued or not. Judge Bronson, however, says that "if, as transfer agent, Schuyler had issued a promissory note in the name of the company, he would have stepped entirely beyond his powers, and would have bound no one but himself." It is consoling to hear from one of the learned counsellors, that there was anything he could not do, as agent of the company; but is it not plain also, that "he stepped equally beyond his powers" when he issued certificates of shares which had no existence in fact, which had and could have no value, and which were prohibited by the charter? And in case he had issued a promissory note in the name of the company, I can see no reason why it would not have been as binding as his issue of these fraudulent certificates, for the purchaser or holder in that case, also, could not have access to the books, and might have supposed that, as he was president of the company, he might have been authorized to issue the note by a special vote of the directors. If the argument be good in the one case, it would seem that it ought to be equally good in the other. You will also have probably remarked that there is a discrepancy in the opinions given by Mr. O'Connor and Judge Bronson. The first says: "I am of opinion, that the directors may refuse to recognize as stock all shares which can be clearly and certainly traced to an origin in the over-issue." The latter, however, speaking of those who are holders of what are called spurious certificates, says, "Those who have, in the usual way, obtained certificates in their own names, are stockholders in the company, and are entitled to be treated as such for all purposes." Such are the contradictions into which even the most learned and ingenious fall, when they undertake to support a doctrine not founded on truth and reason.

"Who shall decide when lawyers disagree,
And learned casuists doubt, like O and B?"

Well, Mr. Chairman, if I have succeeded in making myself understood, it will have been readily seen that, in my opinion, this question can be settled only by the judicial tribunals of the country, and there, I hope, we shall leave it. I have no fears of the result, if the case can only be brought fairly under their cognizance. But to depreciate the stock two-fifths of its value by assuming the fraudulent shares, is what, I trust, we shall never consent to do. I believe we have no right to do so, if we would. At the same time, unless compelled, I see no good reason for taking a formal vote upon the question. It was a remark of the late Mr. Webster, in his celebrated speech of the 7th of March, that "it was not expedient to re-enact a law of God." May we not say, with equal truth, that it is inexpedient "to re-enact" a law of the sovereign state of Connecticut? The shares which Robert Schuyler issued by excess are, in my opinion, null and void by the charter, and let that content us. By refusing, however, to assume them, we do not (as some have erroneously stated) refuse to pay a debt, for we do not owe one. We repudiate only the fraud of the transfer agent. But since the directors informed us, at our last meeting, that they wanted our advice, if it be your opinion that there is the remotest danger of their assuming the fraudulent certificates, or making a compromise; and that our omission to take a formal vote on the subject might be considered an implied approval, on our part, of such a course, in that case, my opinion is, that the sooner we settle the question by a stock vote, the better.

But whatever, Mr. Chairman, we may decide to do, let us reject the pernicious counsel of those who would recommend a compromise. Indeed, I cannot but express my wonder that any one should make such a suggestion. Coalition in politics, and compromise in the payment of debts! Such are the proposals which we too often hear made in these degenerate days, and which may be considered as one of the worst omens for the future. Who does not perceive at once that this company is liable, or that it is not liable? And if it be liable, has it come to this, that we are ready to compound a fraud, and, instead of paying what we owe, to make a compromise, and, like unfortunate or dishonest debtors, pay but a part of what is due our creditors?

There may be those who would recommend such a course; but I cannot believe they can be found in Connecticut, the state so distinguished for religion, morality, and high commercial honor. We are out of the atmosphere of Wall street now, and who does not feel that he breathes a purer and a freer air? When I contemplate the character of the state and of the city in which we have met together to-day, consecrated by the memory of so many illustrious, good, and distinguished men, I would say to each one of you, in the language once addressed from heaven to the Hebrew prophet, "Put off thy shoes from off thy feet; for the place whereon thou standest is holy ground." Remember that we are not acting for ourselves alone, but for the widows, orphans, poor clergymen, and savings banks, which have placed their confidence in the honor and safety of this company, and have invested their hard earnings in its stock. They look to us to do them justice, and can you doubt that they are watching our proceedings here to-day with the most painful solicitude? The tidings of what we do will soon cross the Atlantic, and be made known in England, France, Germany, and even amidst the smiling valleys and snow-capped mountains of Switzerland; for we have stockholders in all these countries, and also in the East Indies.

Let me implore you, then, so to act to-day, that, if their property is to be taken from them, the blame may not be laid to our charge, but rather to that of the established judiciary of the land. They are ready and willing to assume the responsibility, and in their hands, I hope, we shall leave the case.

Mr. Chairman, I need to say but a very few words in respect to the resolutions that I am about to offer. One should speak of himself as little as possible; but perhaps there is a propriety in my presenting these resolutions, as it is well known that I entered the campaign against Robert Schuyler as long ago as 1849, and have never taken off my armor since. Let it not now be said that I would kick the dead lion after having encountered him in his very den. If the resolutions offered by Mr. Young, at the meeting held in 1849, had been acted upon and followed, we should have been saved all this trouble to-day, and the road would, in all probability, now have been in the most prosperous condition. These resolutions not only meet my own approbation, but also that of every member of the committee. They are as follows:

Whereas, it is apparent that, to promote the prosperity and success of the New York and New Haven Railroad Company, its affairs should be conducted by managers or directors enjoying the full and entire confidence of the stockholders, and it is believed that the gentlemen at present holding the place of directors do not possess that confidence believed to be so essential; therefore,

Resolved, That the directors be, and they are hereby requested to form a new board, by successive resignations, and by filling vacancies, agreeable to the sixth section of the act of incorporation.

Resolved, That the following persons be, and they are hereby proposed, as suitable persons to fill such vacancies, viz., James J. Roosevelt, New York; J. Phillips Phenix, do.; George N. Miller, do.; Dennis Kimberly, New Haven; Nathaniel A. Bacon, do.; Moncure Robinson, Philadelphia; William L. Lyon, Greenwich; Peter T. Homer, Boston; William W. Billings, New London.

Resolved, That the directors be requested to engage the services of the Hon. Roger S. Baldwin, of New Haven, as associate counsel with Messrs. Noyes and Wood, to defend the corporation in all actions which have been, or may be brought against it.

Resolved, That we approve of the course of the directors, in having submitted the question of liability to the eminent counsel, Messrs. Noyes and Wood, and we recommend said opinion as a safe guide for their future action, and that it would be unwise, inexpedient, and hazardous for this meeting, this corporation, or its directors, to attempt, in any form, to subject the stockholders to a burthen which neither the law nor equity impose upon them.

THE PLUMMER PROFESSORSHIP.

[The following are the remarks made by Hon. S. D. Bradford, in the Board of Overseers of Harvard College, on Thursday afternoon last, on the question of confirming the appointment of Rev. F. D. Huntington to be Plummer professor. —*Boston Daily Advertiser, April 14th*, 1855.]

Mr. President,—I rise with great reluctance to offer a few observations upon the question now under discussion, viz., the confirmation by this board of the nomination of the Rev. F. D. Huntington, as Plummer professor in the University at Cambridge.

Finding that great injustice was done to the motives which governed the vote I gave upon the confirmation of another nomination, that of Judge Loring, upon a recent occasion for another professorship, I am unwilling by giving a silent vote to-day, to subject myself to a repetition of the same difficulty. On that occasion, my vote was declared, by one part of the public press, to have been in favor of Judge Loring, and, by another, against him, which could not have happened had a discussion taken place as I considered most expedient; but other counsels prevailed. The question before us to-day must, I think, on many accounts, be considered as the most important which has been brought to the notice of the board for a great number of years.

It seems to me to open the whole question of the establishment of sectarian religion in the college at Cambridge.

I intend to use the word sectarian in no offensive sense,

but as indicating certain opinions in religion, entertained by a party which has separated itself from the established church, (where one exits,) or which holds tenets different from those of the prevailing denomination in a kingdom or state.

Perhaps, to prevent all misconception, I ought rather to have said that it opens the whole question of uniting religious with secular instruction in the university.

I would not, on any account, impute to the government of the college the design of establishing sectarian religion there, for I believe there is nothing more remote from their intentions or wishes; but I may, I hope, be permitted to express the strong fears I have that, if the Plummer professorship be established, they will be suspected, if not actually charged, with such a design; and that it may lead to consequences of the most injurious character to the prosperity and welfare of the university.

No one can have attended to the reading of the statutes or rules of the proposed professorship, without perceiving that they establish a religious teacher in the university. The professor is to officiate at morning and evening prayers, to preach to the government and students on Sundays, to deliver lectures, and to cultivate with the students habits of the closest intimacy, with a view to their religious and moral improvement.

I remember that, during a discussion at Cambridge, in 1853, upon the question of appointing a pastoral teacher for the college, when the question was asked, by a member of the board, why, if such a proceeding were expedient, measures were not taken to re-establish or revive the Hollis professorship, the answer was, that the very name had such an effect upon the religious sensibilities of some persons, it was dangerous even to speak of it; and now, as I am obliged to look upon the question, the proposition before this board is to supersede the Hollis professorship, and establish another in its place, with duties, responsibilities, and functions, of a greatly extended character.

I was four years at Cambridge, under the late Professor Henry Ware, who was then Hollis professor of Divinity; but, if I understand the statutes or rules of the Plummer professorship, they require double the duty to be performed by Mr. Huntington which was ever performed by the late Dr. Ware, with the exception of hearing the students recite.

In those days, there was very little of any personal intercourse between the Hollis professor and the undergraduates; and the sight of a professor in a student's room was as rare and uncommon as that of a bishop, a few years since, in some of the rural districts of England.

I can speak feelingly on this subject, for, having been appointed, in my junior year, to deliver a sermon before a certain religious society, to which I belonged, we invited the Hollis professor to be present; and, much to my astonishment and dismay, he attended, but never can I forget the effect it produced on me. *Vox hæsit faucibus.*

Now, Mr. President, if the consequences of having had a Hollis professor, (with the limited duties he had to perform,) have been such, formerly, that it is dangerous even to allude to the subject, may we not anticipate still more serious consequences from the proposed establishment of the Plummer professorship, upon the more extended scale I have mentioned? It seems to me it cannot be otherwise, and that such a state of things must be prejudicial to the interests of the college, which I am most anxious to preserve from being charged with sectarian influence of any kind.

It is but a short time since the complaint was frequently heard, that there was little if any addition, from year to year, to the number of students at Cambridge, and the question was often asked, how happens it, when every thing else in this state has increased so much, (the population having then reached nearly a million,) the number of students at Cambridge is almost stationary?

Now for the last few years we have witnessed a most gratifying change. The students have greatly increased in number, and are beginning to be sent there in an increased ratio, by Orthodox, as well as Unitarian, parents; and I had fancied it was partly because our Orthodox friends, (a good number of whom are now members of this board,) have inquired into the matter for themselves, found all right at Cambridge, and have made a favorable report to their brethren, that there really is no religious test at the college, and that each and every sect is fairly dealt with. I believe this has always been the case, but I have heard that, at one time, a different opinion prevailed in the country, and that it was supposed to have had an injurious effect upon the prosperity and growth of the college.

Some persons may perhaps think that I am unnecessarily alarmed on the subject of sectarian religion as connected with education; but it has been my fortune to witness the evil effects of attempting to unite religious with secular instruction, not only in my own country, but in Great Britain also, where it has defeated every attempt of the government to establish a system of national education. Ministry after ministry has brought forward its plan to accomplish an object of such vast importance, but every one has failed on this account.

Most educationists agree that religion is too important a part of education to be omitted in any complete system, if men could only agree in defining religious truth, and the proper mode of imparting it; but this agreement seems to be utterly impracticable.

In a debate, some time ago, in England, on this subject,

Lord Brougham addressed the House of Lords in a speech of great power, a few paragraphs of which, with your permission, Mr. President, I will read to the board. It was during a debate on education.

The Marquis of Lansdowne intimated that the government had seriously considered the practicability of a plan which had been proposed, but had given it up on account of the religious dissensions which stood in the way.

Lord Brougham exposed this mischievous *odium theologicum* very happily.

> "But why," said he, "could not such a system be adopted? He could tell their lordships frankly, very frankly; it was because they had two classes of the community, for both of which he had the most profound and inviolable respect, he meant the members of the church and members of dissenting congregations, each in their sphere, great promoters of education, and deeply interested in the training of youth. He was not speaking of the clergy, but of the community, although the clergy were most sedulously bent on the promotion of education. But there was one thing which both the church and the dissenters preferred, and that was controversy, which made them neglect the great object of education, and made them prefer, more than anything else, victory. They lost sight of the main object in the glory of the victory. That was what he universally found. The church would not have any system which was so comprehensive as not to allow of any clerical interference; the dissenters would not have any system that allowed the least interference on the part of the church; and, therefore, unhappily between the two, education went more or less to the wall."

Since the delivery of this speech, various plans have been proposed, especially one by Mr. Cobden, dividing the kingdom into districts, appointing in each nine commissioners of education, no two of which should be of the same religious opinions; but all have failed, for the reasons given by Lord Brougham; and the work of national education stands still.

Such have been the effects of attempting to unite religious and secular education in England, and against which I wish, if possible, to guard our beloved university.

My desire is to open its gates as wide as possible, that students of all denominations may come in and share the great advantages it affords, without distinction of sect or party.

The picture I have drawn so feebly, is no fancy sketch, but a similar state of things may arise amongst ourselves sooner than we anticipate.

I have already said, that I consider the Plummer as superseding the Hollis professorship; and when I reflect how generously that noble benefactor, Hollis, bestowed his money upon the college, (commencing in 1719 and ending only with his life,) having given it a sum valued at six thousand pounds, (a vast amount in those days,) I cannot help feeling that a professorship bearing his venerated name is the last one which should be permitted to fall into abeyance, or be superseded by another.

I would not express any opinion upon the right or propriety of appropriating funds, not otherwise disposed of, to increase the income of some particular professorship, but, if this be ever done, I can conceive of no case which has such claims as the Hollis professorship.

When I consider, too, the noble liberality of Hollis, so that, when preparing the rules for his professorship, he required no subscription to a creed, nor any confession of faith, except that "the Scriptures of the Old and New Testament are the only rule of faith and practice;" and that, though he was a Baptist himself, all he asked was that a person's being one might not operate to his exclusion as a candidate for the professorship, I cannot express the admiration I feel for the character of such a Christian; and I have long thought that to have appointed one of his own sect to the professorship he established, (had it been deemed proper by the corporation,) would have been a most appropriate tribute to the universal respect and esteem which every one has for his memory.

Mr. President, I would, on no account, find fault with the corporation for the interpretation they have put upon the words of Miss Plummer's will to establish a professorship "upon the Philosophy of the Heart." I can easily imagine their task to have been anything but an easy one, and that, had the duty been assigned to seven different persons having no communication with one another, each might have produced several pages of statutes or rules having nothing in common, and each differing from the other. I will add that it is with much regret I find the words have been construed in such a manner that I cannot vote in the way I could have wished.

After due deliberation and reflection, is the necessity of making this appointment so urgent as some have supposed? And here I cannot avoid expressing the surprise which has filled me when I have heard some persons speak of the religious and moral condition of the students at Cambridge, lamenting that there were "no religious influences in operation there." No religious influences at Cambridge! Is that fiction, or is it fact? Are there not religious exercises in the chapel twice a day? Is there not divine service on Sundays also in the chapel? Do not the students use the works of Paley, Butler, and other writers on religion or morals as text-books? And do not their teachers always impress upon them, when they can, the necessity of religion and good morals?

There are some persons of such looks and manners, you cannot come into their presence without feeling that they exercise a religious and salutary influence over you; and I have always felt that the president of the university was one of that number, and I doubt not many others have had that feeling, and the students also, whose conduct, at the present time, I am firmly convinced, would bear a favorable comparison with that of any former period in the history of the college.

We ought to think of the unruly part of the students, (and there will be some such in every college,) as Burke said during the French revolution the people of England should think of certain persons in that country, "Because," says he, "a parcel of grasshoppers, on a summer's day under a fern, make a whole field resound with their importunate clink, whilst hundreds of noble cattle under the British oak chew the cud and are silent, we must not think that they are the only tenants of the field."

No doubt there is room for improvement there, and the attempt, on the part of the corporation, to improve the moral condition of those entrusted to their care is praiseworthy in the highest degree. I can also easily believe that Mr. Huntington is eminently qualified for the office it is proposed to assign him; but I cannot permit this consideration to influence me so far as to give my vote in favor of establishing this new professorship, which afterwards we may have reason to regret.

The moral propriety of separating secular from religious instruction is gaining advocates, I think, everywhere. Some time ago it received an unexpected sanction, as it were, from the other world, in a posthumous declaration of the late Dr. Chalmers in favor of the separation.

It required some moral courage to express such an opinion, in Scotland, too, a country in which, I remember, some years since, that the works of Sir Walter Scott were voted out of a circulating library at Aberdeen, as of an irreligious tendency on account of the manner in which he had written concerning the Covenanters, nor is it probable Dr. Chalmers would have ever expressed such an opinion had it not been forced upon him by the conviction that otherwise the work of education would continue to stand still. No one, I believe, dared to apply to him the epithet of infidel, though it had been applied to so many others who had ventured to advocate the same doctrine.

Should there appear to be any inconsistency on my part in favoring the reëstablishment of the Hollis, whilst I oppose the establishment of the Plummer professorship, I would remark that many reasons might be assigned in favor of an ancient professorship which formed a part of the college for so many years, which do not apply to the one last named; but they are so easily perceived, it is not necessary to name them.

There are other suggestions, Mr. President, I might make in favor of the view I have felt constrained to take of the question before us, but I have already occupied too much time, and will conclude by again expressing my regret that I cannot cast my vote in favor of the proposition laid before this board by the corporation.

CONDUCT OF THE PRESS.

REMARKS MADE AT THE ANNUAL MEETING OF THE NEW YORK AND NEW HAVEN RAILROAD COMPANY, HELD AT NEW HAVEN, MAY 10, 1855.

MR. PRESIDENT,—It gives me great pleasure to meet you and our other fellow stockholders once more in this good city of New Haven, not upon any extraordinary call of the directors or shareholders, as happened last year, but at our annual meeting, as prescribed in the charter.

I do not know that there is any particular reason why I should make any demand upon your time and patience upon this occasion, but, as some too partial friends have suggested that my silence might be misunderstood, I propose to make a few observations, to which your attention is respectfully invited. You may probably recollect that, when we assembled here on the eighth of November last, it devolved upon me, as chairman of a committee, chosen in New York, to make a full and particular report upon the affairs of the New York and New Haven Railroad, past, present, and future; but that, for want of time, it was not forthcoming.

It was perceived that a new board of directors would probably be chosen soon; that then a thorough examination would have to be made, and could be prosecuted under their direction at the office in New York, and without the large expenditure that the investigation first called for must have cost.

By the printed report of the president and directors just published, you will have seen how thorough and searching their examination must have been, and what a full statement of facts they have been able to lay before us, especially as relates to the stupendous fraud of Robert Schuyler, which seems to increase in magnitude as the investigation proceeds.

The results at which the directors have arrived, are deduced from an examination of the books of the company, and answer some of the resolutions which were passed at the meeting in New York in October last, but there are others which could be answered in a satisfactory manner, only by having the power to send for persons and papers under the authority of a subpœna, which the directors had no right to use. Further important disclosures may, perhaps, be made during the trial of cases now in progress in the courts at New York.

It gives me great pleasure to state that, so far as I have been able to ascertain the sentiments of the numerous stockholders, (whose proxies I hold,) they highly approve of the injunction obtained on the 30th of January last, to prevent the holders of the fraudulent certificates commencing any new suits, (which would have been attended with great expense to the company,) and obliging them all to come in under the general bill of interpleader, prepared by our distinguished and vigilant counsel, Messrs. Noyes, Powers, and Tallmadge.

With respect to the course adopted here in November, in voting not to assume the spurious shares, or to appoint a committee of compromise, I think I may safely say that, whatever doubts there may have been in the minds of some persons, upon the expediency and justice of the decision then taken, there is now almost a universal consent amongst people of reflection, everywhere, that the plan adopted was just, honorable, and the only one likely to lead to any satisfactory result; that the idea of a compromise was impracticable, if not degrading and utopian; and that, if there ever was a case in which an appeal to the judiciary was imperatively called for, this was that case. I will add, that amongst all the stockholders in New England, with whom I have conversed on the subject, only one has suggested an adjustment by compromise.

We were told, you may perhaps remember, at both our meetings, by certain gentlemen, that, if we would only assume the fraudulent shares, (as the stockholders in the Parker Vein Coal Company, and the Vermont Central Railroad had done, upon discovering the frauds of which they had been the victims,) all our difficulties would disappear, we should regain the confidence of the public, and our stock would rise to a high figure in the market.

How this prediction has been falsified in the cases cited, I need not relate. The prices at which such scrip is selling, speak in a language which none can misunderstand, and warn us, in a manner we should never forget, that the advice of interested parties should always be received with great caution, and be well considered before adopting it. The last quotation I have seen of Vermont Central, was two dollars and eighty-seven and a half cents a share! Corporations, deeply indebted, and not knowing which way to turn, may feign to act with liberality in assuming debts which legally they do not owe; but they should always be just before they are generous, and pay their old debts before they incur new ones. The New York and New Haven Railroad Company have no occasion or desire to buy a credit on such conditions.

You may, perhaps, remember also, that a day or two previous to our meeting at the Apollo Rooms, in New York, there was a public notice given in the *New York Herald*, that a numerous committee had been appointed by the Board of Brokers, "to fight the New York and New Haven Railroad Company," with ample funds, which had been provided for the purpose.

It was not particularly stated in what manner the contest was to be carried on, whether through the press, or the method usual in such cases, the courts of law. The notice was no doubt official, and, from the violence and malignity of the newspaper communications, which appeared between our first meeting in New York and that which took place on the eighth of November, at New Haven, it would now appear that the press was the principal organ selected for carrying on the war, together with the circulation of certain legal opinions which had been purchased for the same purpose, and sent broadcast through New York and Connecticut. It happened, however, that, soon after the signal defeat which the holders of spurious shares met with at New Haven, little was said upon the subject in the newspapers, and many persons supposed that the firing had ceased for want of ammunition, or that they had changed their opinions as to the validity of their shares. Recently, however, the attacks have been repeated, with increased virulence; and I presume you must all remember the pathetic appeals, which were made a few weeks ago in the *Herald*, to some of "the prominent merchants and citizens of New York" who were shareholders, to stop the bill of interpleader, and to force a compromise; and you must also have observed what a withering reproof they received in the perfect apathy of the stockholders, and in their determination not to interfere.

It is painful to paint such a portrait of the press as it exists in our country, because, with all its defects, we are so much indebted to it for our civil and religious rights. Every one knows what good it is capable of achieving when guided by justice and truth, and that, fortunately, in the minds of respectable persons, it signally defeats its own object when it becomes venal, false, and malicious.

If, however, when a case involving a large pecuniary sum is soon to be acted upon in the courts of law, the custom is growing up in New York (as is daily asserted) of prejudging it by means of newspaper communications, by personal attacks of the most malignant character upon one side or the other, with the intention of influencing not only public opinion at large, but the judges and juries also who are to try the cause, I say, if such a practice is to be tolerated, we may retain the forms of justice, but the spirit will leave us, and our boasted freedom will be only a name. It cannot fail, unless reprobated and put down, to deteriorate the character of the Bench, of which we have long been so justly proud, and to which we are all so much indebted, for no country can have any great reason to complain when the judges are governed by the principles of truth and justice, and when the law is equitably administered. It was the purity of the ermine, which probably preserved England from a revolution, previous to the passage of the Reform Bill in 1832; for a people will endure a great inequality in their civil rights so long as they can look up to the judges on the bench as equally the defenders of the rich and the poor, the high and the humble. May our judges ever remain just and true men, so that each may be able to exclaim, in the words of the poet,

"Welcome business, welcome strife,
Welcome the cares of ermined life;
The visage wan, the purblind sight,
The toil by day, the lamp by night,
The tedious forms, the solemn prate,
The pert dispute, the dull debate,
The drowsy bench, the babbling hall,—
For thee, fair Justice, welcome all!"

What I have said of the press in general will not apply

to all the public journals, for the *Journal of Commerce*, and a few others, have pursued a course, as respects this contest, of which no one could justly complain.

And now, for a moment, let us inquire what have the shareholders of the New York and New Haven Railroad Company done to call down upon them the denunciations of the press? They have charged Robert Schuyler with forgery; with procuring money upon false pretences; and with having exceeded his power as transfer agent, but in a manner not binding upon the corporation. They have lost, by their connection with him, at a moderate estimate, a million of dollars, for it has been computed, by a competent engineer, that his having accepted the road, before it was properly completed, has probably cost the company half a million, not to mention other heavy losses, as is proved by the books. Who will deny these charges? In consequence of Mr. Schuyler's having left the company, with a floating debt of four hundred and forty-three thousand dollars, instead of one hundred and forty thousand dollars, (as stated by him on the eleventh of May, 1854) they have still a debt of one hundred and twenty-six thousand dollars, and yet these holders of spurious certificates turn round and abuse the company, because they will not acknowledge them, and speak of them as retaining dividends which should be distributed, when they ought to know there is no money on hand to divide, nor is there likely to be any soon. They know they cannot be admitted as stockholders, without violating the charter, even if they had any right to be so admitted, and they confess it would reduce the value of the shares to sixty cents upon the dollar; and yet the Mechanics Bank of New York, in its action against the company, have demanded payment at the rate of ninety-four cents on the dollar of the spurious stock, being upwards of fifty per cent. more than the genuine shares are worth, if the principle the bank contends for, prevails.

Unjustifiable and disgraceful, however, as the assaults have been, I am glad the company have preserved a dignified silence, trusting to the justice of their cause; and I am not aware of the expenditure of a single dollar on their part to influence public opinion one way or the other. They have acted, from first to last, upon the principle,—" *Virtus tutissima cassis.*"

They have appealed to the established tribunals of the country, not doubting that they will decide the question at issue according to justice and the law.

The principle involved in the decision, whatever it may be, is second, probably, in importance to none which has ever before exercised the legal acumen of the Bench, and no doubt they so consider it. If decided against the company, no prudent man will ever invest again in a corporation of any kind. He will also dispose of any property he may hold thus situated with the least possible delay; but a decision drawing after it such consequences I trust we are never destined to deplore.

Mr. President, I am gratified to see around me such a general attendance of stockholders, and I hope this will continue not only during the difficulties under which we labor at present, but also when those embarrassments shall have passed away. I have not attended the annual meetings as I should have done. It is true I had great fears for the safety of the corporation for several years before the forgery and escape of Schuyler were discovered, and communicated them to other shareholders. I had no personal acquaintance with the president, but it required very little foresight to perceive that he must soon break down, with four railroads upon his back; and then I hoped there would have been an end to his mismanagement of our property. I was active, also, in coöperation with Mr. Henry Young, of New York, and other stockholders, in November, 1849, in the attempt to get rid of him; but we were outvoted, principally by proxies in the hands of Schuyler and his particular friends, and so his power was prolonged until these embarrassments have come upon the company.

It has been said, by a profound moralist, that no man becomes a villain all at once, and by that rule it is reasonable to suppose that Schuyler commenced his nefarious practices long before he became connected with the New York and New Haven Railroad Company, and probably continued them during the eight years he acted as president. The annual meetings, I have heard, were not well attended; and thus we may all learn a lesson, that it is by vigilance only we can maintain our liberty or our prosperity.

Permit me, before I take my seat, to thank you, fellow stockholders, for the patience with which you have listened to my remarks upon the present and upon prior occasions. I believe it is known to most of you already, that I was no volunteer in the war now being carried on between the company and the holders of the fraudulent certificates of shares. The laurels to be gained by a contest with Wall street, are not of a character which my ambition has ever coveted. You may remember, perhaps, the report of the Schuyler directors, which was read at the Apollo rooms, to which was annexed the opinion of two most eminent counsel of New York, that the company were in no way liable for the fraudulent issues; but when, after reading the report, the president rose, and said he considered it was a case for compromise, I could remain silent no longer. Although a stranger to almost every one in the room, my remarks were received with favor, and, from that time to the present, I have done what I could to keep the company out of the hands of the Philistines; and have labored, that equal justice should be done to all. My course on that occasion was also approved by the shareholders in Boston and its vicinity, so that, at the next meeting, without any solicitation on my part, they sent me their proxies to vote upon nearly two thousand shares.

I have reason to believe that a legal decision will be given in the suit of the Mechanic's Bank, in the course of a few weeks, by the Superior Court of New York, consisting of six judges, presided over by that distinguished jurist, Judge Oakley; and I trust that, in due time, the New York and New Haven Railroad may be extricated from all its difficulties, and become, not only one of the best conducted, but also one of the most profitable thoroughfares in the country.

CHARACTER OF MRS. GREENWOOD.

[We published, a few days since, a notice of a venerated and much-beloved lady, and from another friend we have received the following.—*Boston Daily Advertiser.*]

DIED, in this city, on Tuesday, June 5th, Mrs. Mary Langdon Greenwood, widow of the late W. P. Greenwood, and mother of the late distinguished divine, F. W. P. Greenwood.

Several days have elapsed since the papers announced the decease of this excellent woman, and, on Thursday last, her remains were conveyed to their final resting-place, at Mount Auburn, followed by many of her attached relatives and friends. It was on a summer's day, when all nature was radiant with beauty and loveliness, and seemed to rejoice amidst the richness of the verdure, and the fragrance of the blossoms and flowers, which, by contrast, seemed, if possible, to increase the sorrow which weighed so heavily upon the hearts of the mourners. The country, on some accounts, appeared more lovely than ever before; as if nature intended to make amends for the length and severity of the last tedious winter. Autumn, towards its close, would have been a more appropriate emblem of the scene; for then the decay of vegetation, and the falling of the leaves, are significant of death, and remind us all that "our life is a shadow which continueth not."

Every thing without indicated joy and happiness; every thing within, that a beloved relative and friend had departed for another and better world. Every eye was moistened with tears, whilst every tongue spoke of the uncommon virtues and excellences which distinguished the character of the deceased; and who can wonder at this, that ever enjoyed the privilege of her acquaintance, or was favored with her confidence and regard? To describe her domestic life and character would be to present a portrait of most of the virtues which are most valued and esteemed in the world. Benevolent to a degree seldom witnessed, she was never so happy as when she could do a kindness to another. Hospitable in the largest sense of the word, she was always gratified when she could receive and entertain her friends. She was a noble specimen of a woman; such as is but seldom seen, and can never be forgotten. Nature had endowed her not only with one of the kindest of hearts, but also with remarkable mental powers, so that her conversation instructed whilst it delighted the hearer. In early life, she evinced a decided talent as a writer, especially as a discriminating reviewer of the compositions of others; and, had her domestic occupations permitted, it is not doubted she might have gained an enviable reputation as an author. Her reading was extensive, and there was a discrimination about her mind, which is found but in few persons. Her conversation was various, discursive, and highly entertaining, but always marked by wisdom and goodness. Her perception was quick and discerning, and this continued to the last. The body only seemed enfeebled by disease, and not the mind; for the decay of physical strength, and the want of her usual activity, seemed rather to increase the powers of her mind. Her interest in the happiness and welfare of others appeared to become greater as her own strength and health continued to fail; and she thought more of others at the time when most people think more and more of themselves. Nothing could exceed the cares she manifested for the happiness of her children and grandchildren; and their love and attachment for her seemed always in proportion to the kindness conferred, and gratified her much. Her manner towards the young proved that she had explored every avenue to the youthful heart.

It has been said, by a beautiful German writer, that "a contemplative, meditative, and evective life is the most exalted state of existence, and that it is only in old age it can be fully enjoyed; as at an earlier period it is constantly coming into collision with our necessities and active duties." Our departed friend was a striking example of the correctness of this; remark and, if it be true that it sometimes requires a hundred years for the oak to come to perfection, it may also seem sometimes to require a period of nearly the same length to produce such a woman as Mary Langdon Greenwood.

"The spirit increases in perfection," says Comaro, "as the body grows older;" which was also illustrated in her life; and if the theory of a recent French writer be true, that "the second period of old age begins at eighty-five," it may be safely affirmed that, in this case, the mind was fully equal to another term, and required only a new body. Even her memory was quick and retentive to the last. Her countenance was full of intelligence, and very pleasing; her figure was noble and commanding; and the soul, the spirit within, was worthy of the form which contained it.

It has pleased a wise and just, but merciful Providence, to take her from us in a good old age, honored and esteemed by all; but those who have been benefited by her counsels and example; the poor, who for so many years have shared her bounty; the young, who have been guided and cheered by her wisdom and advice; her bereaved children, grandchildren, and other relatives and friends who have always taken so much delight in her society, and to whom she was so much attached; in short, every one who had the good fortune of knowing her will never forget the exemplary Christian and friend, whom they have lost. Her surviving relatives may think that such various excellences of character require no monument of brass or marble; and when those who knew her in life shall recognize her resting-place in Mount Auburn, they may be reminded, perhaps, of one of the apothegms of Lord Bacon, who relates that, " when Cato the elder, at a time when many of the Romans had statues erected in their honor, was asked by one in a kind of wonder, why he had none, he answered, 'He had much rather men should ask and wonder why he had no statue, than why he had a statue.' "

S. D. B.

VINDICATION OF THE OVERSEERS OF HARVARD COLLEGE.

[At the meeting, Thursday afternoon, of the overseers of Harvard College, while the report of the committee, recommending a concurrence with the corporation in the establishment of a new professorship in the Law School was under consideration, Samuel D. Bradford, Esq., a member of the board, made the following remarks in vindication of the action of the overseers upon the nomination of Judge Loring.
Boston Atlas.]

Mr. President,—I rise with some reluctance to offer a few observations upon a subject not now before this board, but upon which so much has been said by the press and the public generally, that I may almost claim a portion of your time and attention for the sake of making a personal explanation.

I allude to the rejection of the nomination of Edward Greely Loring, Esq., as lecturer in the Law School at Cambridge, on the 15th of February last, concerning which such bitter complaints have been made, and such unworthy motives imputed to the members of this board, who voted in favor of that rejection.

As one of that number, I have long desired an occasion for stating the motives which governed my vote, and I avail myself of this first appropriate opportunity of doing so.

In order, however, to have the question fully understood, it will be necessary to recite briefly the history of the case, and to begin with Mr. Loring's first connection with the Law School, which dates from the 31st of January, 1852, on which day it appears that, at a meeting of the president and fellows, the following votes were passed, viz.:

Voted, That the Honorable Edward Greely Loring be appointed lecturer in the Law School for the remainder of the academical year.

Voted, That the compensation of the law lecturer be at the rate of one thousand dollars per annum.

This nomination was presented to the board of overseers, at their meeting, held on the 5th of February, 1852, and, at an adjournment of said meeting, on the 19th of February, 1852, was confirmed, and was, of course, to continue for a little over six months, viz., to the end of the academical year.

When this appointment was first announced, nearly four years since, it would be no exaggeration to say that it produced not a little surprise amongst some of the members of the Suffolk bar, and it is confidently believed that the public generally regarded it as one of doubtful expediency, and there is reason to believe, also, that many, amongst the overseers themselves, were in great doubt how they ought to vote.

The fact of his being judge of probate for the county of Suffolk was considered, by many, as a weighty objection, and this may have made a deeper impression on their minds from the circumstance that there had been one or more attempts made to raise his salary, as judge of probate, and much had been said, in the public journals and before the legislature, concerning the multifarious and severe duties of that office; and it actually appears by the record that, when the vote was finally taken, of the thirty members of the board who were present, four abstained from voting, one cast a blank vote, and seven voted in the negative.

If the nomination had been for a longer term, or had it, after a discussion, been referred to a committee, it may be a question if the nomination would have been confirmed.

On the 23d of December, 1853, Mr. Loring had been law lecturer sixteen months after his term had expired, by its own limitation, and now a second time our attention is called to him. On that day the corporation established a new professorship in the Law School, and elected Mr. Loring university professor of law, with a salary of twenty-five hundred dollars per annum.

These proceedings were laid before the overseers, at their meeting, on the 25th of January, 1854, and at an adjourned meeting, on the 9th of February following, the whole subject, on the suggestion of Mr. Winthrop, and on the motion of Mr. Bassett, was referred to a committee appointed by Governor Washburn, then in the chair.

This committee made a very elaborate and thorough examination of the whole subject, and, at an adjourned meeting of the board, held the 9th of March, 1854, presented, through Mr. Bassett, their chairman, a very able report, and unanimously recommended that the overseers should not concur with the corporation.

After having given some account of the Law School from its commencement, and of the course of education there, and made some remarks on the question of the expediency of establishing a new professorship, they proceed as follows:

"There are some views which might be taken with regard to the proposition to establish a new professorship, if that proposition stood alone, detached from other propositions. But it does not stand alone. The subject of a professorship comes to this board with a professor to occupy it, already elected on the part of the corporation. The committee have felt obliged to consider the choice of the professor as bearing directly on the question of a professorship.

"Of the terms and conditions upon which the office is tendered to the professor, the committee must freely and fully speak, and they require the careful attention of this board.

"It is well known that the gentleman elected now holds the important and responsible office of judge of probate for the county of Suffolk, and your committee have been informed and believe that he is to continue to hold that office. The proposition, therefore, is to establish a new professorship, with a gentleman to fill the office, who is charged with all the duties and responsibilities of the judge of probate for the county of Suffolk.

"The duties of the judge must of course take precedence of the duties of the professor. To form some idea of the extent to which the duties of the judge will interfere with the duties of the professor, it may be needful to refer briefly and generally to the duties of the judge of probate for the county of Suffolk.

"There are, within his jurisdiction, one hundred and forty or fifty thousand inhabitants, with more than two hundred millions of taxable property. The annual number of deaths of these inhabitants is about four thousand, and the number of estates to be annually settled must be large. For several years, the annual amount of property entered in the probate of Suffolk is believed to have been about seven millions of dollars; and, the last year, it may probably have been ten millions. The amount of property, therefore, which comes within the jurisdiction of this judge is immense, and, in regard to it, he has great duties to perform. Grave and difficult questions of law and equity are to be examined and settled. Contested matters of fact are to be patiently heard and decided. Administrators, and guardians, and trustees, are to be appointed; bonds to a great amount are to be approved and taken; and complicated accounts are to be examined and allowed; and there is a great amount of other matters, which need not be particularly mentioned.

"The relation of the judge of probate to the inhabitants is peculiar, and requires that he should be within its jurisdiction, and always accessible to the bereaved and friendless, the widows and orphans who are particularly under his care and protection. From this brief view, it would seem quite apparent that the duties of the judge cannot be fully and faithfully performed without much time and labor, and great and constant care and watchfulness.

"But, besides matters of property, the judge of probate has jurisdiction of questions deeply affecting personal liberty. Applications are made to him to place under guardianship persons who are alleged to be insane; and also persons who are spendthrifts. These are often cases of great delicacy and difficulty, requiring long and patient hearing, and most careful and thorough inquiry and research. If a professor is required and expected to perform his duty in the school, it would seem hardly suitable to select a person encumbered with such additional duties, unless, from his character and standing, he could render as much aid and assistance to the school as another man without these incumbrances. Such was the case of Judge Story. His great fame, great talents, and great attainments, enabled him to do more for the school, with all his judicial duties upon him, than could be done by any other man, who was free from such other labors. But Judge Story was an extraordinary man, and his case forms an exception, not a rule."

No part of this report has been ever published. It was known at the time, that this portion of it was written by the distinguished gentleman who had then recently retired from the bench of the Supreme Court.

The report gave rise to an animated and protracted discussion. No definitive vote was taken; and, on the motion of the Rev. Dr. Worcester, of Salem, who desired to express his views in favor of the report, the same was laid aside without being disposed of, and the board adjourned to March the 23d. Every appearance, however, indicated that it would have been accepted by a decisive vote, had it been taken.

At the adjourned meeting, on the 23d of March, the president of the university laid before the board a vote of the corporation, rescinding their former votes to establish a new professorship, and nominating Mr. Loring as its occupant, and withdrawing the same altogether; and the overseers took no further action as to said report.

But, Mr. President, we have not yet done with the Hon. E. G. Loring; for, on the 25th of January, 1855, at the annual meeting of the overseers, a vote of the corporation was laid before the board, nominating him as lecturer in the Law School, but without mentioning any term for which he was to hold the office.

This nomination, with others, was postponed till the adjourned meeting on the 15th of February, when Mr. Loring was rejected by a vote of about two to one.

Such is a brief and concise statement of the case; and who, after hearing it, will venture to affirm that those gentlemen who voted in the negative on the 15th of February, did so without the most substantial and satisfactory reasons? I can speak for myself, at any rate, and will say that, before I cast my vote, I made the most particular inquiries, from various members of the bar, as to Mr. Loring's qualifications, all of whom expressed the opinion, that the nomination ought not to be confirmed. Being personally unknown to the gentleman, I availed myself of the information of others, who had always known him in his profession.

They all spoke highly of him as a gentleman and estimable citizen, but did not consider him as well adapted to the office of law lecturer. No doubt, other members of the board were equally diligent in their inquiries, and voted against his nomination for the same reasons which influenced me; and yet, we all remember what unworthy motives were assigned to them by the press, and they were condemned at a meeting of the law students at Cambridge, no doubt because the young gentlemen there were unacquainted with the facts in the case; for I would not do them the injustice to suppose they would have passed the resolutions they did had they known all the particulars.

But, besides the objections already named, there was another, entitled to no small consideration, to the appointment of Mr. Loring as law lecturer at Cambridge. This was the circumstance, (since become so prominent,) that he was, at that very time—the 15th of February, 1855, a commissioner of the Circuit Court of the United States, to perform various duties pursuant to several acts of congress; and, by the act passed in 1850, was intrusted with large powers and duties. In that capacity, he is liable at all times to be called upon to act in cases of extradition of fugitives from justice from foreign countries, with whose governments we have treaties on the subject; also, as relates to revolts and mutinies on board of ships, and crimes on the high seas; and, by the act of 1850, called the Fugitive Slave law, according to Mr. Loring's own construction of its provisions, (as appears by his remonstrance to the last legislature):—

> "The duty of commissioners of the Circuit Court of the United States is imperative upon them; for, by the terms of the act, they are not merely authorized, but they are expressly required, to exercise and discharge all the powers and duties conferred by the act. An application made, pursuant to law, to any commissioner, fixes that duty on him, and, after such application, he can neither decline nor evade it; for, if he could legally do so, all others might: and then not only the statute, but the constitution of the United States, would be violated, and the public faith pledged to it, and the oaths taken to support it, would be broken."

I am sure, Mr. President, I need not enter into all the particulars of what Mr. Loring may be called upon at any time to do under such a commission; for I cannot doubt it will be seen at once, that holding such an appointment may become at any time quite incompatible with his duty of lecturing or holding moot courts at Cambridge.

Let it not, however, be understood that I find any fault with Mr. Loring's course in relation to these matters. So long as he holds the important office, which he has always indicated it was his intention to retain, I trust he will always discharge his duty in the same fearless, upright, and independent manner on all occasions, as he has done heretofore; and I will venture here to add, that, when upon a recent occasion an attempt was made to deprive him of the office, the duties of which he had so conscientiously performed, I believe that no one in the commonwealth rejoiced more than I did, that the executive power was in the hands of a chief magistrate who had the moral courage to support the independence of the judiciary, the bulwark of our safety, and to sustain Judge Loring for having been true to the constitution, the Union, and the laws. At the same time, were I called upon to act on his nomination again, I would not confer on him an important office in the college, the performance of the duties of which might become, at any time, incompatible with his other great and onerous duties.

Before I take my seat, Mr. President, there is one other subject on which I would say a few words, and that is the imperative duty of the members of the corporation, as also of this board, (whatever we may do,) to be governed always by considerations only of what is right, and will promote the best and highest interests of the college; but never to act with reference to the interest of personal friends or connections. Let us abjure the spirit of nepotism, that we may avoid the fatal consequences which it never fails to produce.

Now, may Heaven forgive me if I do injustice to any one by the suspicion, but it did seem to me that in the case of Mr. Loring there must have been influences at work which caused his nomination to be pressed upon the board with so much pertinacity beyond any intrinsic merits which any candid person could assign to him. I am confirmed in this opinion by the unusual, and I must call it unwarrantable, course, pursued by his friends.

When his nomination was finally rejected, on the 15th of February last, was it such a course as a true regard for the welfare of the college dictated, or such a one as it was supposed would most promote the private interests of Mr. Loring? It was at once proclaimed by his friends, in the newspapers and elsewhere, that his rejection was to be attributed wholly to his decision in the case of Burns, the fugitive slave; a statement, in my opinion, without the least foundation, but one at the same time better calculated than any other, to injure the Law School, by preventing young gentlemen from the South connecting themselves with it; and, if there has been any decline in the number of the students, it may probably be imputed to this cause.

This statement was sent broadcast through the land, and I noticed was copied *in extenso* by those editors in New York and other places, whose religious sentiments were opposed to those which, it has sometimes been asserted, are most favored at Cambridge.

Had the charge been true, instead of being, (as I believe,) wholly unsupported by evidence, no true friend of the college would have aided in giving it circulation, as was done by the friends of Mr. Loring, in such a persevering and determined manner. It certainly seemed as if an attempt was made to make it appear that he was a persecuted and injured man, and had been rejected for having done his duty as United States Commissioner; and as this was a subject which touched the sensibility of so many persons, the country or the government at Washington were perhaps expected to compensate him for his loss.

Mr. President, I will here conclude the remarks I proposed to offer on this subject, in order to remove the wrong impression under which the public mind has labored heretofore. I have long felt that a vindication of the conduct of the overseers who voted to reject Mr. Loring against such unjust charges was imperatively called for, and I regret it has fallen into such feeble hands.

I thank you for the patience and attention with which you have listened to my defence, and I shall have been well rewarded should it be admitted hereafter, (as I think it ought to be,) that the overseers acted with becoming firmness on the occasion, and would have surrendered rights and privileges incontestably belonging to them, had they voted otherwise.

LETTER TO PRESIDENT JACKSON.

West Roxbury, (near Boston,)
February 16th, 1837.

My Dear Sir,—I have long wished to have the date of the visit, with which you were pleased to honor me on the first of July, 1833, at Roxbury, engraved upon some tablet more durable than that of memory.

During my recent extensive tour in Europe, as I was walking one day through the Royal Museum, at Naples, my attention was arrested by a portrait of Columbus, by Parmigiano, who died in 1540. As I gazed on the picture of that great man, I began to think of my country, and of you, who have twice saved it; once by the valor of your arms, when it was attacked by a powerful foreign enemy; and again, upon an occasion more recent, but of danger not less imminent, when its union was threatened to be dissolved by a combination of powerful individuals in a southern state.

It occurred to me, that you might like to have a correct likeness of the discoverer of that country, over whose destiny you have presided so long, with singular wisdom, prudence, and good fortune. The original could not be had, for it belonged to the government of Naples; but I was able to find an artist on the spot, who could take a copy, and who has succeeded so well in the task, that it is said, by some, to be superior to the original.

I have had inscribed upon one corner of the canvass, the name of my native town, and the date of your visit.

I have sent the portrait to your address at Washington, and ask the favor of your acceptance of the same, as a testimonial of the gratitude I feel for the honor you conferred upon me by the time you passed with me at Roxbury, and as a proof of the admiration and respect with which I remain

Your much obliged friend, and
Most obedient servant,
S. D. BRADFORD.

To ANDREW JACKSON,
President of the United States, Washington, D. C.

(COPY.)

REPLY OF PRESIDENT JACKSON.

WASHINGTON, February 21, 1837.

MY DEAR SIR,—Your letter of the 16th instant, communicating the flattering feeling under which, when abroad, your heart prompted the noble offering of the portrait of Columbus, is received at a time to make such gift most welcome.

Returning to the Hermitage, to see its walls adorned by the likeness of the heroic discoverer, and that by the hand of a too partial friend, who has deemed the destiny which I have fulfilled somewhat worthy to associate me, in his thoughts, with the firm, daring, lofty spirit which gave a continent to civilization, and liberty a land to abide in, while it must fill me with humility by the comparison, cannot but be gratifying to that pardonable feeling which has animated me, through a long career of unceasing labor, in the hope that I might live in the good opinion of my country.

I thank you, my dear sir, for your much esteemed present. I shall look upon it with pride while I live, for the sake of the gift and the giver, and shall leave it as a relic never to be removed from the halls of the Hermitage, where, I trust, the memorial will be considered well placed, as showing that I could fully appreciate, however feebly communicate, my sense of the sublime genius it calls up to mind.

Be so kind as to present to your amiable sister, my kind salutations, and believe me,

Very respectfully
Your friend,
ANDREW JACKSON.

To Samuel D. Bradford, Esq.,
Roxbury, Mass.

COURT OF APPEALS.

THE PRESIDENT, DIRECTORS, AND COMPANY, OF THE MECHANICS' BANK, IN THE CITY OF NEW YORK, AGAINST THE NEW YORK AND NEW HAVEN RAILROAD COMPANY.

[This cause was heard at the last April term of this court, at Albany, before Hon. Hiram Denio, Chief Justice, and Hons. A. S. Johnson, G. F. Comstock, Wm. B. Wright, Wm. Mitchell, and F. Hubbard, Justices; and was argued by Messrs. William Curtis Noyes and George Wood, (with whom was associated Nicholas Hill, Jr., Esq.,) for the defendants; and by Messrs. E. S. Van Winkle and Daniel Lord, for the plaintiffs. It was kept under advisement until the 17th of June, 1856, when the following unanimous opinion of the court was delivered.—*New York Times, June* 26, 1856.]

Comstock, J.—This is an action for damages founded on a certificate for eighty-five shares of stock in the defendants' corporation, issued to Alexander Kyle, upon the security of which the plaintiffs loaned to that person a sum of money; and the first inquiry naturally is, what was the force and effect of the certificate in his hands? The mode of presenting this inquiry most favorable to the plaintiffs is, to consider it as free from the difficulty that there was no power in the corporation, its board of directors, or any of its agents, to create the shares of stock in question. Assuming that the corporation had stock at its own disposal, and that Robert Schuyler, as agent, had full power to sell it in market, and issue the proper certificates therefor, it is clear that any person dealing with him in good faith, and paying value, would become entitled to all the rights and privileges of a stockholder, although the agent, by a secret fraud, intended the transaction to be for his own benefit, and used the funds which he received for his own private purposes. In such a case, the acts of the agent being such as the corporation was competent to perform, and strictly within the powers delegated to him, upon principles entirely familiar, the law would not permit third persons to suffer by a secret abuse of the trust.

But it is equally clear, that no rights would be acquired by a party not dealing with the agent in good faith, and receiving a certificate of stock without paying any value therefor. To say that the original holder of such a certificate could not be admitted to a participation with the genuine and *bona fide* stockholders in the property, franchises and revenues of the corporation, is a proposition so plain that it needs only to be stated. Such was the situation of Alexander Kyle, the original holder of the certificate now in question. To what extent he was implicated in the frauds of Schuyler, is not material. The certificate is admitted to have been issued fraudulently, and he paid nothing for it; on this ground it was in his hands spurious and void; and this is a conclusion which is reached without calling in question the power of the corporation to create the stock, or of Schuyler, as agent, to issue the proper evidence thereof to a purchaser in good faith.

The certificate in the hands of Kyle was also void, for the reasons which will now be mentioned:

First, Schuyler, as the agent of the company, had no power to issue a certificate for shares of stock, except upon the conditions precedent of a transfer on the books by some previous owner, and the surrender of that owner's certificate. He was the transfer agent merely, and his powers were expressly limited to that department of the business of the corporation. He had no general certifying power, nor any power at all to certify, except as *incidental*, to a transfer of stock by its owner to some one else, and, as an incidental power, it could only be exercised upon the conditions named.

Second, Neither the board of directors by whom Schuyler was appointed agent, nor the whole body of the corporation, had power to create the stock which the certificate issued to Kyle professed to represent; and if the stock itself could not be brought into existence by the whole power of the corporation, the certificate issued as the evidence of its existence, and the right of the holder thereto, was necessarily void. Upon the premises last stated, the conclusion would be the same, even if Kyle had paid to the transfer agent the full value of the stock. He could purchase stock of any person who owned it, but he could not, under any conditions, obtain it from the corporation or its agents, because there was none to be had, and none could be created.

Thus far, I do not understand that my conclusions differ essentially from the views of the counsel who have argued the cause for the plaintiffs; and, if I was not mistaken in regard to the general scope of their argument, they conceded the further result, that the plaintiffs, holding the certificate by transfer from Kyle, have no rights as *stockholders*, merely for the particular reason, that the stock cannot exist under the charter; the essential ground of the action in the view of the counsel, being the injury sustained by dealing upon the faith of the false representation of stock which the certificate contains. The opinions, however, of the judges in the court below, are before us for examination, as well as those of eminent lawyers, who have not appeared upon the argument, and I think it proper to refer to these opinions for the purpose of bringing into view all the theories upon which, it has been supposed, the plaintiffs' rights depend.

Mr. Justice Hoffman, in the opinion pronounced by him, holds that the certificate was not void, as transcending the powers of the corporation in the creation of stock and issuing certificates therefor, or those delegated to Schuyler as the transfer agent. He, therefore, considers the obligation to be one which the defendants can perform, and ought to perform, according to its terms. He admits that the effect of an over-issue is to increase the number of shares, but not the actual capital; and, according to his view, the spurious certificates are to be made good by a reduction in the actual value of those that are now genuine. He holds, therefore, that the defendants were bound to admit the plaintiffs as stockholders, and to register their shares on the books accordingly; and that this suit depends, purely and simply, on the non-performance of that duty, after being requested to perform it. "Without a demand," he says, "and refusal to transfer, there would be no *ground of action whatever.*"

Directly opposed to these views are those of Chief Justice Oakley. He holds the certificate utterly void, because it transcended the powers of the transfer agent, whose commission, he thinks, was special, and not general; and, if the action depended on the validity of the certificate, he says, the following questions would have to be answered: First, Whether the plaintiffs, as *bona fide* holders, could acquire any rights under it superior to those of Kyle, in whose hands it was void? And, secondly, Whether the plaintiffs can be considered as *bona fide* holders?

As to the last point, he inclines to think that the plaintiffs were bound to see that Schuyler, as agent, did not exceed his special powers, and, therefore, if they chose to deal in the stock without inquiring as to that fact, they took the certificate from Kyle at their peril. But the learned chief justice, nevertheless, holds the defendants liable, on the ground that the certificate was a false representation that Kyle held stock, when in truth he did not. He thinks that Schuyler, the agent, had an implied authority from the company to make such a representation—an authority resulting from his constant habit of issuing certificates in the same form in the course of the regular business of the corporation. If, as he assumes, the certificate was void, tested simply by the authority given to the agent, and if, as he also assumes, the plaintiffs were bound to take notice of the want of authority, with deference, it appears to me, that they are affected by the same considerations when they change the grounds of complaint to misrepresentation and fraud. Can an agent's authority to misrepresent, in the course of a dealing, be inferred, when it is admitted he has no authority to enter into the dealing at all?

Justices Bosworth and Slosson, if I do not misunderstand them, both admit, that there was no power in the corporation to create the shares of stock which the certificate professes to represent, and that the instrument, considered as a real representation of stock, was void for that reason; thus discarding the only ground upon which, in the opinion of one of their brethren, the action can be maintained. They nevertheless hold, that the suit is not founded upon the motion of misrepresentation and fraud, thus as distinctly rejecting the theory of the other. They appear to me to have found a middle ground of liability, which is, perhaps, fairly expressed in the following language of Justice Bosworth: "The certificate," he says, "so far as any inferences can be drawn from its terms or appearance, purports to be, and is as much the act of the defendants, as any certificate that has been issued by the company representing genuine stock. The plaintiffs took it, believing it to be what it purports to be, and their action is based on the theory that, as between them and the defendants, it is, in judgment of law, *the act of the defendants;* and that the defendants are *estopped* from asserting the contrary, so far as the question of their liability for refusing to reimburse to the plaintiff the amount of their loan to the extent of the value of the stock is concerned." And again, he says: "The action is based on the assumption, so far as the right to be compensated in damages is concerned, that the company has given *an assurance* that Kyle owned the stock, which the certificate represents stood to his credit on its books." The reasoning by which these results are reached, is, in substance, that the act of Schuyler, in issuing the certificate, was within the apparent scope of his powers, and, therefore, although the contract was void, because it transcended all the powers of the corporation, and was impossible to be performed for the same reason, the defendant must, nevertheless, make it good *in damages* upon an *assurance* that it was valid; the assurance being a part of the contract itself. I confess my own impression to be, that this reasoning is too refined. Admitting that the agent acted within the scope of the power delegated to him by the board of directors, I do not clearly see how certificates of stock, which they themselves had no authority to issue, void in their origin, and under all conceivable circumstances, can be made the basis of a liability ruinous to the genuine stockholders, by turning the spurious instruments into a *promise* or *undertaking* that the stock in fact existed.

The extreme difficulty which has been encountered in endeavoring to find a principle on which to rest the action, may be further illustrated by reference to the professional opinions which have been submitted to our examination. In one of them—certainly entitled to the very highest respect, the reasoning of which, I think, must have been in substance approved by Mr. Justice Hoffman—it is claimed that all the over-issued certificates are valid, so far as question of corporate power is concerned; that the multiplication of shares did not increase the capital stock, but merely reduced the value of the shares; that the acts of Schuyler, in issuing such certificates, were done within the scope of his authority as agent; and, as a conclusion from these premises, that all the holders in good faith, who had not already received new certificates in their own names, were entitled to receive them, and so to be admitted to all the rights and privileges of stockholders. In another of these opinions, distinguished by great acuteness and force of reasoning, the clear and emphatic concession is made, that the defendants have no corporate right to create a valid title to a single share of stock beyond the prescribed number; that the corporation, being prohibited from issuing more than thirty thousand shares, was, by necessary consequence, forbidden to recognize, as a part of its stock, any share known to have been issued contrary to that prohibition, and consequently, that the directors might refuse to recognize all shares which could be clearly traced to an origin in the over-issue. In respect to all such shares it is claimed, however, that compensation in damages must be made by the corporation to the innocent holders, who, by dealing in them, have suffered pecuniary loss. The issue of false certificates, it is insisted, was a failure of *corporate duty*, an act of *negligence* by the corporation, for which it is liable to the party injured. The company, it is also said, is bound by an *estoppel* in favor of the innocent shareholder, and must either recognize him as a stockholder, or respond in damages as a wrong-doer for withholding his apparent right.

If those who assert that this action can be maintained, had been able to agree upon a reason for that opinion, there would be fewer propositions to discuss than I shall feel obliged to examine.

I have already stated, in general terms, my own conclusion to be on the side of the invalidity of the so-called spurious shares, upon the ground of a want of corporate power to create them, and I will now give some further expression to my views on that question. By the charter of this railroad company, its capital stock was limited to three millions of dollars, to be divided into shares of one hundred dollars each. It is admitted that the whole capital was subscribed and paid in, and that certificates of stock were issued representing the thirty thousand shares actually subscribed and paid for. Now if it is plain, as all concede, that the capital could not be increased beyond the three millions, it seems to me equally plain, that no more than thirty thousand shares could be created Both are unalterably fixed by the charter; the capital, by expressing the aggregate amount, and the number of shares by expressing the amount of each. The whole capital is divided into shares of one hundred dollars each, and the mathematical result is thirty thousand in all. Viewing the question, therefore, as one of abstract power, nothing appears to be wanting to a complete demonstration that additional shares could not be created. There is, under the charter, no more capacity to increase the nominal capital by multiplying the shares to an indefinite extent, than to increase the real capital by an actual subscription indefinitely beyond the specified limit.

But it is important to observe that the question has other relations than those which belong to it as one of simple capacity and power. The thirty thousand shares of original stock, subscribed and paid for by the persons to whom the genuine certificates were issued, belonged to them in their individual right, and were as much their separate and individual property as any other possession which they could acquire. The entire capital was represented in the property and franchises of the corporation, and the owner of each share was entitled to a fixed and unalterable proportion of that capital. And from this it follows that any attempt to create a greater number of shares by the issue of additional certificates, is not only a violation of the organic law of the corporation, but a direct invasion of the contract between it and each holder of its original stock. Now, while it cannot be denied that the value of every share may be reduced by misfortune or accident in the management of the business of the corporation, or by the neglect and misconduct of its agents acting within their acknowledged powers, it is equally plain that this result cannot be effected by a change in the fixed proportion which each share bears to the aggregate number. It has been said, that the limitation of the capital and the number of shares, was imposed from considerations of public policy alone. This is not so. Those who asked for the charter, and proposed to invest their private capital in the enterprise which it contemplated, required such a limitation for their own protection; and every individual who subscribed and paid for shares of stock must be deemed to have done so relying upon the charter for the safety of his investment.

The conclusion to which I am brought upon this question, is not impeached by the consideration (if such is the fact) that there are shares and certificates of stock, beyond the original limit, which cannot be traced to an over-issue by the fraudulent agent of the company. I know not how the facts may be in this respect, nor is it material to the argument. The corporation may be compelled to respond to the holders of certificates, amounting in the aggregate to more than its capital, because it cannot distinguish those which are spurious and those which are genuine. Thus the number of shares to be recognized may be practically increased, not for the reason that all over-issues are not void, but because, in a given instance, the corporation cannot show that the shares claimed are of that character. No question of this kind arises in the case before us.

I have also stated, in general terms, as one of my conclusions, that the certificate issued to Kyle, was void in his hands, upon the more special ground that the agent could not certify, except upon conditions which did not exist in respect to that transaction. I observe now, further, that a third person, dealing with Kyle, and taking from him a transfer of the certificate, doubtless had reason to suppose that it had been duly issued. Whether a dealing with him under that belief, created new rights against the corporation, I shall presently examine. But Kyle himself dealt directly with the agent of the company, and he knew the conditions had not arisen, on which the power to certify depended. He knew this, because he surrendered no previous certificate, and had no transfer on the books, or otherwise, from any actual shareholder. Now, I do not understand it to be claimed, on the part of the plaintiffs, that the acts of the agent, in issuing the spurious certificates, were within any actual power which the corporation ever attempted to confer upon him, nor, that all persons proposing to deal in the stock, were not chargeable with a knowledge of the extent and limit of his authority. He was known to be a transfer agent, merely of existing and genuine shares, and in that character his name was signed to the certificate in question, and all others. What is claimed I understand to be precisely this:—That the false certificates, being regular on their face, and the same in form, as those which were genuine, presented to third parties dealing in them, all the appearances of having been duly issued, although, in fact, the agent had no authority to issue them, and although the exact extent of his authority was known. But these appearances were known to be false, by those who dealt directly with the agent; and with that knowledge it is not pretended that they can assert any claim against the corporation. Such was the situation of Kyle.

It is as well, in this connection as any other, to notice a special feature of the transaction, which, I think, imparts neither strength nor weakness to the plaintiff's case. The facts as they appear in the finding of the judge are, that Kyle received the certificate, not for his own but the agent's use, and having negotiated with the plaintiffs a loan, by pledging it as security, paid the proceeds of the transaction over to the agent. But these facts were not known to the plaintiff. They dealt with Kyle as the owner. Upon that theory they have a right now to rely, and I understand them to do so. It is the best the case will admit of. If they choose to take the facts as they actually are, and to regard Kyle as a negotiator merely between them and the fraudulent agent of the corporation, they would then stand in the position of an immediate dealer with the agent, receiving from him a certificate of stock issued without authority; and this position, as I have shown, would be fatal to their claim. They justly prefer to be regarded, and I do regard them, as third parties, dealing with Kyle as the apparent owner of stock.

In order to keep in view the exact conditions of the general question, I think it proper to state the conclusions which I consider thus far established. They are as follows: First. The certificate was void in the hands of Kyle, the first holder, because it was fraudulently issued, and he paid nothing for it. Second. It was also void in his hands because issued by an agent without authority, there being no surrender of a previous certificate, and no transfer to him on the books of actual stock; and this want of authority was known to him. Third. It was void because the stock it professed to represent had no existence, and could not exist under the charter of the company; all the powers of the corporation in the creation and issue of stock being exhausted. In respect to the conclusion last mentioned, it must be, and I think is conceded, that, as a further result, the certificate is void under all possible circumstances, so that no person, in whatever situation, can claim under it the rights of a stockholder, or damages on the ground of a refusal to admit him to such rights. As the law will not require the defendants to violate their charter by creating an excess of stock to supply this spurious certificate, so it will not punish them in damages for refusing simply to be guilty of such violation. I consider this result so necessary and so evident as not to require further discussion.

I will proceed, however, to a more particular examination of the plaintiffs' rights as the transferrees of Kyle; and, giving them the most favorable view of the case, will consider the certificate as void in his hands only on the grounds that it was issued fraudulently, without consideration, and without any authority contained in *the terms* of Schuyler's appointment as transfer agent. In this view, the defendant's corporation is regarded as competent to recognize the certificate, and, if they are bound to do so, they must respond in damages upon their refusal. The question, therefore, will be, Are they so bound, or, to state it in another form, are the plaintiffs in a situation to assert any rights against the company which Kyle, their assignor, did not possess.

By the charter of this corporation the shares of its capital stock were made transferable in such manner and in such places as the by-laws should direct; and the by-laws declared that all transfers should be made in the transfer-book, kept at the proper office; and where a certificate of the stock had been issued, that the same should be surrendered prior to the transfer being made. The certificate now in question, as all others, declared on its face the same conditions. This certificate has, in fact, never been surrendered, and no such transfer has ever been made. The plaintiffs, on making their loan to Kyle, took from him an assignment and power of attorney in blank, but paid no regard to the fundamental conditions on which alone a legal title to the stock could be transferred. Of these conditions of course they had notice.

I am aware it is common to deal in this manner in the stock of corporate companies, and I do not say that any rule of law or of public policy is violated by it. The dealer undoubtedly acquires an equitable title to the stock of his vendor, and, if the vendor's title is open to no impeachment, he has a right to call upon the corporation to clothe him also with the legal title by permitting a transfer to himself on its books, and to demand a new certificate in his own name. But the question here is, not whether the purchaser is clothed in equity with all the rights of the seller, but whether, by a transfer not made, according to the laws of the corporation, he acquires new and superior rights as against the corporation itself; in short, whether his title is good when that of his vendor was good for nothing.

So, too, it is common to deal in this manner with respect to obligations of every description. If extreme caution is exercised, the purchaser will inquire of the maker of the obligation, and procure his admission of its validity, and his assent to the transfer; and have ing done so, an estoppel will arise in his favor, not because he has invested his money in the purchase, but because he purchased after procuring such admission or consent, and upon the faith thereof. Where there is no estoppel of this sort to rely upon, then the question whether the transferree of an obligation apparently sound, and from the apparent owner, acquires any better right to enforce it than his assignor had, depends on the nature of the obligation itself. The general and familiar rule is, that he does not. If the instrument has negotiable qualities, then he may. In the case of negotiable instruments, the legal title passes by mere indorsement or delivery. When they are not negotiable, an equitable title is all that can be acquired; and this suggests the further observation that, as between equities merely, the prior one, as a general rule, prevails. The prior equity, as well as the law, is in favor of the party who made the obligation, if, for any good and valid reason, he ought not to be bound by it. The principle is so familiar that authorities need not be cited. It seems to me, therefore, that we are brought directly to the question whether certificates of stock in the defendants' corporation are to be regarded as negotiable instruments in the sense of the commercial law, so that, by their indorsement and delivery to a purchaser in good faith, a title to the stock they profess to represent may be acquired, although in the hands of the vendor they are spurious and void, and although the company itself has never recognized the transfer. This question, I think, must be answered in the negative. They contain, in the first place, no words of negotiability. They declare simply that the person named is entitled to certain shares of stock.

They do not, like negotiable instruments, run to the bearer, or to the order of the party to whom they are given. They commence, it is true, with the words, "Be it known," but such words have no tendency to show that they possess the quality claimed for them. A phraseology quite similar may be found on bonds and other instruments which no one ever thought to be negotiable.

But, aside from the absence of any language of these certificates which can impart to them a negotiable character, both the laws of the corporation, and the certificates themselves, contain special restrictions, which seem to me to put this question at rest. I do not suppose that a corporation, without something very extraordinary in its charter, can place such restraints upon the sale of its stock, that the individual holder may not transfer as good a title in equity as he himself possesses, by any mode of assurance good upon general principles of law. But, if a natural person has an undoubted right so to express the terms of his obligation that it shall not be negotiable in the commercial sense, or in any sense which can give to the purchaser a title superior to that of his vendor, I see no reason to doubt that corporations possess the same right. Have the defendants so expressed themselves in these certificates of stock? I think they have. They have distinctly declared, both in their by-laws, and on the face of the certificates, that shares can be transferred only on the books, and on the surrender of the evidence of the previous owner's title. If an illustration were wanting of the value of such a restriction, it is furnished in the present case. But, whatever its value, the restraint is lawful in itself, and one which the corporation had an undoubted right to impose. I do not say that it prevents the owner of stock from selling his shares by an outside transfer, so that his vendee will acquire in equity his own rights; but to say that the holder of a false and fraudulent certificate, by indorsing and delivering it to another person, can create a title hostile to the corporation itself, would be to deny to the restriction any meaning or effect whatever.

I have examined attentively the authorities cited upon the question, but do not find that the doctrine contended for, has in them the least support. In the case of *Kortright* vs. *The Commercial Bank of Buffalo*, (20 Wend., 91, L. C. in error, 22 Wend., 348,) it was held that an action of assumpsit, will lie against a corporation in favor of the assignee of a stock certificate, for refusing to permit a transfer on the books. This and the class of cases to which it belongs, prove that a transfer not made according to the charter or by-laws of a corporation, confers upon the transferree, in an equitable sense, the title of the previous owner; that, being thus clothed with the equitable title, it is the duty of the corporation to permit him to take a legal transfer on the books; and that the law will imply an assumpsit for the performance of that duty. For a breach of this duty, actions of assumpsit and case have been indifferently maintained. In principle, the remedy should have been a special action on the case. Such was the opinion of Chief Justice Nelson in the case referred to—but he adds, "It being once settled, (that assumpsit will lie,) there is no occasion for disturbing it." It is only material to observe that the *assumpsit* is not in the certificate itself, and so passing by indorsement and delivery to the transferree, but is implied *after the transfer*, from the duty of the corporation to clothe the equitable owner with the legal title. Such cases, so far from tending to show that a dealer in certificates acquires rights better than those of the person with whom he deals, seem to me to justify quite an opposite conclusion. They necessarily assume that the change of title is incomplete, until the proper transfer is made on the books.

In the case of *Fatman* vs. *Loback*, (1 Duer, 354,) no question arose involving the rights of the corporation. The decision is directly opposed to that of Chancellor Walworth in *Stebbins* vs. *Phenix Bank*, (3 Paige, 350,) and my own impression is, that it cannot be sustained. I find in it, however, nothing which can affect the question I am considering. The case was disposed of upon principles which were not asserted as having any peculiar application to dealing in stocks or negotiable securities. The case of *Stoney* vs. *The American Life Insurance and Trust Company*, (11 Paige, 635,) only held that the *negotiable* security of a corporation, appearing on its face to have been duly issued, was valid in the hands of a *bona fide* holder, although, in fact, issued contrary to law. The case of *Delafued* vs. *The State of Illinois*, (2d Hill, 159,) related to state bonds, payable to bearer, and strictly negotiable. Such securities are sometimes called stocks, but a confusion of terms should not involve principles in obscurity.

In the case of *Fisher* vs. *The Morris Canal and Banking Company*, (3 Am. Law Reg., 423,) the question was, whether the bonds of a railroad corporation, payable to bearer, issued for the purpose of raising money, with interest coupons annexed, also payable to bearer, were negotiable in such a sense, that a purchaser for value took them free from any equities between the company and the seller. The decision was in favor of the purchaser, and I fully concur in the doctrine. The distinction between such a security and a stock certificate, which by its very terms is not negotiable, and which is not a security for money at all, it seems to me, is too plain to escape observation.

These are the only authorities cited in favor of the doctrine contended for. It is quite evident that they have no tendency in that direction. I will now mention some which are decisively the other way. In the case of the *Union Bank of Georgetown* vs. *Laird*, (2 Wheaton, 390,) the stock was transferable only on the books of the corporation. The precise propositions decided were, that no legal title to shares could be acquired except by a transfer made according to the requirement, and that the equitable title of the transferree was subject to all the rights of the corporation against his assignor. The same doctrine was held by Chancellor Walworth in *Stebbins* vs. *Phœnix Fire Insurance Company*, (3 Paige, 350.)

In the State of Connecticut, there have been a series of cases going still further. There the registry on the books, when required by the charter or by-laws of a corporation, is deemed the originating act in the change of title to stock, and a transfer not so made, is regarded as ineffectual for any purpose. (2 Cown., 529; 3 ib., 544; 5 ib., 246; 6 ib., 552.) So rigorous a doctrine has not been followed elsewhere, and I think the established rule now is, that a transfer of stock not made in the manner prescribed is, nevertheless, valid so as to pass in equity all the rights of the seller, but no greater. (See further, Angell and Ames on Corporations, 352, 353, 3d ed., where the rule is stated, and the cases cited.)

Looking at the question upon principle, I am not aware of anything in the nature or uses of this kind of property which requires an application of the rules which belong to negotiable securities. Stocks are not, like bank bills, the immediate representative of money, and intended for circulation. The distinction between a bank bill and a share of bank stock is not difficult to appreciate. Nor are they, like notes and bills of exchange, less adapted to circulation, but invented to supply the exigencies of commerce, and governed by the peculiar code of the commercial law. They are not like exchequer bills and government securities, which are made negotiable either for circulation or to find a market. Nor are they like corporation bonds, which are issued in negotiable form for sale, and as a means for raising money for corporate uses. The distinction between all these and corporate stocks is marked and striking. They are all in some form the representative of money, and may be satisfied by payment in money at a time specified. Certificates of stock are not securities for money in any sense, much less are they negotiable securities. They are simply the muniments and evidence of the holder's title to a given share in the property and franchises of the corporation of which he is a member. The primary use and design, I must be allowed to say, of this species of property, is to afford a steady investment for capital, rather than to feed the spirit of speculation. I am aware that people will speculate in stocks, as they sometimes do in lands, and there is no law which absolutely forbids it; but such, I am persuaded, is not the use for which we should hold them chiefly intended.

The question is capable of some further elucidation, by attending to the rules which have been settled in regard to the transferability of other instruments and the effect of transfer. A certificate of stock is, in some respects, like a bill of lading, or a warehouse or wharfinger's receipt. Each is the representative of property existing under certain conditions, and the documentary evidence of title thereto. They are all alike transferable by indorsement and delivery, and the title to the property, thus represented, passes by such transfer. So far, they resemble each other, but there are distinctions to be noted. Bills of lading and wharfingers' receipts, are commercial instruments, and their transferability, or, as it is sometimes termed, their "*quasi*-negotiability," depends on the custom of merchants, and the conveniences of trade. Certificates of stock are not commercial instruments, and the title to the property they represent, passes in equity only by indorsement and delivery, where, by any law or rule of the corporation, the transfer is required to be made on the books. With these resemblances and these distinctions, if a bill of lading is not negotiable, in the sense which must be contended for in the present case, there is much greater difficulty in affirming that such a quality belongs to a stock certificate.

In the great case of *Lichbarrow* vs. *Mason*, (2 Term Rep., 63; 5 id., 367,) it was held that the consignor of goods had lost his right of stoppage *in transitu*, when the consignee, holding the bill of lading indorsed in blank by the consignor, delivered it to a third person, who received it in good faith, and made advances upon it. This has been the settled rule ever since. But, in such cases, it is to be observed, the legal title to the goods has vested by the sale and consignment in the consignee, subject only to the peculiar and anomalous right of arresting their delivery, in the event of insolvency. If, therefore, before this right is exercised, the consignee transfers the bill of lading to another person, who takes it in good faith and for value, the latter acquires the title which his vendor had at the time of the transfer, and which the consignor cannot afterwards take from him, by stopping the goods before they have reached their destination. In this doctrine, which was settled after a very remarkable contest in the courts of England, is contained all the negotiable quality that belongs to a bill of lading, and it requires but little discrimination to see that this is not negotiability in any just sense of that term. On the other hand, it has been held by the Supreme Court, and the late Court of Errors of this State,—(*Saitus* vs. *Everett*, 15 Wend., 475; 20 id., 267,) that a bill of lading, covering goods shipped, but made without the owner's authority, cannot affect the owner's title, into whatsoever hands the instrument may come. So it has been lately held in the English Queen's Bench, (*Gurney* vs. *Behrend*. 3 Ellis and Bl., 622,) that, if a bill of lading is misappropriated, as if it be indorsed in blank by the consignor, and sent to his correspondent, but not intending thereby to have it transferred, and the person receiving the bill transfers it for value, the title to the goods is not affected by the transaction. Lord Campbell, in delivering the judgment in that case, very explicitly denied the negotiability of such instruments. In *Covill* vs. *Hill* (4 Denio, 323,) Chief Justice Bronson had occasion to say, "If the master of a vessel, after signing a bill of lading to the owner of the goods, should give one to another person, it would confer no rights upon those who were misled by the false and fraudulent paper." See also *Thompson* vs. *Dominey*, (14 Mees and W., 402,) *Zachrisson* vs. *Ahman*, (2 Sand, 68,) *Commercial Bank of Rochester* vs. *Cole*, (15 Barb., 506.)

It is conceded that Kyle, the first holder of the certificate in question, could assert no title to the stock it appears to represent, and that, in his hands, it was spurious and void, for all the reasons which have been mentioned. Before its transfer to the plaintiffs can be admitted to confer any better title upon them, it must be shown to have not only all the negotiable qualities of a bill of lading, but others also which that instrument does not possess.

Testing this question, therefore, in any conceivable mode, whether by the express terms of these certificates, by their general nature and character, by the authority of adjudged cases, or by the most favorable anologies, I have no hesitation in saying, that the doctrine contended for, is entirely without foundation. It is mainly by assuming, for these instruments, the possession in a greater or less degree of the peculiar qualities of negotiable securities, that the plaintiffs claim to have acquired, by transfer, better rights than their assignor had; and, as that assumption fails, this claim must fall to the ground.

It was also said, on the argument, that those certificates of stock are in the nature of general letters of credit, on the faith of which any one might act; and upon this idea, it was insisted that the defendants are in some way bound by the obligation in the hands of the plaintiff. I am unable to see the analogy suggested. By attending to a mere definition of a letter of credit, it will be seen there is no resemblance. Thus, in *McCulloch's Commercial Dictionary*, it is defined to be "a letter written by one merchant or correspondent to another, requesting him to credit the bearer with a sum of money." Or, to take the further definition of another writer, it is "an open or sealed letter from one merchant in one place, directed to another in another place, requiring him, that, if the person therein named, or the bearer of the letter, shall have occasion to buy commodities or to want moneys, he will procure the same, or pass his promise, bill, or other engagement for it, on the writer of the letter, undertaking that he will provide him the money for the goods, or repay him by exchange, or give him such satisfaction as he shall require." (3 Chitty, Com. Law, 336; Bouvier's Law Dictionary.)

Now, while it may be the *effect* of a stock certificate to give the holder a credit, its terms do not request, invite, or guarantee it. So the possessor of property of any description, or of the evidence and muniments of title thereto, in their effect give to the possessor a credit with other men. In this sense, every chose in action invites a credit in favor of him who holds it, and so do the title-deeds of his real estate. Innocent parties may deal with him and be deceived. They may lend their money and lose it. Nothing more than this can be said of a certificate of the ownership of stock in a corporation. Regarded as a *promissory* instrument, imposing obligations to be performed by the artificial person which makes it, it is like any other chose in action, except as greater restrictions may be placed upon its transfer and sale. Regarded as a muniment of title merely, it is like any other instrument by which title is manifested. But to say that, like a letter of credit, it contains a request, express or implied, addressed to any one in particular, or to the community in general, to deal with, or advance money to, the holder, or that it contains any assurance or guarantee addressed to the dealer, of the safety of the transaction, is, in my judgment, to confound plain and long-settled distinctions.

I will now briefly examine the validity of the plaintiffs' title in another aspect, still keeping out of view, however, the absolute want of power in the corporation to create the stock in question. It has been mentioned as one of the reasons why the certificate was void in the hands of Kyle, that Schuyler, the agent, was not acting within the scope of his powers when he issued it. The full effect of this particular objection upon the plaintiffs' rights as the transferrees of Kyle, has not been considered. And I observe now, in the first place, that if, upon a vague theory of negotiability, (already examined,) they could overcome the difficulties arising out of the fraud of the agent toward the company as his principal, and out of the want of consideration, this objection would still have to be removed. It is obvious, upon a moment's reflection, that negotiability can impart no vitality to an instrument executed under a power where the agent has exceeded his actual or presumptive authority. Whoever proposes to deal with a security of any kind appearing, on its face, to be given by one man for another, is bound to inquire whether it has been given by due authority, and if he omits that inquiry, he deals at his peril.

It is not denied, that the plaintiffs, in taking the certificates in question, were chargeable with notice of the extent and limit of the powers of Schuyler as transfer agent. All that is claimed in their behalf is, that his act in issuing it was apparently and presumptively, although not actually, within his authority. Upon this ground it is urged, that, according to the rules which govern the relation of principal and agent, the defendants are bound in some way to make the obligation good. The extent of the authority, it is admitted, the plaintiffs knew, or were bound to know; but it was not known, they say, that the act done was not within such authority.

There are, in the books, many loose expressions concerning the distinction between a general and special agency. The distinction itself is highly unsatisfactory, and will be found quite insufficient to solve a great variety of cases. It is not profitable to dwell upon that distinction. Underlying the whole subject, there is this fundamental proposition, that a principal is bound only by the authorized acts of his agent. This authority may be proved by the instrument which creates it; and beyond the terms of the instrument, or the verbal commission, it may be shown that the principal has held the agent out to the world, in other instances, as having an authority which will embrace the particular act in question. I know of no other mode in which a controverted power can be established. But in whichever way this is done, it cannot be limited by secret instructions of the principal on the one hand, nor can it be enlarged by the unauthorized representation of the agents on the other. These principles, I think, are elementary.

But suppose an agent is authorized, by the terms of his appointment, to enter into an engagement, or series of engagements, on behalf of his principal, and while the appointment is in force, he fraudulently makes one in his own or a stranger's business, but in the form contemplated by the power, and which he asserts to be in the business of his employer, by using his name in the contract, can the dealer rely upon that assertion, and hold the principal, or is he bound to inquire and to ascertain at his peril whether the transaction is, not only in appearance but in fact, within the authority? According to the decision of the Supreme Court of this State, in the case of *The North River Bank* vs. *Aymer*, (3 Hill, 362,) he can. There the agent was authorized to draw and indorse notes in the name and for the benefit of his principal. He drew various notes, which in their appearance were within the power, but really had no connection with the business, of his principal. The plaintiff's bank, which had the letter of attorney in its custody, discounted them, and it was held they could be recovered against the principal. Justice Cowen and Chief Justice Nelson delivered opposing opinions, in which the question is very elaborately discussed. The decision was reversed in the Court of Errors, but the case is not reported in that court. If the reversal proceeded, as I suppose it must, upon a doctrine directly opposite to that held by the Supreme Court, then the case certainly suggests a limit of great importance to the liability of principals, the recognition of which would be decisive of the present controversy. So in *Grant* vs. *Norway*, (10 Com. Bench, 665,) it was held, after full discussion, that the master of a ship signing a bill of lading for goods not actually shipped, was not to be considered the agent of the owner of the vessel, so as to make him responsible to one who made advances upon the faith of the bill. That is a strong case. The master is the general agent of the owner as to all matters within the scope of his duty and employment; and has unquestionable power to sign bills of lading for goods shipped; and every bill asserts, as it did in that case, that the goods are received on board. The act, therefore, judged by its appearance and the representation of the agent, was strictly within the power. But the principal was held not to be liable, because it was not so in fact. The doctrine of that case was affirmed by the English Court of Exchequer in *Hubertsey* vs. *Ward*, (8 Exchequer Rep., 330, S. C., 18 Eng. Law and Eq. Rep., 551;) and again with great deliberation by the Common Pleas in *Coleman* vs. *Riches*, (29 Eng. Law and Eq. Rep., 323.)

The distinction is not always attended to between the apparent *powers* of an agent and his *acts* apparently but not really within the power. An agent's apparent powers are those which are conferred by the terms of his appointment, notwithstanding secret instructions, or those with which he is clothed by the character in which he is held out to the world, although not strictly within his commission. Whatever is done under an authority thus manifested is actually within the authority, and the principal is bound for that reason. But it is obvious that an agent may clothe his act with all the *indicia* of authority, and yet the act itself may not be within the real or apparent power. The appearance of the power is one thing, and for that the principal is responsible. The appearance of the act is another, and for that, if false, I think the remedy is against the agent only. The fundamental proposition, I repeat, is, that one man can be bound only by the authorized acts of another. He cannot be charged because another holds a commission from him, and falsely asserts that his acts are within it.

Cases may often arise, which, to a casual observation, might appear to be within the principles stated, but which really are not. Thus an agent may be authorized to give notes for his principal in order to raise money to be used in the business of the latter. A third person may inspect the power, advance the money in good faith, and the agent appropriate it to his own use. In such a case, I should hold the principal responsible, not because the act of the agent *appeared* to be within the authority, but because the authority actually included the transaction. A power given to an agent to borrow money upon notes, or otherwise, implies that the money may be paid to him, and so the whole transaction is strictly and literally authorized. But suppose the power to give the note is on its face conditional. It then has no existence until the condition has been fulfilled. To a confiding dealer who believes that the agent would not do an improper act, the note will certainly carry the appearance of due authority, but if it turns out that the conditions had not occurred, on which the exercise of the power depended, then he was trusting to the representation of the agent, and, I think, must look to him alone. As the principal never authorized the transaction at all, he is bound neither by the contract, nor by the representation. If not by the former, then it is extremely plain he is not by the latter.

Connected with the observations last made, it is proper, though, perhaps, scarcely necessary, to notice another doctrine which has been much urged, under some disguise, it is true, but, in effect, that the very employment of an agent in situations of trust and confidence is a recommendation and certificate of his character, so that, if he deceives others to their injury, the principal must make compensation. If by this it were only meant, that, where the agent is guilty of fraud or deceit in doing his employer's business, the latter is responsible, the doctrine is entirely true. —(Story's Agency, § 462, and cases cited.) But, in all its other aspects and forms of statement, the doctrine is unsound. If the agent, in dealing for his principal, and within the power, commits a fraud, the principal is liable; not upon the ground that he holds the agent out to the world as an honest man, but because the fraud enters into and is a part of the authorized transaction.

If the agent deals dishonestly for his principal, it is in a just sense a wrong done by the principal himself, although unknown and unauthorized. But the dealing itself must be authorized. If the transaction is not within the power, then, as the dealing is imputed to the agent personally, so necessarily are all the circumstances attending it, and all the means and instrumentalities by which the fraud is consummated. The power of the agent to charge his principal by doing a wrong must be traced directly to his authority, and it cannot be referred to an increased facility for imposing on the credulity of others derived incidentally from his appointment to a situation of trust. If the fraud consists in an over-representation of his power to act, by which others are drawn into dealing with him, then it is a self-evident proposition, that a man can no more enlarge than he can create a power by such a representation.

Applying the principles which have been stated in this branch of the discussion, they are decisive against the plaintiff. If the corporation had held stock, and Schuyler had been the agent to sell it, and issue certificates therefor, a sale and a certificate issued by him would have been valid against his principals, although, by a private fraud, he applied the proceeds to his own use. The transaction with the purchaser, in all its branches, the sale, the certificate, and the payments to him of the money, would have been not only apparently but actually within the powers. His misappropriation of the proceeds would have been a mere breach of trust, relating to moneys in his hands, and upon the principles of trust, his intention to misappropriate would not affect an innocent party.

But such were not the relations between Schuyler and the corporation, nor was he held out to the world as standing in such relations. He had no power to sell stock at all, and none to issue certificates, except as incidental to a sale between existing stockholders; and then, it depended on the conditions precedent of a transfer on the books, and a surrender of a previous certificate for the same stock. The authority which he assumed to exercise, therefore, confessedly, never had an actual existence, and, within the principles which have been stated, it never had an apparent existence. His appointment in its very terms, which all dealers are supposed to have been acquainted with, did not include his acts, and there is no pretence that the authority it conferred was ever enlarged by any holding out or recognition of such acts. All that can be said in behalf of the plaintiffs is, that the certificate itself implied a representation or assurance that it was issued within the power; in other words, that the conditions on which the power depended had been fulfilled. Even this representation, when closely scanned, was no more than an inference of the dealer, that, as the agent had no authority to certify, except under conditions, those had been in fact performed. But the conclusive answer is, that the defendants never authorized any such representations. To say that they had, would be simply saying that they authorized the certificate, because the representation was contained in that, and existed nowhere else, and this would be assuming the very point in dispute. The representation or assurance, therefore, if such we call it, was the unauthorized act of the agent. Upon this the plaintiffs naturally, no doubt, relied, and so, doubtless, the dealer did upon the bill of lading, in *Norway* vs. *Grant*, (*supra*,) which contained an express declaration that the goods were shipped. The precise difficulty is, that they relied upon the appearance which the agent gave to the act, and by that they were deceived. They were under no deception as to the power in its real or apparent scope. Testing the question by any rule of agency with which I am acquainted, the defendants were not bound by the transaction.

If any one of the main conclusions, at which I have arrived in this discussion, is sound, there is no remaining ground on which the action can be sustained. Viewing the certificate in question, as unaffected by the want of power in the corporation, to create or recognize the stock it appears to represent, we have seen that it was void in its origin, because issued without consideration, and in fraud of the defendants' rights. We have, also, seen that those objections were equally fatal to its validity in the hands of the plaintiffs, as the assignees of the first holder. It has been further shown, that the instrument imposed no obligation or duty on the defendants, upon the more special ground, that the act of Schuyler, in issuing it, was not within any authority which they ever, in fact or in pretence, conferred upon him as their agent; and, if this objection is sound, the further observation has been made, and, I doubt not, assented to, that it cannot be overcome, by allowing to the certificate, the transferable quality and immunity which belongs to negotiable paper. Unless these conclusions can be overthrown, they are subversive of the entire ground of action.

The notion of estoppel which has been advanced in the argument, not as a distinct ground of liability, but blended with other principles, deserves by itself very little consideration. Every corporate as well as private obligation or instrument undoubtedly contains an express or implied representation of facts upon the faith of which innocent parties may deal. If it be a promissory note, value received is a fact expressed or implied, and, although the fact may not be so, the maker is bound to pay the obligation in the hands of an innocent third party, not upon any theory of estoppel, but upon principles peculiar to that species of security. Where the instrument is not negotiable, the maker may, as I have heretofore observed, be affected by an estoppel *in pais*, if it be transferred upon his representation of its validity, and the dealer acts upon that representation. But to say that he is estopped by the instrument itself simply because he made it, and a third party has dealt with it, is only asserting in another form that fraud, mistake, duress, illegality, want of consideration, or want of authority, when the act is one of pretended agency, is no defence. This would subvert the settled maxim that the assignee or purchaser takes subject to all equities between the original parties. It would also subvert another maxim which belongs to the doctrine of estoppel itself. That maxim is, that an admission or representation is no estoppel in favor of a stranger to whom it is not made, and whose conduct it was not expressly designed to influence. (3 John's Cases, 101; 6 Hill, 534; 3 Id., 215; 7 Barb., 644.) The result is, that before the principles of estoppel can be applied to this controversy, it must be asserted and proved, that a certificate of stock, differing from all other modes and forms of obligation used in the transactions of men, contains within itself a representation or admission of facts which any dealer, however remote from the original parties, may accept as addressed to himself, and intended to influence his conduct. For such a doctrine no authority has been cited, and it has no foundation in any principle hitherto recognized.

As I have once mentioned, a theory of the action prominently urged upon the argument, assumed, that the corporation had no power to create more than the original three millions of stock, or to issue certificates for a greater amount. That this is so, I think I have demonstrated. But, assuming these premises, it was then insisted that the certificate in question was, therefore, false, and that the action would be on this ground. The essential principle of the case in this view would be, that as the defendants, for want of corporate power, *cannot* recognize the certificate as the true representation of stock, and so respond to the engagement which it implies, they must make compensation in damages for the injury sustained in consequence of the representation regarded as false.

Now, by presenting the *falsehood* alleged in the certificate, and the consequent injury as the ground of the action, a plausible appearance is given to this view of the case. But it is essentially illogical. The falsehood, viewed in this aspect alone, really consists in a want of corporate power to enter into the engagement, and that, instead of being a *cause* of the action, is a serious difficulty to be removed. If an agent, irrespective of all questions arising out of the special limitations of his own authority, as derived from the board of directors, cannot bind a corporation, or affect the rights of its genuine stockholders by the *terms* of an over-issued certificate, there is great difficulty in affirming that the result may be indirectly reached by thus changing the ground of liability. If a corporation has received the benefit of its agent's misrepresentation or fraud in a transaction unauthorized by its charter, I will not say there is no mode of redress. I am not an advocate of the doctrine that a corporation cannot be responsible for a wrong, or may not in some form be liable when its agents enter into engagements which its charter forbids, and the benefits of the transaction can be traced to its stockholders, or are held for their benefit. But such is not the case before us. The stockholders of this corporation are in no wise connected with the misconduct of their agent, nor have they been benefited by it. It is true, they trusted him, but it is not alleged that they had not ample reasons for so doing. Conceding that Schuyler's authority, derived from his appointment as transfer agent by the board of directors, might apparently include his fraudulent acts, the difficulty is only removed one step further back. The directors themselves were not the corporation, but its agents only. It may be granted that they wielded all the corporate powers, but among those powers the one in question is nowhere to be found. It did not even have *apparent* existence. The argument concedes this absolute want of power, and I have yet to discover the principle on which the genuine stockholders can be made liable in any form for an attempt to exercise it, by any of their agents, for their own individual benefit.

But such a point need not be determined. Before reaching this ultimate question, the action fails upon the special grounds which have been examined at large. Conceding to the defendants the power, if they so elect, to recognize and perform the obligation under which their agent attempted to place them, then, if they are not liable upon their refusal to do so, for the reasons which have been stated, it is extremely plain they are not if the power to do so is wanting. To say that their agent's false representation of stock, which did not and could not exist, can render them liable to dealers in the spurious certificates, when they would not be bound to recognize the same dealers, if the stock in fact existed, and the representations were therefore true, involves a fallacy so evident, that it needs only to be suggested. This is the error in the argument which places the defendants' liability on the simple ground that the certificate is a fraudulent representation of non-existing stock; the alleged fraud consisting in the statement of that falsehood alone. In this view of the controversy, the other fatal objections to the action are overlooked. If I have been successful in showing that the plaintiffs can have no title to the shares of stock mentioned in the certificate, for the particular reasons which have been given, then manifestly the non-existence of the shares, or the false assertion of their existence, is no ground of. complaint.

In concluding, it is proper to say, that the case of *The Bank of Kentucky* vs. *The Schuylkill Bank*, (1 Parsons' Select Eq. Cases, 180,) has not been overlooked. That case has been much relied on as an authority in point upon the general question before us, and it is certainly true, that in the opinion delivered on pronouncing the judgment, some principles were stated scarcely reconcilable with the conclusion to which we have come. In that case, however, the suit was brought by the corporation against its own fraudulent agent, after it had recognized the spurious issue under an enabling act of the legislature; and in many essential circumstances the controversy differed from the present one. After a careful consideration, we are unable to yield to that decision any controlling influence upon the question now to be determined. We are all of opinion that the judgment should be reversed, and a new trial granted. Ordered accordingly.

A Copy. F. KERNAN, State Reporter.

Tracy, Powers and Tallmadge, defendants' attorneys; E. S. Van Winkle, plaintiffs' attorney.

www.ingramcontent.com/pod-product-compliance
Lightning Source LLC
LaVergne TN
LVHW021142110826
845150LV00005B/1098

9781425549169